Chaplaincy

A COMPREHENSIVE INTRODUCTION

MARK A. JUMPER

STEVEN E. KEITH

MICHAEL W. LANGSTON

Baker Academic
a division of Baker Publishing Group
Grand Rapids, Michigan

© 2024 by Mark A. Jumper, Steven E. Keith, Michael W. Langston

Published by Baker Academic
a division of Baker Publishing Group
Grand Rapids, Michigan
www.bakeracademic.com

Printed in the United States of America

Library of Congress Cataloging-in-Publication Data
Names: Jumper, Mark A., 1954– author. | Keith, Steven E., author | Langston, Michael W., author
Title: Chaplaincy : a comprehensive introduction / Mark A. Jumper, Steven E. Keith, Michael W.
    Langston.
Description: Grand Rapids, Michigan : Baker Academic, a division of Baker Publishing Group,
    [2024] | Includes bibliographical references and index.
Identifiers: LCCN 2023035150 | ISBN 9781540964045 (paperback) | ISBN 9781540966513
    (casebound) | ISBN 9781493441587 (ebook) | ISBN 9781493441594 (pdf)
Subjects: LCSH: Chaplains.
Classification: LCC BV4375 .J76 2024 | DDC 253—dc23/eng/20230927
LC record available at https://lccn.loc.gov/2023035150

Unless otherwise indicated, Scripture quotations are from The Holy Bible, English Standard Version® (ESV®), copyright © 2001 by Crossway, a publishing ministry of Good News Publishers. Used by permission. All rights reserved. ESV Text Edition: 2016

Scripture quotations labeled NIV are from THE HOLY BIBLE, NEW INTERNATIONAL VERSION®, NIV® Copyright © 1973, 1978, 1984, 2011 by Biblica, Inc.® Used by permission. All rights reserved worldwide.

The information contained herein is not intended to render legal advice. Factual and legal issues may arise that must be considered in each circumstance. If legal advice is necessary, the services of a competent attorney should be sought.

Baker Publishing Group publications use paper produced from sustainable forestry practices and post-consumer waste whenever possible.

24   25   26   27   28   29   30   7   6   5   4   3   2   1

To all faithful chaplains—
past, present, and future

CONTENTS

PREFACE

We believe it is time for chaplaincy to be given its full and rightful place in the panoply of professional ministry. Among Protestant Christians, clergy are typically seen as either pastors or missionaries—or maybe theological teachers. Many a chaplain, at clergy gatherings, has been asked, "When are you coming back to ministry?" Such sentiments reveal the view that clergy ought to either minister as pastors within the church or go forth as missionaries to build new church groups that also minister within the church. Chaplains indeed minister "outside" the churches they represent and are endorsed by. But our true measure is to minister continually within the (mostly secular) bodies we serve. We are thus defined by our location not outside something but inside something—with unparalleled access to people's lives. Our paradigm is to serve in the workplaces of those outside the church with all the ministry that's possible, rather than going on mission to attract people to our church or to build new churches. Chaplains are inherently more missional than attractional. We hope this book will help many more see and support the amazing ministry that is being given by chaplains as insiders who minister with all they can give.

The authors thank God and country for the opportunity to serve as evangelical chaplains for twenty-four years in the Navy (Mark), thirty years in the Air Force (Steve), and thirty-six years in the Marine Corps and Navy (Mike). We also gratefully acknowledge the support of our wives, who inspired and motivated us: Ginger Jumper, Delta Keith, and Kathy Langston. None of us would trade our chaplaincy for any other ministry. We all had the opportunity to bear the presence and message of Christ with thousands of military members and their families and were able to see hundreds come to Christ as Savior and grow in him and his Word as we served many types of units and pastored congregations at installations stateside, overseas, and in war zones. It was our privilege to care for the dying, honor the dead, and nurture the living. There is no higher or more fulfilling calling. If the Lord is calling you to chaplaincy, do not hesitate to leave the trinkets of this world on the street behind you and follow him (Matt. 16:24–25)!

ABBREVIATIONS

ACPE	Association of Clinical Pastoral Education
BOP	Federal Bureau of Prisons
CPE	clinical pastoral education
DOD	Department of Defense
EMS	emergency medical services
FFC	Federation of Fire Chaplains
HR	human resources
ICPC	International Conference of Police Chaplains
KSAs	knowledge, skills, and abilities
MA	master of arts
MDiv	master of divinity
MRE	Military Rule of Evidence
NCMAF	National Conference on Ministry to the Armed Forces
RFRA	Religious Freedom Restoration Act
RLE	Religious Leader Engagement
SCOTUS	Supreme Court of the United States
VA	Veterans Affairs

Chaplaincy Examined

Theology, Theory, and Application

Part 1 covers the basics. In our years of chaplain service, we have led and been on staff at military chaplain schools. One of us taught at a service academy. We have also been training chaplain students in master of divinity, doctor of ministry, and doctor of philosophy programs at our three schools—Columbia International, Liberty, and Regent—for a decade, with a combined annual enrollment of well over one thousand. We have learned much in our student encounters. We have also received much positive feedback regarding our graduates, especially those in military and clinical pastoral roles. We have spent much time as a team discussing what should be covered here. This book is the result.

We offer biblical, theological, philosophical, historical, and legal underpinnings of chaplaincy in chapters 1 through 4. Every chaplain needs knowledge in these areas. Our book is noticeably American in context and outlook. However, we hope that those of other nations may glean valuable insights from how chaplaincy has developed in the US. This book is also evangelical in basis and outlook. We hope those of other beliefs will find some commonalities and some understanding of us and our place among you, our valued colleagues.

Chapter 5 addresses the evangelical chaplain to consciously prepare for next steps from the basics. Chaplain endorsement (chap. 6) is a mystery to many who seek to be chaplains and often invisible to those who encounter chaplains. Yet we consider it a crucial component mediating between faith groups and the institutions that use their clergy as chaplains.

We next move in chapter 7 to the person of the chaplain. Our times have revealed horrifying abuses by clergy, including chaplains, who prey on those they are supposed to serve. We pray that every chaplain maintains consistent self-care and accountability so as not to cause such cruelties. Not only is the estimable character of the chaplain a preventive against such; it is also an essential foundation for faithful, fruitful ministry.

Chapters 8 and 9 dive deep into the chaplain's needed knowledge, skills, and abilities that translate into practical, effective ministry. These skill sets and practices differ from those of pastors and missionaries. Those who wish to serve as chaplains should recognize this difference and not just think that they are "missionaries to the military" or "pastors to patients" (as has often been said). No, they are *chaplains*: a specialized professional category that requires its own status and standards. This is what we hope to show.

Finally, we note in chapter 10 that while chaplains seldom hold institutional leadership positions, they are always moral and spiritual leaders who significantly influence both the institutional leaders and the people they lead. Also, chaplains often have input into institutional policies and practices and thus have substantial long-term leadership influence.

We hope this introductory book is experienced as comprehensive if not exhaustive. There are more categories we could cover, and much more we could say about each area addressed. For those wider and deeper treatments—perhaps in journals and compendia—we rely on you, the reader, to be inspired to add to chaplaincy's riches.

A Brief Introduction
to Chaplaincy

Welcome to chaplaincy! The world is entering a "chaplaincy moment" that increasingly recognizes the importance of chaplains and takes advantage of what they offer. We invite you to join the journey of discovering and practicing chaplaincy in all its fullness. Our hope is that as you read, you will be not only informed and educated but also inspired to seek your own chaplain service.

But first, what is a chaplain? A chaplain is a minister (or priest or holder of another such office) who represents a recognized religion and who joins an institution or organization, usually secular, as one of its people in order to support and minister to its members from the inside.

Next, what is chaplaincy? Chaplaincy involves chaplains providing religious ministry and service for all people in the context of their organizations.

Even as the world seems to be secularizing, the types and number of institutions that use chaplains are growing. We have identified ten "functional areas of chaplaincy" in which chaplains are active. These functional areas include military, healthcare, education, community, public safety, and others. Some governments, even formerly communist ones, have begun chaplaincies or added to their existing positions. Many organizations worldwide understand that chaplains add value to their operations. Some of this value comes from chaplains' success in preventing and addressing people's problems, which minimizes costly adverse effects. The chaplain often provides a relief valve for

those who feel battered by the pressures of life and work. People need someone
to patiently listen to them vent and help them assess their situation in a quiet,
private place. More than that, a chaplain's presence, prayers, and words bring a
better spirit to everyone. The chaplain's presence alone reminds people of "the
better angels of our nature," to use Abraham Lincoln's phrase, when all around
seems coarse and cutthroat. Bringing wisdom and encouragement, chaplains
help life go smoother and better throughout the organization. They keep people
in tune with the higher ideals that they can easily forget about in the daily grind:
God, truth, goodness, love, morality and ethics, kindness, peace, comfort, help,
character, and human connection that diminishes isolation. Institutions are taking notice and increasing the number of chaplains to serve in more places—in
secular corporations, community organizations, and governments—even as the
world seems to be secularizing.[1]

The growth of chaplaincy in an increasingly secular society may seem counter-
intuitive. But we believe that chaplaincy is expanding *because of* secularization—
because chaplaincy holds a key to meeting that secular challenge. Religious
attendance has drastically decreased in many industrialized or cyberized nations.
The religiously stubborn United States has lagged behind this general trend but
has not been immune. According to a comprehensive poll, while 73 percent of
Americans claim to be Christian, only 31 percent of Americans attend religious
services at least once a month.[2] There is an increase of agnostics, atheists, natu-
ralists, humanists, nones, spiritual-but-not-religious, moral-therapeutic deists,
and those who claim to love Jesus but not the church. These developments mean
that more people have little or no connection to a religious leader and often
no religious group to provide social support, guidance, and accountability. Yet
because people are created by God, people's spiritual needs and their need to
deal with ultimate questions remain. These needs are part of what we sometimes
call the God-shaped hole in every human heart. As Ecclesiastes 3:11 says, God
"has made everything beautiful in its time. Also, he has put eternity into man's
heart." As Augustine says:

> And man desires to praise thee, for he is a part of thy creation; he bears his mor-
> tality about with him and carries the evidence of his sin and the proof that thou
> dost resist the proud. Still he desires to praise thee, this man who is only a small
> part of thy creation. Thou hast prompted him, that he should delight to praise

1. John D. Laing, *In Jesus' Name: Evangelicals and Military Chaplaincy* (Eugene, OR: Resource,
2010), 2.
2. "The State of the Church 2016," Barna Group, September 15, 2016, https://www.barna.com
/research/state-church-2016.

thee, for thou hast made us for thyself and restless is our heart until it comes to rest in thee.[3]

Given this ultimate reality to which Christians witness and that all people live, what happens when ultimate questions and needs arise and a person has nowhere to turn? A chaplain can be a helpful person to have nearby. As people have holes in their hearts that only God can fill, so secularizing society has a void that chaplains can help fill.

We therefore believe that chaplain ministry will grow in the coming years. As chaplains operate within institutions and organizations, they continue to practice a whole-life, full-immersion ministry that resonates with many people as authentic, available, and valuable.

The Chaplain's Identity

A chaplain is a bearer of the image and message of God who cares for, comforts, and serves all the people connected with an organization. Some people expect chaplains to hide their particular faith tradition. We, by contrast, hold that chaplains should be who they are: first, persons who do not lose their identity in the organization they serve and, second, faithful representatives of particular religious bodies, or "faith groups." A certain cultural expectation paints chaplains as low-energy, low-content empty suits who believe little and stand for little, doing "all religions" as needed but with few convictions of their own. This idea is reinforced by the common secular notion that all religions are essentially the same and can therefore be practiced by a single professional. This damaging stereotype helps no one in practice, as it refuses to recognize the real identities and differences of real people. Low-content chaplaincy thus undermines the proper recognition of diversity.

A foundational problem of this approach to chaplaincy is that it refuses to recognize the real differences between religions and beliefs and therefore the differences between members of various religions and faith traditions. The truth is that religions are not all essentially the same, and the denial of this truth undermines the proper recognition of diversity within an institution or organization. Since religions are not fundamentally the same, a chaplain cannot practice any and every religion; a chaplain must represent a particular, legitimate religious group. A genuine evangelical chaplain could not, for example, authentically lead a Buddhist service, even if Buddhists wanted someone outside their own faith to do so. There is no such thing as a multifaith clergyperson. Therefore, each

3. Augustine, *Confessions* 1.1, trans. Albert C. Outler (Gainesville, FL: Bridge-Logos, 2003), 11.

religious group must certify that its representatives will faithfully represent its beliefs and practices. The groups do this by providing an "endorsement" (see chap. 6) of their chaplains.

Religious Endorsement Standards

To be recognized as an endorser requires adherence to certain standards and requirements as a religious group. While it is difficult to define a legitimate religious group, the US government, between its bureaucracy and courts, has arrived at an admittedly imperfect standard used by the Internal Revenue Service to help adjudicate tax status for claimant groups. The idea is that most of the following fourteen points should be practiced in some way by a given group:

1. Distinct legal existence
2. Recognized creed and form of worship
3. Definite and distinct ecclesiastical government
4. Formal code of doctrine and discipline
5. Distinct religious history
6. Membership not associated with any other church or denomination
7. Organization of ordained ministers
8. Ordained ministers selected after completing prescribed courses of study
9. Literature of its own
10. Established places of worship
11. Regular congregations
12. Regular religious services
13. Sunday schools for the religious instruction of the young
14. Schools for the preparation of its members[4]

Some may quibble with some of the points, but they reflect real-world practice and are workable in our diverse society. The government is reluctant to proceed beyond these points, as it is liable to transgress the Free Exercise Clause of the US Constitution's First Amendment (see chap. 4).

4. Internal Revenue Service, *Tax Guide for Churches and Religious Organizations*, last revised August 2015, 33, https://www.irs.gov/pub/irs-pdf/p1828.pdf. This list appears to flow from a federal district court decision, *Malnak v. Yogi* (1977), in which Circuit Judge Arlin M. Adams wrote a thorough concurring opinion that sought to find a single modern definition of religion that might not be necessarily theistic.

However, the US government maintains lists of recognized endorsers for its military and Veterans Affairs (VA) chaplains.[5] These endorsers also typically endorse chaplains in areas other than the military. Requirements for becoming an endorser are more rigorous than the Internal Revenue Service standards of merely existing as a recognized religious group. These requirements include high educational standards and a solid commitment to provide supervision of endorsed chaplains. A chaplain who loses endorsement is required to cease ministry immediately and will be separated from government employment. Only ecclesiastical endorsers—not the government—are given the power to determine whether a chaplain truly represents them.

The US government also works, through the Armed Forces Chaplain Board, with an institution that mediates between church and state, the National Conference on Ministry to the Armed Forces (NCMAF). NCMAF, composed mostly of endorsers of military, VA, and Federal Bureau of Prison (BOP) chaplains, is the largest interfaith group in the world. Its members work cooperatively to ensure that every legitimate group that meets the high standards of endorsement status has the opportunity to be represented in military, VA, and BOP chaplaincy. It claims the following mission and vision:

> Mission: NCMAF connects member faith groups with military and VA chaplaincies, and celebrates the religious diversity of the United States of America.

> Vision: NCMAF will advocate for the First Amendment and provide a unified voice on religious freedom and religious diversity.[6]

NCMAF works closely with the Armed Forces Chaplain Board and the chiefs of chaplains of the Army, the Navy, the Air Force, VA, and BOP to ensure evenhanded representation and collegial, accountable religious ministry.

While many chaplains are not engaged in military ministry, those principles of high standards, diverse representation, collegiality, and accountability are good models for chaplaincy across the board. Some organizations that use chaplains do not maintain such standards, advocating for chaplaincy without endorsement and other problematic practices. Such practices open the floodgates to waves of unqualified applicants, who may not even represent a religion.

5. See "DOD-Listed Religious-Endorsing Organizations/Agents," Office of the Under Secretary for Personnel and Readiness, accessed January 19, 2023, https://prhome.defense.gov/M-RA /MPP/AFCB/Endorsements. See also "Ecclesiastical Endorsing Organizations," US Department of Veterans Affairs, November 2022, https://www.patientcare.va.gov/chaplain/docs/Ecclesiastic alEndorsing/Ecclesiastical-Endorsing-Organizations.pdf#.

6. National Conference on Ministry to the Armed Forces (website), accessed July 31, 2023, www.ncmaf.com.

What, then, is the religious legitimacy of chaplaincy as it is practiced in secular environments? Beginning with chaplains' commitment to God paves the way to understanding the religious focus of chaplains as they work within their chosen area.

Starting with God

Evangelical chaplains, as with all clergy, must have a firm foundation for the work of ministry if they are to thrive. Chaplains can have many responsibilities and serve in many ways, but unless they are first focused on God, the essence of chaplaincy is absent. Without God in the mix, chaplains bring no lasting presence to people. Chaplains represent God's explicit presence and help in an organization. Evangelical chaplaincy is first about God.

There are movements that de-emphasize the God core of chaplaincy and replace it with the vague notion of spirituality. Some propose de-emphasizing the term "chaplain" or even replacing it with "spiritual-care provider." We agree that every person has a spirit that is expressed—spiritually! But the definition of "spiritual" can vary so widely as to become unclear and even devoid of content. As Christian chaplains, we prefer to deal with the whole person—body, mind, and spirit. Simply being a spiritual care provider or offering spiritual care does not, by definition, address the whole person. We define ourselves by our relationship with God, Jesus, and the Holy Spirit.

As orthodox Christians of evangelical Protestant conviction and identity, we believe that God himself is the right place to start the chaplaincy endeavor. Who is God, and how does he love? What has he done, and how does he work? The answers to these and similar questions form the foundations of evangelical Christian chaplaincy. The journey toward chaplaincy begins with the understanding that our loving God is personal. In love, he created people in his image, so humans' very existence witnesses to his personhood. But his personhood is infinitely greater than people's personhood in scope, strength, and reach. He is the infinite reference point that our finite souls need if they are to find their whole reality. Without this reference point, people are adrift without purpose or help on the random seas of life. Those who do not acknowledge God or worship him may possess and use the many talents and gifts they have received from him but can never realize their full potential, having cut themselves off from their divine source and design. By living and working with God as the source, model, and lodestar, Christians have identity, purpose, and direction. Such a rock-solid foundation gives the chaplain a steadiness and consistency that will quickly become noticed and depended on in the ever-changing dynamics of a purpose-based group.

The Great Commandment

Evangelical chaplains operate according to God's strategic principles. The first is the Great Commandment, Jesus's answer to critics based on the Scriptures they held in common:

> And one of them, a lawyer, asked him a question to test him. "Teacher, which is the great commandment in the Law?" And he said to him, "You shall love the Lord your God with all your heart and with all your soul and with all your mind [Deut. 6:5]. This is the great and first commandment. And a second is like it: You shall love your neighbor as yourself [Lev. 19:18, 34]. On these two commandments depend all the Law and the Prophets." (Matt. 22:35–40)

Jesus knows that people naturally love themselves. Treating others with that same love limits selfishness and builds community. Loving one's neighbor as oneself can also be seen as an expression of the universally acknowledged Golden Rule, which Jesus similarly confirms from Hebrew Scripture: "So whatever you wish that others would do to you, do also to them, for this is the Law and the Prophets" (Matt. 7:12).

We note, then, three facets of the Great Commandment. All of them involve *relationships*. The first is often passed over, but if it is omitted, the second and third are impossible to fulfill. This first facet is to love God with all of one's heart, soul, and mind. In other words, God first. The singular purpose and mission of the evangelical chaplain is to help people have a personal relationship with God and to assist them in having godly relationships with one another. Those called to chaplaincy must immerse themselves in a personal, loving relationship with Jesus Christ (Gal. 2:20) and be willing to stand as shining lights before others, "that they may see your good works and give glory to your Father who is in heaven" (Matt. 5:16). As chaplains yield to the Holy Spirit's filling and strength, they exhibit the fruit of the Spirit: "love, joy, peace, patience, kindness, goodness, faithfulness, gentleness, self-control" (Gal. 5:22–23). This kind of loving relationship with God lays the foundation for the chaplain to accomplish the mission. Without it, the chaplain's ministry would simply be a facade. The chaplain's authentic relationship with the Lord is ground zero for integrity and effectiveness. All that the chaplain is and does must be rooted in a personal, loving, and holy relationship with God. Everything that flows from the chaplain's heart, soul, and mind must be anchored to the source of all that is good (James 1:17).

Second, the words "You shall love your neighbor as yourself" (Matt. 22:39) call chaplains to establish selfless relationships with people and to help individuals enjoy God-based relationships with one another. Much of the chaplain's ministry is focused on helping people with their relationships, whether in the workplace, at home, or in their play. Often chaplains are called on to provide relational counseling for individuals struggling with marriage, family, work, and spiritual and emotional issues. Chaplains freely refer those they serve to other professionals in the fields of mental and physical health, social work, addictions, abuse, human resources, and other specialties. They understand themselves to be part of an integrated care team and see these other professionals as colleagues, not competitors. But they also believe that God's selfless love offers substantive help to struggling people that is found nowhere else and that only through Jesus's redeeming love can a person's soul be healed and made well (John 3:16). Scripture reminds its readers that God calls believers to model Jesus's humble, selfless love, to see others as better than oneself, and to be concerned for their needs (Phil. 2:1–8). This kind of love for others truly represents the heart and voice of Jesus. The goal of every evangelical chaplain should be to bear the presence and message of Christ, a presence of selfless love and a message of God's redeeming love.

The third facet of the Great Commandment is the Golden Rule: "Whatever you wish that others would do to you, do also to them" (Matt. 7:12). This requires mentally putting yourself in another person's place, seeking to understand and help that person by picturing what you yourself would want, and then meeting the needs and wants of that person as appropriate. Chaplains who make a habit of this exercise and encourage others in it can quickly build positive community, even in a secular organization, because they are committed to the common good of all. The resulting atmosphere is contagious—in the best way!

The Great Commission

Evangelical chaplains further remember that Jesus gave them a Great Commission when he told his disciples before his ascension:

> All authority in heaven and on earth has been given to me. Go therefore and make disciples of all nations, baptizing them in the name of the Father and of the Son and of the Holy Spirit, teaching them to observe all that I have commanded you. And behold, I am with you always, to the end of the age. (Matt. 28:18–20)

The Great Commission's object and goal is discipleship. Evangelical chaplains consider evangelism to be the first step in making a disciple, as a person begins a personal and eternal relationship with God on the journey to be conformed to the image of Christ (Rom. 8:29–30). A person must first accept Jesus Christ as Lord and Savior to start a relationship with God and begin striving to be a

Christ follower (Rom. 10:9–10, 13). They are then given a new Christlike nature and a desire to become like Jesus (1 Cor. 5:17), becoming indwelt by the Holy Spirit (1 Cor. 3:16) and gaining a new capacity through the Spirit to understand the things of God (1 Cor. 2:14). As a new creation in Christ, a believer receives the forgiveness of God (Heb. 10:14) and begins the challenge of becoming like Christ in thought, word, and action (Rom. 12:1–2). Yet evangelism and the moment of belief in Christ are only the beginning of making disciples. Many Christians use conversions as their measure of success, but the Great Commission measures success by discipleship. Discipleship is well suited to chaplaincy, as chaplains have a unique opportunity to live and work relationally among people within an organization or setting for an extended period of time. Conversion is a wonderful start, but it is only a moment, even if it is the culmination of a long process. Discipleship is a lifelong process. Chaplains are continually available, strategically placed, and ready to assist those who seek help.

The Great Commission also entails an emphasis on ethics, which is centered on observing the commands of Christ. Jesus affirms God's law even as he demonstrates that humans cannot keep it to gain God's favor and can make progress in it only with God's help. God's law, summarized in the Ten Commandments, is recognized in substance by most of humanity. Its principles, starting with God's transcendence versus human transience in the introduction, relate to (1) divine reality versus relativism, (2) spirituality versus materialism, (3) suitable speech, (4) Sabbath rest and worship, (5) generational respect and honor, (6) sanctity of life, (7) sexual fidelity, (8) protection of property, (9) truth versus lies, and (10) an inner life of ethics versus outward rules. All these commandments represent qualities that most people want to affirm. Chaplains in secular spaces can show organizations or communities, along with their people, the advantages of accepting these principles as the ground for normative ethics that work well in the real world. For those who are willing, chaplains can also point expressly to God's presence to help them live by those principles—which were originally given to help people who had been released from bondage as a way to retain God's gift of freedom.

Anyone who attempts to fulfill God's law or just lead an ethical life will fail without God's help. That is why the Great Commission's promise of Jesus's presence is so important. The chaplain, as a person of faith intentionally roaming an organization's or setting's precincts and places, represents and reminds people of God's presence. Evangelical chaplains depend on the Spirit's presence and guidance—promised and given by Jesus—to lead them to just the places and people that need them most. They then convey and share that precious gift, even among those who do not yet know God but can still feel something special (which we attribute to the presence of the Holy Spirit) surrounding the chaplain.

GC²

GC² reflects the combination of the major concepts of each principle. First, we combine the two "greats": the Great Commandment and the Great Commission, each abbreviated as GC. These two concepts mutually reinforce and grow each other into a complete package. However, we are not simply adding them together. Rather, their cumulative effect is *exponential*. Their combination creates a spiritual dynamic that produces abundant fruit in and for the lives of our people—"far more abundantly than all that we ask or think, according to the power at work within us" (Eph. 3:20). GC² is accessible, understandable, and usable for the chaplain's people.

GC² ministry is ultimately about relationships—starting first with God and extending to others. Chaplains are called to be centered in God and his divine nature. At the very essence of his being is a divine relationship between Father, Son, and Holy Spirit. God is one God in three persons, reflecting unity. God also created Adam and Eve to be in relationship with him and one another (Gen. 1:26–27), reflecting his divine community in human community. Chaplains help people live in life-giving relationships with God and others.

Summary

To summarize, the GC² ministry mindset can serve as both an entry point and a goal as chaplains meet individual needs and build community—with God's help. Chaplains perform ministry functions that organizations and their people greatly need and that no one but chaplains can fulfill. Accordingly, chaplains play an important role, which they can use to the full benefit of the organizations or communities and the people they serve.

2

Biblical, Theological, and Philosophical Foundations of Chaplaincy

Chaplains, being action oriented, tend to move straight toward chaplaincy's tasks. But a careful examination of chaplaincy's theological and philosophical foundations is necessary to a strong chaplain ministry. This chapter begins with the Bible as its basis, starting with theology as our application and philosophy as our outlook for practice. Laying these firm foundations allows chaplains to move forward with more substance and ministry fruit.

The Nature of God and the Nature of Chaplaincy

The chaplain, as with any member of the clergy, must have a firm foundation if the work of ministry is to thrive. This foundation includes theology that is based on the Bible. The Greek word *theologia*, dating back at least to Plato, does not itself appear in the Bible. However, its root words, *theos* ("God") and *logion* ("sayings, utterances, or general words of Scripture [Heb. 5:12]"[1]), do

---

1. William F. Arndt and F. Wilbur Gingrich, *A Greek-English Lexicon of the New Testament and Other Early Christian Literature* (Chicago: University of Chicago Press, 1957), s.v. "*Logion, ou, to.*"

appear in Scripture. "Theology" thus implies a systematic study of God from divine words and texts. But theology is more than words describing God. It is discourse or discussion about God's person, presence, and work. Such talk cannot remain solitary but requires communal interaction, including the living presence of God himself. The chaplain who brings good theology to people builds community and brings the palpable presence of God to a place and a people that need him.

God's Word in the Holy Bible is the only reliable source of God's special revelation of himself to humans. His general revelation appears in creation, and we gladly refer to it in our chaplain ministries. But apart from Scripture and the Holy Spirit's enlightenment, the works of creation are insufficient to bring the knowledge and offer of salvation. We therefore turn to the Bible for our theological foundations of chaplaincy, and we start with creation in Genesis, which could not happen without God's existence and action. Creation shows that everything and everyone is made by God and owes him recognition and praise. Therefore, any organization that does not in some way recognize God's presence is out of tune with the core realities of the world and its people. It will therefore experience structural difficulties and relational impediments that flow from that omission. On the other hand, an organization that recognizes God's presence and sovereignty—for example, by providing chaplains—has already put itself in a better place regarding the world's realities. God is the source of all. Without him, there is nothing and no meaning. Our thesis here is that chaplaincy is rooted in the nature of God, as it represents and applies God's presence in every possible setting. Chaplaincy, to be effective, must be God based and God centered.

Chaplain ministry is rooted in several key attributes of God's nature as found in Scripture. These include God's eternal nature, relational nature, holy nature, loving nature, humble nature, incarnational nature, supernatural nature, and evangelistic nature. We present these to you with the Scripture references that underscore them.

God's Eternal Nature

Chaplain ministry is rooted in the eternal nature of God. All that matters in life is joined to God's identity as the one who is without beginning or end (Gen. 1:1; 21:33; Ps. 90:2). God is an eternal being who created people in his image with eternal souls (Gen. 1:26–27). His eternal reality gives our finite lives a necessary reference point of structure and meaning. Chaplain ministry is focused on caring for the eternal souls of people. It is focused on bringing God to people and people to God. Moreover, it is focused on helping people have godly relationships with one another (Matt. 22:37–39). *Chaplaincy is an eternal mission.*

God's Relational Nature

Chaplain ministry is rooted in the relational nature of God. God by his eternal nature is one God in three persons. God is in relationship with himself as Father, Son, and Holy Spirit (Matt. 3:16–17; 28:19; 2 Cor. 13:14). This triune God created man and woman in his image so he could enjoy a personal relationship with them (Gen. 1:26–27; 2:7; 3:8). Chaplain ministry focuses on people's relationship with God. Further, God created the man and woman to be in relationship with each other (Gen. 2:21–24). Accordingly, chaplain ministry focuses on helping individuals have a holy and loving relationship not just with God but also with one another (1 Pet. 1:22).

Indeed, God created man and woman in his moral likeness to be holy and loving creatures capable of relating to his holiness and love. The fall of Adam and Eve into sin (Gen. 3) separated them from God and from each other. Moreover, Adam's sin nature passed on to all his descendants (Rom. 5:12), resulting in all people being born sinful and separated from God and the capacity for eternal life (Rom. 3:9–20). Evangelical chaplains are thus not surprised or shocked when people do bad things. They are able to enter a situation and bring help that works. This realistic view of human nature is the only one that fits the full facts of human behavior and history.

God has put into action his rescue plan to provide salvation and the restoration of an eternal relationship with people (Rom. 5:8; 10:9–13). Each person of the Trinity has played an integral part in the mission. God the Father sent his Son to pay the penalty for sin (John 3:16); Jesus the Son humbled himself to die a vicarious death to atone for sin (Phil. 2:5–8); the Holy Spirit raised Jesus back to life to conquer sin and death (Rom. 8:11; 1 Pet. 3:18) and has provided a living presence in each believer, empowering them to live God's way (Rom. 8:11; 2 Tim. 1:14).

The Father's love, the Son's obedience, and the Spirit's power provide a pathway to a holy and loving relationship with God, and the chaplain's purpose is to assist people in understanding this pathway (Acts 1:8), which requires faith (Eph. 2:8–9). Chaplains build relationships with people so they can show them the way to a relationship with God. One further relationship needs to be mentioned here: the chaplain's own relationship with God. Chaplains can show people the pathway to a relationship with God only if they are already walking it. As they walk this pathway, they understand that there is no greater good than sharing the good news of Jesus Christ (Mark 16:15). *Chaplaincy is a relational mission.*

God's Holy Nature

Chaplain ministry is rooted in the holy nature of God. The standard for goodness and rightness is based on the holiness of God (Gen. 3; Rom. 5). God created man[2] to be like him and to be a morally pure creation reflective of God's moral nature. Adam and Eve chose to act contrary to God's standard of right and became immoral and unlike God in their thinking and actions (Gen. 3:1–7; Rom. 1–3). Chaplain ministry focuses on the restoration of God's holiness and moral standard in the lives of people (Rom. 6, 8, 10). *Chaplaincy is a holy mission.*

God's Loving Nature

Chaplain ministry is rooted in the loving nature of God. God is the source of all love (1 John 4:7–11). True love is based not on feelings but on God's ultimate nature. He created man and woman to be like him, to be loving in thought and conduct (Gen. 1:26–27). Adam and Eve enjoyed a loving relationship with God and one another but then chose to dishonor their love for God (Gen. 3:1–7). Nevertheless, out of his love for humanity, God sent his Son, Jesus Christ, to offer himself as a sacrifice for sin and to provide the opportunity for individuals to be restored to a loving relationship with God (John 3:16). Chaplain ministry is focused on the restoration of God's loving image in the lives of people (Rom. 8:29; Eph. 2:4–10; Col. 3:10). Additionally, chaplains seek to help people love one another with the love of God (Matt. 22:37–40). *Chaplaincy is a loving mission.*

God's Humble Nature in Christ

Chaplain ministry is rooted in the humble nature of God as seen through the life of Jesus Christ (Phil. 2:1–11). God humbled himself and left the wonders of heaven's glory to become a man. Further, as a man Jesus humbled himself to the point of dying on the cross. There is no greater example of humility and love than Jesus giving himself to redeem others. "Meekness"—meaning not weakness but strength under control—is another word that applies here. Chaplains are to model Jesus's humility and to humble themselves to be the servants of others, using gentle power, not *gentile* power (Mark 10:42–45), to bring people to Jesus as Lord and Savior and to help them live godly, loving lives for the glory of God. It is with a humble, serving spirit that chaplains seek to minister in meekness, to "count others more significant than [themselves]" (Phil. 2:3–4). *Chaplaincy is a humble mission.*

---

2. We hold that the term "man" retains its usefulness to characterize and personify humans as a whole, believing that since the substitutes "humankind" and "humanity" still have a "man" in the middle, they offer no substantive improvement.

God's Incarnational Nature in Christ

Chaplain ministry is rooted in the incarnational nature of Jesus's earthly ministry. In fact, Jesus's incarnational ministry lays the foundation for chaplain ministry in all its forms. "The Word became flesh and dwelt among us" (John 1:14). The Great Communicator, who spoke the universe into existence, became human (Gen. 1–2; John 1:1–3). Jesus's earthly mission was fulfilled through his physical presence, teaching, healing, provision, and more. Through his sacrificial ministry of presence, Jesus purchased salvation and eternal life for those who would believe (John 3:16). Through his words, Jesus announced the message of salvation and called people to receive it (John 3:3, 15–17). Within this grand mission of saving people, the incarnational presence and words of Jesus made forgiveness possible and brought hope to the hopeless, healing to the sick, comfort to the brokenhearted, peace to the tormented, strength to the weak, and joy to the tearful (Ps. 147:3).

Chaplains are likewise called to a form of incarnational ministry. The term "incarnational ministry," when applied to Christians rather than Christ, is often used to refer to ministry that resembles Christ's incarnation in some ways. As Jesus is fully God and fully man, so the chaplain belongs fully to the kingdom of God, as certified by an endorsement, and to the secular organization or setting in which they serve. The chaplain's ministry, like Christ's, has two aspects: bearing the presence of Christ and communicating the message of Christ. As in the ministry of Jesus, both aspects are necessary and equally important. Neither presence nor verbal communication alone is sufficient for a full-fledged ministry. But together they enable a chaplain to serve as a purveyor of God's grace (John 1:17) and a bearer of God's light amid darkness (Matt. 5:14).

The idea of incarnational ministry is often used in conjunction with the idea of a ministry of presence, which says that simply being present with someone can powerfully help that person. There is much truth to that conception, and we will explore it in more depth below (see chap. 9). For now we note that presence is an excellent start for effective ministry but that it must not involve just human presence; it must mean representing and mediating the presence of God through the indwelling of the Holy Spirit as well as the use of words—as appropriate—since Jesus is himself the Word of God (John 1:1). We remember as well that this entire concept is based on the incarnation of Jesus. *Chaplaincy is an incarnational mission.*

God's Supernatural Nature

God is all powerful (Ps. 147:4–5). His strength has no limits (1 Chron. 29:11; Eph. 1:19). His creation is a testimony of his incredible might (Rom. 1:20).

He is the source of all strength, and he is anxious to provide believers with supernatural power to carry out his divine mission (Isa. 40:28–31; John 1:12; Acts 1:8; Eph. 3:20). Simply put, without God's power the chaplain cannot accomplish the mission (Matt. 19:26). Chaplains who seek to find strength within themselves will fall short of carrying out anything of eternal value (John 15:4–5). Conversely, chaplains who rely on God's strength can do "all things" (Phil. 4:13) and understand that God's "divine power has granted to us all things that pertain to life and godliness" (2 Pet. 1:3). The evangelical chaplain relies on the Holy Spirit to supply the power and strength to do God's work (Acts 1:8) and wisely chooses to operate in this divine power by walking in the Spirit (Gal. 5:16–26). It is the indwelling Holy Spirit who enables the chaplain to walk, talk, and minister like Jesus (Eph. 3:20; 2 Pet. 1:3) and thereby influence people for eternity. Further, the chaplain recognizes that human effort is essential to fulfill God's plan but that it is God's supernatural work through the Spirit that achieves God's "good pleasure" (Phil. 2:13). *Chaplaincy is a supernatural mission.*

God's Evangelistic Nature

The word "evangel," a synonym of "gospel," comes from a Greek word meaning "good news." We believe that God offers to all people "a future and a hope" (Jer. 29:11)—which is good news indeed! He, the Great Communicator (Ps. 33:6), has chosen to offer this good news through words. People receive the future and the hope—that is, they are saved—when they hear this message and then have faith (Rom. 10:17; Eph. 2:8–9). The sharing of the message, called "evangelism," is entrusted to all believers (Matt. 28:19), and it is especially a responsibility for chaplains, who bear the presence and message of Christ in secular settings. If chaplains do not have good news to share, what good are they in the midst of demanding, difficult, and depressing circumstances? On the other hand, if they proclaim the message with divine authority (Acts 1:8) and in a sensitive and respectful manner (1 Pet. 3:15), they can have a tremendous positive impact.

Many in secular society bristle at evangelism, claiming it to be oppressive and manipulative. We contend, however, that proper evangelistic activity must involve voluntary consent by the hearer—not coerced, pressured, or manipulated—which means an invitation from the person that enables the chaplain to offer, in turn, God's invitation. Proper evangelism also respects the response of the listener, even if it is a rejection of the message. It takes into account the context (both situational and personal), personal capability (important in healthcare settings), and consent. These principles for evangelism rest on a conviction that the Holy Spirit goes before the chaplain. The Spirit works in people's hearts, and chaplains are anxious to follow the leading of the Spirit—rather than trying to be the Holy Spirit. We prefer the term "proselytism" for the kind of sharing that lacks consent and involves manipulation. We disapprove of proselytism and insist on a method that remains ethical while sharing the message with the conviction that it is truly good news. *Chaplaincy is an evangelistic mission.*

Chaplaincy as the Fulfillment of GC²

We have already mentioned GC² as referring to the Great Commandment (Lev. 19:18; Deut. 6:4–5; Matt. 22:37–40; Mark 12:28–31; Luke 10:25–28) and the Great Commission (Matt. 28:19–20). Essentially, GC² is all that God calls chaplains to do. The Great Commandment directs the chaplain to enjoy an all-consuming love relationship with God and then to share that love relationship with others—a task that is accomplished by fulfilling the Great Commission. At the root of GC² chaplaincy is the desire of God to build eternal relationships with people and for people to build godly relationships with one another. Thus, GC² chaplain ministry can be summarized in one word: relationships. The singular purpose and mission of the evangelical chaplain is to help people have a personal relationship with God and to assist people in having good and godly relationships with one another.

Chaplains accomplish their GC² mission by living the Great Commandment. Jesus gave the Great Commandment when he summarized the Ten Commandments and said, "You shall love the Lord your God with all your heart and with all your soul and with all your mind. . . . You shall love your neighbor as yourself" (Matt. 22:37, 39). These words call every individual into a personal relationship with God that holds nothing back. Those called to chaplaincy must immerse themselves in such a relationship and, from it, attain a godly character and manner of living (Rom. 12:1–2; Eph. 4:12) that provide a clear reflection of his love and holiness (Matt. 5:14–16).

Chaplains accomplish their GC² mission by living the Great Commandment, which leads to a desire to do the Great Commission—to "make disciples of all nations, baptizing them in the name of the Father and of the Son and of the Holy Spirit, teaching them to observe all that I [Jesus] have commanded you" (Matt. 28:19–20). The supernatural result of enjoying a loving relationship with God and people is the desire to share that amazing relationship with those whom one loves.

The Common Good of All

Chaplains perform many good works for the sake of people's physical, mental, and spiritual welfare. The biblical basis of this God-inspired service to all for the common good includes Abraham praying for the sparing of Sodom (Gen. 18:17–33), Joseph serving the Egyptians to save them from famine (Gen. 41:25–57) and teaching wisdom to Pharaoh's elders (Ps. 105:16–22), Daniel serving the Babylonians (Dan. 1–2), and Paul praying for the good of his shipmates (Acts 27:21–44). When chaplains offer prayer for organizations and people, it is not done in a manipulative way, with material support being offered in exchange for a spiritual response. Rather, the support is given freely for the common good of the people, with prayer that the doors of their hearts will open to God. A positive response cannot be forced by expectations or coercion; it must happen because of the genuine will of the person. *Chaplaincy seeks the good of all.*

The Trinity and Chaplaincy

God Our Source

We affirm that our one God consists of three distinct yet united persons: the holy Trinity of Father, Son, and Holy Spirit, each and all joined relationally in eternal love. God's triunity offers the highest example of a union between the personal and the communal. People's lives tend to become unbalanced in one direction or another. Some view life as "all about me," regardless of what that means for others. Others see life as all about the group, to the extent that the individual is lost or squashed in corporate identity and demands—a frequent problem in chaplaincy venues. The beauty of God lies much in the full expression of both emphases—personal and communal, neither at the expense of the other—in a marvelous unity that humans find so attractive yet so elusive. The chaplain finds a great ministry application of God's person as three in one when ministering to members of a large purpose-based group. Chaplains help each person find meaning amid collective emphasis, and they help each person unite with disparate members in common purpose.

This active, relational, eternal love among the persons of the Trinity also models the reality of love that corporate life and lonely individuals can quickly lose. Love is a quality much desired and much in demand in the world, yet it is often scarce, with poor substitutes often filling the vacuum and people "lookin' for love in all the wrong places" as a result.[3] With the prevalence of humans failing to gain, give, or keep love, many people feel a deep need to find an alternative way. That can be a particularly frustrating quest in a secular purpose-based group. The chaplain is in a perfect place to minister the love of

3. Johnny Lee, "Lookin' for Love," track 9 on *Urban Cowboy* (soundtrack), Full Moon Records, 1980.

God, which remains firm, real, and ready to fulfill that quest with a love-filled divine-human relationship that brings mercy, grace, and peace. Here again the essence of God's character gives the foundation for a ministry that fills the gaps of a lonely, lovelorn world.

This theological exploration thus takes its form first from God himself and his trinitarian nature. However, we will construct our framework not just from theology proper (the study of God himself) or philosophy, which includes topics such as epistemology (the study of knowledge) and ontology (the study of being), but also from applied theology—the application of God's actions as Christians experience them through his presence. This approach is especially appropriate given the action-oriented nature of chaplaincy. We will thus look at *creation* as the Father's action, *incarnation* as the Son's action, and *impartation* as the Holy Spirit's action. We will next proceed to theological anthropology, considering the human trinity of body, soul (mind, will, emotions), and spirit.

This brief review of God's trinitarian nature—including his demonstration of personhood, community, and love—can be carried further as we draw out functional implications for the chaplain's ministry from the identity and work of each person of the Trinity.

God the Father: Creation

Scripture, which begins, "In the beginning, God created . . ." (Gen. 1:1), reveals the ultimate source of the universe, the earth, creatures, and humans. God created the earth as a purpose-designed home, and he designed humans to live in that home. This method of creation means that there is an underlying unity—and that there should be harmony—between people and creation, since God made both. We say the same regarding relationships between people: that there should be harmony due to the common Creator and the shared creation. However, the first humans' sin became the lot of all humanity, as humans can at least partially perceive in the processes of epigenetics. That inherited sin nature destroys harmony and brings destruction and death to people and the rest of creation. But a turn toward God is a turn toward the restoration of that which was lost. That restorative turn, modeled and mediated by a chaplain, can bring peace and harmony to an organization that experiences the standard ills of conflict that are common for a fallen world and humanity.

God the Father's creation—both place and people—also emphasizes the essential respect that people owe both to him and toward the place he has made. This respect for place entails an ethos of "creation care" that God gave humans at the start. Adam and Eve's first work, given by God, was that of creation care—to tend the garden of Eden. The "cultural mandate," as it is often called, of man's dominion in Genesis 1:26–28 states:

> Then God said, "Let us make man in our image, after our likeness. And let them have dominion over the fish of the sea and over the birds of the heavens and over the livestock and over all the earth and over every creeping thing that creeps on the earth."

> So God created man in his own image,
>   in the image of God he created him;
>   male and female he created them.

> And God blessed them. And God said to them, "Be fruitful and multiply and fill the earth and subdue it, and have dominion over the fish of the sea and over the birds of the heavens and over every living thing that moves on the earth."

This original action and declaration of dominion, far from dominating creation with destruction, as some claim,[4] is designed to encourage the growth and sustainable nurture of creation. Otherwise, the mandate to fill the earth with offspring would leave those offspring with no sustainable earth to fill. The chaplain, then, should have an acute sense of place—concerning not only the earth itself but also the structures people build and the works they do there, individually and in groups. Chaplains should honor and respect the place where God has put them—wherever that might be—including its purpose, people, and proper activities. They are to stand for the care, respect, and nurture of the place and people when many have lost their sense of place and identity. Chaplains' rootedness will be attractive and helpful to those living in rootless times. Beyond that, chaplains dare to bring a sacred presence to any place. They are about far more than the temporal: they bring not just a spiritual dimension but also the eternal presence of God. Chaplains roam among many seemingly godforsaken places but believe they can make God's presence felt there by their own presence. Such presence can be of inestimable value, as it brings positive ambiance—and results—to any place and people.

Evangelical chaplains recognize God's creation of man—male and female—in his image (*imago Dei* in Latin). This understanding of human origins assigns to a person a dignity that surpasses that assigned by any other explanation. Because they understand the divinely based value of each person, God-believing chaplains treat everyone with sensitivity and respect. The alternatives are tragically

4. See Lynn White Jr., "The Historical Roots of Our Ecologic Crisis," *Science*, n.s. 155, no. 3767 (March 10, 1967): 1203–7.

shown in the mass murders committed by history's utopians at their philoso-phies' behest and in the modern mass abortions, conducted in denial of both biological facts and moral truths. The chaplain brings to the people and their group a divine understanding of their source and potential, which is rooted in the creative action of God and his ongoing presence and which is desperately needed by people dehumanized by the horrors of the present time.

Thus, it can be seen that the knowledge of God the Father and his acts of cre-ation has tremendous importance that reaches the roots of the human condition. Chaplains have the privileged opportunity to convey these creation blessings of the Father where they are needed most.

God the Son: Incarnation

The coming to earth of God the Son in the person of Jesus Christ is the central event of human history. Nothing else comes close in importance or significance. His name reveals his role and acts. "Jesus"—the English version of the Hebrew *Yeshua*—means "savior," which implies that the human condi-tion requires saving. All people, however reluctant to admit this, know deep within themselves that the reality of the human condition imposes this need. This name also indicates that Jesus, being divine, has the only power that can save people and, being human, is the only one who could adequately apply that power to save humans from their fallen status and their sinful thoughts, words, and deeds.

"Christ"—the English version of the Greek *christos*—is a title that means "anointed one," "messiah," the divine King who shall one day rule the earth directly. Such anointing could come only from God, and such a rule could be claimed and accomplished only by God himself. No human ruler can claim or take such a role. Such attempts always devolve to the abuse of those ruled. But "Christ" is a title of great hope, as it tells that God will, in the end, make all things right.

We pause here to note that the name "Jesus Christ" comes from two lan-guages: Hebrew and Greek. The same is true of the ancient Greek version of the name that was used in the early church and in the New Testament: *Iēsous Christos*. The name *Iēsous* is a foreign (Hebrew) name that is slightly modified to sound more natural in Greek. *Christos*, on the other hand, is different. It is a Greek *translation* of the Hebrew and Aramaic terms meaning "anointed one." Therefore, it is a mix between Hebrew and Greek. This name told early Christians that whether they were Jews or Greeks (the latter standing in for all gentiles), they all had access to Jesus and his salvation. That is the multiethnic, multicultural offer to all people that chaplains still make today.

We also use the term "Lord," which, in its basic sense, indicates Jesus's active rule over the world. The term, however, does much more than that. Since it is used of God throughout the Bible, its application to Jesus in the New Testament asserts his divinity. The chaplain, operating in tune with the Holy Spirit, has the privilege to represent the claims, invitation, benefits, and responsibilities that come with this divine rule.

"Immanuel" is another name for Jesus, meaning "God with us." That is, God the Son is immanent—present, in our midst, constantly coming among us (first as the Word, then in the flesh, now through the Spirit, and later in triumph)—rather than far off, not involved. This is good news that chaplains can share with those who are lonely or alienated: Jesus is available to them, willing to come to them, ready to take up his residence with them. God in Jesus is near, not far. He heals, forgives, helps, protects, and more—all in a most intimate way through a personal relationship. The offer of this relationship is revolutionary to those who think or fear that God doesn't care. The reality is that Jesus, through his life, words, actions, death, resurrection, ascension, and coming return, always cares and is always close. This is good news for those who feel alienated and stymied in organizations. Jesus can be their friend and on their side. A chaplain who shares this news offers hope that can come from nowhere else.

We return now to the subject of God's incarnation in the person of Jesus. Jesus is God come in the flesh, both fully God and fully man. This reality is an astounding affirmation of the human body around which so much of people's lives revolve. Some philosophies and religions denigrate the body as evil or a burden to shed. Christianity, by contrast, exalts humans—as a unity of body, soul, and spirit—in the image of God, as embodied and modeled by Jesus himself. Chaplains thus affirm the value of the body and the need to care for it through feeding the hungry, healing the sick, clothing and providing shelter for the needy, and so forth. God's creation of the body as good is a truth that is desperately needed when people hate or harm their bodies or feel hopelessly unable to meet their culture's views of attractiveness. The chaplain's affirmation of the goodness of the body can make a lifesaving difference to those in bodily need, doubt, or despair.

God the Holy Spirit: Impartation

We begin with the basics: the Holy Spirit is a person, not a force, thought, or mode of showing and knowing. For example, the Spirit can be grieved (Isa. 63:10; Eph. 4:30). And he is not just any person but a person of the Trinity, a divine person who is the source and model of the human spirit rather than a reflection of it. The Bible shows that he can be blasphemed (Mark 3:29). Such an action is possible only toward God. This reality of the Holy Spirit's personhood is very helpful to a chaplain seeking to explain spiritual realities in secular settings. The triune God—including the person of the Holy Spirit—is personal and relates on a personal level to all who seek to relate to him.

Scripture refers to the Holy Spirit as "him" and "he," and we believe it is imperative to take Scripture's lead in this matter; we have nothing else to offer than what God states in the wisdom of his Word. Some have sought to identify the Spirit as female and thus to make possible the *imago Dei* in women. We respond that God's essence and mystery are far beyond such small attempts to create one-to-one correspondence and that every woman fully represents God's image, as does every man. God, then—Father, Son, and Holy Spirit—is not, as some say, beyond sex or gender but includes in his nature the full reality and expression of both male and female—far more than humans can imagine.

The theologian J. Rodman Williams can help Christians understand what it means for the Holy Spirit to be, as his name indicates, spirit: "The word *spirit* conveys the note of intangibility, incorporeality, thus *immateriality*. . . . Spirit is not substance—even substance in its most rarefied or shadowy form. Yet it represents the essential reality of human existence, operating through soul and body." He also says that the word "signifies *freedom of movement*" and "represents energy, drive, and dynamic movement."[5]

The Spirit was present at the world's creation: "And the Spirit of God was hovering over the face of the waters" (Gen. 1:2). His presence in the world is his constant gift that keeps the world going. Apart from the Spirit's action, entropy would stop it all. The Spirit's presence filling Christian believers is his eternal gift of relationship that never stops giving. Chaplains depend entirely on the Spirit filling them and working through them to inspire, protect, bless, and grow their ministry. This reliance is especially true when chaplains move in secular circles seemingly bereft of any godly presence or influence. As Paul preached to a secular audience in Athens, "Yet [God] is actually not far from each one of us, for 'In him we live and move and have our being'" (Acts 17:27–28, likely quoting Epimenides of Crete). This gives evangelical chaplains great confidence to know that the Spirit is present in all the world, supernaturally perceiving all things and helping humans as he wills.

The Holy Spirit has been active in the world since the first verses in Genesis and will close earth's age with an invitation: "The Spirit and the Bride [the church] say, 'Come.' And let the one who hears say, 'Come.' And let the one who is thirsty come; let the one who desires take the water of life without price"

5. J. Rodman Williams, *Renewal Theology: Systematic Theology from a Charismatic Perspective*, vol. 2, *Salvation, the Holy Spirit, and Christian Living* (Grand Rapids: Zondervan, 1996), 137–38.

(Rev. 22:17). Knowing this, that no place is hidden from the Spirit's presence or bereft of him at any time, chaplains minister in confidence as they move in harmony with that Spirit wherever they are.

It may seem basic to state that the Holy Spirit is holy, but that word is needed. "Holiness," in the Hebrew, refers to separating something from the general grouping. Indeed, God's people are set apart by God from fallen humanity, to love him and serve him with holy lives and works that are sourced in God, far above and beyond "the common." That is not to say that Christians are not part of humanity; rather, it is to say that believers, sharing in the common humanity, have been called to something higher, purer, and better: holy lives that satisfy humanity's highest aspirations. To be holy is to be the best in God that one can possibly be. It encompasses other meanings as well; Williams writes that the word "holy" "stresses *sacredness*," "connotes utter purity and righteousness," and "expresses the high note of *majesty* and *glory*."[6]

Holiness is not a popular concept in the ways of the world. Yet God made people to live it and experience it, now on earth and later in heaven. There is thus something inherently attractive in the concept, even when it is presented to people who seem to dislike it, fear it, and oppose it. Chaplains, then, may feel that they face a headwind when presenting the Holy Spirit and the invitation to holy living. They must take special care, in secular environments, to resist the temptation to join the crowd and leave holiness behind when that very crowd depends on the chaplain's holy presence and witness for its welfare. But they can take comfort in knowing that God's undercurrent of human creation is stronger than the forces of entropy and dissolution. In the task of offering holiness, the chaplain is not alone, as it is the Holy Spirit himself who is drawing people Godward.

The Holy Spirit shares his power as a gift for Christians. Humans are limited, burdened, and hindered by sins, and this fact gives believers both the feeling and the reality of weakness. People in themselves are often not up to their assigned tasks in life. But Jesus told his disciples that they would receive power from the Holy Spirit, who came at Pentecost (Acts 2:1–4) and invested that power into the church so they would spread the gospel and work God's works. Christians understand that they are not limited to human power alone but, rather, have ready access to the Spirit's divine power as he makes it available. Thus, a chaplain in a place of weakness has strength from the Holy Spirit, a chaplain in lonely witness finds friends, and a chaplain in the face of negative reactions to God, from shrugs to denial to hostility, has the resources needed to share God's gospel, which transforms people, places, and situations. This

---

6. Williams, *Renewal Theology*, 2:138.

power is provided through the agency of God's powerful, wonderful Holy Spirit, who supplies strength that allows them to stand up to the dark powers of every age.

It can thus be seen that the Holy Spirit imparts many helps and advantages to those who minister his presence in his power. A Christian chaplain who imparts a fully trinitarian ministry offers a beautifully balanced message and witness that glorifies God in his fullness and serves exactly the full needs of every person that the chaplain encounters.

Philosophies of Chaplaincy

Chaplains need certain points of view regarding the people they serve and the place where they minister. These philosophies of chaplaincy are the underpinnings of a practical theological approach to chaplaincy.

God and Anthropology

We have already looked at some aspects of man—male and female—as a creation made in the image of God. One such aspect that deserves further comment is the unity of the human person: body, soul, and spirit. People are not fundamentally souls or spirits imprisoned in a body. When God creates, redeems, and fills a person, he does so with respect to the whole person, not just a part. We thus reject the "shell view" of man, which says that a body in a casket is just a shell that has been shed and is no longer needed as the spirit flies free. The bodily resurrection of Jesus cements this understanding of the unified person and offers a preview of believers' glorious destiny in him.

Every person is wonderfully made in God's image and is able to exist and thrive in both the physical realm and the spiritual realm. C. S. Lewis did well in using the analogy of humans being like earth's amphibians. Here he speaks in the voice of Screwtape, a fictional demon:

> Humans are amphibians—half spirit and half animal. . . . As spirits they belong to the eternal world, but as animals they inhabit time. This means that while their spirit can be directed to an eternal object, their bodies, passions, and imaginations are in continual change, for to be in time means to change.[7]

The human body is a marvel of design that firmly roots humans in the physical world. Yet people are not just about the temporal but, rather, are also about the

---

7. C. S. Lewis, *The Screwtape Letters* (1942; repr., San Francisco: HarperSanFrancisco, 2001), 37.

eternal. God, who is infinite, relates to his finite image bearers and offers them eternal life in addition to the temporal life he has already given. Even the fact of God's relating to people is a great hope for chaplains to share, for it offers a revolutionary breakthrough to address people's problems.

The classic Christian orthodox view of man says that humans, though created wonderfully and beautifully, have chosen sin, are fallen into sin, and live in sin—indeed, that all people are born into the sin that flows from Adam and Eve's horrendous legacy. When they ate the forbidden fruit (often depicted as an apple), all evils gained entrance into the world for all time until Christ returns. Thus, in that single disastrous moment was contained, potentially, all the horrors the world has known since. In that apple was Auschwitz.

Thus, man needs deliverance in order to be saved from sin, to return to a relationship with God and his goodness. Jesus Christ is that divine Savior, the only sinless human who could perform that task by his costly sacrifice on the cross. God's people, the church—which Christian chaplains represent—share God's invitation to turn from sin; accept his offer of grace, mercy, and salvation; and live in his love. In doing so, chaplains invite people to be more human: to come to a greater understanding of God's great plans, blessings, and delights for their lives and to live accordingly while receiving divine help to meet life's challenges, pains, and diseases and the reality of inevitable death.

Chaplains mediate that help, and they do so with respect and relationship as fellow humans made in God's image; with God's love and care for the whole person—body, soul, and spirit; with God's invitation to enter into relationship with him; and with the rich community of God's people, the church. This is all done in the midst of an environment that may hinder or oppose a person's positive response. But many institutions, seeing the positive results of chaplains' presence and ministry in their midst, give them a chance to give that care and make that offer. Indeed, there are times when chaplains may be the only ones or among the few who offer this dignity, respect, relationship, and opportunity. It is an offer that many are glad to accept, whether in whole or in part.

God and Work

God gave humans, even before the fall, the gift of work. That first work was the care of God's creation; they were to tend the garden of Eden—lit by the moon, sun, and other stars and planets—as stewards of God's gifts. This work assignment from God has meant that humans have an intimate relationship with the physical cosmos, from earth to space, all created by God. People are made for earth and its care, even as it is made to support people with its bounty, which man is charged to wisely attain, receive, store, and use. By extension, humans are intended to explore the physical creation, discover its treasures, and use them well as God's gifts. This use and exploration require work. Thus, an amazing partnership develops between humanity's care *for* creation and humanity's care *by* creation, both of which are mediated by work. Work as God's gift gives people a stake in both their world and their own well-being. As such, work gives people not only harmony with creation and sustenance for their lives but also satisfaction, dignity, and meaning. The chaplain, almost always ministering in a work environment, can use these understandings to help people better appreciate and attain the benefits of work's high value—in and of itself.

Work is needed not just for human survival but also for human flourishing and fulfillment. Dorothy Sayers explains:

> I urged . . . a thorough-going revolution in our whole attitude to work. I asked that it should be looked upon—not as a necessary drudgery to be undergone for the purpose of making money, but as a way of life in which the nature of man should find its proper exercise and delight and so fulfill itself to the glory of God. That it should, in fact, be thought of as a creative activity undertaken for the love of the work itself; and that man, made in God's image, should make things, as God makes them, for the sake of doing well a thing that is well worth doing.[8]

Good work well done brings a sense of satisfaction and well-being. Its craft and its art can be admired in and of themselves. A chaplain who admires someone's excellent and beautiful work is paying tribute not just to the work but to the essence of that person. Such admiration and praise are not always as prevalent as they should be, and it is a gift that a chaplain can give.

The chaplain, to give that gift well, should take a personal interest in the conditions, equipment, economics, hours, social structure, atmosphere, and so forth that combine to form the work environment for the people they serve. Taking an interest in these things displays an interest in the people whose lives are so driven by them.

Work also almost always requires cooperation and coordination among various people to accomplish results. Even small tasks unavoidably involve the intricate web of human relationships that provides supplies, places, timing, markets, and more. Such dependence on community for work's success means that, ideally, work should build community. This realization gives the chaplain—a community builder by vocation—strong motivation to help people work together with goodwill and to great effect. In this endeavor people not

8. Dorothy Sayers, "Why Work?," in *Creed or Chaos?* (New York: Harcourt, Brace, 1949), 46.

only find God's common grace but also may glimpse the greater joys of communing with God himself, who offers to work with all who seek him. The chaplain, in building this community of work, also supports that community's productive purpose, which is why being an insider, part of the community, is so crucial. The chaplain makes the same commitments, pays the same price of those commitments, and enjoys the same benefits as others. These prices and benefits differ, of course, from environment to environment. But the chaplain, as an integral part of the community, joins all others in being subject to its existence, purpose, and rules. This participation always involves some kind of work, and that is ground on which the Christian chaplain is comfortable while ministering as one of the fellow workers.

Access

Chaplaincy offers unparalleled access to people's lives and access by those people, regardless of their religious beliefs or affiliation, to a clergyperson serving as a chaplain. This access is perhaps one of the greatest privileges of chaplaincy: that ministers can freely be with people in their place of service (or where they receive other services, as with students and healthcare patients). They are not limited to religious buildings, chapels, and so on. Yes, chaplains use those facilities, but chaplaincy moves far beyond them to be available to all people anywhere, anytime. Chaplains have access to everyone, and everyone has access to their chaplains—regardless of their religious affinity, belief, or membership. In that regard, chaplains must have a mindset of being a chaplain every minute as they witness to God's nature and presence everywhere, all the time. It is common for chaplains to be approached for ministry matters, large or small, at times having nothing to do with formal ministry programs. This availability is the beauty of chaplaincy: the chaplain's access to people and people's access to the chaplain.

Inclusiveness

Chaplains believe that all the people in their secular organizations should have their spiritual and religious needs met. "Spirituality" and "spiritual care," while highly important, do not fully address the reality of human life or chaplain service. "Religion" has acquired a negative connotation in much of the world— admittedly due to the failings of many religious people—but it really just refers to the formal beliefs, practices, and actions that people of faith maintain and live out. It is not uncommon to hear religion scorned from buildings that are, in reality, religious. But chaplains realize that every system of ultimate thought

will take some form of religious expression. These forms require tangible structures, items, and personnel, such as a sanctuary or meetinghouse, a sweat lodge,
candles, sacramental elements, an altar, a sound system, musicians and musical
instruments, and so forth. Spiritual care tends toward the individual and the
intangible, while religious support tends toward the communal and the tangible.
Both are important, and a good chaplain will go to great lengths to support both.

We completely support the philosophy of meeting the needs of all religions
when possible. An inclusive culture creates room for all to practice their religion freely, unlike a cancel culture that excludes those deemed to be unworthy
because of their beliefs. In other words, we support free exercise (see chap. 4).
Some evangelicals are shocked at this stance, which involves providing equipment and opportunities for other groups, deemed to be in error, to meet. We
answer that the job of chaplains is not only to provide for their own people
but also to facilitate for others and to care for all. We have a threefold justifica-
tion for this philosophy. First, God gave freedom of choice to the first humans,
Adam and Eve. He gave them a command and told them what would happen
if they broke it, thus giving them freedom (Gen. 2:15–17). Who are chaplains
to deny people the same freedom that God gave from the start? Second, when
chaplains protect the freedom of others to practice their religious faith, they
also protect their own freedom. They take their place with everyone else as
wanting to have free exercise of religion in a relatively restricted work environment. When chaplains help others get it, they are glad to get it too. Third, we
believe that when an interfaith environment offers a truly level playing field, in
which all have the freedom to practice their faith and invite others, the gospel
of Jesus Christ will do well and bear fruit.

Interfaith Etiquette

Chaplains, unlike pastors, expect to practice their ministry within an interfaith environment. While pastors conduct mission into the general world, they
do so from a home base—a church—in which their faith is practiced. Those
who are out in the world and wish to receive the full ministry of the pastor
must ultimately come to that pastor's community, whether it is in the context
of a building or through a website. Such ministry, therefore, must be primarily
attractional—even if supported by a missional mindset and methods. Chaplains, on the other hand, live, minister, and stay in their secular and interfaith
environments. They are by definition missional. They therefore have to be far
more sensitive to the thoughts, feelings, and practices of others.

That is why chaplains are willing and ready to be immersed, on a daily
basis, in a variety of viewpoints without feeling uncomfortable or out of place.

They are willing to interact openly and winsomely with others, whatever their beliefs and practices, all the while avoiding proselytism and being open enough to listen and establish warm, long-term relationships. The good chaplain does not just show respect for all but takes the trouble to hear deeply and learn who others are, whatever their beliefs or religion. The good chaplain serves as a via media, a "middle way": a person who, while standing strong in their own faith, can love those of other faiths while daily living and working with them as a colleague. Thus, the chaplain offers an attractive way for them to explore that chaplain's faith when they wish.

Love, Enjoyment, and Integrity

Good chaplains should love the people to whom they are assigned. That love is not only the self-giving *agapē* love of God that chaplains offer as their explicit ministry. Every Christian minister should have that kind of love. But in the chaplain's case, another step is needed: *phileō* love—that is, brotherly love of fellow feeling with other people. In other words, the chaplain needs to *enjoy* being with, working with, and living with secular people and people of other faiths. The love of bringing God's news needs to be complemented by a genuine love for people themselves as beings made by the Lord. This means liking them too—including the ones who do not like the chaplain. Some chaplains miss this step in their rush to bring their religious mission and ministry to the "heathen." But they need to know that they should commit to being *with* the people, whether or not the people like or accept the chaplain. That is the test of true love.

In doing this, however, chaplains must take care not to lose their own identity by slipping into the enculturation of their environment. It is easy for a chaplain to succumb to wanting to be accepted as "one of the gang." Chaplains will be watched closely—and tested—to see if they will stay true to their Christian beliefs and practices or only give them lip service. Chaplains will want to be social and should take care to attend social gatherings—but they must not ruin their testimony with coarse words or ribald behavior. Chaplains will want to be *with* the people in the workplace but not *like* them. In fact, the people will hope that the chaplain will show, when tested, that he or she is *not* like them in terms of belief and practice, even though he or she is like them as a human and as a part of the same organization or community. They *need* the chaplain to be different, because, secretly or not, that is their true and deepest hope: that the minister will offer hope in that place as a redemptive person and presence. So, yes, a chaplain can be advised to hang out with the folks and be at ease, to listen and show love and acceptance instead of disgust and rejection. But the chaplain who does this must maintain his or her testimony too. Then the people will know that the minister in their midst has something that is better than not just their banter and antics but also the problems they have in life.

Summary

In this chapter, we have discussed the biblical, theological, and philosophical bases of chaplaincy. These areas overlap and reinforce each other, forming a foundation for holistic chaplain ministry.

3

Chaplains in History

To better understand chaplaincy, it is essential to have a clear description and explanation of its origin and historical framework. From where does chaplaincy come? How has it evolved through the centuries to reach its present-day roles and practices? Lastly, how can chaplains understand the modern functional areas of chaplaincy in terms of its origins and development?

Chaplaincy is steeped in a rich history that has accumulated as chaplains have served militaries, hospitals, businesses, and other organizations throughout the centuries. Chaplains have long existed because people and organizations felt a need for them. This chapter focuses on the historical growth of chaplaincy and on the expansion of modern chaplaincy in the United States.

The Mists of Time

Soldiers in battle have always desired religious support for their safety and success. Various types of priests, seers, prophets, and similar religious leaders have joined armies on the march, in camp, and in battle. Military victory is the ultimate goal, and anything that does not support that goal is considered dispensable. Why, then, have chaplains always been part of fighting forces? Fighting power comes from physical supplies that provide everything from food, sanitation, and healthcare to transportation and armaments. Leadership, diplomacy, planning, organization, morale, strategy, and tactics follow.

How is it that these protochaplains have always been included in armies, even when resources have been at a premium? A military force's spirit and morale are crucial, indispensable supports that chaplains help fulfill. Chaplains meet a basic need among military members who are deployed far from home and struggle with issues of life and death. Military members often feel an acute need to receive spiritual support and opportunities for religious practice. Chaplains also help make sense of life and death in light of life's ultimate significance. They meet this need by providing worship, prayer, and a personal touch of care, assurance, and meaning. They inspire the group and advise soldiers and leaders. Finally, they have often provided a public reinforcement of an army's cause in ceremonies and services. While the saying "There are no atheists in foxholes" is demonstrably false, it is largely true that soldiers are glad to have a chaplain nearby who represents and mediates the presence of the divine.

Homer's epics the *Iliad* and the *Odyssey* and Virgil's epic the *Aeneid* focus on war and how people behave before, during, and after battles. Many modern people fail to realize that these are also fundamentally religious texts demonstrating the involvement of the gods, who determine and drive human life. Apart from the religious interactions between humans and the gods, these epics would make little sense. They consistently and convincingly demonstrate the essential link between military actions and some higher, divine support. Chaplains, though not known by that name until the eighth century, embody the essence of that link.

Likewise, healthcare and healing practices have long sought partnership with divine presence, comfort, and intervention. Ancient temples—such as those to Asclepius, the Greek god of medicine—touted divine healings, and many healers represented a religion of some sort. Disease, sickness, and injuries brought closer the boundaries between life and death. As with soldiers, those who were sick, wounded, or knowingly near death often wished to have divine comfort and health. Thus, healing practices have long had a close connection with religious faith and practice. Religious ministers were often present and practicing in the various places of healing. They, too, would ultimately develop chaplaincy.

Not surprisingly, the development of modern chaplaincy—from the early modern period of the Reformation until the present—has found its primary examples of chaplaincy in the military and the field of healing. Examining chaplaincy from the time of antiquity yields insights into a modern understanding of the chaplain's work.

The Old Testament depicts the Israelite priests accompanying the Israelite army into battle, as depicted in Joshua 6 when the Levites (the priests' practical

assistants) carried the ark of the covenant at the successful siege of Jericho.[1]
Today, people would refer to these Levites as military chaplains. There are
many other biblical passages in which priests accompany the army of the Lord
into battle.

The Romans, led by Virgil in this respect, attributed their origins to survivors
of the Trojan War who, through divine guidance given to Aeneas, found and
founded a new home. Because the Trojan War involved the Greeks, Rome's
religious expressions tended to reflect the pantheon of Greek gods. It is well
known that Roman armies and those they fought were accompanied by priests
who invoked those gods and sought their signs (in animal entrails or natural
events) for advice, information, and favor concerning various plans. Ralph
Mathisen states that within the Roman army, some military officers provided
ministry for the state religion's cultic requirements to the groups of soldiers
under their command.[2] There is evidence that by the early 400s, after the shift
from pagan Rome to Christian Rome, a form of military chaplaincy existed in
the Roman army. The bishop Eusebius of Caesarea reports that Constantine,
in order to meet spiritual needs, had a "tent of meetings" set up for his soldiers
to worship in.[3]

St. Martin of Tours

St. Martin of Tours is a key link in understanding the genesis of the term "chaplain" and the foundational development of the Western nomenclature of chaplaincy. Martin was born in 336 in Szombathely, Hungary, into a military family.[4]
He lived most of his formative life in Italy and later became a soldier himself.
Suplitius Severus reports that it was during this time that Martin had an encounter with Christ. During most of his army career, Martin was stationed in
Gaul (modern-day France). On a cold winter day just outside Amiens, Martin
encountered a beggar asking for alms at the city gate. Martin had compassion
for the beggar, since it was the middle of winter. Removing his cloak, he cut it
in half, gave one piece to the beggar, and wrapped the other piece around his
own shoulders. That night, in a dream, Christ came to Martin wearing the same

1. Ralph W. Mathisen, "Emperors, Priests, and Bishops: Military Chaplains in the Roman
Empire," in *The Sword of the Lord: Military Chaplains from the First to the Twenty-First Century*, ed.
Doris L. Bergen (Notre Dame, IN: University of Notre Dame Press, 2004), 29–43.
2. Mathisen, "Emperors, Priests, and Bishops," 30.
3. John D. Laing, *In Jesus' Name: Evangelicals and Military Chaplaincy* (Eugene, OR: Resource,
2010), 27.
4. Fernando Lanzi, *Saints and Their Symbols: Recognizing Saints in Art and in Popular Images*
(Collegeville, MN: Liturgical Press, 2004), 104.

half cloak he had given to the beggar at the Amiens gate. Christ said, "Martin, who is still but a catechumen, clothed me with this robe." When Martin awoke, the cloak was restored to its original wholeness.[5] The connection to chaplaincy came as the cloak became a "relic of the Catholic Church during the reigns of the Merovingian Kings."[6] Its importance gradually grew as its continual bequeathment became part of the royal tradition and legitimacy.

The term "chaplain" first appeared in the fourth century in its Latin form, *capellanus*. It describes the priests who carried into battle the relics of saints, especially St. Martin's cape (*cappa*). The cloak was later brought into battle by the priests of Charlemagne to protect the French armies.[7] The priests who cared for the cloak in the reliquary had the Latin name *cappellanu*. As they went into battle, the tent in which the cloak was housed and protected was called a *capella*, which means "little cape" or "chapel."[8] The priests who served in the military and carried the cloak into battle were called *cappellani*. Chapels were not formal churches. They were temporary structures or tents built by the king (not the church or clerics) to house the cloak (*capella*). Gradually, chapels became places of gathering and worship in the context of chaplains' work.

Thus, the identifying terms "chaplain" and "chapel" have ancient history and usage. Some have objected to the term "chaplain" on the grounds that it is a solely Christian artifact. While it originated in a Christian context and refers to the caring actions of a Christian soldier who later became a priest, bishop, and saint, it is not exclusively a Christian term, as it relates to an item of clothing and its generous sharing. The word may thus be agreeably used by those of other religious traditions. Also, as has been seen, the chaplain's function goes back much further than the name, into deepest history.

Crowns and Chaplains

While chaplaincy began primarily in the military and, to some extent, in healing endeavors, it began to expand into other venues. Christendom's royalty and nobility typically had household priests who had great influence in their

5. Suplitius Severus, *Saint Martin of Tours*, chap. 3, in *A Select Library of Nicene and Post-Nicene Fathers of the Christian Church*, 2nd series, ed. Philip Schaff and Henry Wace, 14 vols. (1890–1900; repr., Peabody, MA: Hendrickson, 1994), 5. See also "Saint Martin of Tours," Saint of the Day, Franciscan Media, accessed January 19, 2023, https://www.franciscanmedia.org/saint-of-the-day/saint-martin-of-tours.

6. Laing, *In Jesus' Name*, 30.

7. J. P. Brunterch, *Un village au temps de Charlemagne*, 90–93, cited in François-Olivier Touati, *Maladie et société au Moyen Âge* (Brussels: De Boeck Université, 1998), 216n100.

8. Thomas Benson, *American Rhetoric: Context and Criticism* (Carbondale: Southern Illinois University Press, 1989), 269.

personal lives and governmental operations, often becoming government officials themselves, like Joseph, Mordecai, and Daniel in the Bible. The royal, the noble, and the wealthy would often erect chapels within their domiciles (such as castles) or on their grounds to minister to their families and retainers within the precincts. Kings, having taken chaplains into battle, also wanted them in their presence at home. The practice of naming household and court priests "chaplains" soon grew widely in Western Christendom and continues to the present.[9]

The Crusades and Beyond

At the Concilium Germanicum in the year 742, Catholic bishops discussed the spiritual care of soldiers in the army. David Bachrach states that the Concilium Germanicum is "the legal origin of the chaplain's office in the Latin west."[10] By around 850, during the Carolingian era, chaplaincy had become more formal and specialized. Benedict the Levite led the way, establishing protections for chaplains from abusive secular leaders. Chaplains were prohibited from bearing arms, shedding blood, and taking life.[11] The infamous Investiture Controversy (ca. 1076–1122) began in earnest when Henry IV, Holy Roman emperor, named his court chaplain Tedald as bishop of Milan—in opposition to Pope Gregory VII. When the Crusades began in 1095, chaplain duties were specifically defined and established as preaching, celebrating Mass, carrying relics to the field of battle, and providing caring ministry for the dying and dead.[12] By that time it was standard practice to have the troops offer confession prior to battle to free them of their sins and to assure them of heaven should they die. In addition to these duties, chaplains blessed the soldiers en masse, encouraged and inspired them, and were present with them throughout their wartime ordeals.

Chaplaincy continued to develop and became a strong ministry within the Christian community. In 1215, at the Fourth Lateran Council, Pope Innocent III presented an updated list of chaplain duties. In 1238, Pope Gregory IX clarified even more chaplain duties in a papal bulletin. By the time of the Protestant

9. *Encyclopedia Britannica* (online), s.v. "chaplain," last updated March 31, 2023, https://www.britannica.com/topic/chaplain.

10. David S. Bachrach, "The Medieval Military Chaplain and His Duties," in Bergen, *Sword of the Lord*, 76.

11. Laing, *In Jesus' Name*, 28.

12. Laing, *In Jesus' Name*, 28; Bergen, *Sword of the Lord*, 6. The dynamic, conflictual tenor of the times is captured in such significant events, rapidly following each other, as Christianity's Great Schism between East and West (1054), the Investiture Controversy (beginning in 1076), and the First Crusade (called for in 1095).

Reformation, chaplains were regularly going into battle with their country's armies and ministering to the soldiers they served.[13] Ulrich Zwingli, one of the great Swiss Reformers, served in the military as a chaplain and was the first Protestant chaplain killed in combat, at the Battle of Kappel on October 11, 1531.[14]

During the English Civil War (1642–51), military chaplains served on both sides. Royalist chaplains emphasized allegiance to the king, while the parliamentary chaplains taught that it was acceptable to disobey the king. During England's war against Ireland, Cromwell's chaplains, as anti-Catholics, found it easier to preach violence against Irish Catholics than against Scottish Presbyterians. Chaplaincy in England continued to flourish, and in 1796 the English Parliament established the Royal Army Chaplains Department.[15] Before then, by the early 1600s, a great migration toward the New World was beginning to take shape. In the eastern part of the county of Sussex, England, a group of people were forming an expedition to the New World. Robert Hunt, a Church of England clergyman and the vicar of Heathfield, became the chaplain of the expedition that resulted in the founding of Jamestown, Virginia. As the first chaplain at Jamestown, "he lit the candle for the Anglican Church in Virginia (United States); he first lifted his voice in public thanksgiving and prayer on April 29, 1607, when the settlers planted a cross at Cape Henry, which they named after the Prince of Wales."[16]

> Once settled in the fort, the whole company, except those who were on guard, attended regular prayer and services led by . . . [Chaplain] Hunt. Captain John Smith described worship services that took place in the open air until a chapel could be erected. Captain Smith's religious feelings were conventional but deeply felt. His piety asserted itself in his writings constantly; he saw the hand of God at work in his life, and he believed it had intervened to save the colonies. "He concluded that God, who had thwarted Spanish attempts to settle North America, had reserved that Region for the Protestant English." . . . Captain John Smith described . . . [Chaplain] Hunt as "our honest, religious and courageous divine." The Reverend Hunt was a peacemaker, often bringing harmony to a quarreling group of men.[17]

13. Laing, *In Jesus' Name*, 29.
14. Laing, *In Jesus' Name*, 29; Stephen Brett Eccher, "The Bernese Disputations of 1532 and 1538: A Historical and Theological Analysis" (PhD diss., University of St. Andrews, 2011), 26.
15. Bergen, *Sword of the Lord*, 7; Michael Francis Snape, *The Royal Army Chaplains' Department, 1796–1953: Clergy under Fire*, Studies in Modern British Religious History 18 (Rochester, NY: Boydell, 2008), 15; Christopher Swift, Andrew Todd, and Mark Cobb, eds., *A Handbook of Chaplaincy Studies: Understanding Spiritual Care in Public Places* (Burlington, VT: Ashgate, 2015), 203.
16. "The Reverend Robert Hunt: The First Chaplain at Jamestown," Historic Jamestowne, National Park Service, last updated September 4, 2022, https://www.nps.gov/jame/learn/history culture/the-reverend-robert-hunt-the-first-chaplain-at-jamestown.htm.
17. "Reverend Robert Hunt."

Chaplain Hunt's expansion of duties to include meeting the community's felt needs has been a hallmark of chaplaincy.

In 1637, chaplains were a vital part of the British settlement in the New World. The Connecticut Legislature gave authority to raise a local militia of ninety men and appointed Samuel Stone as its first chaplain for that militia.[18] In England chaplaincy was growing as well. In 1773 John Howard, high sheriff of Bedfordshire, established the first prison chaplaincy in England. He was an advocate for clean living accommodations, for religious services, and for the segregation of the prison populations by gender, age, and the offense of which they were convicted.[19]

Military Chaplaincy in America

As the American colonies began their revolt against British rule, the Continental Congress established the first funded army chaplaincy position on July 29, 1775—almost a year prior to the Declaration of Independence.[20] This date is established as the birthdate of the US Army Chaplain Corps. General George Washington was an emphatic supporter of the religious ministries provided by chaplains and of chaplains accompanying troops in military operations.

After the Revolutionary War, General Washington commenced provisions to add chaplains to each regiment in the new American army. John Hurt of Virginia, having served as a chaplain to the Sixth Virginia Regiment during the American Revolution, became the first chaplain appointed to the newly formed position on March 4, 1791.[21] By an act of Congress, authorization for the formation of a second infantry regiment in the regular army was established in law. The act of Congress authorized the commissioning of a new brigadier general, a quartermaster, and a chaplain. Today, chaplain John Hurt is recognized officially as the first United States Army chaplain.[22]

18. Israel Drazin and Cecil B. Currey, *For God and Country: The History of a Constitutional Challenge to the Army Chaplaincy* (Hoboken, NJ: KTAV, 1995), 6.

19. Laing, *In Jesus' Name*, 31.

20. Laing, *In Jesus' Name*, 32; Robert D. Crick, *Outside the Gates: The Need for, Theology, History, and Practice of Chaplaincy Ministries*, with Brandelan S. Miller, rev. ed. (Oviedo, FL: HigherLife Development Services, 2011), 126; Angela L. Caruso-Yahne, "Spiritual, but Not Religious: Fostering Conversations in the Military System," Upaya Zen Center, December 2013, 8, https://upaya .org/uploads/pdfs/CarusoYahneThesisFinal.pdf; Ed Waggoner, "Taking Religion Seriously in the US Military: The Chaplaincy as a National Strategic Asset," *Journal of the American Academy of Religion* 82, no. 3 (2014): 705.

21. Frank Moore, ed., *The Patriot Preachers of the American Revolution, with Biographical Sketches, 1776–1783* (New York: Charles T. Evans, 1862), 143.

22. Moore, *Patriot Preachers*, 143.

TABLE 3.1

Establishment Date for Military Branches and Chaplain Corps

Branch	Date Established	Chaplain Corps Established
Army	June 14, 1775	July 29, 1775
Navy	October 13, 1775	November 28, 1775
Marine Corps	November 10, 1775	Uses Navy chaplains
Coast Guard	August 4, 1790	Uses Navy chaplains
Air Force	September 18, 1947	September 18, 1947
Space Force	December 20, 2019	Uses Air Force chaplains

The Continental Congress adopted the second article of Navy regulations on November 28, 1775, indicating that a clergyman was authorized to be part of a Navy ship's company, thus establishing the birthdate of the US Navy Chaplain Corps.[23] On November 15, 1776, Congress fixed the base pay of the chaplain at twenty dollars a month, a Navy lieutenant's salary. This newly adopted Navy regulation additionally authorized chaplains to receive a share of the prize money of any ship or booty taken in battle. The first chaplain known to have served in the Continental Navy was Harvard-educated Congregational minister Benjamin Balch of Barrington, New Hampshire, who was assigned to the frigate *Boston* after receiving the first written commission for a chaplain in the Continental Navy, on October 28, 1778.[24]

His father had served as a chaplain in "King George's War" in 1745. Prior to becoming a Navy chaplain, Rev. Balch had fought at Lexington as a Minuteman and served as an Army chaplain during the siege of Boston. . . . Chaplain Balch . . . served aboard her until her capture during the siege of Charleston, South Carolina in 1780. He then served aboard the frigate Alliance under the command of Commodore John Barry. Because of Chaplain Balch's being active amidst Alliance's sea battles, he earned the nickname "the Fightin' Parson."[25]

23. William F. R. Gilroy and Timothy J. Demy, *A Brief Chronology of the Chaplain Corps of the United States Navy*, Navy Personnel 15506 (1983), 1, available at https://ia803208.us.archive .org/5/items/a-brief-chronology-of-the-chaplains-corpsof-the-united-states-nay/A%20Brief %20Chronology%20of%20The%20Chaplains%20Corpsof%20The%20United%20States%20 Nay_text.pdf; Lawrence P. Greenslit, *Religion and the Military: A Growing Ethical Dilemma* (Carlisle Barracks, PA: Army War College, 2006), 4.

24. Gilroy and Demy, *Brief Chronology*, 1.

25. Bryan J. Dickerson, "The Navy Chaplain Corps: 230 Years of Service to God and Country," Marines, October 27, 2005, https://www.2ndmaw.marines.mil/News/Article-View/Article /522775/the-navy-chaplain-corps-230-years-of-service-to-god-and-country.

Military chaplains were prominently present with their soldiers and sailors in the War of 1812, the Mexican War, and that great cauldron of American crisis, the Civil War.

The Civil War saw chaplains meeting the spiritual needs of soldiers on American battlefields by caring for the living, praying over the wounded, and burying the dead. Further, chaplains often led evening worship services, gathering up to two thousand soldiers to pray, read Scripture, sing hymns, and hear sermons. Of special note are the chaplain-led evangelical revivals that broke out in camps. As chaplains preached the gospel, thousands responded and gave their lives to Christ. Chaplains baptized many of those who accepted Christ in the camps. A poignant example is the Great Revival of 1863/64, during which approximately 10 percent of the soldiers in the Army of northern Virginia made decisions to commit their lives to Christ.[26] Eyewitnesses reported:

> The great body of soldiers in some regiments meet for prayer and exhortation every night, exhibit the deepest solemnity, and present themselves numerously for prayers of the chaplains. . . . The audiences and interest have grown to glorious dimensions. . . . You behold a mass of men seated on the earth. . . . The Spirit of God went with the preached word and . . . the heads of many of the most hardened sinners were bowed down as they became convicted of sin. . . . Those that tasted of the love of Christ showed the greatest eagerness to lead others to the same precious fountain.[27]

Meanwhile, African American chaplains—many of them formerly enslaved— served their segregated units with distinction in combat.

Navy chaplains successfully ended punishment by the lash and replaced the daily issuing of rum with a daily issue of coffee. They were also foremost in providing education and literature to make sailors' lives more productive. Army chaplains, during the Indian Wars, offered priceless ministry to soldiers and their families at isolated frontier outposts.

The Spanish-American War and the First World War began to bring military chaplaincy into a much more formal organizational practice. The industrial, institutional nature of modern warfare—and the societies supporting it—meant that military organizations were becoming even more reflective of that nature. Chaplains' ranks, assignments, and institutional requirements were laid out with increasing detail and accountability. The first Navy chief of chaplains, Captain John B. Frazier, Chaplain Corps, was named in 1917,

26. Bergen, *Sword of the Lord*, 110–11.
27. William J. Jones, *Christ in the Camp; or, Religion in the Confederate Army* (1887; repr., Harrisonburg, VA: Sprinkle, 1986), 284–88.

and the first Army chief of chaplains, Chaplain (Colonel) John T. Axton, was named in 1920.

Military chaplaincy gradually expanded its representative ranks as well. The first rabbis were commissioned during World War I. During World War II, the newly founded National Association of Evangelicals successfully sought to place its chaplains alongside the traditionally represented Catholic, Lutheran, Presbyterian, Methodist, and other mainline representatives. African American chaplains were also appointed to serve not just those of their ethnicity but all those in a given ship or unit.

Clinical Pastoral Education

The 1920s also saw a revolution in pastoral care for chaplains working in health-care settings. William A. Bryan, superintendent of the Worcester State Hospital in Worcester, Massachusetts, hired Chaplain Anton T. Boisen to "break down the dividing wall between religion and medicine." Boisen believed that

> crisis periods in life have creative possibilities. He associated crisis with religious "quickening." He writes, "In times of crisis, when the person's fate is hanging in the balance, we are likely to think and feel intensely regarding the things that matter most." Amidst such circumstances new ideas flash into the mind so vividly that they seem to come from an outside source. For Anton, crisis periods had creative possibilities. They are moments bringing forth change either for better or for worse.[28]

The formal training of theological and pastoral students to research these possibilities began in 1925, later transitioning, with Boisen's departure in 1931, to a more pastoral emphasis that included both action and reflection in the care of patients. Clinical pastoral education (CPE) has expanded dramatically in practice and influence since its founding almost a century ago. Many areas of chaplaincy encourage CPE qualifications, and some—especially healthcare chaplaincies—require it. Many seminaries now require a CPE internship for all their students, making it a prominent and sometimes primary component of chaplain practice. Still further, a few seminaries have become ACPE centers and melded CPE into graduate-level courses that are included in master of divinity degrees.

28. Robert Leas and John R. Thomas, "Association for Clinical Pastoral Education, Inc.," Association for Clinical Pastoral Education, accessed January 19, 2023, https://acpe.edu/docs/default-source/acpe-history/acpe-brief-history.pdf. This history is the major source for this paragraph.

Chaplaincy's Expansion

After centuries of chaplaincy's development, primarily in military and health-care settings but also in prisons and among the royal, the noble, and the wealthy, the twentieth century saw chaplaincy's dramatic expansion into further fields, fields we will explore in detail in the book's second half. Chaplains were invited to serve with police officers and firefighters, in civic organizations, in various government agencies from town councils to the US Senate, and in general work-place and corporate settings, such as factories, national parks, sports teams, cruise lines, and communities. Chaplaincy, in recent years, has moved into maturity in its traditional areas and is expanding rapidly in the nontraditional ones. In contrast to the secularization of American society, chaplaincy is just beginning to hit full stride as it moves confidently into a future in which chaplains are increasingly needed and welcome.

4

The Constitution and Religious Freedom in Chaplaincy

Since chaplaincy involves a crossover between religious and secular organizations, it inevitably raises some difficult questions about law and ethics. In this chapter we will provide a wealth of information that will help chaplains navigate these difficulties wisely and appropriately. Our focus here is on the United States, but we hope that the information given provides a helpful model for other places as well. We will begin by delving into the history of the United States and exploring its Constitution and the First Amendment, and with this foundation laid, we will address a number of important concerns for chaplains.

The Constitution and the First Amendment

Religious freedom is arguably one of the most important principles that Americans hold dear in terms of their foundational rights. This principle, enshrined in writing more than two and a half centuries ago, is as important today in its meaning and application as it was at the establishment of the Constitution of the United States of America.

The Founding Fathers and Freedom of Religion

The Founding Fathers of the United States founded the nation and its government on religious freedom, which is based on personal conscience and individual choice. By that point the millennia-old church-and-state model of the Western European community, which established one form of Christianity as the religion of the land and enforced it by penalty of the law, had proved to be unjust, corrupt, and repressive. Thus, the timing of religious freedom in the history of Christianity and the establishment of the United States created an opportunity for the freedom of religious expression or the lack thereof, with no penalties from a government or church. The Founding Fathers' concern for religious freedom was supported by their recognition, drawn from the historical record and from their own experience, of the vital importance of religion in the life of the individual and in society. Dennis J. Goldford notes the impact of religion in the society and culture of the United States, offering a reminder that "religious beliefs, by their very nature, form a central part of a person's belief structure, his inner self. They define a person's very being—his sense of who he is, why he exists, and how he should relate to the world."[1] This is, in essence, the foundational thought process behind the enshrinement of freedom of religion in the US Constitution.

Religious Freedom

The Protestant Reformation, initiated by Martin Luther in 1517, severed the unity of Western Christendom, paving the way for religious pluralism. What emerged from this disruption were four patterns of Protestant faith: the Lutheran Reformation, the Anglican Reformation, the Anabaptist Reformation, and the Calvinist Reformation.[2]

The Founding Fathers understood that diversity would be a feature of their new nation and that they would need to take steps to ensure that the people would remain united despite their differences. Religion would naturally factor into this project. Goldford notes, "A society can hold together in its diversity only if conflict is channeled into institutions and processes that can resolve it peacefully. . . . Perhaps in no area of human life are our possible differences more important than religion, which is among the most fundamental causes of social conflict."[3] Hence, the framers of the US Constitution began with the most

1. Dennis J. Goldford, *The Constitution of Religious Freedom: God, Politics, and the First Amendment* (Waco: Baylor University Press, 2012), 24.
2. Whit Woodard, *Ministry of Presence: Biblical Insight on Christian Chaplaincy* (North Fort Myers, FL: Faithful Life, 2011), 16–17.
3. Goldford, *Constitution of Religious Freedom*, 21–22.

prevalent and pressing concern of their day regarding social unity and the preservation of individual rights: religious freedom. William R. Clough writes that "the Constitution itself is basically procedural. It lists the branches of government and their responsibilities. Freedom of religion is the first freedom specified."[4]

Behind the First Amendment were four contrasting views of religious liberty. The first viewpoint was the Puritan one, which held that church and state were two distinct covenantal associations under the authority of God and that, as such, "each did its part to establish and maintain the community and its founding moral and religious ideas."[5] In essence, the Puritan view allowed for "both the coordination and cooperation of church and state."[6]

The second view was the evangelical one, in which religious liberty found its roots in sixteenth-century European Anabaptist groups like the Mennonites. "They emphasized that religion was a voluntary choice signaled by adult baptism and that the church was an independent institution protected from the state by a 'wall of separation.'"[7] In comparison to the Puritans, the evangelicals sought a more defined separation of church and state. According to Witte, "Evangelicals sought a constitutional means to free all religion from the fetters of the law and to release all churches from the restrictions of the state."[8] The evangelical viewpoint emphasized freedom from the constraints that society and government would place on the free practice of religion.

The third view was that of the Enlightenment, which in America was championed by the Constitution writers Thomas Jefferson, Benjamin Franklin, and James Madison (as a political comparison to the evangelical view) and was explained in a letter written by James Madison to Jasper Adams: "The tendency of usurpation on one side, or the other, or to a corrupting collation or alliance between them, will be best guarded against by an entire abstinence of the government from interference in any way whatever, beyond the necessity of preserving public order, and protecting each sect against trespasses on its legal rights by others."[9] The Enlightenment supported the government staying completely out of church dealings.

The fourth viewpoint was the civic republican view, promoted by George Washington, John Adams, Benjamin Rush, Samuel Adams, and others. They promoted the separation of church and state but held that "religion, particularly

4. William R. Clough, "The First Freedom: Religion in the American Republic," *Journal of Interdisciplinary Studies* 30, no. 1/2 (2018): 5.

5. John Witte Jr. and Joel A. Nichols, *Religion and the American Constitutional Experiment*, 4th ed. (New York: Oxford University Press, 2016), 26.

6. Witte and Nichols, *Religion*, 27.

7. Witte and Nichols, *Religion*, 29.

8. Witte and Nichols, *Religion*, 32.

9. James Madison, letter to Jasper Adams, September 1833, in Witte and Nichols, *Religion*, 34.

Christianity, was foundational for the prosperity and happiness of citizens and the efficacy and efficiency of good government."[10] The civic republicans viewed society as needing Christianity as a modifying factor in government.

John Witte Jr. and Joel Nichols write that "the founders' original understanding regarding government and religion cannot be reduced to any one of these four views. It must be sought in the tensions among them and in the general principles that emerged from their interaction."[11] As these four viewpoints were synthesized, they came together to form a whole in terms of guiding governmental ideology that could be applied in a manner supported by all. Thus, a constitutional guarantee of religious freedoms for all US citizens developed from an interplay of the four viewpoints that are foundational to understanding and protecting religious diversity in America.

The opening of the First Amendment clearly says that "Congress shall make no law respecting an establishment of religion or prohibiting the free exercise thereof." This statement contains two distinct clauses: the Establishment Clause and the Free Exercise Clause. The Establishment Clause prevents government from establishing a state religion and forbids the government from acting in favor of one religious group or view over another.[12] Conversely, the Free Exercise Clause severely limits and generally prohibits government from infringing on anyone's freedom to practice their religion, spiritual convictions, or lack of faith.[13] The key to the wording in these religious clauses is that only Congress or the federal government is expressly prohibited from prescribing or proscribing religion. This wording left the writers of the state constitutions with the autonomy to interpret the First Amendment in light of the Puritan, evangelical, Enlightenment, and civic republican viewpoints.

However, there was still a potential danger under federalism with the separation of powers—namely, that states might share the same or similar majorities. Legislatures could potentially discriminate against a minority view, with the executive or executives signing off on that view (or the view being overridden by sufficient votes from the legislatures) and the judiciaries allowing and even approving such discrimination. Religious freedom was seen as particularly significant in this area, and the First Amendment was fashioned to protect minorities from religious persecution or coercion by a majority.[14]

10. Witte and Nichols, *Religion*, 32.
11. Witte and Nichols, *Religion*, 25.
12. "Establishment Clause," Legal Information Institute, Cornell Law School, accessed January 19, 2023, https://www.law.cornell.edu/wex/establishment_clause.
13. "Free Exercise Clause," Legal Information Institute, Cornell Law School, accessed January 19, 2023, http://www.law.cornell.edu/wex/free_exercise_clause.
14. Goldford, *Constitution of Religious Freedom*, 33–36.

Thus, state legislatures needed to be prevented from overriding federal protections that, to this day, use the Supreme Court to interpret the application of these rights. The tension that arises between groups holding various personal beliefs finds its solution conveyed within the context of the Supreme Court.

Principles in the First Amendment Religion Clauses

Whit Woodard introduces six principles that are part of the First Amendment clauses:

1. Liberty of conscience
2. Free exercise of religion
3. Religious pluralism
4. Religious equality
5. Separation of church and state
6. Disestablishment of religion[15]

These six principles are the foundational axioms in the formation and amendment of the constitutional Bill of Rights.[16] Each is worth examining in detail.

Liberty of Conscience

The underlying moral bedrock of the Founding Fathers' belief systems was a simple understanding of liberty of conscience, which "was the right to be left alone to choose, to entertain, and to change one's beliefs without coercion by the state."[17] Witte and Nichols note that the Founding Fathers realized the growing pluralism in America would challenge every religious faith represented. Regarding the abolition of a state-enforced penalty for religious choice, Thomas Jefferson argued for "equal liberty as well religious as civil to all good people."[18] Thus, liberty of conscience became part of the Constitution's First Amendment.

15. Woodard, *Ministry of Presence*, 2.
16. Woodard, *Ministry of Presence*, 4.
17. Thomas S. Kidd, *God of Liberty: A Religious History of the American Revolution* (New York: Basic Books, 2010), 43.
18. Thomas Jefferson, quoted in Kidd, *God of Liberty*, 43.

Free Exercise of Religion

Free exercise of religion was protected as long as this exercise didn't infringe on the rights of other people, disturb the public peace, interrupt harmony, or disrupt community law and order. The free exercise of religion and religious expression included "religious worship, religious speech, religious assembly, religious publication, religious education and more."[19]

George Washington exemplified this principle in his historic and famous letter to the Jewish Community at the Touro Synagogue in Newport, Rhode Island. This synagogue was the first Jewish synagogue in Newport and was founded in 1677. Some say it might even go back as far as 1656. In this letter, President Washington pledged that this new nation would "give to bigotry no sanction, to persecution no assistance." This was his way of assuring the synagogue that it would be free to practice its faith, not just believe something different secretly. To "exercise" one's faith means to put it into practice. Thus, the Free Exercise Clause was intended to allow those who believed, for religious reasons, that they should dress, act, or worship in a certain way to fulfill these requirements of their faith.[20]

Religious Pluralism

The Founding Fathers understood the need for and impact of religious diversity in the American experiment. They defined two types of religious pluralism: confessional and structural. Confessional pluralism is the maintenance and accommodation of a plurality of forms of religious expression and organization in the community.[21] Structural pluralism encourages each community to maintain and accommodate a variety of social units that foster religion, such as families, schools, charities, churches, and synagogues.[22] The Constitution was written in part to support religious pluralism in the United States.

Religious Equality

Religious equality guaranteed the equal standing and protection of all peaceable religions before the law. Kidd notes the phrasing of the First Amendment clauses regarding religious equality: "Nor shall the full and equal rights

19. Kidd, *God of Liberty*, 46.
20. George Washington to Hebrew Congregation of Newport, Rhode Island, 1790; see "Washington's Letter," George Washington Institute for Religious Freedom, accessed January 19, 2023, https://www.gwirf.org/washingtons-letter.
21. Kidd, *God of Liberty*, 47–48.
22. Kidd, *God of Liberty*, 47–48, 242–44.

of conscience be in any manner or on any pretext infringed."[23] Protections for all beliefs and religions were inserted into the First Amendment to guarantee religious equality for all Americans. No religion was to be favored over another.

Separation of Church and State

For the Founding Fathers, the long history of church-state relations cataloged the destructive influences that inevitably accompanied the blending of church and state and the resulting impact on religious and civic liberties. However, they were cognizant of the need to seek God's blessings. There were five major motivations in the Founding Fathers' decisions leading to the religion section of the First Amendment:

1. Protecting the church from the state
2. Protecting the state from the church when necessary
3. Protecting the individual's liberty of conscience from intrusion by either the church or the state
4. Protecting individual states from the federal government in its governing of local affairs
5. Protecting society from unwelcome participation in religion, religious activity, or morals interpreted from religion[24]

The idea of a wall of separation between church and state is an extraconstitutional idea expressed in a presidential letter to a particular group. That letter had no public or legal authority and has led to many misunderstandings that tend to stifle religious practice in the public square in ways that would have dismayed the founders.

Disestablishment of Religion

The disestablishment of religion is, at its core, the guarantee that the state will not mandate or prefer one religion over another. The First Amendment states, "Congress shall make no law respecting an establishment of religion, or prohibiting the free exercise thereof." The Constitution prevented the establishment of an official religion for the country from the outset of its existence.

Religious liberty was foundational to the expression of freedom both individually and in civic society. Witte and Nichols aptly state, "Religious liberty was

23. Kidd, *God of Liberty*, 52.
24. Witte and Nichols, *Religion*, 54–57.

too foundational for other civil rights and liberties to be in any way deprecated; it was, as Thomas Jefferson said, 'the most inalienable and sacred of all human rights.'"[25] Protecting religious beliefs from governmental control was crucial for the Founding Fathers.

For the chaplain, these six essential principles of religious freedom must be committed to memory and protected in practice. The chaplain must stand as a bulwark against the degradation of such inalienable rights. The chaplain becomes the first line of defense against all who would challenge the constitutional rights concerning religious freedoms for all. One specially protected group or favored ethnicity does not receive all the freedoms, but all religious groups who fall under the jurisdiction of the Constitution receive these freedoms. If the freedom is applied to one group or person, it must be applied to all.

Principles for Chaplaincy

Cooperation without Compromise

Christian chaplains have a unique way of ministering in a pluralistic society. Of course, all ministers in America who are called to preach, teach, or lead in gospel ministry have the opportunity to do so in a pluralistic setting. In cities and towns across America today, there are families of various nations, cultures, and races all living together. However, places of worship are not as integrated. Pastors minister to the people who walk through the doors for their times of worship, and the makeup of the congregation rarely, if ever, changes. By contrast, the congregation of the chaplain is always changing. Evangelical chaplains need to be prepared to embrace this reality, for they have opportunities to reach outside the church doors in multicultural venues. Chaplains need to be prepared to rise to the challenge.

The chaplain's opportunity is unique indeed. Chaplains may be able to minister to those who would never walk into a place of worship. Michael Milton, in his book *Cooperation without Compromise*, refers to stepping foot in India and meeting people of various sects and cults. Milton compares his experience in India with America today. "Increasingly, that is our world today, not only in metropolitan areas, but in almost every community in America."[26] He continues, "Today those same places are home, in an increasing way, to Muslims, various Eastern cults, Mormons, and of course, there seem to be more secularists and

25. Witte and Nichols, *Religion*, 63.
26. Michael A. Milton, *Cooperation without Compromise: Faithful Gospel Witness in a Pluralistic Setting* (Eugene, OR: Wipf & Stock, 2007), 6.

atheists."[27] The United States is not the same as it was a generation or even a decade ago.[28] The melting pot is growing more diverse on an almost daily basis. Being prepared to minister faithfully in an ever-changing society is essential for today's chaplain.

Milton describes "cooperation without compromise" as a primary motto of chaplaincy. This phrase originated in the US Army, but it is applied throughout all other branches of the military.[29] It is an apt picture of and motto for chaplaincy in general. A chaplain is to cooperate by honoring those of other faiths without coercion. However, there is no requirement or expectation that a chaplain or anyone else should compromise his or her own faith to do so. The non-Christian chaplain is not required to pray in Jesus's name, and the Christian chaplain is not required to use the term "Allah" or "Vishnu" in speaking about God. Everyone holds to their own religious beliefs without facing punishment or abuse, and everyone allows the same freedom to others without implying a tacit approval of their religion. If someone wants access to a chaplain or other spiritual leader from their own religion, we would be expected to cooperate in seeking someone qualified and available to pray or study their holy book with that person, but we cannot be required to do it ourselves.

Religious Plurality versus Religious Pluralism

The term "pluralistic" refers to a society or other community that has "an undeniable plurality of beliefs and ideas and even the customs and cultures that are derived from those ideas." Milton distinguishes pluralistic as "a matter of numbers," while pluralism is "a matter of ideology." The United States today is a pluralistic society. Pluralism, on the other hand, is something totally different from plurality. Another definition of pluralism, according to John Stott, is an affirmation of the "validity of every religion, and the refusal to choose between them and the rejection of world evangelism," and others see pluralism as "all spiritual paths . . . finally leading to the same sacred ground."[30] In a pluralistic society, the resulting attitude of love and respect demonstrated toward those who disagree is significantly different from the attitude of pluralism. Yet there is no denying the presence of pluralism, and there is no going back. "Every chaplain has been confronted with pluralism; sometimes as an encouragement; sometimes as a warning; and sometimes as a weapon."[31] Adapting to change

27. Milton, *Cooperation without Compromise*, 6.
28. Milton, *Cooperation without Compromise*, 2.
29. Milton, *Cooperation without Compromise*, 7.
30. Milton, *Cooperation without Compromise*, 6–7.
31. Woodard, *Ministry of Presence*, 96.

is a necessity for evangelical chaplains in today's American culture. Thankfully, they can cooperate without compromising. Lesslie Newbigin explains the concept of pluralism:

> I . . . believe that a Christian must welcome some measure of plurality but reject pluralism. We can and must welcome a plural society because it provides us with a wider range of experience and a wider diversity of human responses to experience, and therefore richer opportunities for testing the sufficiency of our faith than are available in a monochrome society. As we confess Jesus as Lord in a plural society, and as the Church grows through the coming of people from many different cultural and religious traditions to faith in Christ, we are enabled to learn more of the length and breadth and height and depth of the love of God (Eph. 3:14–19) than we can in a monochrome society. But we must reject the ideology of pluralism.[32]

Chaplains need not object to America being a pluralistic society. The Christian faith does not require its members to live in a religiously homogeneous society or to set up political or social penalties for those who do not accept the tenets of the religion. On the other hand, evangelicals need not accept pluralism. Christian chaplains and all believers should be welcoming of all. They should not, however, as devout followers of Christ, compromise their faith by affirming that all faiths lead to the same place. Such a claim denigrates the particular beliefs of most other faiths—and it is thus not really inclusive, projecting its assumption on all. One's faith in Christ should be firm. Chaplains are to represent their own denominations and faith groups. Evangelicals, for example, hold strong biblical-doctrinal stances. Jewish rabbis and Catholic priests should be just that: rabbis and priests representing their own faith groups. "Chaplains are empowered and guided by the regulations of the faith group that ecclesiastically endorses them and then sends them out to faithfully minister in a manner that is in accordance with their respective faith group and doctrinal foundations."[33] One can both claim that another group is wrong and still respect that group as a valid group. When each group is respected for what it is, all can respect one another.

In our combined ministry experiences, some have told us at different times that they could not be a chaplain because they could not compromise the message of the gospel in their ministry. They could not, with a clear conscience, for example, provide materials, information, or names of local clergy for those of a different faith. "There is little doubt that the perception of pluralism has

---

32. Milton, *Cooperation without Compromise*, 7.
33. Milton, *Cooperation without Compromise*, 3.

unnecessarily driven many ministers away from consideration of chaplaincy."[34]
Cooperation without compromise is essential to be effective in the faith of one's
calling. There is no middle ground. Milton points out that cooperation without
compromise includes the following tenets:

- Respect for others
- Support of others
- A refusal to proselytize unless invited into the holy places of the other's life
- A refusal to compromise one's own religious values and practices[35]

As already seen, Milton carefully distinguishes between the terms "pluralistic"
and "pluralism" with regard to religious views.[36] In a pluralistic society, the
resulting attitude of love and respect demonstrated toward those who disagree
is significantly different from an attitude of pluralism—namely, in which either
there is no final underlying truth to be found anywhere in religion or all religious
ideas are to be considered equally viable or equally true. Milton articulates that
we need to recognize and honor people from many religious views, including
those with whom we may strongly disagree. However, the clear and absolute
contradictions between religious beliefs cannot be simply ignored or somehow
thrown out in order to create some crude amalgam of shared religious beliefs
(or some ridiculous claim to such), and no attempt should be made to do so in
the name of religious pluralism.[37]

Evangelism versus Proselytization

Earlier in the book, we noted the difference between evangelism and proselytism. We use the terms "evangelism" and "proselytism" as functionally defined,
rather than using technical theological categories. "Evangelism" simply refers
to the sharing of God's good news, whereas "proselytism," as it is commonly
understood today, conveys a sense of coercion or pressure toward changing
one's religious beliefs. The major difference between the two is that evangelism
involves consent that is freely given without outside manipulation. Proselytism
involves pressure, repeated reminders, initiated arguments, and religious discussions at inappropriate times. Evangelical chaplains should practice evangelism
without slipping into proselytism, and they should always be sure to abide by
the rule of cooperation rather than compromise. However, those who believe

34. Woodard, *Ministry of Presence*, 112.
35. Milton, *Cooperation without Compromise*, 10.
36. Milton, *Cooperation without Compromise*, 5–9.
37. Milton, *Cooperation without Compromise*, 7.

that coercive pressure is used in any attempt to convince others to convert are quick to accuse. Evangelicals do well to trust the Holy Spirit as the one who moves people to invite our words. We thus have no need to push our way into someone's heart and mind.

Without legal protection, the distinction between these two terms could easily be a slippery area of interpretation, as the word "proselytism" technically means attempting to convince someone to convert from one religion to another—which is much the same thing as evangelism. "The 'no proselytizing' value of cooperation without compromise simply means that, in our case [that is, the case of evangelical Christian chaplains], the gospel may be presented when there is an invitation for us to speak in chapels or as military members come to us for counsel, especially dealing with spiritual or religious issues."[38] In a corporate setting, it may not be appropriate to approach someone with the sole intention of convincing them to convert to Christianity. The chaplain should build a relationship first; then all kinds of doors open for further conversations on a variety of subjects, including religion. If an individual approaches the chaplain for help, the door to the gospel opens. In essence, this person has just invited the chaplain into the holy places of their life.

> The effective [evangelical] Christian chaplain must become adept at obtaining permission to share his faith in considerate [relational] evangelism. Forcing his views upon someone or insisting that they are mandated by public or workplace policy introduces the element of coercion and crosses the line to what would then correctly be considered proselytizing—a practice that is almost universally prohibited in chaplaincy.[39]

By taking the time to build relationships with people, the chaplain will be invited into the holy places, where the gospel can be shared.

Milton gives an excellent biblical example of this approach—namely, in how the apostle Paul cooperates without compromising. In Acts 17 readers find the account of Paul preaching in Athens. Milton notes that "the condition of that city was both pluralistic and obviously committed to pluralism."[40] Paul "was greatly distressed to see that the city was full of idols" (v. 16). Paul takes his distress and turns it into an opportunity to share the gospel. One can learn from Paul's example by looking at the things he does and does not do:

38. Milton, *Cooperation without Compromise*, 10.
39. Woodard, *Ministry of Presence*, 162.
40. Milton, *Cooperation without Compromise*, 12.

- Paul does not denounce their culture. He quotes their poets.
- Paul does not retreat to safety. He goes along with them to the Areopagus.
- Paul does not destroy their altars. He studies them.[41]

"At the Areopagus, Paul did not rail as an angry prophet against their idolatry, . . . nor did he protest their paganism, . . . but he approached the Athenian religious plurality with the care that God did when he sent Jonah to Nineveh."[42] Paul does not endorse their gods. He uses the inscription on one particular altar, "To the unknown god" (v. 23), as a bridge for his introduction of the one true God. In Acts 17:24–29 Paul establishes things he has in common with his audience by identifying things they agree on about God. Then, in verses 30 and 31, Paul moves on to the message of Christ and his resurrection. Woodard writes, "The faith of which we speak is no mere intellectual ascent; it is a deep-seated trust in the redemptive work of Jesus Christ in his death, burial and resurrection."[43] It is the Holy Spirit who convicts the human soul. God, not man, brings individuals to him. Jesus said, "No one can come to me unless the Father who sent me draws him. And I will raise him up on the last day" (John 6:44). It is the ministry of the Christian chaplain to comfort, to care for, and to serve all who are in need, wherever needed.

Religious Diversity within Chaplaincy

Diversity is a result of the First Amendment, since the amendment allows employees to exercise their personal rights in the workplace even if doing so means differing from their peers. Diversity entails recognizing the differences inherent in the workplace to include religion, gender, race, age, disability, and sexual orientation and then accepting the inclusion of these differences in the workplace on the basis of federal statutes and standards.

Evangelical chaplains practice their ministry in a religiously diverse environment consisting of many Christian groups (over two hundred are recognized by the Department of Defense [DOD]), world religions, and people of no faith at all. In this diverse community, chaplains must be mindful of each person they are talking to, as well as the person's religious background or lack thereof,

41. Milton, *Cooperation without Compromise*, 12–13.
42. Milton, *Cooperation without Compromise*, 13.
43. Woodard, *Ministry of Presence*, 180.

in interacting with them. Chaplains are expected to know how to respond to everyone in respectful, uplifting, and interactive ways.

Confidentiality for Chaplains

Confidentiality involves a private conversation with a chaplain, pastor, or missionary (a recognized clergyperson) in which the details of the conversation are not disclosed to anyone else for any reason. The person who is communicating owns the confidence. The clergyperson who is receiving the information generally is required to safeguard the information and to keep it confidential. Under the priest-penitent rule, chaplains are not considered mandatory reporters; however, some states require chaplains to report child and elder abuse. Federal law overrides state law. Federal law and the Supreme Court uphold chaplain confidentiality. In chaplaincy, the most confidential information is gathered through times of confession or counseling.

Confidential communication is generally considered to carry both an ethical and a legal responsibility for clergy. Clergy have a moral responsibility to maintain confidentiality. A chaplain does not have to be in a paid position to honor confidentiality or confidential communication. The fact that a chaplain is endorsed by a faith group, ordained and licensed by a church, and recognized by a civilian organization to provide chaplain services validates their authority to practice and maintain confidentiality. So a volunteer chaplain has to respect confidential information just as much as a full-time, employed chaplain. However, some state laws consider chaplains to be mandatory reporters of certain conditions or statements. Great care must be taken to understand and properly respond in every situation.

Privileged Communication

Only one exception to the rule of privileged communication exists, and it is found in the military. If military personnel declare themselves to be conscientious objectors, they must undergo a mandatory interview with a chaplain. Before the interview takes place, the chaplain must explain that the conversation is not covered under privileged communication. Everything that is said in the conversation between the service member and the chaplain will be disclosed by the chaplain in a written report detailing the interaction. This is the only instance in which privileged communication is not afforded to the person seeking assistance. In all other chaplain conversations, a strict confidentiality is practiced. The chaplain in most cases cannot even affirm that they met with the person counseled.

Priest-Penitent Privilege

Priest-penitent (or clergy-penitent) privilege is the legal mechanism that prevents the clergyperson from being called to court to disclose confidential information in a legal proceeding. The privilege of disclosure belongs to the person who is disclosing the information in confession or in the counseling session with the chaplain. This rule is designed for the protection of that person.[44] It is not designed for the protection of the clergyperson. Legally, chaplains cannot disclose in any way any of the information that someone tells them without that person's explicit permission, preferably in writing. The law of South Carolina upholds priest-penitent privilege in this way:

> In any legal or quasi-legal trial, hearing or proceeding before any court, commission or committee no regular or duly ordained minister, priest or rabbi shall be required, in giving testimony, to disclose any confidential communication properly entrusted to him in his professional capacity and necessary and proper to enable him to discharge the functions of his office according to the usual course of practice or discipline of his church or religious body. This prohibition shall not apply to cases where the party in whose favor it is made waives the rights conferred.[45]

Each state has confidentiality guidelines and laws, and these laws may vary from state to state. However, each state has laws regarding privileged communications made to clergy in the context of their professional duties (e.g., confession or penitential communication). It is always prudent to check the current laws of the state where one is practicing chaplain ministry. Communications made to chaplains employed by the federal government (via the military, federal agencies, and federal institutions) are protected under federal law with regard to confidentiality.

Reporting Child Abuse and Neglect

Chaplains employed by the federal government are protected from mandatory-reporting laws. All other chaplains must follow state laws, which vary across the country. Mandatory-reporting statutes in some states specify the circumstances

44. David O. Middlebrook, "Pastoral Confidentiality: An Ethical and Legal Responsibility," Assemblies of God (website), February 2, 2010, https://news.ag.org/features/pastoral-confidentiality-an-ethical-and-legal-responsibility.

45. South Carolina Code of Laws, title 19, chap. 11, § 19-11-90, "Priest-Penitent Privilege," https://www.scstatehouse.gov/code/t19c011.php.

under which a communication is "privileged," or allowed to remain confidential. In privileged communications, clergy may be exempt from the requirement of reporting suspected abuse or neglect. The right to maintain this confidentiality under state law must be provided by statute. Most states do provide the privilege, typically exempting clergy from providing evidence in trials and civil procedures. If the issue of privilege is not addressed in the reporting laws, that fact does not mean that privilege is not granted; it may be granted in other parts of state statutes.[46]

This privilege, however, is not absolute. While clergy-penitent privilege is frequently recognized within the reporting laws, it is typically interpreted narrowly in the context of child abuse or neglect. If a clergyperson learns of the abuse outside of direct priest-penitent interaction, such as through secondhand information or by witnessing it, then the clergyperson is a mandatory reporter because it is not revealed to the clergyperson in confidence. The circumstances under which clergy-penitent privilege is allowed vary from state to state, and in some states it is denied altogether in cases of child abuse or neglect. For example, among the states and territories that list clergy as mandatory reporters, Guam, New Hampshire, and West Virginia deny the clergy-penitent privilege in cases of child abuse or neglect. Four of the states that indicate that "any person" is a mandatory reporter (i.e., North Carolina, Oklahoma, Rhode Island, and Texas) also deny clergy-penitent privilege in child-abuse cases.[47]

Lieutenant Shane Cooper, Judge Advocate, General Corps, US Navy, explains the significance of Military Rule of Evidence 503 as it relates to chaplain confidentiality and privileged communication:

> The morale of our military's men and women is the backbone of a successful fighting force. The Chaplain Corps is an invaluable asset, crucial to maintaining and gauging morale, as chaplains tend to the needs of service members stationed throughout the world. Chaplains provide a rare conduit for military service members to discuss their deepest problems regarding military, personal, emotional, financial, or family issues. All branches of the Armed Forces regard the penitent-clergy privilege as "absolute" both in-court and out-of-court. Within the military court setting, Military Rule of Evidence 503 (MRE 503) prohibits a chaplain or a chaplain's assistant from divulging a privileged communication without the consent of the penitent. Furthermore, military regulations have expanded upon the theory behind MRE 503 and also bar the chaplain

46. "Clergy as Mandatory Reporters of Child Abuse and Neglect," Child Welfare Information Gateway, April 2019, https://www.childwelfare.gov/topics/systemwide/laws-policies/statutes/clergymandated.
47. "Clergy as Mandatory Reporters."

from disclosing these privileged communications in out-of-court contexts as well. In sharp contrast to the military's treatment of the penitent-clergy privilege, an increasing number of states are overriding their respective penitent-clergy privileges by requiring clergy to be mandated reporters in cases of child abuse and molestation. In these states, it is a misdemeanor criminal offense for clergy who fail to report such cases. The possible conflict between the military's "absolute" penitent-clergy privilege and various states' "mandatory" reporting laws begs the question: When a military service member confesses to a chaplain that he or she has abused or molested a child, what does the chaplain do?[48]

First, MRE 503 provides a thorough and informative background and history regarding the clergy-penitent privilege in the civilian community as well as the privilege currently embodied by military regulations. Second, it identifies the competing legal, moral, and ethical considerations that confront the chaplain when faced with possibly conflicting child-abuse mandatory-reporting laws at the state level. Third, this note provides a framework for chaplains and judge advocates that may help them identify when a conflict exists and suggests possible methods of settling this conflict. Finally, the note answers the question facing the chaplain establishment:

1. Military chaplains have a legal obligation to maintain the confidentiality of privileged communications under all circumstances, civilian or military, in court or out of court.
2. Military chaplains will likely prevail in dismissing an attempt by a state to prosecute under its child-abuse mandatory-reporting laws.

This last point is subject to debate, with credible arguments favoring both sides; furthermore, arriving at an answer necessarily involves an unexpectedly tedious analysis of jurisdictional and federal supremacy-clause issues.[49]

Supreme Court Decisions concerning Religious Freedom and Chaplaincy

The Supreme Court of the United States (SCOTUS) has noted that military chaplaincy is supportive of the Free Exercise Clause, which is in place to complement the Establishment Clause. "Unless the Army provided a Chaplaincy

48. Shane Cooper, "Chaplains Caught in the Middle: The Military's 'Absolute' Penitent-Clergy Privilege Meets State 'Mandatory' Child Abuse Reporting Laws," *Naval Law Review* 49 (2002): 128.
49. Cooper, "Chaplains Caught in the Middle."

it would deprive the soldier of his right under the Establishment Clause not to have religion inhibited and his right under the Free Exercise Clause to practice his freely chosen religion."[50] Chaplaincy is needed in the military and public sectors, and it is guaranteed by the First Amendment Religious Clauses. These clauses enable the chaplain not only to minister to all religions but also to stand with others, whether religious or nonreligious, when their religious freedoms may be challenged.

The Autonomy of the Military

In *Orloff v. Willoughby* (1953), the Supreme Court upheld a high level of autonomy to the Uniform Code of Military Justice in First Amendment cases involving military personnel because of the military's exclusive culture and function in national security, using descriptive wording like "separate society" and "military necessity."[51]

The Supreme Court normally gives preference to the government's interest and discretion when hearing cases involving US military personnel and First Amendment rights. "The Supreme Court seems to use lower levels of review or operates from the strong presumption that 'military necessity' or the military interests in governing its unique, 'separate society' tend to override or outweigh the speech and religious rights individuals ordinarily hold."[52] In *Katcoff v. Marsh*, the court rejected an Establishment Clause challenge to the Army's chaplaincy program, finding that chaplains enabled soldiers to practice the religions of their choice.

The Lemon Test

The *Lemon* test is derived from the 1971 *Lemon v. Kurtzman* SCOTUS case, which applied the watershed 1947 *Everson v. Board of Education* SCOTUS ruling and a developing test from the 1970 *Walz v. Tax Commission* SCOTUS case. In its interpretation of the First Amendment, SCOTUS applied a three-pronged test to determine whether government aid or action could be applied to religious entities. If it failed any of these tests, it could not be applied.

1. The aid or action includes a clear secular purpose.
2. The primary effect does not directly advance or inhibit religion.

50. Katcoff v. Marsh, 755 F.2d 223 (2d Cir. 1985), https://casetext.com/case/katcoff-v-marsh.
51. Elizabeth Beaumont, "Rights of Military Personnel," First Amendment Encyclopedia, 2009, https://www.mtsu.edu/first-amendment/article/1131/rights-of-military-personnel.
52. Beaumont, "Rights of Military Personnel."

3. The aid or action does not create an excessive governmental entanglement with religion.[53]

The difficulty in applying this test consistently lies largely in the third prong, in which justices treat lack of "entanglement" to mean that the government needs to maintain a complete separation from any kind of religion (i.e., a wall keeping a religious entity from influencing the state or the state from supporting a religious entity, as opposed to Jefferson's idea of a wall protecting a religion or denomination from the state). By contrast, those who interpret a lack of entanglement to mean the state can and should accommodate religious practices (rather than leave them hindered or abandoned) would apply it as protective of religion. This contrast in application has many calling it "a lemon of a test" that tends to result in significant inconsistency as a precedent.[54]

After another landmark case, *Agostini v. Felton* (1997), the *Lemon* test saw a modification from the entanglement clause into a primary-effects basis. That case focused on the primary effect in part 2, where the primary effect doesn't directly advance or inhibit religion. However, the consistency problem will continue on account of lower courts still utilizing the *Lemon* test as their primary method for Establishment Clause cases.

The Rights of Military Personnel

While it is true that everyone within the United States holds the same freedoms and rights, there has always been an inside joke within the military that this view does not apply to military personnel. Surely, when one sees the command structure and the rules and regulations, the joke seems accurate to an extent. However, there have been several instances in which the courts have become involved with the armed forces to institute change and assimilation. One of these instances pertains to the conscientious-objector policies within the US military. Before the Second World War, those who believed that directly engaging with an enemy force was against their beliefs were dismissed and prevented from serving or even jailed. Following key cases before the Supreme Court and various tribunals, these policies were adapted to allow noncombatants into the military ranks.[55]

The 1985 case of *Katcoff v. Marsh* challenged the practice of having military chaplains on the grounds that it indicated an establishment of religion. However,

53. Richard L. Pacelle Jr., "Lemon Test," First Amendment Encyclopedia, 2009, https://www.mtsu.edu/first-amendment/article/834/lemon-test.
54. Pacelle, "Lemon Test."
55. Beaumont, "Rights of Military Personnel."

the practice of chaplaincy, as it existed both before and after the establishment
of the Constitution, was determined to be an accepted and essential form of
religious accommodation for the members of the armed services. Included in
the argument are the following direct quotations:

1. "The great majority of the soldiers in the Army expresses religious
   preferences."
2. "The problem of meeting the religious needs of Army personnel is
   compounded by the mobile, deployable nature of our armed forces,
   who must be ready on extremely short notice to be transported . . . to
   distant parts of the world for combat duty in fulfillment of our nation's
   international defense commitments."
3. "In the opinion of top generals of the Army and those presently in the
   chaplaincy, unless chaplains were made available in such circumstances
   the motivation, morale and willingness of soldiers to face combat
   would suffer immeasurable harm and our national defense would be
   weakened accordingly."
4. "Many soldiers in the Army also suffer serious stresses from other
   causes attributable largely to their military service, which can be al-
   leviated by counseling and spiritual assistance from a leader of their
   respective faiths. Among these are tensions created by separation from
   their homes, loneliness when on duty in strange surroundings involving people whose language or customs they do not share, fear of facing
   combat or new assignments, financial hardships, personality conflicts,
   and drug, alcohol or family problems. The soldier faced with any of
   these problems at home would usually be able to consult his spiritual
   adviser."[56]

Through this key decision, even though it did not go through the Supreme Court,
the basis of chaplaincy within the military was cemented and reaffirmed. This
case also led to Justice Department and Department of Correction cases being
rendered in favor of the chaplaincy programs and positions.

Because of the nature of military representation, the military is given a unique
degree of leeway to apply its own Uniform Code of Military Justice to guarantee readiness for war and defense and support of the government and nation
among the military. The military is perhaps the clearest example of a uniquely
recognized environment "in which standard First Amendment protections do

56. Katcoff v. Marsh, 755 F.2d 233.

not apply to the same extent" as in general society.[57] One major area where the military have less freedom is that of political expression. Military personnel cannot speak publicly against the president of the United States, their commander in chief.

This more settled nature provides the military with a higher resistance to enforced change than other areas of society, although they are not completely beyond the reach of the courts. This plays a role in military chaplaincy being recognized as an intended and necessary practice from the very beginning of the United States, which in turn significantly affects the idea of chaplaincy in general across all institutions.

The unique status of military chaplaincy sets the tone for and gives an example of the purpose and essential nature of chaplaincy in the formation of the states. It demonstrates the value and necessity placed on the provision of spiritual and religious support to those in stressful and life-altering situations and those away from their normal means of receiving spiritual care. There is no greater need for someone undergoing deep struggle, aloneness, and highly stressful situations and grief than to experience the presence of God and receive God's love through his representatives. This is the role of the chaplain, and it is a divine calling of the highest honor. Chaplains should not take such a mantle lightly, and they must practice their profession confidently, honoring it as a profession designed by God and the founders of the United States and protected by people's right to have their acknowledged spiritual needs met.

Prayer at Government Meetings

When chaplains pray in public places, they have a captive audience. Inviting people to pray in the form and manner of their tradition as the chaplain prays in the form and manner of their tradition generally sets people at ease. In *Marsh v. Chambers* (1983), a member of the Nebraska state legislature filed a lawsuit against his own political body for employing Robert Palmer,[58] a Presbyterian minister who had overseen the opening prayer of the legislature for almost twenty years. Even though the Eighth Circuit Court agreed that this employment violated the *Lemon* test, the Supreme Court ruled in favor of Palmer in a 6–3 decision, observing that the emplacement of clergy within the legislature was deeply ingrained in the country's persona. Chief Justice Warren E. Burger even noted that a minister was employed by the Continental Congress three days before the Declaration of Independence was signed, demonstrating the importance of the

57. Beaumont, "Rights of Military Personnel."
58. John R. Vile, "*Marsh v. Chambers* (1983)," First Amendment Encyclopedia, accessed August 21, 2023, https://mtsu.edu/first-amendment/article/456/marsh-v-chambers.

position throughout American governmental history. In a similar case, *Town of Greece v. Galloway* (2014), prayers before monthly town board meetings were challenged. The case went to the Supreme Court, which applied the findings of *Marsh* to uphold the town's practice of praying before meetings.

Burwell v. Hobby Lobby Stores *(2014)*

In *Burwell v. Hobby Lobby Stores*, the Supreme Court ruled in favor of Hobby Lobby. The company could be exempt from the Affordable Care Act contraceptive requirements that violated their religious principles.[59]

Under the Patient Protection and Affordable Care Act (ACA), employment-based group healthcare plans must provide certain types of preventive care, such as FDA-approved contraceptive methods. While there are exemptions available for religious employers and nonprofit religious institutions, there are no exemptions available for for-profit institutions such as Hobby Lobby Stores, Inc. The plaintiffs argued that the requirement that the employment-based group healthcare plan cover contraception violated the Free Exercise Clause of the First Amendment and the Religious Freedom Restoration Act of 1993 (RFRA). "The Court held that Congress intended for the RFRA to be read as applying to corporations since they are composed of individuals who use them to achieve desired ends."[60] Thus, SCOTUS supported the Green family and their corporation, Hobby Lobby, in their freedom to exercise their religion in their provision of healthcare to their employees.

Congressional Acts and Regulations

Chaplains have often been involved in standing up for the religious rights of the people they serve. In 1964 Congress passed the Civil Rights Act, protecting a number of basic rights under the Constitution, of which religion was one. Throughout the ensuing years, other regulations were enacted, including the 1993 RFRA.

The Civil Rights Act, Title VII (1964)

The Civil Rights Act (Title VII) prohibits employers from discriminating against their employees on the basis of their religion.[61] This statute requires

59. Burwell v. Hobby Lobby Stores, Inc., 573 U.S. 682 (2014), https://casetext.com/case/burwell-v-hobby-lobby-stores-inc-1.
60. *Burwell*, 573 U.S. 682.
61. Matthew D. Staver, "Religious Rights in the Workplace," Liberty Counsel, 2000, https://lc.org/religious-rights-in-the-workplace.

employers to make reasonable accommodations for the religious practices of their employees, unless doing so creates some kind of undue hardship on the employer, organization, company, or business. Examples of reasonable accommodation include granting a day off for a religious holiday or sacred observance, excusing one from work on the Sabbath, allowing religious apparel at work, and permitting employees to observe religious practices during the work day, such as specific prayer times in accordance with one's faith practices.

This prohibition of discrimination pertains to all parts of religion and practice. People who feel that their rights have been violated and need justice can file a claim with the Equal Employment Opportunity Commission. A claim would involve "the employee's sincerely held religious belief, the employer's accommodation of that belief, and the employer's defense that it cannot accommodate the belief because the accommodation would result in an undue hardship."[62] This act is very important because it allows employees to practice their religion without fear of discrimination or dismissal. For example, if an employee is religious and asks their boss for time off to go to church, they are protected by this law. The employee must be allowed to go to the church of their choice, even if that church only offers one service. Another example involves a Muslim employee who wants to observe the required time of prayer during work hours. Under the Civil Rights Act, the employee is allowed to pray, and the employer must provide a place to pray. Similarly, this act also applies to religious garments worn during work hours, as long as they do not interfere with the job needing to be done. According to this law, if it is a "sincerely held" religious belief, the employer must accommodate it and allow it.

Religious Freedom Restoration Act (RFRA) (1993)

The RFRA was enacted to override the Supreme Court and provide more protection of free exercise. This act requires "strict scrutiny" and "prohibits any agency, department, or official of the United States or any State (the government) from substantially burdening a person's exercise of religion."[63] This law restricts courts from meddling with individual free-exercise rights, unless they violate "religious-neutral criminal laws." This law was applied to the previously discussed *Hobby Lobby* case of 2014. Hobby Lobby said that providing coverage for abortion and contraception for their employees would go against their

---

62. Staver, "Religious Rights."
63. Religious Freedom Restoration Act of 1993, H.R. 1308, 103rd Cong. (1993–1994), https://www.congress.gov/bill/103rd-congress/house-bill/1308.

religious conscience. The court determined that no criminal law was violated and therefore allowed their religious views to stand. The same law was applied to different effect in the case of two men who were dismissed from their jobs as drug counselors because they used peyote. The men used it during a Native American religious ceremony. Because of this law, the court applied "strict scrutiny," and their firing was justified because they had violated existing criminal laws.

Military chaplains are unique because they have government restrictions in addition to their rights as citizens of the United States. For example, a Catholic commander cannot order a non-Catholic chaplain to offer a Catholic blessing. Chaplains do not have to obey this order. Chaplains are protected by the Civil Rights Act. If they are following their sincerely held beliefs, if their actions are part of their religious duties, and if their actions do not pose undue hardship on their commander, they are within their rights to refuse. In the case of sports chaplaincy, a team chaplain could pray over the team before an event and not be persecuted for it. The chaplain could even pray in Jesus's name. The chaplain would be operating within their sincerely held beliefs and would have the right to pray and do so in whatever manner they think appropriate.

The RFRA's primary legal standard of individual rights is fully applicable to chaplains and passed in the National Defense Authorization Act and its associated service policies. *City of Boerne v. Flores* declared the RFRA unconstitutional as applied to states. As a result, the RFRA required the courts to use strict scrutiny regarding laws that may restrict religious freedom. The strict scrutiny employed by the Supreme Court has guided decisions in protecting religious freedoms under the RFRA, while other decisions have held the RFRA to be unconstitutional, spurring many states to draft their own "mini-RFRAs" to address free-exercise cases before they reach the federal level.[64] For the chaplain, the RFRA is also a call to strict scrutiny when advising individuals of their religious freedoms and avenues of appeal, as well as the chaplain's own rights and responsibilities with respect to accommodation.

The RFRA requires federal and state courts to apply the principle of strict scrutiny when examining the application of rules or laws affecting religious freedom.[65] The principle of strict scrutiny typically leads directly to the question of whether a law should be struck down, and it can generally be defined as follows:

64. David Schultz and David L. Hudson Jr., "Religious Freedom Restoration Act of 1993 (1993)," First Amendment Encyclopedia, last updated September 2017, http://www.mtsu.edu/first-amendment/article/1092/religious-freedom-restoration-act-of-1993.
65. Schultz and Hudson, "Religious Freedom Restoration Act."

Strict scrutiny is the highest form of review that courts use to evaluate the constitutionality of laws. Under a strict scrutiny analysis, a law that restricts freedom of speech must achieve a compelling government interest and be narrowly tailored to that interest or be the least speech-restrictive means available to the government. Strict scrutiny also is used when a law targets a specific religious faith.[66]

Despite the overwhelming bipartisan congressional support of the RFRA, SCOTUS did not allow the RFRA to stand for application at the state level. Four years later, in the 1997 *City of Boerne v. Flores* case, the court explicitly quoted and refuted state application of the federal RFRA as an unconstitutional federal overreach into the authority of states. SCOTUS determined that its intervention in the earlier *Smith* case had fallen under the acceptable role of federal-government intervention "to remedy or prevent unconstitutional actions." However, Congress's enforcement of RFRA over states was considered to have crossed a line, creating "a substantive change in governing law" that went beyond appropriate federal authority over states.[67]

Conclusion

As chaplains work for institutions, the general guidelines, rules, and bylaws of those institutions are expected to apply equally to chaplains as to other staff. This would include HIPAA laws regarding patient confidentiality in healthcare institutions, the military code of conduct, and so on. However, it would seem impermissible for an institution to institute a new rule or bylaw specifically targeting the use of chaplains or the freedom of chaplains to represent their beliefs whenever invited to do so, since this rule would cross the line of the strict-scrutiny principle regarding free exercise of religion. It would also not be considered legally or ethically appropriate for one chaplain to push out a chaplain of a different faith whom a care receiver had explicitly requested or who would be more in accordance with the beliefs of the care receiver. Nor would it be appropriate for a chaplain to repeat overtures to a care receiver who already had chaplain services. The freedom and protection of the care receiver would supersede the freedom of the chaplain.

From the foundations of the nation, the Founding Fathers, who had differing religious beliefs, worked together to protect the rights of Americans to worship freely and equally. Establishing the First Amendment to guarantee

66. Schultz and Hudson, "Religious Freedom Restoration Act."
67. Schultz and Hudson, "Religious Freedom Restoration Act."

freedom in religious belief systems was crucial to the Founding Fathers and early Americans. In like manner, chaplains respect the rights of all people to worship freely within the context of their belief systems. To remain faithful to their own religious commitment, however, chaplains abide by the concept of "cooperation without compromise," a key component to working successfully with diverse groups in workplaces. It is essential for chaplains to understand the laws that protect confidential communication and how these laws apply to the chaplain's work setting, protecting both themselves and those they help. To be effective in their ministry, chaplains must also understand the essential protections that the US Constitution provides for Americans' religious rights.

5

Evangelical Identity
and Practice

Evangelical chaplains make up a large percentage of the chaplains serving in America today, in both sacred and secular settings. Over two hundred religious groups sponsor chaplains for governmental, community, and private entities, and a sizable number consider themselves to be evangelical. Some observe that evangelicals are overrepresented in chaplaincy due to their understanding of biblical ministry and their mission-mindedness as compared to progressives, who may steer more toward social-justice roles. This chapter defines evangelical chaplains and explains their identity and ministry, including their beliefs, authority to accomplish the mission, characteristics, and challenges.

Beliefs of the Evangelical Chaplain

An evangelical chaplain is a born-again believer and follower of Jesus Christ who is called, prepared, and sent out by the church to bear the biblical presence and message of Christ in sacred and secular settings. Evangelical chaplains need a clear descriptive understanding of the term "evangelical," which itself is rooted in the Greek noun *euangelion*, which means "glad tidings," "good news," or "gospel."[1] It is the basis for the Greek word *euangelistēs*, which is translated

1. Gerald R. McDermott, "The Emerging Divide in Evangelical Theology," *Journal of the Evangelical Theological Society* 56 (2013): 357.

as "evangelist," the one who preaches or proclaims the Word.[2] Martin Luther identified the term with the church, and his Lutheran followers took the name "evangelical" to distinguish themselves from Catholicism. The term was also embraced by John Calvin, who led the Evangelical Church of Geneva. The use of the term expanded over time among Protestants, encompassing to some degree groups such as Pietists, Dissenters, Quakers, Puritans, Methodists, revivalists, Holiness believers, and others.[3]

The definition and history of evangelicalism is complicated. The term is difficult to define, mainly because it refers not to a Christian denomination or a church but rather to a movement within Christianity that encompasses many different denominations that have similar doctrinal beliefs.[4] Evangelicals, according to Whit Woodard, are Christians who are Bible believers and hold to six foundational precepts: "(1) The deity of Jesus Christ, the Son of God and God the Son; (2) the virgin birth of Christ; (3) the death of Christ as a vicarious blood atonement for sin to satisfy the righteous justice of God; (4) the bodily resurrection of Christ from the dead; (5) the inerrancy of the Bible; and (6) the personal bodily return of Christ to earth."[5] These theological markers set the stage for the behavioral and organizational characteristics mentioned below.

Scholar David Bebbington, seeking to define evangelicalism, proposes four qualities that are generally accepted as special marks of evangelical religiosity: "*conversionism*, the belief that lives need to be changed; *activism*, the expression of the gospel in effort; *biblicism*, a particular regard for the Bible; and what may be termed *crucicentrism*, a stress on the sacrifice of Christ on the cross."[6] Together, these four terms form what is called the "quadrilateral of priorities that is the basis for Evangelicalism."[7] These four concepts—conversionism, activism, biblicism, and crucicentrism—form a foundational understanding, known as the Bebbington Quadrilateral, that clearly articulates a widely accepted description of evangelicalism.[8] We synthesize these and other writings to provide the following list of six tenets of evangelicalism:

2. McDermott, "Emerging Divide," 357.

3. Mark A. Noll, David W. Bebbington, and George M. Marsden, *Evangelicals: Who They Have Been, Are Now, and Could Be* (Grand Rapids: Eerdmans, 2019), 195.

4. Lawrence P. Greenslit, *Religion and the Military: A Growing Ethical Dilemma* (Carlisle Barracks, PA: Army War College, 2006).

5. Whit Woodard, *Ministry of Presence: Biblical Insight on Christian Chaplaincy* (North Fort Myers, FL: Faithful Life, 2011), 176.

6. David W. Bebbington, *Evangelicalism in Modern Britain: A History from the 1730s to the 1980s* (Grand Rapids: Baker, 1989), 2–3.

7. Brian Harris, "Beyond Bebbington: The Quest for Evangelical Identity in a Postmodern Era," *Churchman* 122, no. 3 (2008): 202.

8. Mark A. Noll, David W. Bebbington, and George A. Rawlyk, eds., *Evangelicalism: Comparative Studies of Popular Protestantism in North America, the British Isles, and Beyond* (New York: Oxford University Press, 1994), 181–84.

1. The need for personal conversion, which is not necessarily an emotional experience but at least involves personal repentance and trust in the person and work of Christ, not simply intellectual adherence to doctrine[9]
2. Commitment to evangelism and missions[10]
3. The supreme authority of Scripture as a source of knowledge of God and a guide for Christian living[11]
4. The majesty of Jesus Christ, both as incarnate God and Lord and as the Savior of sinful humanity[12]
5. The lordship of the Holy Spirit, who is necessary for the application of the presence and work of Christ[13]
6. The importance of religious community for spiritual nourishment, fellowship, and growth[14]

Point 5, regarding the Holy Spirit, especially reflects the massive Christian renewal movement that includes Pentecostals, charismatics, and third wave groups. Many among these renewal groups, such as the Assemblies of God, are willing to include themselves under the evangelical banner. Overall, these evangelical theological precepts emphasize a unique biblical faith and the way in which it is understood in the forming, believing, and acting out of a Christian spirituality.

In contrast, a liberal-progressive understanding of Christianity would place a premium on personal autonomy and would appeal to internal norms, which appear in one's conscience and individual religious experience,[15] while focusing externally on matters of social witness, justice, and action. However, one area of service shared by evangelicals and progressives has to do with relieving suffering through ministries that address hunger, housing insecurity, disease, addictions, domestic violence, forced migration, and other urgent concerns.

Karl Barth, the influential twentieth-century theologian, presents another perspective on evangelicalism. Barth understands evangelicalism to be "informed by the gospel of Jesus Christ, as heard afresh in the sixteenth-century

9. Noll, Bebbington, and Rawlyk, *Evangelicalism*, 181.
10. Noll, Bebbington, and Rawlyk, *Evangelicalism*, 181.
11. Noll, Bebbington, and Rawlyk, *Evangelicalism*, 182.
12. Noll, Bebbington, and Rawlyk, *Evangelicalism*, 183.
13. Alister McGrath, *Evangelicalism and the Future of Christianity* (Downers Grove, IL: Inter-Varsity, 1995), 56.
14. McDermott, "Emerging Divide," 359.
15. McDermott, "Emerging Divide," 362.

Reformation by a direct return to Holy Scripture."[16] Klaas Runia compares
Barth's position to the Reformation's focus on *sola scriptura*: "The Reformation
was a movement 'back to Scripture' and to the gospel proclaimed in it."[17] Albert
Mohler explains that the evangelical movement "was driven by an explicit commitment to stand for biblical truth, even as that truth was under assault by the
modern, secular, and anti-supernaturalistic world view."[18] Gerald McDermott
offers a reminder that the "'new evangelical' theology (led by E. J. Carnell, Har-
old Ockenga, and Carl Henry, and inspired by Billy Graham) was committed to
engaging with culture in an attempt to transform it through the gospel."[19] This
approach stood in contrast to that of the fundamentalists, who stood against
engaging with the things and ways of the world.

Evangelicals have been part of the American story since its beginnings,
and they remain prominent in the country today. Researchers Sang-Ehil Han,
Paul Metzger, and Terry Muck have identified evangelical Protestantism as
the largest Christian religious group in the United States.[20] Kim Hansen's research indicates that the scope of evangelicalism comprises over 30 percent of
Americans in the United States, surpassing Roman Catholicism as the largest
religious group in North America.[21] Han, Metzger, and Muck indicate that this
does not mean that evangelicalism is unified in its "polity and faith doctrinal
positions."[22] Evangelicalism as it exists today has achieved "such a degree of
political and cultural power that liberals [are] alarmed and academics working
on the assumption of inexorable secularization [are] thrown into confusion."[23]
The assumption is that, by this point, religion, especially evangelicalism, should
have retreated into a private place where individuals, families, and the local
church can engage with each other confidently without encroaching on the
larger populace. The message that evangelicals preach in this postmodern
world, however, does not fit nicely with privatized religion that is separated
from church and state.[24]

Many African American Christians in the United States, with a long history
of separate ecclesial life due to racial discrimination but also, later, to self-

16. McDermott, "Emerging Divide," 358.
17. Klaas Runia, "What Is Evangelical Theology?," *Evangelical Review of Theology* 21 (1997): 269.
18. R. Albert Mohler Jr., "The Eclipse of God at Century's End," *Southern Baptist Journal of Theology* 1 (1997): 8.
19. McDermott, "Emerging Divide," 358.
20. Sang-Ehil Han, Paul Louis Metzger, and Terry C. Muck, "Christian Hospitality and Pastoral Practices from an Evangelical Perspective," *Theological Education* 47, no. 1 (2012): 11–31.
21. Kim Philip Hansen, *Military Chaplains and Religious Diversity* (New York: Palgrave Macmillan, 2012), 167.
22. Han, Metzger, and Muck, "Christian Hospitality," 11.
23. Hansen, *Military Chaplains*, 166.
24. Hansen, *Military Chaplains*, 166.

sustainability, share evangelicalism's precepts but also understand the urgent need for social witness, justice, and action. Mark Noll, in *The Scandal of the Evangelical Mind*, describes evangelicalism in the United States as composed of mainly white Protestants who hold to Bebbington's four key components of evangelicalism, but Noll also includes "black Protestants" who hold to the same beliefs but avoid applying the term "evangelical" to their denominations or to themselves.[25] Noll resists the term "evangelicalism," arguing against the "-ism" applied to "evangelical." Instead, he proposes the following understanding in lieu of a definition:

> "Evangelicalism" has always been made up of shifting movements, temporary alliances, and the lengthened shadows of individuals. All discussions of evangelicalism, therefore, are always both descriptions of the way things really are as well as efforts within our own minds to provide some order for a multifaceted, complex set of impulses and organizations.[26]

Thus, evangelicals are more of a movement than a concrete denomination or organization like the Catholic Church, the Orthodox Churches, and so on.

A thorough understanding of evangelicalism and what it means to individuals' religious faith in American society provides a way to understand the unique challenges "evangelical Christians face in Chaplaincy and other religious environments. . . . It is unrealistic to expect the spiritual beliefs of Christian citizens to vanish as they spend time at work or other community activities."[27] Most people who are from an evangelical tradition want to engage their faith not only in their private lives but in the public sector and on the job as well. They desire the opportunity to act out their own traditions whenever there is a need and wherever they are. The chaplain offers the religious support, guidance, security, and sustenance for that to happen in the workplace, where people spend 30 to 40 percent of their lives.

Evangelical Chaplains' Authority to Accomplish the Mission

Chaplains have two major sources of authority by which they minister: constitutional authority and religious authority. The first of these was discussed in the previous chapter. This section will address the evangelical chaplain's greatest authority: God.

25. Mark A. Noll, *The Scandal of the Evangelical Mind* (Grand Rapids: Eerdmans, 1995), 8–9.
26. Noll, *Scandal of the Evangelical Mind*, 8.
27. Hansen, *Military Chaplains*, 168.

Over the years many questions have arisen about evangelical chaplains' ability to accomplish ministry in secular settings. There is a widespread misunderstanding that chaplains and their religious ministry efforts are controlled by their employer. Often, evangelical pastors and leaders think that chaplains must surrender their biblical beliefs, ministerial practices, and spiritual convictions to serve within, for example, the military, VA hospitals, or federal prisons. The fact is, evangelical chaplains in America have tremendous authority from God, recognized by the government and many institutions, to be who God called them to be, adhere to their biblical beliefs and practices, and minister according to their religious convictions.[28]

It is essential to understand that the chaplain's religious authority comes from God and not the government, the military, or civilian institutions. God grants the authority, and that authority is recognized by the Declaration of Independence, the Constitution, laws, governmental policies, and military regulations, as well as civilian organizations that employ chaplains. To explore this truth further, we will focus on the chaplain's authority granted by God and then on the authority recognized by the government and civilian employers.

The Scriptures reveal that God, the Creator of the universe, is the rightful authority over all his creation (Gen. 1–2). Jesus reveals that his all-encompassing authority, "in heaven and on earth," is given to him by God (Matt. 28:18). Likewise, the chaplain's authority to accomplish God's mission is given by God (Matt. 28:19–20; Luke 10:19). This God-given authority may be understood to flow from the chaplain's personal salvation, the indwelling of the Holy Spirit, the Word of God, biblical convictions, a calling to chaplaincy, seminary education, pastoral ordination, ecclesiastical endorsement, and ministerial experience.

Salvation provides the foundational source of authority for the evangelical chaplain to accomplish the mission. As a born-again believer, the evangelical chaplain is a child of God and a member of the heavenly household, the "royal priesthood," and God's "holy nation" (1 Pet. 2:4–10). The chaplain's relational status with respect to God is at the core of their ministry and authority to accomplish the mission. The three dimensions mentioned here (membership in the heavenly household, membership in the royal priesthood, and membership in the holy nation) deserve to be examined in detail.

First, God has gifted the believing chaplain with the relational status of a son or daughter who has been adopted into his family (Rom. 8:15; Gal. 4:5; Eph. 1:5). Expansive rights, privileges, and authority come with this relationship. God has redeemed born-again believers and granted them membership in the

---

28. DOD Instruction 1304.28, "The Appointment and Service of Chaplains," § 2.2.b, https://www.esd.whs.mil/Portals/54/Documents/DD/issuances/dodi/130428p.pdf.

spiritual household, even giving them a positional seat of authority in heaven (Eph. 2:6). The evangelical chaplain ministers on earth, understanding that this ministerial authority comes from God in heaven, where the chaplain is positionally seated in the throne room.

Second, God has granted the believing chaplain the status and authority of a royal priest (1 Pet. 2:9). The purpose of the royal priest is to bring God to people and people to God (Rev. 1:6; 5:10). Likewise, the primary mission of the evangelical chaplain is to bear the presence and message of Christ to bring God to people and to bring people to God through Jesus Christ the High Priest (Heb. 9:11–15).

Third, God has raised up born-again chaplains to be members of God's holy nation (1 Pet. 2:9). This is a nation made up of all believers and followers of Jesus Christ. It is a righteous nation authorized by God, paid for with the blood of Jesus, and empowered by the Holy Spirit dwelling in God's chosen people (1 Cor. 2:12; Eph. 1:3–7). It is a nation that enjoys being in a loving relationship with God, serving under the authority of God, and being empowered by God to invite others into the nation through Jesus Christ (Matt. 22:37–40; 28:19–20).

The indwelling Holy Spirit is a source of authority and power for born-again chaplains as they seek to accomplish their mission (Acts 1:8). When a believer receives Jesus as Lord and Savior, the Holy Spirit comes into their soul and lives in that person (1 Cor. 2:12; 6:19; 2 Cor. 5:5). This indwelling of the Spirit seals the eternal relationship of the believer with God (2 Cor. 1:22; Eph. 1:13) and results in the yielded believer being empowered with the fruit of the Spirit for Christlike living and relational ministry (Gal. 5:22–23). God Almighty, the source of all authority, dwells in the born-again chaplain and authorizes and empowers that chaplain's ministry.

The Word of God, too, is a powerful source of authority for the chaplain. The evangelical chaplain believes that "all Scripture is breathed out by God and profitable for teaching, for reproof, for correction, and for training in righteousness, that the man of God may be complete, equipped for every good work" (2 Tim. 3:16–17). Likewise, the evangelical chaplain understands that "the word of God is living and active, sharper than any two-edged sword" (Heb. 4:12). It is the power of the Word of God that generates saving faith in a person's heart. Without hearing the good news of Jesus's death and resurrection, a person cannot be redeemed (Rom. 10:17; Eph. 2:8–9). Sometimes chaplains are told they are welcome to bear the presence of Christ silently but are asked not to share the gospel. Chaplains need to understand that the power of salvation rests not in their silent godly example but in the powerful Word of God. The chaplain's words carry the authority of God when they match the Word of God. When the chaplain speaks the words of Scripture, they are a powerful source of authority for the chaplain.

There is a popular saying widely attributed to Saint Francis, "Preach the gospel at all times. If necessary, use words." It is unlikely that Francis said this. If anything, he preached repeatedly to many people. The use of words is absolutely necessary to communicate the gospel in its fullness. John 1 says that Jesus himself *is* the Word of God and thus his Word is necessary to salvation. Actions of love by Christians, even toward their enemies, are a fine witness to God's love. But it is ultimate vanity to think that as sinful humans—even if redeemed—we have the authority or power to convert others to Christ.

Biblical convictions are another powerful source of authority in the accomplishing of the chaplain's mission. As one studies God's Word, one will treasure its truths and desire to apply them to life (Ps. 119). This application will lead to the formation of personal biblical convictions. One's conscience may also come into play when forming and applying personal convictions (John 1:9; Rom. 2:15). While the authority of God's Word is not always accepted in secular society, one's conscience is usually honored as a legitimate authoritative source for personal and religious actions.[29]

God's ministerial call is a deep-rooted source of authority. A clarion call from God makes it clear to chaplains that they are on a mission from God and are sent with the authority of God (Isa. 6:8–9). I (Steve) recall being sent on a mission by a four-star general to investigate the increase in suicides at a particular military installation that had a two-star general in command. When I, a chaplain lieutenant colonel at the time, asked the four-star what kind of authority I had in confronting the two-star, he gruffly replied, "My authority!" He then told his secretary to get the two-star on the phone and promptly told him that he was sending the chaplain with his "stars on"! When I arrived with a team to investigate and develop solutions, I was treated like a four-star general. The two-star understood that even though the chaplain was a much lower-ranking officer and was not in the chain of command, he came with all the authority of the four-star general. Likewise, when chaplains understand that they are sent with the authority of the Commander in Chief of the universe, they have great confidence to accomplish God's mission and will have great respect among most who understand that calling.[30]

Seminary education with a master of divinity (MDiv)—or equivalent, as applicable—provides authoritative confidence for the chaplain, from both a knowledge basis and a respect basis. A person who is called to chaplaincy and

29. DOD Instruction 1304.28, "The Appointment and Service of Chaplains," § 3.1.g.
30. See chap. 6 under the section "Call to Chaplaincy."

follows that call with academically strenuous seminary studies will have a sense of religious authority and expertise. A seminary education provides one with the conviction and confidence to handle God's Word rightly (2 Tim. 2:15) and to minister effectively in secular and pluralistic settings. Furthermore, a seminary degree calls for respect from the chaplains one seeks to minister among; an MDiv speaks loudly to the authoritative expertise of the person who holds the degree.

Ministerial ordination is a biblical and traditional human source of authority for the chaplain. God created the church to be the vehicle by which he orchestrates his work on earth (Matt. 16:18). Further, he designed and gifted various church offices and functions. The underlying church office of the chaplain is that of the pastor, who is called to shepherd the people of God and prepare them for spiritual ministry (Eph. 4:11–12). Not all chaplain ministries require pastoral ordination, but pastoral ordination powerfully extends the church's authority to the chaplain as a servant who will care for the souls of people (1 Tim. 3:1–2; John 15:16). Many chaplain employers require pastoral ordination, especially when the chaplain's endorser requires it.

Ecclesiastical endorsement is yet another recognized source of authority (Heb. 13:17). For evangelical chaplains, ecclesiastical endorsement is provided by various consolidated church groups, fellowships, or denominations. Essentially, a single representative of the church group is given the endorser title and the authority to endorse and oversee chaplains in their service as religious caregivers. In military and governmental chaplaincy positions, the endorser has complete religious authority over each of his or her chaplains. This authority is the result of the First Amendment of the US Constitution and its stance on the separation of church and state (see chap. 4).

Pastoral experience provides a chaplain with further authority. In fact, experiential authority may provide the greatest measure of gravitas for the chaplain. When a seminary-trained and ordained pastor has served as a local-church minister for an extended period, they will have a greater sense of authority and be recognized as a trusted agent in matters of faith and practice. Experience provides a powerful source of authority for the chaplain, and there is no replacement for it. For this reason, the military requires two years of post-MDiv experience for those who want to become chaplains.[31] This experience is never waived for active-duty chaplains, although sometimes pastoral experience before and during seminary is allowed to fulfill the requirement. Those headed into military chaplaincy will want to pursue pastoral ministry opportunities while in seminary. A pastor-mentor will be of utmost importance in applying

31. DOD Instruction 1304.28, "Appointment and Service of Chaplains," § 3.2.

the knowledge and skills learned in the classroom. Experience in preaching, teaching, counseling, advising, baptizing, leading communion, performing weddings, and leading funerals will be invaluable in the development of pastoral skills and a foundation for ministerial authority. Healthcare chaplains will glean experience and authority from completing four units of CPE and becoming board-certified healthcare chaplains. The VA healthcare chaplaincy requires two years of professional pastoral experience, including four units of CPE and board certification. (Requirements for other types of chaplaincy vary and appear in more detail in part 2.)

Characteristics of Evangelical Chaplains

Chaplains are called by God to be people of godly character. Those who look to chaplains for spiritual guidance count on them being like God: relational, holy, loving, humble, and selfless.

Relational

God, in his very essence, is relational. The triune God, being in an eternal relationship with himself, created humans in his image to be in relationship with him and with one another (Gen. 1:26–27). This relational design set the foundation for how God ministers to us and how chaplains should minister. God desires to have an eternal relationship with every person (2 Pet. 3:9). To this goal, evangelical chaplains strive to befriend every person, to reach out first, and to pull others into their inner circle as Jesus did (Luke 7:34). They help people enter into an eternal relationship with God (Matt. 28:19–20) and have godly relationships with others (Matt. 22:37–39).

Holy

God, in his very essence, is holy (Isa. 6:3). All that God thinks and does is an expression of his holiness (Exod. 15:11). Evangelical chaplains understand that a commitment to follow Christ means a call to holy living (1 Pet. 1:15–16). Still, the challenge for chaplains ministering in secular settings is to avoid being pulled into the unholy behaviors of those to whom they are called to minister (1 John 2:15–17). It is exceedingly difficult for chaplains to provide incarnational ministry, to become part of the group, and at the same time to act differently. Still, the chaplain must stand firm in the Lord to provide effective ministry. A chaplain cannot lead people in the light if they are personally walking in darkness (1 John 1:5–7). From personal experience, I (Steve) recall the challenge of living a holy life while stationed in Greenland, where I was confronted with numerous temptations to fall into sin. By God's grace I stayed true to the Lord and to my wife. At first, I thought I would be rejected by those I came to serve. Instead, I was respected and found many opportunities to lead people to Christ and disciple them to also live a godly life in Christ (Mark 16:15). Every chaplain is called to live a holy life and to lead by example.

Loving

God, in his very essence, is love. All that God thinks and does flows from a heart of love (1 John 4:8). Evangelical chaplains strive to emulate God's love, knowing there is no more powerful force in all the universe than the love of God (John 3:16; Rom. 8:35–39; Eph. 3:17–19). God's love drove him to send Jesus to die for sinners and to be raised from the dead, thereby offering everyone eternal life (John 3:16; 1 Cor. 15:3–4). Therefore, it is through God's love that individuals are offered the opportunity to enjoy an eternal relationship with God (Rom. 5:8; 10:9–10). Likewise, it is through the loving leadership of chaplains that individuals are guided to God and into an eternal relationship with him (see Rom. 10:14–17). Evangelical chaplains understand that even though people are created in the image of God, every person is by nature a sinner, separated from God, and in need of God's loving forgiveness (Rom. 3:23; 6:23). Understanding that the mission of God is to forgive sins and to have a relationship with all who believe, it is paramount that chaplains allow God's love to flow through them by the power of the Holy Spirit (Acts 1:8). A chaplain who demonstrates love in word and deed draws people who wish to experience and follow that love (see John 13:34–35). No doubt, relational leadership is a powerful and wonderful way to guide struggling individuals to experience God's forgiveness and enjoy a relationship with him. Loving leadership is also a superior way for chaplains to approach and care for people in crisis and in failing relationships. Much of the counseling the chaplain does will be focused on helping people experience the love of God and share that love with others.

Humble

Jesus exhibited humility and sets the example for chaplains to do the same (Phil. 2:5–8). He humbled himself in servitude to the Father, who sent him to earth to die for the sins of humanity (John 3:16). He, being very God of very God, chose to "[empty] himself, by taking the form of a servant" (Phil. 2:7). Jesus sets the example as one who understood how to humble himself and serve under the authority of the Father. He knew that he needed to humble himself to accomplish the mission, a sacrificial mission of dying (Phil. 2:8). Likewise, chaplains are called by God to humble themselves under his authority and to be willing to serve him, even unto death. This is exactly what Jesus called his disciples to do when he said, "Let him deny himself and take up his cross and follow me" (Matt. 16:24). This humble self-denial fits in beautifully with servant leadership. Sometimes chaplains become prideful and let their rank, awards, and status go to their heads. Doing so is a complete failure to model Christ and his humility. Chaplains need to examine themselves daily and follow the apostle Paul's challenge to die to self every day to serve Christ and accomplish the mission (1 Cor. 15:31).

Selfless

Selfless service is an outflow of humility and love. The Scriptures make clear that sacrificial service happens when we avoid "selfish ambition or conceit, but in humility count others more significant than" ourselves (Phil. 2:3). Chaplaincy is not about putting on a uniform and rank or a lab coat with a cross on it, nor is it about being given a title or being given special privilege or a paycheck. Rather, it is about humble service before God and man. For nobody can serve oneself and serve God (cf. Matt. 6:24). Humble servant-chaplains cry out, "Here I am! Send me" (Isa. 6:8). "Send me to the hungry and thirsty. Send me to care for the stranger. Send me to help the destitute. Send me to minister to the sick. Send me into the prisons" (see Matt. 25:35–36). "God, send me to the place you need me most so I can bear your presence and message." However, far too often, chaplains get caught up trying to convince God and those in charge as to where they should serve. Too few chaplains let God direct their paths. The truly humble chaplain has but one desire for their next assignment: to be right in the middle of God's plan, faithfully serving (Prov. 3:5–6).

Various Challenges Evangelical Chaplains Face

Evangelical chaplains are challenged on many fronts when ministering in pluralistic and secular settings. Seeking to minister in an ever-changing humanistic culture makes it a tremendous challenge to share the gospel, to be salt and light, and to provide spiritual care for all.

Facing the Culture

The chaplain's commitment to the Lord and biblical convictions will be challenged when facing the culture. America's God-centered foundations have been under attack for many years, and the shift away from biblical values is quite advanced. Many date the foundational shift to June 25, 1962, when the US

Supreme Court ruled, in *Engle v. Vitale*, that prayer in public schools violated the First Amendment, and to a subsequent ruling in 1963, *Abington School District v. Schempp*, when reading the Bible in public schools was declared unconstitutional.[32] The void created by the removal of God from classrooms has been filled with secular humanism, with each person determining what is right in their own eyes (see Prov. 14:12). Traditional biblical values proclaim God to be the author of right and wrong (see Exod. 20:3–17). However, in America the culture has shifted so far away from God as the source of truth and righteousness (cf. John 14:6) that each person is now thought to possess the authority to determine what is true and right for themselves. Of course, this is a spiritual attack from Satan on America that has its origins in the garden of Eden, when Lucifer lied to Eve and convinced her that if she disobeyed God and ate from the tree of the knowledge of good and evil, she would be like God and could determine what was right and wrong for herself (Gen. 3:1–6).

Many are living this idolatrous lie today and will not be anxious to hear an evangelical chaplain proclaim God as the only source of truth and the only authority of what is right and wrong (John 14:6). The Scriptures aptly describe what is true for many when it says, "Since they did not see fit to acknowledge God, God gave them up to a debased mind" (Rom. 1:28). Therefore, chaplains with a biblical worldview and Christian values may be rejected and maligned by those without God in their minds. Nevertheless, God sends chaplains as "sheep in the midst of wolves" (Matt. 10:16). Still, God isn't sending chaplains on a suicide mission; he is sending them on a rescue mission. God wants to see the wolves become sheep (2 Pet. 3:9). Knowing this, the Bible reminds chaplains and all believers to "be wise as serpents and innocent as doves" and to beware of those who seek to harm them and destroy their God-given mission (Matt. 10:16–23). Chaplains need to be aware that the enemy is not the person rejecting Christ but is, rather, the evil one, who is on a seek-and-destroy mission against those the chaplain is called to help rescue (see Eph. 6:12–20). "Be strong in the Lord and in the strength of his might. Put on the whole armor of God, that you may be able to stand against the schemes of the devil" (Eph. 6:10–11).

Sharing the Gospel

Sharing the gospel is the most important challenge the chaplain will face. It is the primary mission God gives to the chaplain, because without the gospel no one can be saved and enter an eternal relationship with God. God has chosen to use the words of the gospel to generate saving faith in the hearts of people, and

32. Engel v. Vitale, 370 U.S. 421, 82 (1962), https://casetext.com/case/engel-v-vitale.

without the opportunity to hear the message of Christ, a person cannot be saved. "Faith comes from hearing, and hearing through the word of Christ" (Rom. 10:17). Nevertheless, the consistent drumbeat of many in authority over chaplains is that sharing the gospel is not acceptable, that chaplains must surrender God's command to share the good news at the door. Many believers have been deceived into agreeing with this idea. In reality, God calls chaplains to bear his presence *and message*, and it is not enough to bear the presence of Christ alone.

Salt and Light

Being salt and light (Matt. 5:13–16) in an increasingly godless society is a tough challenge. Those who have decided to make up their own truth and morals will have little tolerance for chaplains who proclaim Jesus as "the way, and the truth, and the life" (John 14:6). They will not want the chaplain to share the eternal truths of God and his righteousness, but they may want to indoctrinate the chaplain with their ideologies and morals. They may even file official complaints when the chaplain cannot assist them in same-sex relational counseling or perform their same-sex wedding (Gen. 1:26–27; 2:24). Still further, evangelical chaplains may face pushback and rejection when they refuse to buy into transgender ideologies and indoctrination. Nevertheless, God lovingly sends chaplains into the darkness to bear the light of Christ. Some chaplains may have the desire to flee from the darkness or to hide the light of Christ, but the challenge of Jesus is to bear the light of Christ and his standard of right (Matt. 5:14–16). The moral structure the Lord has put in place cannot be changed because it is rooted in his eternal, immutable character (James 1:17). Bible-believing chaplains are called not only to share the gospel but to proclaim the whole counsel of God (Acts 20:27). It is not the chaplain's words that serve as preserving salt and lifesaving light, but rather God's penetrating and powerful Word (Heb. 4:12). So it should come as no surprise that Satan and his emissaries desire to stop the chaplain from sharing God's Word. Chaplains will fail the mission to be salt and light if they rely on their own strength and words. To this point, the evangelical chaplain is challenged to take the following words to heart: "Do your best to present yourself to God as one approved, a worker who has no need to be ashamed, rightly handling the word of truth" (2 Tim. 2:15).

Providing Spiritual Care for All

Employers of chaplains expect their chaplains to make sure everyone's spiritual needs are addressed.[33] No doubt, evangelical chaplains serving in secular

33. DOD Instruction 1304.28, "Appointment and Service of Chaplains," § 3.1.f.

pluralistic settings will find it challenging to provide spiritual care for individuals who are members of different faith groups, especially non-Christian ones. Still, sometimes evangelical chaplains will find that they can offer spiritual care in such cases. For instance, during times of crisis, the chaplain may be able to provide a ministry of presence, spiritual advisement, or prayer. However, when a request is made that the chaplain cannot fulfill because of religious conviction or because of theological or ministry-practice differences, the chaplain should refer the person to another minister who can meet that need. Chaplains should perform or refer in accordance with their endorser's requirements and conscience as recognized by law.

Chaplains should never attempt to provide a religious service they are not ordained or endorsed to offer. For instance, a same-sex couple may ask the evangelical chaplain to provide marriage counseling and perform their wedding. That chaplain should not feel pressured to provide the counseling or perform the wedding, as doing so would be against their theological beliefs, conscience, and ordination vows and against the endorser's policies. Other times, chaplains may simply be challenged with matters of religious practice. For example, a Baptist chaplain may be asked to do an infant baptism that they cannot accommodate. In this case, the chaplain can simply give a referral to a chaplain or minister who can. However, it is recommended that the chaplain explain what they can do and offer the requesting person that option. Baptizing the baby might not be an option, but the chaplain can dedicate the baby and ask God's blessings on the parents. This may be sufficient for the parents.

Conclusion

In this chapter the evangelical chaplain has been defined as a born-again believer and follower of Jesus Christ who is called, prepared, and sent out by the church to bear the biblical presence and message of Christ in sacred and secular settings. Several aspects of evangelical chaplains' identity and ministry have been discussed, including their beliefs, God-given authority, godly character, and challenges.

6

Endorsement
and Employment

People contemplating service as a chaplain need to know what requirements must be met to become a chaplain. There are two entities that play into the overall requirements: the ecclesiastical endorser and the employer. Because chaplaincy is a form of pastoral ministry, ecclesiastical requirements are paramount. Chaplaincy is not a secular occupation one might pursue out of personal desires or a preference for an interesting career. Rather, chaplaincy is a calling of God on one's life and must be approached as such. This chapter will explore what ecclesiastical endorsement is, the need for endorsement, the authority of the endorser, the requirements of the endorser, the value of the endorser, the importance of a positive working relationship with the endorser, employer-based requirements for various chaplaincies, and endorser support organizations. We will conclude with a historical example of pluralistic cooperation among chaplains.

Ecclesiastical Endorsement Defined

Each recognized religious organization that endorses chaplains is represented by a single endorsing agent who is authorized to provide ecclesiastical endorsements on behalf of that organization. The endorsement confirms that the chaplain is properly educated and has the ecclesial experience to function as a clergyperson representing that group in a particular field of chaplaincy. The endorsement may also confirm that the chaplain is ordained, though not all chaplains have to be ordained. Over two hundred recognized endorsers from denominations and world religions are authorized to provide chaplains to the military, government agencies like the Veterans Administration, the Federal Bureau of Prisons, civilian hospitals, and other civilian organizations.[1] Each of these endorsing bodies is authorized to oversee (though not directly supervise) its chaplains' ministries. Endorsed chaplains provide ministry for their employer under the religious authority of their endorsing agent. Later parts of the chapter will clarify some details of this arrangement.

The Necessity of Ecclesiastical Endorsers

Ecclesiastical endorsement of chaplains is a requirement of the US government and several civilian organizations that employ chaplains. The government mandates ecclesiastical endorsement for all chaplains serving within government organizations. This requirement is rooted in the US Constitution's First Amendment, which states, "Congress shall make no law establishing religion." Ecclesiastical endorsement provides the government with a means of employing chaplains without the government attempting to decide the validity of a chaplain's religious identity or faithfulness. The government is not qualified to make such judgments, and therefore it properly turns those judgments over to the endorsing faith groups, all of which meet the same basic requirements of being recognized religious organizations (see chap. 1). Additionally, ecclesiastical endorsement is required by many civilian organizations; endorsement allows them to employ chaplains without providing religious supervision.

Further, officially recognized religious organizations mandate ecclesiastical endorsement to ensure denominational authority over their chaplains in matters of faith and practice, whether employed by the government or by civilian organizations. Church endorsement ensures both that the chaplain's First Amendment rights are upheld as they perform ministry according to their organization's theological and religious practices and that they are not religiously

---

1. DOD Instruction 1304.28, "Appointment and Service of Chaplains," § 4.1, https://www
.esd.whs.mil/Portals/54/Documents/DD/issuances/dodi/130428p.pdf; 38 U.S.C. § 7405, https://
casetext.com/statute/united-states-code/title-38-veterans-benefits/part-v-boards-administra
tions-and-services/chapter-74-veterans-health-administration-personnel/subchapter-i-appoint
ments/section-7405-temporary-full-time-appointments-part-time-appointments-and-without
-compensation-appointments.

directed by the government or a secular civilian organization.[2] Both church and state have a vested interest in employing chaplains who faithfully represent their faith tradition and provide ministerial care for military members and their families, federal and state employees, and so on. This approach maintains publicly accountable quality control of chaplains' activities. The First Amendment speaks to this when it says, "Congress shall make no law prohibiting the free exercise [of religion]." Making best use of these arrangements, chaplains provide positive ministerial care and enable the free exercise of religion for thousands of individuals around the globe. This is to the eternal benefit of all involved.

Legal Necessity

The First Amendment of the US Constitution makes clear that the government cannot make laws establishing religion. Therefore, organizations connected to the US government cannot make rules and regulations dictating what a chaplain should believe or how the chaplain should conduct ministry. In 1901 the US War Department decided to require ecclesiastical endorsement.[3] Today the government relies on recognized religious bodies to endorse qualified individuals for chaplain service to the Army, the Navy, the Air Force, VA hospitals, federal prisons, the State Department, the FBI, the CIA, Secret Service, and other federal entities. Various nongovernment organizations, such as hospitals, hospice-care organizations, and community groups, also understand the legal value of ecclesiastical endorsement and require their chaplains to be endorsed. Additionally, various chaplain healthcare certification groups, like the Association of Professional Chaplains, require ecclesiastical endorsement before they will board-certify a chaplain.

The endorsement of chaplains by federally recognized religious groups allows the government to ensure that the First Amendment right of free exercise of religion is afforded to military members, hospital patients, and many other people, while at the same time not establishing religion. To this end the ecclesiastical endorser serves as the sole religious authority for chaplains. The military, for example, has no religious authority over the chaplain; instead, the endorser is the director of the religious administration and the religious speech of the chaplain. Chaplains who discern that their ministerial authority is being usurped without resolution should bring the matter to their endorsers.

---

2. DOD Instruction 1304.28, "Appointment and Service of Chaplains," § 4.2.
3. National Conference on Ministry to the Armed Forces (website), accessed August 21, 2023, https://www.ncmaf.com.

Ecclesiastical Necessity

The endorsement of chaplains places the authority of recognizing whether a person is a bona fide minister in the hands of religious bodies and not the government. Endorsers ensure that the chaplains they approve for the federal system, the state system, hospitals, or other entities have met all the requirements of their faith group and are prepared to serve in chaplaincy, and they also ensure that their chaplains' theology and practice of ministry are in line with those of their religious group.

When companies and organizations do not require ecclesiastical endorsement for their chaplains, the employer must provide religious oversight. This oversight is a task that most secular organizations are not qualified to do, and the Scriptures make clear that such oversight belongs to the church (Acts 20:28; Eph. 4:11–12). For the evangelical, the church is at the foundation of chaplaincy. The church in its various expressions—people, congregations, regional and national networks and denominations—is ordained by God to accomplish God's work on earth: that is, the fulfillment of the Great Commandment (Matt. 22:37–39) and the Great Commission (Matt. 28:19–20). Chaplain ministry is necessary for accomplishing the fullness of this mission. Therefore, every evangelical called to chaplaincy should be rooted in the body of believers. It is in and through the church that a person may hear the gospel, commit their life to Jesus Christ as Lord and Savior, be discipled in faith and doctrine, be called to chaplaincy, be sent to a seminary to prepare, be ordained, serve as a pastor, and be endorsed by the overseeing religious group to which the church is connected.

The Endorser's Authority

Religious organizations that choose to send chaplains into the government or civilian organizations to perform pastoral ministry select a single individual to represent them as their ecclesiastical endorsing agent. This person is empowered by the denomination to select, endorse, and oversee chaplains and to revoke endorsement when appropriate, and the government recognizes the agent's authority. The endorser may also be given authority to establish an endorsing team to best accomplish the mission. Ecclesiastical endorsers are thus the gatekeepers for all government and civilian employers that require endorsement.[4]

Normally, endorsements are withdrawn when a chaplain's theology, practice of ministry, or lifestyle no longer represents the religious organization's beliefs

4. DOD Instruction 1304.28, "Appointment and Service of Chaplains," § 4.2 (b. 2).

and doctrinal stances. When the endorser chooses to withdraw an endorsement, the action normally follows conversations conducted in hopes of rectifying areas of concern. Once the endorser determines that the chaplain's endorsement must be withdrawn, the endorser will formally notify the government or civilian organization in writing. For military and government employees, this withdrawal will result in a loss of employment within ninety days. However, if the chaplain can procure another endorsement within those ninety days, they may be allowed to continue serving, depending on the discretion of military and government officials. Within the military, chiefs of chaplains of the Army, Navy, and Air Force normally examine whether the current endorser and future endorser agree concerning the proposed future employment.

Evangelical Endorser Requirements

At this point, the reader may still be asking, "So, how do I get endorsed?" Those pursuing chaplaincy should start by asking their pastor if their local church is affiliated with a group that endorses chaplains. If not, aspirants will need to do some research to find an endorsing agency of like faith and practice. They may want to check with their seminary to see whom the school can recommend. Evangelical seminaries, especially those specifically training chaplains, often provide a service to match students with endorsers. Once an aspirant is connected with a religious body that endorses chaplains, they will be guided through the qualification process. Evangelical endorsers will want to hear a clear testimony of the aspirant's salvation, spiritual walk, calling to ministry, and plan for ordination if they are not already ordained. Endorsers will be anxious to hear whether an aspirant's doctrine and practice line up with the group's statement of faith and ministry policies. Additionally, they will want to hear how the aspirant has been serving in pastoral roles in their local church and community. The endorsers will be interested in the seminary education of the inquirer, including their grade point average. Finally, if the aspirant is married or engaged, endorsers will want to ensure that their spouse is called to serve alongside them in chaplaincy.

The main requirements of typical evangelical groups for endorsement deserve further attention. We will explore them in detail in the following pages.

Personal Salvation Testimony

Chaplain ministry might be defined in one word: relationships. The chaplain's mission is to help people have an eternal and loving relationship with God and to help people love one another with the love of God (Matt. 22:37–

39). It is paramount that the chaplain know Jesus as personal Lord and Savior and follow him (Matt. 16:24–26). Evangelical chaplains understand that "all have sinned and fall short of the glory of God" (Rom. 3:23) and that "the wages of sin is death [separation from God], but the free gift of God is eternal life in Christ Jesus our Lord" (Rom. 6:23). They also believe that "God shows his love for us in that while we were still sinners, Christ died for us" (Rom. 5:8), and they understand that "if you confess with your mouth that Jesus is Lord and believe in your heart that God raised him from the dead, you will be saved" (Rom. 10:9). Evangelical chaplains have an eternal relationship with God because they have trusted Christ's finished work of salvation and have called on the name of the Lord so they could be rescued from sin and could begin a right relationship with God (see Rom. 10:13). This eternal, saving relationship between God and the chaplain is the foundation of all the chaplain is called to do by the Lord, which is to love God, love people, follow God's commands, and set an example of Christlikeness (see 1 John 5:1–5).

Christlike Living

Chaplains serve outside the church as Christian ministers. Therefore, they must model themselves after Christ and according to biblical standards given to pastors (1 Tim. 3:1–7). They must be spiritually strong enough to maintain their testimony and witness in isolated secular environments. Evangelical endorsers will require those they accept as chaplains to live in a way that demonstrates a new life in Christ, with old things passing away and all things becoming new (2 Cor. 5:17). Further, endorsers will want to know that aspirants are practicing spiritual disciplines to grow in Christ—prayer, meditation, worship, Bible study, Bible memorization, evangelism, journaling, fasting, fellowshipping, or serving (2 Pet. 3:18). Additionally, the endorser will want to hear about spiritual mentors and coaches, as well as accountability partners, who are assisting the chaplain in growing in Christ.

Call to Chaplaincy

Chaplaincy is a calling. A clear call from God that is rooted in one's mind, emotions, and soul is paramount to successful chaplain ministry. A call to chaplaincy is not something one finds by reading a list of professional occupations that people enjoy. Rather, a call to chaplaincy comes to an individual through the Holy Spirit. It is God calling the person to surrender one's life to Christian service. It is a call to "deny [oneself] and take up [one's] cross and follow" (Matt. 16:24). It is a call to a life of service and sacrifice, a call to humble oneself in order to serve others for the glory of God (Phil. 2:1–7). It is a call to bear the presence and message of Christ with all who need to know that God is with them and who desire to hear the good news. It is a call to represent Jesus, driven by a heart of love for God and people. It is a call to leave the trinkets of this life behind on the highway and follow Jesus through the trenches of this world to share the love of God and the gospel of Jesus Christ with the needy. It is a call to minister to those who are spiritually, emotionally, and physically in need. It is a call to visit and care for the hungry, thirsty, sick, estranged, destitute, and lonely (Matt. 25:35–36). A call to chaplaincy is a high calling of God to serve people in their darkest hour and to celebrate the goodness of God in their brightest days.

For military chaplains, a pastoral calling is foundational to one's chaplain calling. The Army, Navy, and Air Force hire only those who are church-ordained and pastorally trained to be chaplains. They then seek to train them on how to provide ministry in the various cultures of the Army, Navy, and Air Force. When military chaplaincy was set up during the American Revolution, existing pastors were invited to join the military to provide pastoral ministry on the battlefields. These chaplains were Christian, possessed a divinity degree and a pastoral-ordination certificate, and were serving as local church pastors.[5] Elements of this historical practice remain today. The military still requires evangelicals seeking to become chaplains to have a clear pastoral calling, clergy ordination, an MDiv degree, and at least two years of full-time pastoral experience following their graduation and ordination.

Seminary Education

A call to be a chaplain is a call to prepare. Different kinds of chaplaincy require different kinds and levels of education, but complete clergy education is always a requirement. An MDiv is required by all endorsers and employers of chaplains serving the US government, whether in the military, Bureau of Prisons, or VA, and it is required for many healthcare and community chaplain positions. However, state-level chaplain positions often require only a master's-level seminary degree, not specifically the MDiv. Positions in this category may include state-prison chaplaincies, police and fire chaplaincies, and various state community chaplaincies. Additionally, sometimes hospice chaplain positions and workplace chaplain positions require only an applicable master of arts (MA).

5. Lawrence P. Greenslit, *Religion and the Military: A Growing Ethical Dilemma* (Carlisle Barracks, PA: Army War College, 2006), 3.

Evangelical Beliefs and Doctrine

Evangelical endorsers will want to know that a prospective chaplain is aligned with them on all major and secondary doctrines. Most evangelical chaplains agree with the following descriptions.

The doctrine of God. Evangelical chaplains believe God is eternal and is a Trinity: one God in three persons, Father, Son, and Holy Spirit. God is the Creator, and all that he created was good. God is holy, and God is love (Gen. 1–2; Isa. 6:3; 9:6; 40:28; Matt. 3:16–17; 1 John 4:8; Rev. 4:8; 22:13).

Evangelicals believe that God the Father is the First Person of the Trinity and that he rules and reigns over all creation with holiness and love, that he was grieved over the broken relationship that Adam and Eve's sin brought, and that both his holiness and his love propelled him to send his only Son, Jesus, to earth to rescue sinners and provide a way of restoring man's broken relationship with him (Gen. 1–3; John 3:16; Rom. 6:23).

Evangelical chaplains believe that Jesus Christ is the Second Person of the Trinity and that as God incarnate, born of a virgin, he lived a sinless life, died a vicarious death on the cross for the sins of all humanity, rose again bodily from the dead, ascended back into heaven, and will return to earth to raise the dead in Christ and transform the bodies of living believers so they can dwell with him throughout eternity (see esp. 1 Cor. 15).

Evangelical chaplains believe that the Holy Spirit is the Third Person of the Trinity and that he was sent by God after Jesus's ascension to dwell in the hearts of believers and to empower them to be witnesses of the gospel and to live godly lives. Evangelicals also contend that the Spirit gives believers the ability to live in love and unity (Matt. 3:16–17; Acts 1:8; Gal. 5:22–25).

The doctrine of man. Evangelical chaplains believe that man and woman were created in the image of God to enjoy an eternal relationship with him. Man and woman sinned and suffered spiritual death and separation from God, which transmitted to all their descendants (Gen. 1–3; Rom. 3:10, 23; 5:12; 6:23). Man was eternally separated from God by sin, but God created a way for man to be redeemed through Jesus Christ (John 3:16–18; Rom. 3:23; 6:23; 10:9–10; 1 John 5:12).

The doctrine of Satan. Evangelicals believe Satan is a fallen archangel, named Lucifer, who rebelled against God and was cast out of heaven with one-third of the angels. He has sought to destroy man's relationship with God (Gen. 3:1–5; Isa. 14:12–17; Ezek. 28:16; Rev. 12:7–9; 20:10) and seeks to stop the saving message of the gospel (2 Cor. 4:4; Eph. 6:11–12).

The doctrine of salvation. Evangelical chaplains believe that God provided a way for man to be reconnected to himself through the sending of his Son, Jesus

Christ, who went on a rescue mission to save people from a Christless eternity. Jesus died a vicarious death on the cross and rose victorious from death to provide the only way of salvation for all who believe (John 1:12; 11:25–26; Rom. 4:24–25; 5:8; 6:23; 10:9–10, 13; 2 Cor. 5:21).

Evangelical chaplains believe that salvation is possible only because of Jesus Christ and only through faith in Christ, and they believe that a person's efforts to find forgiveness of sins or approval from God through personal effort or religion are futile (John 14:6; Eph. 2:8–9; Rev. 20:11–15).

Evangelical chaplains believe that God's message of salvation must be told in order for people to come to a saving knowledge of Jesus Christ (Matt. 28:19–20; John 3:3, 16; Rom. 5:8; 6:23; 10:9–10, 13, 17), that the gospel is not a godly life but is rather the good news of Jesus's sacrificial death for humanity's sin, and that his resurrection must be shared in order for saving faith to be generated in the hearts of people (Rom. 10:9–17; 1 Cor. 15:3).

Evangelical chaplains believe in the resurrection of both the saved and the lost, those who are saved "to the resurrection of life" and those who are lost "to the resurrection of judgment" (John 5:29; see also Rev. 20:11–15).

The doctrine of Scripture. Evangelical chaplains believe that the sixty-six books of the Old and New Testaments are the inspired, infallible, authoritative Word of God; are God's love letter to humanity; are God's guidebook for humanity, which reveals the sinfulness of man, the righteousness of God, and God's plan of salvation for all who believe in Jesus Christ; and are the believer's instructions for righteous and eternally purposeful living (Pss. 18:30; 119:9, 105, 130; Matt. 5:18; 24:35; John 10:35; 1 Thess. 2:13; 2 Tim. 3:16; 2 Pet. 1:20–21; Rev. 22:18–19).

Common ministry practices. Evangelical endorsers vary in matters of practice. Some have divided evangelicals into two groups, "low church" and "high church," based on their positions on infant baptism and believer's baptism, as well as differing liturgical forms. The value of such descriptions among evangelicals may be debated. Nevertheless, aspiring chaplains will want to align with an endorser that best represents their practices regarding baptism, communion, and worship.

Clergy Ordination

Chaplains are often ordained as clergy (to use a term recognized in general society) by the church, which provides the chaplain with the authority to bear the presence and message of Christ (see 1 Tim. 3:1–7; Titus 1:5–9). A call to military chaplaincy as an evangelical is a call to clergy ordination, but other functional areas of chaplaincy may or may not have this requirement.

Ministerial Experience

Endorsers require ministerial experience for their applicants because it helps mold them into chaplains with a clear calling, strong character, greater competence, and improved ability to connect with people. Ministerial experience allows what has been learned in the classroom to be put into action, to be tested and practiced. It also allows new information to be gleaned and ministerial skills to be honed, resulting in more effective ministry.

Experience allows one's calling to be tested and to be made sure. While most ministerial posts offer ministry in Christian settings or organizations, chaplains minister largely to the unchurched and unredeemed. Nonetheless, ministerial experience provides an essential background for chaplains as frontline ministers who often serve people during their worst days and darkest hours. Tough ministry makes for a sure calling.

Experience allows one's character to be developed and tested. Ministering to individuals in times of death, suffering, tragedy, and brokenness, as well as in times of rejoicing and celebration, builds character. One can learn about character in the classroom, but it is through active ministerial service, during good and bad times, that one's character is established.

Experience allows one's competence to grow. As incipient chaplains practice ministry, they will more clearly see their strengths and weaknesses and strive to improve. They will grow in their ability to lead spiritually, provide pastoral care, counsel, preach, and teach. Such competence brings greater trust and confidence from constituents and greater effectiveness in ministry.

Finally, experience allows the chaplain to connect better with people. Living out a ministerial calling can be thought of as the school of hard knocks, but it will result in greater understanding, compassion, and empathy for those God has called the chaplain to serve. This will make the chaplain more relatable. Further, the chaplain's ability to connect well can result in improved pastoral leadership, ministry of care, counseling, and public communication skills.

Chaplain Spouse Preparation

When an individual is called to ministry and surrenders to that call, their entire life will change. It will quickly become clear that there is a world of difference between including God in one's plans and surrendering to God's plan (Prov. 3:5–6). When a person surrenders to the call of chaplaincy and says, "Here I am! Send me" (Isa. 6:8), all of the person's plans change. When people realize their life is not their own—that they have been bought with a price, the blood of the Lord Jesus (Heb. 9:12)—and they surrender all, their entire mission in life changes. If the aspiring chaplain is married, then their spouse should be included in the process of discovery of God's will for their lives together. Chaplaincy requires deep commitment to God and to the people that the chaplain serves. Introducing spouses to the positives and negatives of chaplaincy allows them to be part of the process of discerning God's will for their marriage, their shared ministry, and their family. Open and honest communication regarding times away from home (especially for military chaplains), the costs of dealing with continual trauma (not least for hospital and first-responder chaplains), and other difficulties allows the spouse to join the aspiring chaplain in making a family commitment to God's calling for their lives.

The Value of an Ecclesiastical Endorser

Not only are ecclesiastical endorsers required by many chaplain employers, but they are a valuable resource to the chaplain and to chaplain employers. Endorsers provide religious authority and oversight, offer religious and personal support, and serve as gatekeepers for the religious organization and employer.

Endorsers Provide Religious Authority to and Oversight of the Chaplain

When serving, endorsed chaplains represent not only themselves but also their endorser. The chaplain's theology and practice of ministry will align with their endorser and will be backed by the endorser. Underlying this arrangement is the endorser's, not the employer's, exercise of religious authority over the chaplain. The employer may therefore enjoy the benefits of a chaplain without the worry of trying to provide religious oversight. Additionally, if the chaplain feels their religious rights are being violated, the endorser can provide top cover, insight, and wisdom. Likewise, should the employer feel the chaplain is not providing appropriate ministry, it can consult with the endorser to seek to resolve the issue.

Endorsers Offer Religious and Personal Support for the Chaplain

Endorsers seek to ensure their chaplains are equipped for the pluralistic and secular environment to which God has called them. They seek to ensure their chaplains receive continual training in ministry best practices, ministry challenges, and personal spiritual growth and resiliency. Endorsers build a chaplain community to encourage fellowship, accountability, and mentorship opportunities. Many endorsers even have annual chaplain conferences to encourage continual connectivity with the church, spiritual growth, fellowship among chaplains, and continued training. Many endorsers will visit their chaplains in the workplace to become familiar with their ministry environments and make connections with their supervisors. Finally, larger endorser teams may be made up of associate endorsers, chaplain advisers, chaplain mentors, and administrative assistants to provide the best care possible for the chaplains.

Endorsers Serve as Gatekeepers for the Religious Organization and Employer

Chaplain employers, whether government or civilian organizations, count on endorsers to approve fully qualified chaplains who are properly educated, ordained, experienced, and prepared to serve in pluralistic settings. Likewise, the religious group the endorser represents counts on the endorser to approve only fully qualified chaplains to serve under the banner of their religious organization. We have already discussed the main requirements that endorsers have, but the endorser also needs to make sure that prospective chaplains are willing and able to support the religious needs of all personnel, directly or indirectly. Chaplains working in pluralistic settings should seek to make sure every individual's religious needs are met without violating their own biblical convictions, their ordination vows, or the endorser's policies. When a chaplain cannot provide direct religious care to an individual because of religious conviction or because of theological or ministry-practice differences, the chaplain should seek out another clergyperson to provide the religious care, when the chaplain can do so in accordance with their endorser's requirements and conscience as recognized by law.

The Importance of a Good Working Relationship with the Endorser

Sometimes individuals may think of the endorsement process as "one and done." However, a close working relationship with the endorser is a great advantage for a chaplain in the field. Endorsers are anxious to celebrate ministry successes and to pray with their chaplains about ministry challenges, and when chaplains do face significant ministerial, supervisory, or personal challenges, they will want to include the endorser in the conversation. In fact, in many situations the endorser should be the first person the chaplain calls. The endorser can provide wisdom, encouragement, and top cover when appropriate. Many endorsers require biannual reports so they can stay informed of the chaplain's ministry successes and challenges, as well as personal prayer matters. An endorser should be thought of not as like a high school principal but rather as a godly authority, mentor, and friend.

Employer-Based Requirements for Chaplaincy's Functional Areas

In no small measure, the various religious organizations that employ chaplains determine what they require of their chaplains. Employer requirements typically include individual ecclesiastical and educational requirements and various personal conditions. The employers of chaplains frequently insist that the chaplain complete all the requirements of the chaplain's faith group for chaplain ministry. These requirements may include a certain level of education, ordination, and ministerial work experience. Military chaplaincy has the most stringent qualifications. (See the appendix for website links for many of the organizations listed in the following paragraphs.) The following areas of chaplaincy coordinate with the chapters in part 2 of this book.

Corporate chaplaincy. Requirements for corporate chaplaincy vary depending on the hiring body. Some umbrella groups—such as Marketplace Chaplains USA, Corporate Chaplains of America, Corporate Chaplains Network, and Frontline Chaplains—provide contract chaplain services for corporations and businesses. An MDiv or MA in an appropriate field, along with an endorsement, is sometimes required.

Healthcare chaplaincy. An MDiv, endorsement, and extensive clinical pastoral education (four units is a common standard) are typically required. Several organizations offer CPE. The leading organization is the Association of Clinical Pastoral Education (ACPE). Additionally, several organizations support, accredit, and board-certify healthcare chaplains. The leading organizations are the Association of Professional Chaplains and the National Association of Veterans Affairs Chaplains. Further, the requirements for hospice care, a branch of healthcare chaplaincy, vary widely, as both hospitals and private organizations offer hospice care. Hospice offered through hospitals will have the same hiring standards they have for their hospital chaplains. However, private hospice companies often have less stringent educational and endorsement requirements for their chaplains.

Military chaplaincy. Beyond standard military-officer requirements regarding age and physical, mental, legal, financial, and security matters, military-chaplain requirements are mostly standardized for the Army, Navy (which also covers the Marine Corps, Coast Guard, and Merchant Marine), and Air Force (which also covers the Space Force). Chaplains must have completed specific ecclesiastical requirements, including ordination by their religious organization, endorsement by a recognized endorsing agency, and two years of pastoral experience after the completion of the MDiv. That experience should include conducting worship services, preaching, leading communion, and doing weddings, funerals, baptisms, and pastoral counseling. Additionally, military chaplains must have completed their educational requirements, including a bachelor of arts or bachelor of science degree from an accredited institution and an MDiv of seventy-two credit hours or more from an accredited institution. Each service branch determines its required grade point average for that work. Accession to military chaplaincy is highly competitive. The Military Chaplains Association supports these chaplaincies. While studying in a graduate-degree program, aspiring chaplains can apply to participate in chaplain-candidate programs with the military branch of their choice.

Education chaplaincy. Chaplains have served in Christian colleges and universities for centuries and continue to do so. There are now opportunities for chaplaincies in public and charter schools across the world. The Association for Chaplaincy and Spiritual Life in Higher Education "brings together professionals who are committed to nurturing the religious and spiritual life of students as a critical part of the mission of higher education in the twenty-first century."[6]

Prison chaplaincy. Positions vary from congregation-sourced volunteer chaplaincies to governmental positions that require an MDiv, endorsement, and sometimes other training. Chaplains are part of the institution and minister to staff, their families, inmates, and their families. The American Correctional Chaplains Association and the International Prison Chaplains Association support these chaplaincies.

Community chaplaincy. This kind of chaplaincy is the most open to various levels of definition, education, and endorsement, with volunteers, local churches, and parachurch groups often taking on chaplaincy-type ministries. Legislatures and executive offices often name chaplains for public events and private ministry. Clubs and associations, from local to regional to national ones, often have permanent chaplain positions. Airports often form a local agency to formulate and activate chaplain requirements. Focused Community Strategies and the International Association of Civil Aviation Chaplains support community and airport chaplaincies, respectively.

Disaster relief chaplaincy. A chaplain applicant in this area should first receive training and certification through various courses offered by the Federal Emergency Management Agency and the American Red Cross. The Southern Baptist North American Mission Board provides specific chaplain training from an evangelical viewpoint, as does the Billy Graham Evangelistic Association Rapid Response Team.

6. "Who We Are," Association for Chaplaincy and Spiritual Life in Higher Education, accessed September 20, 2023, https://www.nacuc.net/who-we-are.

Public safety chaplaincy. These chaplaincies vary greatly, from volunteer to full-time paid positions, with requirements ranging up to the MDiv and an endorsement. The FBI and Department of Homeland Security employ numerous chaplains, with rigorous qualifications. The International Conference of Police Chaplains (ICPC), the Law Enforcement Chaplaincy Foundation, and the Federation of Fire Chaplains (FFC) offer support for these chaplaincies.

Recreation chaplaincy. This ministry takes place in national parks, theme or amusement parks, cruise ships, and so forth. Camps, retreat sites, and team-building operations, while not generally thought of as chaplain-ministry venues, do feature total-immersion experiences similar to the dynamic of healthcare chaplaincy, the military, prisons, and some educational institutions. The chaplaincy paradigm offers much to consider for those groups. A Christian Ministry in the National Parks has operated since 1951 with selected volunteers.

Sports chaplaincy. Recent years have seen significant increases in sports chaplaincy at the collegiate and professional levels. While some chaplain organizations focus on particular sports, others—such as Global Sports Chaplaincy—provide general coordination and training for best practices. Teams make chaplain arrangements as best suits the sport, the team, and the locale. Athletes in Action and the Fellowship of Christian Athletes are especially active, both in providing well-equipped evangelical chaplains and in supporting cooperative chaplaincy in general.

Endorser Support Organizations

Ministry in pluralistic settings is one of the factors that make chaplaincy unique and challenging. More than two hundred chaplain endorsers, representing over two hundred religious organizations, send chaplains into the military, healthcare, and community settings to accomplish ministry. Most endorsing agencies choose to cooperate with one another, understanding that they need to set the example for their chaplains.

The largest chaplain endorser support group for military, VA, and Federal Bureau of Prisons chaplains is the National Conference on Ministry to the Armed Forces (NCMAF). This religiously diverse group of endorsers seeks to provide a unified voice to advocate for religious freedom and protect the First Amendment rights of their chaplains. Over 150 faith groups belong to this organization and represent all large religious organizations in America. NCMAF officially started in 1982, but its roots date back to 1901, when the military officially required ecclesiastical endorsement for all chaplains. NCMAF has no doctrinal statement or creed other than to provide a unified effort to protect the religious freedoms their chaplains enjoy within the US military, VA, and Federal Bureau of Prisons. However, NCMAF does have guidelines and a code of ethics. This code clarifies that the authority and autonomy of each member endorsing agency will be respected as they seek to work together to provide a united force for freedom of religion for chaplains.

NCMAF Code of Ethics

I will hold in trust the traditions and practices of my religious body.

I will carefully adhere to whatever direction may be conveyed to me by my endorsing body for maintenance of my endorsement.

I understand, as a chaplain in the United States Armed Forces, that I will function in a pluralistic environment with chaplains of other religious bodies to provide for ministry to all military personnel and their families entrusted to my care.

I will seek to provide for pastoral care and ministry to persons of religious bodies other than my own within my area of responsibility with the same investment of myself as I give to members of my own religious body. I will work collegially with chaplains of religious bodies other than my own as together we seek to provide as full a ministry as possible to our people. I will respect the beliefs and traditions of my colleagues and those to whom I minister. When conducting services of worship that include personas other than my religious body, I will draw upon those beliefs, principles, and practices that we have in common.

I will, if not in a supervisory position, respect the practices and beliefs of each chaplain I supervise, and exercise care not to require of them any service or practice that would be in violation of the faith practices of their particular religious body.

I will seek to support all colleagues in ministry by building consecutive relationships wherever I serve, both with the staff where I work and with colleagues throughout the military environment.

I will maintain a disciplined ministry in such ways as keeping hours of prayers and devotion, endeavoring to maintain wholesome family relationships, and regularly engaging in educational and recreational activities for professional and personal development. I will seek to maintain good health habits.

I will recognize that my obligation is to provide for the free exercise of religion for all members of the military services, their families, and other authorized personnel. When on active duty, I will only accept added responsibility in civilian ministry if it does not interfere with the overall effectiveness of my primary military ministry.

I will defend my colleagues against unfair discrimination on the basis of gender, race, religion, or national origin.

I will hold in confidence any privileged communication received by me during the conduct of my ministry. I will not disclose confidential communications in private or in public.

I will not proselytize other religious bodies, but I retain the right to evangelize those who are not affirmed.

I will show personal love for God in my life and ministry as I strive together with my colleagues to preserve the dignity, maintain the discipline, and promote the integrity of the profession to which we have been called.

I recognize the special power afforded to me by my ministerial office. I will never use that power in ways that violate the personhood of another human being, religiously, emotionally, or sexually. I will use my pastoral office only for that which is best for the persons under my ministry.[7]

A Historical Example of Pluralistic Cooperation among Chaplains

The account of the four chaplains of the USS *Dorchester* can still be heard today at all three chaplain service schools. This immortal story brings together four chaplains from four faith groups in a time of crisis to provide ministry to the members of their sinking ship during World War II. The four chaplains were George Fox, a Methodist minister; Alexander Goode, a Jewish rabbi; John Washington, a Roman Catholic priest; and Clark Poling, a Dutch Reformed minister.

After sunset on February 3, 1943, the Army chaplains' transport ship, the USS *Dorchester*, was hit with a U-boat torpedo and began to sink. During the ensuing chaos, the four chaplains were on deck handing out life jackets until there were no more, and then they took off their own life jackets to give others a chance for survival. The ship had 903 souls aboard, including the crew and soldiers, but only 230 survived. The survivors revealed that the last time they had seen the chaplains, they were singing hymns with locked arms as the ship was going down. The chaplains ministered together to offer others hope, and today they offer an example of pluralistic ministry in settings of all kinds. Indeed, the four chaplains are a reminder that even though they represented distinct religious organizations and had different theologies and religious practices, they came together for the sake of others in a time of crisis.

7. National Conference on Ministry to the Armed Forces, "The Covenant and Code of Ethics for Chaplains of the Armed Forces," November 16, 2015, https://www.ncmaf.com/the-covenant -and-code-of-ethics-for-chaplains-of-the-armed-forces.

Conclusion

This chapter has addressed the importance of ecclesiastical endorsement and the significance of chaplain-employer requirements. More specifically, the chapter has discussed what ecclesiastical endorsement is, the need for endorsement, the authority of the endorser, the requirements of the endorser, the value of the endorser, the importance of a positive working relationship with the endorser, employer-based requirements for various chaplaincies, and endorser support organizations.

7

The Person of the Chaplain

At the end of the day, when the chaplain returns home, changes into casual clothing, and looks into the mirror, what do they see? What does God see? Who is this person? This chapter will delve into the personal life of the chaplain to examine the chaplain's faith, family, friends, mentors, protégés, priorities, character, ethics, and self-care.

Faith

Faith in the Lord Jesus Christ is core to everything for the evangelical chaplain. It is the foundation for an eternal relationship with God. It provides meaning, purpose, and direction for the chaplain. Faith in Jesus Christ is the basis for life and service. Through faith the chaplain lives and ministers, and without faith the chaplain's life and ministry would have no meaning, purpose, or direction. It is the chaplain's mission to help others be people of faith so they, too, can have a personal saving relationship with God and live a life with meaning, purpose, and direction from God.

An eternal relationship. The evangelical chaplain understands that faith is the foundation for an eternal relationship with God. The Bible reveals this foundation when it states, "For by grace you have been saved through faith. And this is not your own doing; it is the gift of God, not a result of works, so that no one may boast" (Eph. 2:8–9). Saving faith, a gift from God, must be acted on, as the Scriptures make clear: "If you confess with your mouth that Jesus is

Lord and believe in your heart that God raised him from the dead, you will be saved. For with the heart one believes and is justified, and with the mouth one confesses and is saved. . . . For 'everyone who calls on the name of the Lord will be saved'" (Rom. 10:9–10, 13). This personal relationship with God is the driving force for the chaplain's ministry.

A call to ministry and chaplaincy. Many in ministry are performance driven. But while great effort is indeed needed in the coming of Christ's kingdom, effort alone is not the measure of success. Rather, it is faith in Jesus that must underlie all else (Phil. 2:12–13). The evangelical chaplain understands that surrendering to Christ as Lord and Savior means becoming a disciple of Jesus, denying oneself, and taking up one's cross to follow Jesus (Matt. 16:24). It means being eager to follow Christ's command to love God completely and one's neighbor as oneself (Matt. 22:37–39). It means being eager to become a disciple maker (Matt. 28:19–20). It also means eagerly seeking the Holy Spirit's direction for one's lifelong calling (Prov. 3:5–6). With outstretched arms and a willing heart, a follower of Jesus ought to be available to discern God's call, into chaplaincy or wherever else (John 10:27). The Holy Spirit generates the aspirations and desires of the surrendered heart. The inner working of the Spirit gives one confidence, assurance, peace, and motivation to pursue the call of the chaplain.

A desire to live a surrendered life. The evangelical chaplain understands that a call to chaplaincy is a call to a sacrificial life because a call to ministry is a call to follow Christ anywhere at any time. Jesus made it clear: "If anyone would come after me, let him deny himself and take up his cross and follow me. For whoever would save his life will lose it, but whoever loses his life for my sake will find it" (Matt. 16:24–25). The sacrifices the chaplain makes seem insignificant compared with the sacrifice Jesus made to accomplish his earthly mission (John 3:16), but they are nevertheless real sacrifices. The chaplain is called to sacrifice personal time, and in a sense, that is all people have to give. This decision to trust God with one's life, time, and direction is a matter of faith and is foundational for serving as a chaplain. Often, the chaplain must take emergency calls, work late nights, go on temporary duty for weeks, deploy overseas for months, or relocate far away from extended family and friends for years at a time (see Luke 14:26). Besides that, the chaplain is often recognized at various places, such as the store, where an impromptu counseling session can occur. Precious moments with one's spouse and children that cannot be recaptured may be missed. First steps, first bike rides, birthdays, ball games, recitals, performances, and Thanksgiving and Christmas celebrations may be sacrificed. However, I (Steve) found that my heart was drawn closer to my wife and kids through times of separation and that God tied our heartstrings tightly during time spent together when I was home (Prov. 13:12).

Courage in times of danger. The evangelical chaplain understands that a call to chaplaincy may be a call to serve in harm's way. The military chaplain is called into dangerous training and dangerous deployment environments. Healthcare chaplains serve in constant risk of infection and disease. Prison chaplains serve at the risk of personal attack and dangerous fighting outbreaks. First-responder chaplains serve in risky situations daily. I (Steve) recall serving in Iraq with missile and mortar attacks hitting in and around our camp nearly every day. Fear struck my heart every time I heard or saw an explosion nearby, but then God gave me a flash of faith and trust for safety in the terror of the moment. A rush of Scripture filled my mind and soul. "He who dwells in the shelter of the Most High will abide in the shadow of the Almighty. I will say to the LORD, 'My refuge and my fortress, my God, in whom I trust.' . . . You will not fear the terror of the night, nor the arrow that flies by day" (Ps. 91:1–2, 5).

Resilience in times of stress and hardship. The evangelical chaplain understands that a call to chaplaincy is a call to be resilient during times of stress and hardship. Chaplain ministry is often demanding, overwhelming, stressful, and just downright hard work. Care for people's souls can be emotionally and physically draining. Chaplains are called not only to celebrate the best of times in people's lives but also to minister during the worst of times: during emergencies, tragedies, crises, sickness, failing health, death, divorce, and brokenness. Frankly, serving as a chaplain can be a tremendous personal drain. While serving in the war zone, I (Steve) had the honor of leading 125 memorial services in the back of airplanes and praying over 600 severely wounded military members in medical tents. While I was in the "Valley of Baca" (i.e., the "valley of tears"), the Lord sustained me and drew me closer to him than I had thought possible (Ps. 84:4–7). God kept my heart and mind focused on him and not the terrors and ravages of war. He is the sustainer and supplier of the chaplain (Ps. 55:22; Phil. 4:19).

Meaning and purpose. The evangelical chaplain sees life and ministry through the lens of Scripture. This is sometimes called "holding to a biblical worldview." It also means trusting in God's sovereignty and providence. The chaplain sees all life as a gift from God, created by God for himself for his glory (James 1:17). God is the one who provides meaning. Without him, nothing would have meaning (Eccles. 1–2).

The evangelical chaplain does not look to the world to find purpose but rather looks to the Scriptures to discover God's design and purpose. God is the one who gives purpose. God's purpose is for people to be found in his image (Rom. 8:29). This was his original intention (Gen. 1:26–27), but Satan interfered, and sin and death entered the world (Rom. 5:12). Nevertheless, "God shows his love for us in that while we were still sinners, Christ died for us" (Rom. 5:8). God provided himself as a sacrifice so people could regain their relationship with him and live lives that are holy and blameless (Eph. 1:4).

A holy and loving relationship with God. Jesus made clear that the greatest commandment is to "love the Lord your God with all your heart and with all your soul and with all your mind and with all your strength" (Mark 12:30). Simply stated, God desires a personal relationship with humans and died and rose again to make that relationship possible (John 3:16). The chaplain realizes that even though one's heart is made clean through salvation, the transformation of the mind is key to being sanctified, set apart unto God. Growing in Christ takes commitment, and it is essential that a person die to self and be transformed by the renewing of the mind through the Holy Spirit (Rom. 12:1–2).

Loving others. "You shall love your neighbor as yourself" (Matt. 22:39). This command puts chaplains on a mission to facilitate God's love to all those around them in a secular organization. The parable of the good Samaritan (Luke 10:29–37) makes clear that we should love all those we encounter, especially by helping those in difficulty. Scripture also instructs, "As we have opportunity, let us do good to everyone, and especially to those who are of the household of faith" (Gal. 6:10). Jesus goes further, instructing, "Love your enemies and pray for those who persecute you" (Matt. 5:44). Chaplains, as with all Christians, will encounter opposition. God's love through us goes out to all, whether they love us back or not.

Serving others. While it is human nature to serve oneself, chaplains strive to serve others. Jesus set the ultimate example of service when he took off his heavenly glory and was born in human flesh and when he suffered a humiliating death (Phil. 2:1–11). It can be tempting for chaplains to become puffed up and think of themselves as above others, especially when receiving promotions, raises, awards, and words and letters of appreciation. In mind and soul, chaplains need to constantly give God all the credit and all the glory.

Sharing the good news. The chaplain's faith in God, belief in the gospel, and calling to chaplaincy will propel one to proclaim the gospel without fear or shame (Rom. 1:16), to seek to make disciples for the Lord. "Go therefore and make disciples of all nations, baptizing them in the name of the Father and of the Son and of the Holy Spirit, teaching them to observe all that I have commanded you" (Matt. 28:19–20). The chaplain understands that it is "through the folly of what we preach" that people come to believe in Jesus as Savior (1 Cor. 1:21). However, conversion is only the open door to discipleship—which is the goal of the Great Commission. The faithful chaplain will exert much energy to disciple those who have come to Christ.

Family

The primary meaning of family is a husband, wife, and children living together—although sometimes in God's providence a family may consist of a single parent with children or a couple without children.

The chaplain's family is of great importance in the consideration of calling, ministry, and personal support. The chaplain who has a family must prioritize family ahead of ministry whenever possible, as chaplaincy will undoubtedly infringe on family time and plans when least expected. Emergencies, deployments, and last-minute mandatory meetings will be a challenge and can cause the chaplain to miss key moments of spousal relationship-building and parenting. Still, chaplains need to strive to make family the first priority after God and to communicate that in word and action to their spouse and children. This should involve sustainable work-life boundaries when possible and extra attention to family during less busy times. The chaplain's family will thereby know they are the highest priority after God in the chaplain's heart—even when it does not appear so.

Calling. As stated in chapter 6, when a married person feels called to chaplaincy, the spouse must feel called by the Lord to serve alongside. Chaplaincy is a whole-family ministry. This is particularly true for those called to military chaplaincy, especially active-duty service. Military assignments will move the family around the globe every two to four years. Deployments for chaplains—whether active duty or reserve—will interrupt the family in cycles, depending on the branch of service. Constant new assignments and deployments create a tremendous challenge for families. The chaplain should pay close attention to ensure that one's family is not pressed to the point of dissolution or destruction. Wise is the chaplain who is willing to even forgo further chaplaincy service if the family's needs require it.

A new assignment involves moving the contents of one's home and sometimes learning a new culture and language. For the spouse, it might mean a new job search, and for the kids it means a new school, tryouts for new sports and music teams, and the challenge of making new friends. If one's spouse does not feel called to support the new assignment, neither the spouse nor the kids will be happy. The spouse's call comes under extra testing during deployments. During deployments, chaplain spouses can help other struggling spouses, offering support to those who are dealing with children or family issues. In all these ways, the whole family is part of the chaplain's witness and ministry.

Praise God, my (Steve's) wife felt called by the Lord to serve alongside me and enjoyed raising five children around the globe in twelve locations over thirty years. Also, the children loved being a part of the family ministry team, and in large measure they credit their military experience for becoming the spiritually rooted, well-rounded, internationally aware, and accomplished servants of God that they are today. In fact, my wife and kids say they would not trade their military experience for anything.

Love and respect. Chaplains need to be loving spiritual leaders in their homes. A chaplain "must manage his own household well, with all dignity keeping his children submissive" (1 Tim. 3:4). With respect to the ordering of priorities, the chaplain understands that it is God first, family second, and chaplaincy third and that family is the first ministry priority. There is no more important ministry than the chaplain's ministry to one's own family, and within the family structure the priority is the spouse. "Let each one of you [husbands] love his wife as himself, and let the wife see that she respects her husband" (Eph. 5:33). This command from God may be the toughest order the chaplain ever receives. As stated earlier in this chapter, the ministry of the chaplain often involves being away from home for extended periods and missing important events and milestones. Further, the ministry of the chaplain may include overwhelming and draining challenges, emergencies, late nights, and changed or canceled plans. Giving the spouse priority may therefore be extremely difficult. Nevertheless, the key to priorities is the heart. If the chaplain's wife knows he deeply loves her with the love of Christ and takes every available opportunity to express it, or the chaplain's husband knows that she respects him and takes every available opportunity to express it, though oftentimes such opportunities are limited and interrupted, the relationship will flourish. Nothing is more powerful than sacrificial *agapē* love and respect (Eph. 5:25–33).

Communicating this love and respect can be difficult amid deployed or late-night ministry. However, phone calls, texts, emails, notes, letters, and flowers can communicate that love is still burning and that the chaplain still hasn't forgotten the spouse as the first ministry priority. I recall being stationed in Greenland with only a MARS (military auxiliary radio system) line to communicate, which presented a serious challenge for me and my wife. The amount of information that could be conveyed with the loud echo was extremely limited. So we decided to write a letter to each other every day. Even though the letters showed up three or four at a time, our relationship flourished. During later deployments, modern communications provided an excellent means to maintain and even strengthen the marriage relationship. Loving communication is vital to a good marriage.

Being a parent. It is a challenge for chaplains to follow the Lord's order when he says, "Fathers, do not provoke your children to anger, but bring them up in the discipline and instruction of the Lord" (Eph. 6:4). A chaplain's kids may feel neglected by their chaplain dad or mom because of ministry assignments that keep them away from home for months or even years. They may feel they are a low priority because overwhelming ministry challenges and emergencies continually arise and leave them disappointed, if not exasperated. I (Steve) recall deciding to work late and showing up at the end of my son's soccer game, only to see him being vaulted into the air after making the game-winning goal. "Dad, did you see the crazy winning goal I made?" I was struck in the heart and vowed to make family the higher priority whenever possible.

The key to raising good kids in a chaplain's home is to build a loving, godly relationship with them. Chaplains who are parents should love their kids fervently with a tender heart (Eph. 4:32; 1 Pet. 4:8). They should spend time with their kids whenever possible and let them know they are prioritized over chaplain duties. This commitment to follow God's command has no replacement for a parent raising up a child in the love of the Lord. A loving, dedicated parent is an insurmountable force in raising a child to be a Christ follower (Prov. 22:6).

I remember being deployed in Iraq on my daughter's eighteenth birthday and feeling bad about not being with her to celebrate. However, I had an opportunity a few weeks earlier to visit a local market and buy a beautiful crystal bowl from one of Saddam Hussein's palaces. The gift, with a card and picture, was mailed to her and arrived just in time. Later, my daughter communicated that when she opened her gift, she broke into tears, and said she felt more loved than if I had been home in person, since she knew I had gone out of my way and even into harm's way to make her birthday special. Praise God, the relationship grew even stronger in Dad's absence.

Ministry with family. When a person is called to chaplain ministry, the entire family is called into that ministry. Depending on the type of chaplaincy, the spouse and kids may choose to be involved directly or indirectly. In military chaplaincy, if the chaplain is assigned to an Air Force chapel or Army garrison chapel or is on Navy shore duty, the spouse and kids' involvement may be similar to that of a pastor's wife and kids. The chaplain's spouse may choose to be involved in various chapel ministries or to lead a Bible study, small group, praise team, or outreach group—or not. Likewise, teenagers may choose to help with the children's ministry, outreach and community service projects, or teen activities—or not. Further, the family may wish to be involved in hospitality and to invite people into their home. Other types of chaplaincies may not have such direct ways for the family to be involved in ministry. Still, when it is not possible to be directly involved, the family can still be involved behind the scenes in prayer, acts of service, and spiritual and emotional support for the chaplain.

Support from family. The chaplain's family should be their number one support team. The chaplain's spouse has firsthand knowledge of the strains of ministry and may be the person best equipped to encourage, pray with, and partner in ministry with the chaplain, as well as the safest person to vent to

(Eph. 5:21). The old saying "The family that prays together stays together" is an excellent guide for the chaplain family. Great strength of soul is generated from a family kneeling together and praying for one another. Verbalized prayer with one's spouse allows for the formation of deep spiritual connections before the "throne of grace," where "we may receive mercy and find grace to help in time of need" (Heb. 4:16). Further, a child's prayers over the chaplain parent will humble and stir the heart in indescribable ways and provide perspective on what matters most (see Ps. 127:3).

Friends

The chaplain needs friends for many reasons, but the most important is to become a sharp instrument for the Lord's use (Prov. 27:17). There is no replacement for "a friend who sticks closer than a brother" (Prov. 18:24), who has the same goals for life and ministry, and who is a constant encouragement to glorify God in word and deed (1 Cor. 10:31). Chaplains normally have a large circle of friends. Some friends will be individuals the chaplain is ministering to, some acquaintances, some secular workmates, some chaplains and pastors, and some family members. However, the chaplain needs to have a few friends in their inner circle who understand the ministry challenges and personal struggles, friends who can keep confidences, friends who desire the chaplain's success and can help them up when they fall (Eccles. 4:9–10). A close friend is a gift from God who should be cherished, and the friendship nourished.

Many chaplains have trouble finding inner-circle friends who truly understand the overwhelming secular and pluralistic pressure cooker in which chaplains serve. Many times, non-chaplains fail to relate to chaplains' struggles and may even question chaplains' ability to serve without compromise in such places as the military, healthcare facilities, prisons, and community settings. I (Steve) have found that fellow evangelical chaplains make the best friends. They can best relate, they maintain confidentiality, and they have the same theology and ministry goals. No one understands the chaplain's struggles and challenges like another chaplain walking the same path with the same calling and agenda.

The following are some of my experiences with good friends throughout my chaplain ministry. When I was struggling as a new chaplain, it was a God-sent, Bible-believing chaplain friend who showed me the ropes. When a liberal senior-ranking chaplain ordered me to stop preaching the gospel in chapel services, another chaplain friend of like faith and conviction encouraged me to keep preaching the good news (see Acts 5:29). I also recall that when I was hurting deeply from the loss of a child, a close chaplain friend cried with me and comforted me. After I was told on Christmas Eve of a cancer diagnosis, a chaplain friend came and prayed over me. When I was stressing about a badly injured child, a chaplain friend comforted me. When I celebrated my children's weddings, dear chaplain friends came long distances to celebrate with me. When I was dealing with the aftermath of the ravages of war in Iraq, a caring chaplain friend encouraged me. When I was seeking God's direction in retirement, chaplain friends surrounded me with prayer and wise counsel (see Prov. 27:9). The value of an inner circle of godly chaplains of like faith cannot be overestimated.

Mentors

Every chaplain needs a mentor, an experienced and trusted adviser. There is no replacement for a more experienced chaplain who has already walked the same path and can provide wise counsel and direction (2 Tim. 2:2). Every aspiring or new chaplain should seek out a godly and well-respected chaplain to be a mentor. A friend can also be a mentor, but a mentor does not have to be a friend. Throughout my thirty-year military career, I had many momentary mentors but none who stayed for any length of time. This stirred up a bit of envy in me toward chaplains who had lifelong mentors. Nevertheless, the Lord heard my prayer and provided a mentor in the midst of battle. After I had been caring for survivors and honoring seventeen fallen soldiers, a C-17 transport carrying those fallen soldiers lifted into the air. A short time later the senior Army chaplain in Iraq rolled into our Air Force camp looking for me. "Chaplain, we just came over to say how much we appreciate you and your Air Force team of chaplains caring for our wounded soldiers and honoring the fallen." The senior Army chaplain then paused and looked me in the eyes, saying, "Brother, *you* need a prayer!" He put his hands on my shoulders, and we knelt in the dirt as he prayed a powerful prayer over me and the Air Force chaplain team. That's when my tears broke through. I greatly needed that prayer at that moment. I thank God for that chaplain's care. From that day Chaplain (Major General) Doug Carver became my mentor and friend. Mentors are a gift from God. Aspiring and new chaplains should pray for a godly mentor who will help guide them and care for them.

Protégés

Just as every chaplain needs to *have* a mentor, every chaplain needs to *be* a mentor. Being a mentor is a biblical way to further the kingdom of God. Even though Jesus was never called a mentor, he set the example for mentors. As the Son of

God, he obviously was older, wiser, and more experienced than anyone on the planet! What a privilege the apostles had to be mentored by God in human flesh (John 1:1) and to glean from his words (John 8:31–36). The best mentors today are those who are guided by the Word and the Spirit. Chaplain mentors have a tremendous opportunity to mentor younger chaplains and Christian servants.

I had the joy of being the mentor for many individuals during my thirty years as a military chaplain, several years as a chaplain professor, and several years as a chaplain endorser. Sometimes mentoring involved helping a person follow Christ, sometimes it involved helping prepare a chaplain for effective ministry, sometimes it involved helping a chaplain discern God's will, and sometimes it involved simply encouraging a chaplain to use the Word as their guide (2 Tim. 3:16–17), to be diligent in prayer (1 Thess. 5:16–18), to strive to be the heart and voice and hands of Jesus (Matt. 25:35–36), to stay focused on the Lord (Col. 3:1–3), and to *submit* to God's plans instead of merely *including* God in their plans (Prov. 3:5–6). There is great joy in serving as a mentor for the glory of God.

Priorities

A priority is something that is important to a person, something one cares about. Multiple requirements and opportunities compete for the chaplain's time and attention, so having clearly established priorities is essential. The chaplain's priorities need to be ordered by the Lord, and this truth calls one to examine the Scriptures and to seek the Holy Spirit's guidance.

Scripture makes clear that the number-one priority for the chaplain is their relationship with God (Matt. 22:37–38). There is nothing more important to God than one's love for him. God's greatest desire for the chaplain is that they love him completely and make him the first priority, that the chaplain "seek first the kingdom of God and his righteousness" (Matt. 6:33). Nothing should compete with the chaplain's daily affection for and allegiance to the Lord, not even family (Matt. 10:37). The apostle Paul simply says, "For to me to live is Christ" (Phil. 1:21). This should be the heart cry of every chaplain. The chaplain should prioritize the calendar to ensure daily relationship-building times with God—time to pray, meditate, read his Word, and enjoy his presence (Ps. 46:10).

The chaplain's second priority is their family, and chaplains should arrange calendars to include family events.

The chaplain's third priority is church and ministry, which are inextricably connected for the chaplain. The church is a group of born-again individuals called out from the world and assembled to accomplish God's mission on earth (Eph. 1:22–23; Matt. 28:19–20) and to care for one another spiritually (Gal.

6:10; 1 Pet. 1:22). The New Testament church was gifted with apostles, prophets, evangelists, pastors, and teachers to equip believers for the work of ministry (Eph. 4:11–12). Chaplains are not mentioned there by name, but our functions blend the qualities essential to apostles, prophets, evangelists, shepherds, teachers, and pastors serving under the authority of the church. Chaplains should never forget that their ministry, in human terms, flows from and is accountable to the endorsers who represent the faith group that sent them forth.

Character

In a general sense, character may be defined as positive moral qualities distinctive to an individual. For the believer, character may be defined as moral qualities distinctive of Jesus Christ. The Lord's goal is for believers to be found in his image (see Gen. 1:27; Col. 3:10). When a person is born again, their soul is redeemed and the stage is set for godly character development. However, character is not an instant process. Godly character takes time, spiritual discipline, and daily devotion. It starts with making God-honoring decisions, which develop over time into good habits, which, in turn, develop over time into good character. Godly character begins at salvation but is realized through sanctification. For the believer, godly character is not an option but rather a certainty predetermined by God (Rom. 8:29–30). Developing Christlike character means seeking to think, feel, and act as God directs. It means setting one's mind on the things above and seeking, with a determined heart, God's will above all else (Prov. 3:5–7; Col. 3:1–3). In the military system, I was forced to realize that true godly character can be scarce and that the standards of the military do not necessarily align with the Lord's. Nevertheless, the chaplain with Christlike character should seek to live by God's standards, thus informing and shaping the institution in which they serve rather than conform to it and its standards. Never underestimate the positive power of a solitary godly witness.

Character development is fraught with challenges for chaplains. Chaplains are often expected to lower their moral standards to conform to the system, unofficial if not official. They may be challenged to ignore their biblical convictions and to perform religious duties that stand outside their ordination vows and their endorser's doctrine and practices. When they are personally convicted to pray in Jesus's name, they may be challenged by others to leave Jesus out of their public prayers.[1] They may be challenged to not evangelize (cf. Acts 5:28–29). They may be encouraged by chaplain peers and workmates to enter into activities they have preached against. Further, chaplains may get caught

---

1. For more on chaplain prayers, see chap. 8, under "Public Prayer."

in the performance trap and seek to please man rather than God (Gal. 1:10). After all, chaplains are graded by their superiors for their performance, not their character, which is much tougher to discern. To imitate Christ's character is never easy, but in secular and pluralistic settings, it becomes drastically more difficult. Nevertheless, godly character does not compromise the truth of God's Word and God's calling to be Christlike (1 Pet. 1:16). Aspiring and new chaplains should be prepared for relentless pressure to lower their personal and religious convictions and should be ready to stand for Christ (see Eph. 6:10–18). God is more interested in character than in performance (1 Sam. 16:7).

Personal Morals and Ethics

Ethics may be defined as the functional application of moral standards and systems to particular situations and dilemmas. Ethics thus flow *from* standards and systems of right and wrong. Chaplains need to be able to think ethically so they can live Christ-honoring lives and assist others in making ethical decisions. Every chaplain needs to develop a clear ethical decision-making model. This model will allow the chaplain to process moral dilemmas through a series of ethical filters, such as insights from Scripture, guidance from the Holy Spirit, conscience, wise counsel, prayer, and the examining of moral outcomes. Important for this process are morals, which are a person's principles of right and wrong given from a higher authority. Of course, the evangelical chaplain's quest for moral answers will be rooted in a biblical worldview that seeks to glorify God. A chaplain's morals also need to be in line with the teachings of Scripture (see 1 Tim. 3; Titus 1:5–16). The chaplain needs to be a person with an impeccable reputation as a spouse, parent, minister, moral leader, and sacrificial servant of God who lives by the highest ethical standards.

Self-Care and Resilience

Chaplain self-care is of utmost importance for successful, resilient ministry. Chaplain ministry can be wearisome and draining, resulting in low-energy ministry or even burnout. Self-care will strengthen chaplains' daily ministry capacity and elongate their career. Chaplain self-care may be defined as the chaplain's taking charge of their own spiritual, mental, and physical health.

Soul care. The chaplain's care for their own soul is of great importance in being spiritually fit to care for the souls of others. Soul care is training for godliness (1 Tim. 4:7), and it strengthens the roots of the tree of ministry. God calls every believer into an ever-deeper relationship with himself, and chaplains should be

living examples of Christians who are striving to know God intimately (Phil.
3:12–14). Unsurprisingly, God supplies chaplains with a set of tools with which
they can work on this relationship. These tools, called spiritual disciplines, are of
significant value in helping chaplains deepen and strengthen their relationship
with the Lord. Ten spiritual disciplines are recommended for chaplains who
seek to master godliness and acquire healthy souls: Scripture reading, prayer,
worship, evangelism, serving, giving, fasting, silence and solitude, journaling,
and learning.[2] Many chaplains find periodic connection with a spiritual director
to help uncover and correct blind spots and go deeper in the Christian walk.
A daily practice of any one of these disciplines or a combination of them will
greatly assist the chaplain in the lifelong spiritual walk and goal of Christlikeness.

Mental care. The chaplain's care of the mind is of extreme importance in
being mentally fit to care for others. The chaplain needs to have a transformed
mind in order to please God and serve others well (Rom. 12:2). The goal for
the chaplain is to have the mind of Christ and to think and feel like God does
(1 Cor. 2:14–16). The challenge, then, is to "prepare your minds for action"
(1 Pet. 1:13 NASB) and to focus one's mind on what is true, honorable, just, pure,
lovely, and commendable (Phil. 4:8). "For as [a man] thinks within himself,
so he is" (Prov. 23:7 NASB). Practicing spiritual disciplines will greatly aid the
chaplain's mental development. "Do not be conformed to this world, but be
transformed by the renewal of your mind" (Rom. 12:2). Reading and meditating
on God's Word is necessary for having a healthy and spiritually fit mind (Ps.
119:9–11). Additionally, studying and learning God's Word is key to a fit mind
ready to engage intellectually as an instrument of the Lord. "Study to show
yourself approved unto God, a workman that needs not to be ashamed, rightly
dividing the word of truth" (2 Tim. 2:15 KJV 2000). Pornography and various
other addictions can snatch away the chaplain's calling. Many chaplains have
benefited from finding an accountability partner and seeking regular counsel
with a qualified counselor or therapist who is willing to patiently work with the
chaplain to gain and maintain good mental health.

Physical care. The chaplain's care for their own body is key to caring for others. The chaplain needs to have their body in subjection to the Lord in order
to please God and be prepared to serve others well. "I appeal to you therefore,
brothers, by the mercies of God, to present your bodies as a living sacrifice,
holy and acceptable to God, which is your spiritual worship" (Rom. 12:1). The
chaplain needs to understand that their body is a temple of the Holy Spirit and
that they must treat it as such (1 Cor. 6:19–20). Temple maintenance, so to speak,

2. Donald S. Whitney, *Spiritual Disciplines for the Christian Life* (Colorado Springs: NavPress,
1997).

takes more time and attention as the chaplain gathers more years. Proper rest, nutrition, and exercise are positive lifelong practices. Great care should be taken to live in a godly manner in spirit, mind, and body. Further, the chaplain needs to understand that their body is a gift from God to be used as an instrument in bearing the presence and message of Christ. It is often through the chaplain's physical presence that God communicates his concern, love, and care. Also, it is through the chaplain's spoken words that the gospel may be shared and words of hope and healing communicated (Rom. 10:13–17). Therefore, chaplains need to take care of not just their spiritual health but also their physical health so that they maintain a healthy, strong, and enduring instrument of service (1 Tim. 4:8).

Conclusion

This chapter has delved into the personal life of the chaplain and looked behind closed doors to examine the chaplain's faith, family, friends, mentors, protégés, priorities, character, ethics, and self-care. The chaplain's healthy personal life, especially their faith commitments, is essential for long-term fruitful ministry.

8

Chaplaincy Care
and Chaplain Skills

O ne of the major themes addressed in this chapter is how an evangelical
theology influences the praxis of an evangelical chaplain's ministry.
We wish here to introduce the concept of chaplaincy care as a supple-
ment to—not a replacement for—pastoral care, since many distinct differences
between chaplain ministry and pastoral ministry exist despite the many areas
of commonality.

Since Scripture has a major influence on the theology of evangelical chaplains, it becomes the cornerstone for a chaplain's praxis of ministry. Scripture
is the primary guideline for who evangelical chaplains are, what they believe,
and how they apply their ministry. Scripture informs their understanding of
evangelicalism, their denominational doctrines, and the way they fit into the
military, healthcare, business, and community cultures. While all evangelical
chaplains are, at times, literal in their interpretations of the Bible, they search for
the right application in ways that honor the scriptural mandate to go to all the
world and teach the gospel. They also seek ways to clarify their understanding
and application of the scriptural mandates that they follow.

Chaplains often speak of not only professional knowledge, skills, and abilities (KSAs) but also different skills and abilities that are a direct result of their
evangelical faith. Experientially, their application of skills and abilities has become
the actual doing of their evangelical theology in practical ways of caring, comforting, and serving the people of a community. While describing the personal and

ministry dynamics of chaplains is beneficial, reporting their actual words and reactions to situations paints pictures of professional and spiritual realities that descriptions can leave out. We have chosen to include quotes from chaplains who were part of a study of practical theology in chaplaincy in order to pass on the actual words that chaplains have articulated when describing their work. Evangelical chaplains articulate in various ways that they are viewed as "a safe space," "a holy space," or "a sacred space" that provides a sense of security, peace, kindness, and acceptance. In this study of chaplaincy, one chaplain indicated, "The presence of the chaplain makes people feel safer, it changes their behavior, and it's comforting for them." Evangelical military chaplains described the safe space that surrounded them as a product of being bearers of the presence of God, an identity that drew community members and their families to the chaplain for help, assistance, care, and religious nurturing. Another chaplain said, "As chaplains in the military, we're called to be the presence bearers, the bearers of the presence of God."[1]

The understanding that chaplains are bearers of God's presence provides a sense of safety in the sacred space as a privileged dialogue takes place. People feel safe to discuss and address spiritual issues, personal problems, and anything else that weighs heavily on their heart. The requirement of confidentiality helps to define the concept of a safe place. Often, individuals interacting with chaplains have commented that there is a sense of God's presence and a peace that radiates from the chaplain. People coming to the chaplain for care recognize a sense of God's Spirit living in and through the chaplain. Many individuals talk of the chaplain's presence creating a sacredness of the place, making it holy ground when the chaplain is present. This change happens not because of the chaplain but because of who lives in and through the chaplain. Chaplains provide a comforting place to seek healing, reconciliation, and compassionate attention. As a result of being cared for in a compassionate manner, many members of communities where chaplains minister will return to the evangelical chaplain's safe place to engage faith on their terms, while seeking answers about life's meaning and an understanding of their own spiritual faith identity.[2]

The Application of Knowledge, Skills, and Abilities

Chaplains demonstrate their KSAs in the area of pastoral care almost immediately when they engage in any of the ten functional areas of chaplaincy (see part 2). In

1. Michael W. Langston, "Establishing the Practical Significance of the Influence of Evangelical Theology on an Evangelical Military Chaplains Praxis of Chaplaincy" (PhD diss., University of Aberdeen, 2019), 175–76.
2. Langston, "Establishing the Practical Significance," 176.

the chaplaincy study mentioned above, three descriptors—caring, comforting, and serving—emerged as key indicators of what chaplains do. These skills become the groundwork for building relationships that allow for future interactions that are more spiritually focused. One of the major descriptors of chaplaincy is that "chaplains care for all"; they are "carers about their people and are comforters."[3] Evangelical chaplains speak regularly of the importance of caring for the men and women they are called to serve. At different points in the study, chaplains indicated that one of the clearest expectations and direct guidance they received from military commanders was to take care of the people in their command. One Navy chaplain stated specifically that when he checked into his new Marine command, the only guidance the commander gave was, "Chaplain, take care of my Marines."[4]

Caring

The Greek verb for "care" is *melō*, which means "to be of interest, to be concerned with, or to be of concern for."[5] The more modern meaning of the word "care," which aligns with the chaplain's application of ministry, is "to be concerned for," giving "attentive assistance," and "paying close attention to or watchful oversight and supervision thereof."[6]

Pastoral or chaplain care is one of the most important skills that chaplains have and use. Chaplains deal with a great variety of problems, issues, and hardships that are both spiritual and nonspiritual in nature. Many times the chaplain becomes the first responder who addresses and deals with death, grief, fear, sickness, marital problems, financial struggle, and other life issues while ministering in the workplace or other settings. Because chaplains provide a place of grace where people can respond naturally—whether addressing anger, fear, frustration, despair, hopelessness, or spiritual needs—they are a common safe place where self-disclosure and honest emotional processing take place. In chaplains' provision of care, the "mere presence of the chaplain is a reminder to the recipient that God is present and available to address spiritual needs, too."[7] Both in the military and in civilian community settings, people dealing with life's predicaments continually and consistently reach out to chaplains for care.

3. Langston, "Establishing the Practical Significance," 177.
4. Langston, "Establishing the Practical Significance," 186.
5. Eric W. Adams, "Care," in *Evangelical Dictionary of Biblical Theology*, ed. Walter A. Elwell (Grand Rapids: Baker, 1996), 82.
6. Adams, "Care," 82.
7. Robert D. Crick, *Outside the Gates: The Need for, Theology, History, and Practice of Chaplaincy Ministries*, with Brandelan S. Miller, rev. ed. (Oviedo, FL: HigherLife Development Services, 2011), 92.

Chaplains continue to emphasize the importance of caring as one of the major expectations that military commanders, CEOs, and civic community leaders have for chaplains as they provide for specific needs, both spiritual and nonspiritual. In several interviews in the study, evangelical chaplains expressed their understanding of the prominence and importance of the concept of care with some version of the following statement: "Caring . . . is obviously one of the biggest things we do. Sincere caring and compassion, . . . that's almost part of the job description."[8]

Evangelical chaplains engage in care by recognizing the presenting issue of the one seeking care. When the one seeking care is welcomed into the chaplain's presence, an immediate connection begins to develop as the chaplain provides hospitality and comforts the individual in a safe place to hear and address the stated problem and immediate need. Active listening by the chaplain gives the individual a sense of being cared for and indicates that the person is being heard and their issues are being addressed. The art of listening, further, provides a sense of being understood and empathized with. By caring for the individual's needs, the chaplain begins developing a relationship that is built on trust. This initial development of mutual trust facilitates the treatment of the care seeker as a person of worth. If the evangelical chaplain cannot meet or provide for the need, they may refer the person to someone who can take care of that specific need, thus showing and demonstrating genuine care. Validation of this concept of caring is found in the following statement from a chaplain: "The one thing I found about practicing an evangelical theology in [chaplaincy] is people really didn't care what you know until they know how much you care."[9]

In the parable of the good Samaritan (Luke 10:25–37), Jesus introduces the disciples to a deeper and more complex application of caring, comforting, and serving. In the parable Jesus addresses the issue of who one's neighbor is and what responsibility one has to this neighbor. Jesus is calling the disciples to move beyond their understanding of who they are in order to serve and be in relationship with others. He challenges his disciples' theology and cultural norms and calls them to a deeper sense of relationship that goes beyond ethnic, religious, and social-identity boundaries. As chaplains encounter the multicultural, pluralistic environment of the world in which people live, work, and play, they learn the lessons of accepting those who help and those who receive help.

Most evangelical chaplains would consider care for souls to be part of their ecclesial calling. This caring for souls includes many levels of responses to religious needs. Sometimes souls are cared for through traditional religious means.

8. Langston, "Establishing the Practical Significance," 178.
9. Langston, "Establishing the Practical Significance," 179.

Chaplains often have the opportunity to serve through chapel services, whether held in a long-term care facility or aboard a Navy ship. In such a setting the primary focus of caring for souls is accomplished via a set liturgy of prayers, Scripture readings, sacraments, hymns, and preaching. Less traditional means include Bible studies, discipleship programs, devotional opportunities, religious education classes, and morning and evening prayer.

Evangelical chaplains also engage personnel in their ministry setting by being among them and available to them on a daily basis. The ministry of presence means being among members of an organization or community as a basis for building close relationships with them in order to know them and become known by them. The more a chaplain is seen and experienced as a safe person to speak to, the stronger the connections are between the chaplain and the people. Once the chaplain has established that relationship by becoming an accepted member of the community, most people begin to see the chaplain as *their* chaplain. In the study, one Army chaplain spoke to this concept: "We are here to speak to the souls of men and women and to reach out to those that may not have a relationship with God and to encourage those that do. So, that's a part of who we are; it is the essence of Christ, who cared enough about us to die on the cross for us. We share that with those we are called to serve in caring for their souls."[10] This chaplain highlighted the emphasis placed on building relationships in a way that allows for spiritual nurturing to take place. He indicated that chaplains want to be out with the troops, to be with their people so they can be seen by them and be available to them when they have specific needs. When a need arises, because they are among the people, chaplains can immediately impart a message that can change their lives for all eternity.

Comforting

The Greek word for "comfort" is *paraklētos*, which is a verbal adjective of the Greek verb *parakaleō*, which has the ancient meaning of to encourage, console, solace, come to the aid of, afford refreshment, or comfort.[11] The more modern meaning of the word "comfort" is "to give strength and hope to" and "to ease the grief or trouble of."[12]

10. Langston, "Establishing the Practical Significance," 191.

11. Otto Schmitz, "παρακαλέω," in *Theological Dictionary of the New Testament*, ed. Gerhard Kittel, Gerhard Friedrich, and Geoffrey W. Bromiley (Grand Rapids: Eerdmans, 1985), 5:778.

12. *Merriam-Webster*, s.v. "comfort," accessed May 17, 2023, https://www.merriam-webster .com/dictionary/comfort.

Chaplains in most settings emphasize the importance of being present with those in need and coming alongside them to respond to their immediate need, to console, reassure, and assist. This is a valued component of the chaplain's skill set and is integral to the overall healing process. In the study, one chaplain articulated this by saying, "Sitting with someone and hearing their story, listening to it, and hearing it to the point where they feel heard, they feel felt, they feel understood, comforting them, so they sense that a person has come alongside them, on their holy ground of suffering, and is companioning them in that experience" is the pinnacle of being a chaplain.

"Rig fenders and prepare to come alongside" is a time-honored phrase and practice within the Navy. When ships are at sea, their food, supplies, and fuel run low and need to be replenished. That replenishment process usually takes place out on the high seas, especially when the ship cannot come into port. As the ship needing supplies prepares to come alongside a supply ship to receive stores, supplies, and fuel, the boatswain's mate gives the command for the ship to rig fenders and prepare to come alongside the other ship or to moor the ship to the side of a pier. In bygone days these fenders were large pieces of wood with rope and canvas wrapped around them, but in modern times they are large rubber bladders that protect the ships as they come together. These devices prevent the ships from scraping each other and punching holes in their sides. As the ships come alongside each other for replenishment, the fenders provide protection.

Traditionally, Navy chaplains, using the same concept, have come alongside those in need and have rendered care, comfort, and service. The chaplain comes alongside the person and acts as a fender for protection as the person leans on the chaplain for help. Evangelical chaplains participate in this tradition whether or not they are aboard ships. As people of the book, they find similar traditions in Scripture. Second Corinthians indicates the importance of comforting others in the same way one has been comforted, by coming alongside those in need, caring for them in the same way the Holy Spirit has previously comforted the one offering the care:

> Blessed be the God and Father of our Lord Jesus Christ, the Father of mercies and God of all comfort, who comforts us in all our affliction, so that we may be able to comfort those who are in any affliction, with the comfort with which we ourselves are comforted by God. For as we share abundantly in Christ's sufferings, so through Christ we share abundantly in comfort too. If we are afflicted, it is for your comfort and salvation; and if we are comforted, it is for your comfort, which you experience when you patiently endure the same sufferings that we suffer. Our hope for you is unshaken, for we know that as you share in our sufferings, you will also share in our comfort. (2 Cor. 1:3–7)

Evangelical chaplains demonstrate their commitment to Scripture as the authoritative Word of God, committing to comfort others as part of their scriptural mandate.

Serving

The Greek verb for "serve" is *douleuō*, which has the ancient meaning "to serve or provide a service to someone." The more modern meaning of the word "serve" is "to yield obedience, submit to, as well as to work for or serve someone in a humble manner."[13]

When, in the New Testament, Jesus introduces his disciples to the concept of service, he demonstrates that physical serving, the acts of caring and comforting, is significant, but the act of serving or being a servant has a deeper implied spiritual connotation. Jesus reminded his disciples that he came not to be served but to serve those he came to redeem. In John 13:1–38, when Jesus washed the disciples' feet, his act of service caught the disciples completely off guard. Jesus acted as a host who invited them to a meal, yet he became a servant who washed their feet. They were accustomed to serving others in a general sense, but washing another person's feet was completely outside their mentality, standing, and experience. It is a nasty, dirty job generally left to the lowest person in the serving ranks. However, Jesus pointed toward a deeper meaning as he bent down on his knees to serve his disciples by washing their feet, taking on the lowest and dirtiest job. The example set before the disciples is that of serving as life's calling in response to following God.

Evangelical chaplains find themselves steeped in and called to this level of servanthood among the communities they serve. During an interview in the study, an Air Force chaplain elaborated on this well, saying, "I'm here to be their servant because Jesus is the greatest servant that this planet has ever known. We serve a humble God who is our servant, and he came to this planet to serve us, and he says, 'Model me.' So, if I'm going to model him and please him, I can't do it without being a servant."[14] The military requires that its chaplains provide care and comfort for everyone within the military community. Most other areas of chaplaincy also require the same emphasis on serving others.

The foundational KSAs of caring, comforting, and serving allow chaplains to acquire other KSAs that are common to most chaplaincy roles, such as evangelizing, praying, preaching, discipling, and advising. Evangelical chaplains

13. James Swanson, *Dictionary of Biblical Languages with Semantic Domains: Greek (New Testament)* (Oak Harbor, WA: Logos, 1997).

14. Langston, "Establishing the Practical Significance."

indicate that they have relied on these skills and abilities in the fulfillment of their ministry requirements in most organizational, institutional, and military contexts.

Evangelizing

Evangelical chaplains are known for their zeal for sharing the gospel of Jesus Christ with the personnel they serve. They view evangelism as an essential aspect of their religious calling. Their focus on caring for souls begins with the belief that anyone without Christ as their personal Savior at death will be eternally separated from God (Rom. 6:23; Rev. 20:11–15). They believe that the greatest care they can provide is to help someone come to faith in Jesus Christ (John 1:12). They understand that all the care they can give to a person is only temporal if that person does not come to know Jesus as Savior. They believe their mission from God is eternal, and therefore their hearts beat for opportunities to communicate the gospel with everyone who desires to listen (1 Cor. 1:18). The evangelical chaplain understands that bearing the *presence* of Christ alone is not enough: bearing the *message* of Christ is essential for a person to experience salvation, and God has chosen to use the words of the gospel to generate saving faith in a person's heart (Rom. 10:17; Eph. 2:8–9).

John Laing states that evangelical chaplains view their search "to lead people to either a deeper relationship with God through Christ, or an initial salvation decision/experience" as paramount.[15] Laing says that "the most important function of ministry is leading souls to peace with God through faith in the crucified and risen Christ."[16] That must be followed, of course, by the Great Commission's goal of long-term discipleship. Many evangelical chaplains in the study indicated that they are very proactive in caring, comforting, and serving as they address the problems brought to them. That kind of ministry to others often leads to a life-changing encounter as the chaplain is asked to share the gospel.

One Army chaplain who participated in the study voiced her commitment to sharing the gospel with her troops, saying, "I think a good evangelical chaplain needs to know the culture in the military, in our country. The Southern Baptist Convention's material clearly says we want to go to evangelize, to share our faith with people who want to hear it."[17] Another chaplain stated his understanding of evangelism a little more emphatically, saying, "Our primary call is to bring

15. John D. Laing, *In Jesus' Name: Evangelicals and Military Chaplaincy* (Eugene, OR: Resource, 2010), 186.
16. Laing, *In Jesus' Name*, 187.
17. Langston, "Establishing the Practical Significance," 188.

people to Christ. That's our primary call, to present the gospel and to call people to a decision to follow Jesus Christ and embrace him as their Lord and Savior, and everything else is on the periphery of that."[18] For evangelical chaplains participating in this study, one of the primary motivations for becoming a chaplain was to provide for the spiritual and religious needs of the men and women working in businesses, hospitals, the military, or other settings. The chaplain is the conduit for the fulfillment of religious freedom rights. The corollary of the requirement to provide for the religious needs of personnel is to abstain from proselytism, understanding this to mean trying to convert people from one faith group to another. Over two hundred ecclesiastical endorsers, representing multiple faith groups that endorse chaplains, agree on the following statement for their chaplains: "I will not proselytize from other religious bodies, but I retain the right to evangelize to those who are not affirmed."[19]

Yet there are many who think it is wrong or against regulations for a chaplain to share the gospel with those who wish to hear it. I (Steve) recall being a new chaplain at the Air Force Chaplain College when a fellow student stood, faced the other students, and stated with some negative energy, "I perceive there may be chaplains among us that have a hidden agenda to share the gospel!" I thought, that's me, but I kept silent, thinking that to share the gospel must be against regulations. At that moment, another chaplain student of large stature slowly stood up and spoke with authority, "Chaplain, it is no hidden agenda with me! The Lord Jesus saved my soul and has called me to share the gospel to help other people do the same!" In the ensuing discussion, I learned that many people have false perceptions about the chaplain's legal authority and biblical responsibility to evangelize and think that to evangelize would be wrong and violate the listener's religious rights. The evangelical chaplain needs to understand the God-given biblical and legal authority to evangelize and not be dissuaded by those who have false perceptions or opposing beliefs. Understanding these things, evangelical chaplains can be confident in their witness and say with the apostle Paul, "I am not ashamed of the gospel, for it is the power of God for salvation to everyone who believes" (Rom. 1:16).

Chaplains practice evangelism as it is prescribed by their denominational faith groups, according to their theological doctrines. The stipulation is that there can be no coercion or forcing of one's belief on another without their consent.[20] Evangelical chaplains consider evangelism a foundational and pri-

18. Langston, "Establishing the Practical Significance," 197–98.
19. National Conference on Ministry to the Armed Forces, "The Covenant and Code of Ethics for Chaplains of the Armed Forces," November 16, 2015, https://www.ncmaf.com/the-covenant-and-code-of-ethics-for-chaplains-of-the-armed-forces.
20. Langston, "Establishing the Practical Significance," 189.

mary responsibility that they are tasked to fulfill in taking care of the souls of the men and women they serve.

Public Prayer

Another skill that is paramount to chaplaincy is leading and conducting prayer, especially in public. All chaplains are expected to publicly pray and to do it well. One chaplain in the study indicated that he "thinks probably the greatest skill and ability that we have as an evangelical chaplain is prayer."[21] Every chaplain's theology, biblical convictions, and practice of ministry will be tested when serving in secular, religiously diverse settings, but possibly the greatest challenge will be navigating public prayer. In the military, for instance, chaplains are often asked to pray at events that require mandatory attendance, and the normal expectation is that the chaplain's prayer be nonsectarian and general, avoiding the name of Jesus. Such expectations are understandable, considering the mandatory attendance of these events. Nevertheless, such expectations have no military authority and may be understood as suggestions, since the religious authority of chaplains is their ecclesiastical endorser.[22] Further, expectations that chaplains should only minister as civil clerics are at odds with the First Amendment Establishment Clause.

Considering these challenges, evangelical chaplains need to establish a rock-solid theology of public prayer to guide them. The following four biblical principles should inform the prayers of the evangelical chaplain, prayers both private and public. First, evangelicals believe that there is only "one mediator between God and men, the man Christ Jesus" (1 Tim. 2:5), that there is no access to God the Father except through prayer to Jesus. Second, evangelicals believe that Jesus only answers prayers prayed through him (John 14:13–14). Third, evangelicals believe that the name of Jesus is "above every name" and should be exalted (Phil. 2:9–11). Fourth, evangelicals believe that to deny Jesus publicly would result in Jesus denying them before God (Matt. 10:32–33). Embracing these biblical principles will guide the chaplain's prayers.

As an endorser, it is my (Steve's) goal to encourage our chaplains to pray according to their biblical convictions and conscience. I encourage each chaplain, first, to honor the Lord Jesus in their prayer and, second, to pray with situational awareness and sensitivity for their audience and the matter at hand. The chaplain's prayer should always be consistent with their pastoral ordination and

21. Langston, "Establishing the Practical Significance," 189.
22. DOD Instruction 1304.28, "Appointment and Service of Chaplains," § 4.2.b.2, https://www.esd.whs.mil/Portals/54/Documents/DD/issuances/dodi/130428p.pdf.

ecclesiastical endorsement. Some evangelical chaplains have found a warm reception among religiously diverse audiences by making the following statement prior to voicing their Christian prayer in order to show respect for all: "Thank you for the opportunity to pray. I will be praying from the perspective of my Christian faith tradition. Please join me as you desire, according to your faith tradition." Additionally, chaplains who choose to pray in Jesus's name before a religiously diverse audience can avoid the plural "*We* pray in Jesus's name" and instead personalize their Christian prayer and state, "I pray in Jesus's name." Chaplains should rejoice at every opportunity to communicate with God and should invite his presence, help, and blessing through public and private prayers.

Chaplains are trained to provide prayer that is consistent with their faith traditions. A Christian, a Jew, a Muslim, and a Buddhist will offer differing prayers—some might even just offer thoughts rather than addressing a deity. It is best to give equal time to all chaplains at an organization, but avoid a low-content mishmash or a parade of diverse prayers at one time, as depicted in one Snickers commercial from years ago.[23] When conducting these prayers, chaplains must be sensitive to the needs of God's people and aware of the community for whom they are praying. Evangelical military chaplains recognize that prayer is important for the life of both the chaplain praying and the individuals who are engaged in the prayer. Chaplains in other settings should consult their endorsers or more experienced chaplains from their faith group for advice in praying as a chaplain. Each chaplain, as they pray, must have an awareness of the engagement that is taking place and whom the prayer is serving.

One chaplain explained, "In the Air Force, we find ourselves doing a lot of invocations, prayers at a variety of different events. I think praying with people, maybe in a hospital setting, on the flight line, or anywhere you are needed is important. Chaplains, I think, have to know how to pray, when to pray in personal settings, as well as knowing and feeling comfortable with public prayer."[24]

An evangelical Navy chaplain highlighted the privilege of praying over the ship's public-address system every night at taps when the ship was at sea. This amazing opportunity blessed the crew by voicing thoughts and feelings they may have been having and by taking them into God's presence for comfort and peace. The chaplain recalled that one grizzled and vulgar officer, a former chief petty officer, told him at the end of a deployment that he had heard hundreds of such prayers but that evangelical chaplain's prayers had reached him in ways

23. See "Snickers Team Prayer," YouTube video, 0:30, posted by Joe Ekaitis on February 3, 2015, https://youtu.be/35U4t8yaZDo.
24. Langston, "Establishing the Practical Significance," 190.

no others had. Within months he became a Christian—and years later even a Baptist deacon!

We note that while Jesus instructs his followers to ask things in prayer in his name (John 14:13), there are various ways of interpreting that instruction that do not include saying the liturgical words "in Jesus's name." In fact, while many of the prayers in the New Testament are christological, none have that liturgical ending. One can also survey prayers in Christian gatherings and find that Christians do not always say those particular words. For Christians, it is understood that Christ is the only avenue for prayer, whether stated or not. We recommend prayers for the good of all provided by forthright Christians in ways that all will understand.

We encourage each chaplain to pray according to their beliefs. True, you may need to modify accustomed prayer forms to meet the needs of a given occasion, as all ministers should always be intentional regarding situational awareness before speaking or praying anywhere. However, do not allow an outside group to tell you how to pray. You are responsible to your faith group, through your endorser, for all your ministry, including prayer. I (Steve) was once confronted by a Muslim officer who was offended by Christian chaplains' public prayers— not because they were Christian prayers but because they were not! He saw that the other faith groups' chaplains prayed in their own ways but that the Christian chaplains held back in the name of inclusiveness and inoffensiveness. He urged that all chaplains be authentic to their beliefs. We concur.

We wish to give some practical guidance to close this section on prayer. First, we consider it a remarkable privilege to be invited to pray publicly. We never take this as just a ceremonious box to check but a genuine opportunity to mediate the presence of God. Any organization that asks for God's public blessings is better off than otherwise. We are intent to fulfill that purpose.

A ceremony at which one would be asked to pray typically involves a change of some sort: a transition of leadership, retirement, dedication of a structure or implement, the commissioning of a vessel, and so forth. The ceremony stands in the present between the past and the future. Let the invocation be about the past events and people—always people, by name or organization if possible— that have led to this moment. It is a prayer of thanks for what God has done, keeping people safe and helping things be accomplished. Ninety seconds is more than sufficient for a prayer of invocation. A benediction is a prayer of supplication and blessing for the future, asking for God's help to strengthen all involved to accomplish all that they hope to achieve. Sixty seconds is more than enough time for this prayer of benediction as people fidget to leave the ceremony. Spend much time and prayer composing your prayer that it would be to the glory of God and the good of the people present. Make every word count. Use words sparingly and avoid unnecessary verbal artifacts ("God, we ask you God to help us God") that belabor too many evangelical prayers. Let your prayer be dignified but also personable, and even humorous as appropriate. I (Mark) provide the person in charge of the ceremony a memo in advance providing several practical notes for success for all. After all, the chaplain is there to bless all—not to argue over their right to say the prayer a certain way!

Private Prayer

Every chaplain finds opportunities to pray privately with individuals and small groups. Healthcare chaplains find personal prayer with patients to be especially appropriate and helpful in ministry. Each patient's situation, relationships (including to God), and hopes for healing can be spoken in prayer. Gratitude and tears are not uncommon in these precious moments. A healthcare chaplain who has the privilege of charting the patient's treatment can make the patient's openness to and requests for prayer part of that program as appropriate. Prayer at the close of a counseling session—whether formal in the chaplain's office or impromptu in a corner of the workspace—can be an ideal time to voice the person's needs to God, asking for powerful divine help. Asking for permission to close a session with prayer should be part of every chaplain's ministry. Sometimes a group will request prayer, especially before a challenging task such as a combat mission, an unusually delicate surgery, an outside inspection, or a difficult corporate program. This is the time for the chaplain to shine with just the right words as God gives them.

Preaching

Preaching is one of the fundamental skills that all chaplains must master as part of their ministerial capabilities if they are to function well. Preaching is a form of communication that communicates God's Word to his people and creates a relationship between him and the people he has called his own (1 Cor. 1:21). In military chaplaincy programs, preaching is a highly coveted skill and can be conducted only by authorized, ordained chaplains. The requirements vary for chaplains in other settings. The chaplain's preaching is seen as proclaiming the Word of God as it is revealed to that chaplain via the Holy Spirit with reference to a specific text of Scripture. Evangelical chaplains are noted for their expository preaching abilities and their commitment to proclaim the whole counsel of God through the spoken word. One Air Force chaplain who participated in the chaplaincy study confirmed this point, saying, "What I have encouraged my chaplains and even myself to do is that when you lead a worship service, you should preach from the whole counsel of God. You should preach everything that's in the Bible."[25]

Communicating God's love and plan for his people is mesmerizing and life changing when done correctly. The words encourage, empower, and transform people when the human means of the chaplain's preaching is coupled with the divine power of the Holy Spirit to convey a truth that validates God's desire for the people receiving the message. The Word is the real power of the proclamation (Heb. 4:12), and the messenger is merely a tool used by the masterful hand of the Spirit. Understanding and seeking the transformative power of preaching, evangelical chaplains love to be used by God in the pulpit. Indeed, God the Great Communicator has chosen to use chaplains and the "folly of what we preach to save those who believe" (1 Cor. 1:21).

The power of preaching is illustrated in a story of one Protestant military chaplain preaching during an Easter sunrise service, which was attended by the Catholic commanding officer at a naval air station. The chaplain preached a sermon titled "Too Good to Be True." One of the statements the chaplain made in the sermon that morning was that "the disciples on the road to Emmaus said to each other, 'You know, we heard that he's risen from the dead, but it seems like that was too good to be true.'" The chaplain reports that the officer picked up on that thought from the sermon. The commanding officer said that it was the best preaching he had ever heard, and for the remainder of the time he worked with the chaplain, he thanked the chaplain every time he saw him and would say, "Too good to be true!" Years later, the chaplain sent the then-retired officer an invitation to his retirement ceremony. He could not come but sent a note saying, "You were the best chaplain I ever worked with." The chaplain said during the interview process of this chaplaincy study, "This is a Catholic witnessing to my enthusiastic preaching from the Word of God, which does not come back void" (Isa. 55:11).[26] The spoken word is powerful when the speaker is in full submission to the working of God's Spirit in the proclamation process.

Evangelical chaplains can be found preaching gospel-centered sermons at military installations, ships, battlefields, remote air bases, hospitals, prisons, sports fields, and countless community settings on Sundays and throughout the week. They are messengers of God seeking to communicate God's redemptive message to all who wish to hear. We encourage evangelical chaplains to follow God's command to "preach the word; be ready in season and out of season" (2 Tim. 4:2), to "not shrink from declaring . . . the whole counsel of God" (Acts

25. Langston, "Establishing the Practical Significance," 193.
26. Langston, "Establishing the Practical Significance," 193.

20:27), and to "proclaim the gospel to the whole creation" (Mark 16:15). No one should be surprised when an evangelical chaplain preaches the gospel in worship settings, nor should they seek to stop them from proclaiming the good news. Nevertheless, misguided supervisors may think it is inappropriate and thus try to stop it. I (Steve) recall such a situation when, as a young Air Force chaplain, my supervisor, a chaplain lieutenant colonel, called me into his office and explained to me that it was not fitting for a chaplain to preach the gospel in an Air Force chapel. I asked why he thought it necessary to have such a conversation with me. He explained that he had heard me preach a few weeks earlier and that I had shared as part of my sermon that everyone needed to be saved. He went on to say that he did not believe people needed to be saved and that if I preached salvation again, I would be leaving the Air Force. He made it clear I would be leaving within the next year as he would not sign my continuation paperwork. At that point I should have called my endorser, but I knew God had commanded me to preach the whole counsel of his Word and proclaim the good news. The next Sunday morning, with about two hundred people present, he was prominently seated in the front to make sure I did not preach the gospel. At that moment I knew my career as an Air Force chaplain was on the line. I contemplated, should I wait to preach the gospel another day when my supervisor is not in the service? Should I wait for my next assignment and pray for an evangelical supervisor who will allow me to preach the gospel? I knew I needed to decide. I had a choice: to obey God or man (Acts 5:29). Humbly, I did make the right decision that Sunday morning, and seven individuals stood and prayed to receive Christ during the invitation. God intervened and the lieutenant colonel was ordered by the chief of chaplains to sign my continuation documents. I retired twenty-eight years later after serving in twelve more assignments and enjoying hundreds of opportunities to preach the gospel and see many come to Christ. Preach the Word and share the good news with all who desire to hear it.

There is an amazing continuation of God's providence in this story. Twenty years later I was invited to give the keynote address at a military function. While speaking, I noticed my former supervisor sitting in the audience, the same one who tried to end my chaplain ministry for preaching the gospel. After speaking, I went over to his table to say hello. Now up in years and in poor health, he slowly rose to his feet and greeted me with these words, "Steve, I've decided the gospel is true!" He then invited me to speak at his men's Bible study and to share opportunities I had to preach the gospel while in Iraq. Two hundred men attended his study that morning. Following the study, he walked me to my car and thanked me for not caving when he told me to stop preaching the gospel. He said that God used my sharing of the gospel that distant Sunday morning to convict him of its truth (John 14:6). He died not long after, but his words still echo in my mind and heart: "Steve, keep preaching the gospel. God uses it to change lives. I am a living witness!"

Evangelical chaplains are authorized to fulfill their denominational expectations, including altar calls at the end of sermons in worship services. This affirmation is established in Title X of the US Code.[27] One chaplain who participated in the study shared an incident in which he was chastised for offering an altar call at the end of his worship service, which was being conducted in the form and manner of his denomination. Yet in reality there were no prohibitions against him preaching an evangelistic sermon and issuing an altar call as part of the worship service. According to Title X, chaplains are expected to be strict representatives of their respective denominations.[28] Further, the evangelical chaplain has a command from God to "preach the word; be ready in season and out of season; reprove, rebuke, and exhort, with complete patience and teaching" (2 Tim. 4:2).

Discipling

Making disciples is the privilege and responsibility of evangelical chaplains (Matt. 28:19–20). The goal of the evangelical chaplain is to assist individuals who have received the Lord as Savior to be conformed to his image (Rom. 8:29). Through the new birth (John 3:3), a person is imputed with Christ's righteousness and forgiven of sin, and their soul is made pure in the sight of God (Rom. 3:25; 2 Cor. 5:12; 1 Pet. 1:9). Still, the challenge of living out one's new identity as a child of God remains (2 Cor. 5:17). It is the chaplain's duty as a disciple maker not only to share the gospel and help individuals come to Christ as Savior but also to guide them in their quest to be conformed to Christ's image in their minds and bodies (Rom. 12:1–2).

Evangelical chaplains are also known for conducting Bible studies and teaching the Bible through courses on the Old Testament, the New Testament, and individual biblical books. A Navy chaplain in the study shared his insights on discipling in the following excerpt:

> Oftentimes when someone gives their life to Jesus Christ, the very next question is always, "So what's next? What do I do next?" The answer for me is first modelling what it means to be a Christian and showing them in my life what

27. 10 U.S.C. (2012), §§ 3073, 3547, 3581, 5142, 8067, https://uscode.house.gov/browse/prelim@title10&edition=prelim.
28. 10 U.S.C. (2012), subtitle C, part 2, chap. 555, § 6031, "Chaplains: Divine Services."

that means. Along the way I will teach them Scripture, answering questions with them, encouraging them to begin to develop the disciplines of their own personal devotion time, their own personal quiet times in the relationship with Christ, listening, hearing, and understanding what he says, you know, developing those skills because it is different for every person.[29]

Discipling is teaching others about the Christian faith and specifically who God, Jesus, and the Holy Spirit are in relation to the disciple. It involves instructing disciples in how to incorporate the message of God's redeeming love into their lives. Additionally, it involves teaching disciples to emulate the great heroes in the Bible. The purpose of discipleship is to help disciples reflect the character of the divine Trinity in their thoughts, words, and actions. Evangelical chaplains carry out their discipleship by using different techniques and materials, all of which are focused on educating others who want to know God in a more intimate, relational manner.

Advising

Chaplains often advise leaders and staff on ethical considerations involved in decision-making and address issues of religion and spirituality. Chaplains often have a pulse on the group's people—their morale, thoughts, and conditions— like no one else. An excellent chaplain performs ministry by "walking around" the entire organization. Many organizational members are limited to their own section, while the chaplain gains an overall picture. Wise senior leaders seek the chaplain's perceptions and evaluations—without breaking confidentiality—to gain better situational awareness and make better decisions. The chaplain may even be asked for a recommendation regarding various policies and actions. Thus, advisement occurs.

Military chaplains are assigned advisement as a formal duty. It is their job to advise the commander as they perceive necessary. Chaplains in other functional areas of chaplaincy will often find their advice sought, perhaps informally but no less important.

Advisers are some of the most influential and powerful people in an organization. The chaplain of good character and competence, having gained trust over time, may be invited into this elite group that bears an awesome responsibility. In such cases the chaplain, by virtue of office, is expected to give advice that deals with morals, ethics, faith, religion, and seeking God's wisdom (James 1:5). The chaplain should not be embarrassed or hesitate to speak of these things

29. Langston, "Establishing the Practical Significance," 195–96.

as the subject matter expert in those areas. That is what the leader expects and needs. In giving advice to leaders, chaplains must protect the confidentiality of those led as well as of the leader. The leader needs to absolutely trust the chaplain's honesty and discretion—as well as loyalty—even when the advice is not followed. Many chaplains develop strong relationships with leaders that continue for years after their formal work together. Thus chaplains, through this positive relationship, help the leader bear burdens that few in the organization may understand or know. Only through God's help, constantly sought and received, can the chaplain fulfill this role well.

Conclusion

Caring, comforting, and serving are the foundational KSAs required when providing for the needs within an organization or community. The chaplain's motivation for providing such ministry is Christ. The art of performing these KSAs develops over time and becomes more finely tuned to the needs of those being served. These KSAs form the foundation for other skills that are required for chaplain ministry, such as evangelizing, praying, preaching, discipling, leading, and advising.

9

The Ministry of Presence
and Hospitality

Chaplains are the designated professional spiritual leaders within the military and various other organizations. To many people in workplaces, the presence of a chaplain signifies the presence of God. Each Christian is a "bearer of the presence of God,"[1] who lives in believers through his Holy Spirit. This sense of presence is referred to in 2 Corinthians 3:18: "And we all, with unveiled face, beholding the glory of the Lord, are being transformed into the same image from one degree of glory to another. For this comes from the Lord who is the Spirit."

Evangelical chaplains focus on Christ-in-me to explain the core of their faith and ministry. The account in Matthew 10 of Jesus sending disciples out is characteristic of the ministry that chaplains conduct. Dietrich Bonhoeffer interprets Matthew 10:40–42 as follows:

> Those who carry Jesus' word receive one last promise for their work. They have become Christ's co-workers and helpmates. They are to be like Christ in all things.

1. Dietrich Bonhoeffer, *Discipleship*, Dietrich Bonhoeffer Works 4 (Minneapolis: Fortress, 2003), 211; Andrew Purves, *Reconstructing Pastoral Theology: A Christological Foundation* (Louisville: Westminster John Knox, 2004), 193.

Thus, for the people to whom they go, they are also to be "like Christ." With them, Jesus Christ himself enters the house that takes them in. They are bearers of his presence. They bring the people the most valuable gift, Jesus Christ, and with him, God, the Father, and the fruit of their work and their suffering. Every service done to them is done to Jesus Christ himself.[2]

Chaplains move among people, bringing the presence of God to those they encounter. Because of this presence, chaplains convey a sense that the healing of the old self is possible and has come, that moral awareness is present, and that a sense of justness and holiness is there.

Evangelical chaplains embody and model God's presence in their daily lives as a result of their spiritual practices, which are carried out in the presence of God and form part of their daily routines. Individuals often notice a charisma in their chaplains. In the chaplaincy study mentioned in the previous chapter, a Navy chaplain shared that many times his Marines have asked him why he is "always so positive, upbeat, and happy, always sporting a smile on his face" when there is so much death and turmoil around them.[3] This chaplain equated that positivity with the inner peace and security he experienced daily as a result of the Holy Spirit filling him with his presence and living inside of him. He was in God's presence daily through prayer and his personal spiritual disciplines. For this evangelical chaplain, the indwelling, personal presence of Christ radiates out from him in a way that is visible to others. As Jesus comes alongside, providing God's presence, comfort, and peace, he allows the chaplain to come alongside others and provide a personal sense of presence to them. The chaplain called this the "Emmanuel factor—God with us!" (see Matt. 1:23).[4]

The very sense of the presence of God being experienced in and through chaplains is powerful. It is contagious in a way that provides a calming effect for those being served. Chaplains often indicate that by their mere presence, hope seems to come alive. In many ways they embody that hope and light and represent all that is good, holy, right, and just. For these reasons the chaplain becomes the visible moral conscience of the organization. As chaplains walk through the workplace with a cross on their uniform and the light of Christ shining from them, people are reminded of what is moral and right, which affects their actions in the workplace.

2. Bonhoeffer, *Discipleship*, 211.
3. Michael W. Langston, "Establishing the Practical Significance of the Influence of Evangelical Theology on an Evangelical Military Chaplains Praxis of Chaplaincy" (PhD diss., University of Aberdeen, 2019).
4. Langston, "Establishing the Practical Significance."

Hospitality

As evangelical chaplains understand their identity as Christians (Christ living in and through them), they reflect Jesus's casual hospitality in their encounters with people. In New Testament times, hospitality set Christians apart from other religions and groups.[5] In the traditional sense, offering hospitality meant offering a safe space where strangers felt welcomed, accepted, and safe from attack. Hospitality included meeting the stranger's needs while guaranteeing their safety. Evangelical chaplains seeking to imitate Christ in their actions, thoughts, and encounters with others become good hosts in the same way that Christ is the Good Host. Chaplains, as bearers of God's presence, usher the individual not only into a free and safe place to deal with the struggles of life but also into the incarnational holy presence of God. In this space, chaplains apply the ministry skills of care, comfort, service, confidentiality, understanding, compassion, and empathy.

In modern commercial culture, the term "hospitality" often refers to the hotel and restaurant industry and its emphasis on customers' comfort. Christine Pohl says, "Understandings of hospitality have been reduced to Martha Stewart's latest ideas for entertaining family and friends and to the services of the hotel and restaurant industry."[6] This form of hospitality involves high levels of comfort and care provided by beds, spas, and other creature comforts, as well as indulgence in rich food and drink. It focuses on physical needs and relaxation.

Christians, historically, have used the term "hospitality" to refer to provisions for the physical, emotional, and spiritual needs of strangers. Pohl refers to the "blessing and mystery that accompany the practice" of hospitality, as she argues for the significance of hospitality. She attempts to counter the modern Christian view of hospitality as a "mildly pleasant activity if sufficient time is available."[7] The "blessing and mystery" of hospitality encompass the commitment and the work of evangelical chaplains. Examining the ancient Christian tradition of hospitality leads to a deeper understanding of the work of chaplains as they stand in the gap between God and people.

In *Making Room: Recovering Hospitality as a Christian Tradition*, Pohl describes the importance of hospitality to Christians by stating, "Hospitality is a way of life fundamental to Christian identity. Its mysteries, riches, and difficulties

5. Christine D. Pohl, "Hospitality, a Practice and a Way of Life," *Vision: A Journal for Church and Theology* 3 (2002): 36.
6. Pohl, "Hospitality," 34.
7. Pohl, "Hospitality," 34.

are revealed most fully as it is practiced."[8] As a Christian concept, hospitality involves being a host as much as it involves being a guest. Christians must be willing to be both a host who provides for those seeking hospitality and a guest who receives hospitality. To fully experience hospitality, people have to both give and receive. A host is responsible for providing care and comfort and meeting the needs of others—that is to say, serving the guest. Jesus often was a guest in a home, but during his time there he transitioned into the Good Host. In like manner the safe spaces that were part of true hospitality would become sacred spaces when he was present in them.

Hospitality entails providing safe spaces for strangers who are wandering in life. Henri Nouwen introduces hospitality as a primary means of creating a "free space where the stranger can enter and become a friend instead of an enemy."[9] When the stranger enters the safe space, the host provides for the needs of that stranger. As the stranger becomes known, the host invites the stranger deeper and deeper into the safe space until the stranger belongs as a member of the group. Thus, the stranger no longer wanders but instead belongs to the group. Jesus used this pattern to transform the world.[10] Evangelical chaplains, as they imitate Christ within them, use the pattern to transform the world in which they minister.

Types of Hospitality

Evangelical chaplains participate in several kinds of hospitality that were also prevalent in the ancient world. Moralists considered hospitality a fundamental moral virtue that facilitated the social process. By the first century, hospitality could be subdivided into five broad categories in the Jewish, Greek, and Roman cultures:

1. Public hospitality: welcoming and accommodating the needs of national guests
2. Commercial hospitality: providing food and accommodations for businesspeople who were traveling
3. Temple hospitality: caring for those on pilgrimages or holy missions
4. Theoxenic hospitality: generosity to gods, heroes, and semidivine guests

8. Christine D. Pohl, *Making Room: Recovering Hospitality as a Christian Tradition* (Grand Rapids: Eerdmans, 1999), x.

9. Henri J. M. Nouwen, *The Wounded Healer: In Our Own Woundedness, We Can Become a Source of Life for Others* (New York: Doubleday, 1972), 79–80.

10. Nouwen, *Wounded Healer*, 79–80.

5. Private hospitality: welcoming a business traveler or someone
   on a pilgrimage into one's home if the person carried a letter of
   recommendation[11]

These types of hospitality appear throughout the New Testament and are a
part of evangelical chaplains' ministry as well. In some cases the hospitality
requirement is part and parcel of the chaplains' directions from a superior.
Evangelical chaplains view hospitality as a "lens through which [they] can read
and understand much of the gospel, and a practice by which [they] can welcome
Jesus himself."[12] For different reasons, evangelical chaplains in the Langston
study reported multiple occasions when they extended hospitality to others.
In each encounter, chaplains responded to the stranger as though they were
welcoming Jesus himself.[13]

Public hospitality. While public hospitality is not stressed in the New Testament, Jesus still tells people to "render to Caesar the things that are Caesar's"
(Matt. 22:21) and to carry a Roman soldier's goods a second mile if the soldier
asks for one mile's work (Matt. 5:41). These examples show Jesus's concern for
providing the government and its representatives with a welcoming and caring
attitude. Jesus also welcomes the centurion, accommodating his needs by healing
his servant. In this case Jesus responds to a government official and his great
statement of faith (Matt. 8:5–13). Thus, Jesus's response to the government and
government officials is to provide for their needs and to welcome the officials
as guests whose needs he can meet. Jesus demonstrates public hospitality as
he, the Good Host, welcomes government officials into the sanctity of the safe,
holy, and sacred space that he provides.

Chaplains can be part of the structure of an organization and can represent
that organization in many environments, including the national government.
Within the military they are relied upon when national guests arrive at a duty
station. Chaplains often find themselves extending public hospitality to congressional guests or other national figures who visit the areas where the chaplain is
stationed. Military chaplains are often encouraged to participate in Religious
Leader Engagement (RLE) toward international clerical leaders in order to
build bridges for new partnerships. Chaplains who work with international
companies can be assigned duties with visiting dignitaries from another country. As relationships are developed from common ground and ties to religious
foundations, new dialogue and conversations are established.

11. Martin W. Mittelstadt, "Eat, Drink, and Be Merry: A Theology of Hospitality in Luke-Acts,"
Word and World 34, no. 2 (2014): 132–33.
12. Pohl, "Hospitality," 35.
13. Langston, "Establishing the Practical Significance."

Commercial hospitality. Commercial hospitality is also not mentioned often in the New Testament, but its existence was an integral part of the world in which Jesus lived. Jesus's own birth contains a story of an innkeeper who has no room left for Joseph and Mary but who sends the small family to a warm, safe space in the stable. Thus, Jesus's birth in a stable is the result of commercial hospitality. During the night, this safe space changes into a sacred space through a blessing and mystery, as the Son of God comes to earth to dwell among man. The concept of a safe space changing to a sacred space is evident throughout the night, as Immanuel brings God's presence to earth, angels sing and praise God before shepherds, and kings begin a journey to find the holy one (Matt. 2:1–12; Luke 2:1–21). Though he has no room in his inn, the innkeeper is a conduit for God's blessing and mystery through his commercial hospitality.

Jesus's parable of the good Samaritan contains an example of commercial hospitality: the good Samaritan leaves the wounded man in the care of an innkeeper, paying for care and comfort until he returns (Luke 10:25–37). The good Samaritan serves the wounded man as he cleans his wounds, provides a place of safety, and feeds him until he is healthy. The innkeeper's commercial hospitality allows the man to heal in a safe place until he can travel. In this story, Jesus confirms people's need to rely on others when they are unable to follow through with helping someone.

Commercial hospitality is an integral part of most chaplains' duties, especially in the military, as they are often tasked with working out the details of functions or entertaining people for their commands. They may also have to find lodging and provide meals and similar requirements for visitors to the commands. These responsibilities can provide evangelical chaplains with opportunities to influence others in the workplace.

Temple hospitality. The journeys of Jesus, Paul, and other early missionaries are filled with stories of temple hospitality. Jesus's mission on earth is a holy mission filled with encounters with people seeking God. The story of the Samaritan woman at the well (John 4:1–43) illustrates this type of hospitality. On a holy mission, Jesus goes through Samaria to reach Galilee when he hears that the Pharisees are displeased with the numbers of people being baptized through his ministry. Traveling through Samaria—an unusual route for a Jew—Jesus encounters a woman at a well, where he asks for water. The woman offers to a weary traveler the hospitality of a drink and a place to rest. Jesus again turns a safe space into a sacred space, as he first accepts her hospitality toward him as her guest and then offers her water that will prevent her from ever being thirsty again. Jesus accepts temple hospitality on a holy mission, and through his teaching the woman becomes a follower.

Paul and many of the other early missionaries report the hospitality they received because of their holy missions. Paul often mentions the people who cared for him, such as Aquila and Priscilla (Acts 18:1–3, 18; 2 Tim. 4:19), who worked with him in his tentmaking. Paul stayed with people in their homes and accepted their food and drink in order to bear witness to the divinity of Christ. Paul appeals to Philemon to prepare a bed for him (Philem. 22), and one of his major complaints is the lack of hospitality he experiences as he moves throughout the Roman Empire (1 Cor. 4:11–13; 2 Cor. 6:4–10; 11:21–33). In Romans 12–15, Paul exhorts people to submit to governing powers, offer their bodies as sacrifices, and follow many other Old Testament precedents. In this section, however, he also instructs people to "practice hospitality" (Rom. 12:13 NIV).[14] This temple hospitality allows Paul to operate in many cities, working a trade by day and preaching when he can.

As a result of their evangelical theological identity, chaplains view their ministry as a way to share Christ with others (evangelism) and to assist, through the relationships they build, in the transformation of the lives of the people they serve. In this sense, they practice temple hospitality with any-one they encounter. By viewing everyone as being on a journey in search of Christ, evangelical chaplains welcome strangers and help them along on their journeys.

Theoxenic hospitality. Examples of theoxenic hospitality exist throughout Jesus's ministry. Many people invite Jesus to their homes, providing dinner, wine, and conversation. Jesus enters their homes as a guest, partaking of the hospitality of the host. As the dinner progresses, the home—the safe space—of the person becomes a holy place and a sacred space in which Jesus transforms into the Good Host. As this transition occurs, people within the safe space be-come aware that they are in the presence of divinity, standing on holy ground. For example, Jesus seeks out Zacchaeus (Luke 19:1–10) for one of these trans-formational encounters, in which a simple invitation turns Zacchaeus into the initial host who offers the hospitality of his home to Jesus. Responding to the divinity of Jesus, Zacchaeus proclaims that he will provide for the poor and pay back anyone he has cheated. Jesus, changing roles from guest to host, of-fers life-changing words to Zacchaeus and all who would hear and accept his words of safety and peace. Jesus's divinity appears and leads to his changing roles from guest to host.

Historically, the Christian praxis of theoxenic hospitality resulted from the awareness that Jesus might take the form of a stranger at the door. St. Bene-dict stressed this approach in Benedictine monasteries, and evangelicals have

14. Mittelstadt, "Eat, Drink, and Be Merry," 133.

stressed it in their daily practice.[15] Evangelical chaplains, in this manner, also act on the idea that they could be hosting Christ as they walk among those who need care, comfort, and service.

   Private hospitality. Jesus relied on private hospitality throughout his ministry. He ate in homes and was welcomed by many who learned that while he begins as their guest, he ends as their host. In his ministry, Jesus changed many safe spaces into holy and sacred spaces as he walked among people. In Mark 6:7–13, Jesus sends the Twelve out two by two, instructing them to carry nothing with them but a cloak. They carry no money, no food, no extra clothing. This state forces the disciples to rely on the private hospitality of those they encounter on their journeys. To eat or sleep in a house, the disciples must form relationships that lead to the extension of private hospitality. Jesus instructs them to stay in a home until they depart; but if they are rejected, then the disciples are to shake the dust from their shoes and continue their journey. During their visits to homes where hospitality is extended, the disciples, like Jesus, change from being guests to being hosts. In this manner, they change safe spaces into sacred spaces.

   Welcoming strangers is a continual part of chaplains' jobs, and evangelical chaplains practice it as an activity connected to their theological identity as bearers of the presence of Christ. Through Bible studies, meals, small groups, workplace conversations, and many other means, they extend private hospitality. Evangelical chaplains do so with the goal of caring for and comforting but also with the goal of building relationships that will lead to evangelistic opportunities. Just as Christ sends his disciples out to rely on the hospitality of others, chaplains seek opportunities to provide hospitality to those seeking it. Pohl affirms that hospitality is "an important way of acknowledging the equal value and dignity of people."[16] Through private hospitality, evangelical chaplains reach those who are struggling and welcome them into a safe, holy, and sacred space.

Bearers of the Presence of God

Chaplains are to provide a place of safety and, more specifically, a holy place and a sacred place, where an encounter with the presence of God can occur. Chaplains refer to themselves as bearers of the presence of God who represent the sacred place through their physical presence. An identity that provides a safe, holy, sacred space, where people encounter the living Christ, is fundamental to

15. Joan Chittister, *The Rule of Benedict: A Spirituality for the Twenty-First Century* (New York: Crossroad, 2002), 227.
16. Pohl, "Hospitality," 35.

the evangelical chaplain and is critically important to the personnel they serve in each organizational context.

Pohl states that good hosts do the following:

- Recognize their own frailties and weaknesses.
- Recognize the woundedness in themselves and their ongoing need for grace and mercy.
- Do not recoil from human suffering.
- Do not insist on quick evidence of success.
- Are willing to be present and share burdens even when they cannot solve problems.
- Understand the value of small acts of grace.
- Choose to distance themselves from prevailing understandings of power, privilege, status, and possessions.
- Cultivate a countercultural identity that nurtures a distinct way of life and a strong commitment to welcome.[17]

Pohl continues, "In offering hospitality, hosts live between the vision of God's kingdom in which there is enough . . . and the hard realities of human life."[18]

Evangelical chaplains realize experientially that as bearers of God's presence, they are viewed as safe people to approach with issues of life. Often in their trek through life's course, people in a workplace with a chaplain seek out that chaplain as a safe person to speak with. Wherever the chaplain is located, there is a safe place to dwell and address the problems, fears, and weariness that life presents. These provisions are the hallmark of a good host. Henri Nouwen offers a reminder that as weary travelers along life's journey, chaplains must recognize that "hospitality is the virtue which allows us to break through the narrowness of our own fears and to *open our houses to the stranger*, with the intuition that salvation comes to us in the form of a *tired traveler*."[19] Chaplains provide a safe space for the care and comfort of the stranger, but strangers, by coming to chaplains, offer them a deeper sense of their own salvation that comes with the recognition of others' needs.

Evangelical chaplains also recognize their own need for a safe and sacred space where they can be accepted, cared for, and comforted. Nouwen asks, "When our souls are restless, when we are driven by thousands of different

17. Pohl, "Hospitality," 41.
18. Pohl, "Hospitality," 42.
19. Nouwen, *Wounded Healer*, 89 (emphasis added).

and often conflicting stimuli, when we are always 'over there' between people, ideas and the worries of this world, how can we possibly create the room and space where someone else can enter freely without feeling himself an unlawful intruder?"[20] Chaplains sometimes need a safe place to unwind, decompress, just be present with another human being, or simply get a fresh drink of water by themselves. When they are refreshed, evangelical chaplains build safe and sacred spaces so they can engage and build relationships with the people to whom they minister.

Chaplains as Theologians in Community

The evangelical chaplain becomes the theologian in residence, so to speak, of the community by bearing the presence of God. They wear a cross on their uniforms, polo shirts, or hats, which is a constant visual reminder of their role as a theologian in the community. This role means that when people face confusion and questions about existence, fairness, God, religion, spirituality, morality, and other issues, they see the cross and respond to it as a place of safety and security, where their needs can be met, and they do not have to be afraid of retribution or ridicule. The chaplain's confidentiality requirements add to that sense of safety. The perception others have of evangelical chaplains is that of a confidential provider of the presence of God.

When I (Mike) was stationed overseas, I was assigned as the deputy station chaplain, the main Protestant chapel pastor, and the hospital chaplain. A family that regularly attended our chapel service had a long-awaited baby who was born with a medical condition that could not be treated. The baby's heart would not sustain life more than a few days. I responded to the family's need at the time of the birth and sat with them through the four days of this baby's life. During this time hospital nurses and doctors sought me out for comfort and care as they, too, walked with this family through the life and death of the child. The family asked me to be with them as the child took her last breath. The entire staff at the hospital was shaken by this infant's death, as was our base military community. As the physical representative of God, I brought the care and comfort of Christ to the family as well as the hospital staff. I, too, struggled to understand this tragedy, but I offered what I could—the care, comfort, and love of Christ.

As I prepared for the memorial service, members of the community came to me, seeking answers as to how God could let this happen. My sermon focused on comfort and care for the family, the hospital staff, and the many members

20. Nouwen, *Wounded Healer*, 90.

of the community that overflowed from the chapel. The perceptions that others had of me as a theologian in this military community were that I would be able to explain the theological reasons for the death of this baby and that understanding this would help them make sense of the loss. Knowing that a tidy explanation for death cannot console a person, I found myself focusing on comforting the community through Christ's love and care for us.

In the military, a military member escorts bodies returning to the United States. This rule applies to family members stationed overseas as well as all active-duty personnel. All such bodies enter through the Mortuary Affairs morgue at Dover Air Force Base in Delaware. In this case the family asked me to be their military escort back to their home state for the burial. After the memorial service the baby was placed on a cargo plane that had brought commissary stores (food and supplies) to the base and was returning to the United States. I boarded the plane in my service-dress blues uniform, which bears the cross on both sleeves, and was greeted by the crew, composed of former military persons, with "Hi, Chaps. Welcome aboard."

During the flight I went to the casket to pray for the baby. The pilot on the plane joined me. He waited until I was through praying and then told me what an honor it was to bring the baby back to the US. He continued talking until he began crying. The pilot had tragically lost several close family members a year earlier. He told me of his anger at God and how he had not talked about the incident with anyone. I became aware of the presence of God in the plane as this man poured out his pain and then stood silently with his hand on the baby's casket. We were standing on holy ground, a safe place that became a holy place and was transformed into sacred space. I prayed with him and for him, but we mainly stood together on this holy ground. This tiny baby's life and death had provided a safe, sacred space for the crew member to grieve for his family. Healing, grace, and closure came from standing over this small casket, praying with me, at the back of a transport plane headed back to the US.

When we landed at Dover Air Force Base, the pilot and crew stood at attention as I accompanied the baby to the morgue. I entered the morgue, and the staff were in tears as her small casket rolled through the hallways. Throughout the next few hours, the staff at the morgue who were processing the baby came to me over and over, seeking care and comfort as they dealt with the infant. As I stood in my dress uniform with the crosses on display, the staff repeatedly came to me and said, "Chaps." The perception of others within the morgue was that I would provide comfort and care for them as they dealt with the loss of this tiny infant.

Upon our arrival at our final destination, I met with the baby's immediate and extended family. We prayed and cried together. The extended family immediately accepted me as a provider of care and comfort and came to me seeking prayer and solace. After the funeral I returned to my base and spent the next few months comforting and caring for the hospital staff and the immediate family. The staff allowed the mother to come into the nursery for as long as she needed. The mother did so for several months, rocking for hours and grieving for her baby. I often went while she was there and prayed with her. The staff, while supporting her, also found her continual presence difficult, as they were unable to get back to work, as it were, with the reminder of a baby's death sitting in the nursery. They also sought me out as a theologian in community to help them understand what had happened and to seek God's comfort in this tragic circumstance. Chaplains act as theologians for the organization's or community's members, their family members, and anyone who perceives them as sources of care and comfort.

During the height of the war in Iraq and Afghanistan, US military leaders were frustrated by their inability to break down communication barriers with leaders in these predominantly Muslim countries. I was a senior evangelical military chaplain in Afghanistan at the time, serving as the theater chaplain for Combined Forces Command Afghanistan, with responsibilities to the commanding general who led the NATO forces. An American Special Forces unit had desecrated dead bodies of Taliban fighters. Riots had erupted throughout Afghanistan, and NATO forces were being hunted and killed by many people who previously had been neutral. Since negotiations were having no effect, the US commanding general sent me to discuss the issues with the Afghan Hajj and Islamic affairs minister.

On the third day of my entering his office, drinking tea and discussing family, cultures, Christian and Muslim theology, and other concepts that build relationship, the government minister asked me what I wanted. I discussed the riots and asked what could be done about them. The minister's response was enlightening for all US military chaplains. He said that, finally, our country understood that his people wanted their religion as well as their civil government respected. The situation was resolved, and as a result, the RLE initiative was moved to a new level.

I entered the office of the minister with respect, but as a US military officer, I felt that I was the host. I quickly understood that I was a guest and the Afghan official was the host in his office, his country, and his government. Because I was willing to be a guest and receive the hospitality of tea and conversation from a non-Christian, non-American "other," an interreligious dialogue characterized by mutual respect was established. During this time of relationship building, I became aware of the mullah's (a Muslim religious official) role as a government official, but I also understood his role as the head mullah of his country.

I viewed our relationship as one between clergy, and this enabled me to establish communication to stop the riots, which had resulted in deaths to NATO forces. My acceptance of my role as guest to the mullah opened doors of mutual respect and established a working relationship between us. This encounter, in which an evangelical chaplain perceived the clergy role of another faith leader, exemplifies positive interfaith communication in clergy-to-clergy interactions.

Chaplains as Moral Compasses

Many times, chaplains are perceived as moral compasses for the organizations or communities they serve. As bearers of the presence of God, evangelical chaplains create a moral atmosphere by their presence among the people. As moral compasses, they illustrate James William McClendon's idea of the "present Christ," who is the "One who confronts the church [or people] today."[21] Chaplains serve to remind people of their moral and ethical responsibilities concerning scripturally based values, and they call the organization's leadership to a sense of moral accountability. Chaplains do not have to say or do anything for requests to come from those around them. When chaplains enter a room, their presence elicits responses from people, including the avoidance of offensive language, the hiding of certain books and magazines under couches, the changing of TV stations, and the cessation of negative behaviors. People respond as if Christ is entering the room. Through evangelical chaplains, God's presence calls people to a sense of accountability.

Relationship Building

Evangelical chaplains speak about providing for the needs of the men and women they serve. They emphasize using hospitality to welcome the men and women they serve as strangers, thus creating openings for them to engage with the chaplains. The sense of being cared for *as* a stranger and *by* a stranger is life-changing for many people, and it creates a bond between the individual and the chaplain. Even if they do not belong to the same faith group or religion, individuals often engage with the chaplain and indicate that the chaplain has helped them.

Because of this act of caring, the people often seek out the evangelical chaplain again to address their spiritual needs. The act of coming back to the

21. James William McClendon Jr., *Systematic Theology*, vol. 2, *Doctrine* (Nashville: Abingdon, 1994), 239–40. See also John D. Laing, *In Jesus' Name: Evangelicals and Military Chaplaincy* (Eugene, OR: Resource, 2010), 20.

chaplain demonstrates the power of the relationship that is established in the initial act of caring without pushing a religious agenda. People who do not share the chaplain's beliefs can start a conversation, trusting that their own faith, beliefs, and dignity will be respected. As a result, they may want to know more about why the chaplain is providing care for them, even though they are not of the same religious persuasion. In this encounter, the people receiving care, by asking the chaplain specific questions about their faith, are inviting the chaplain into the sacred spaces of their life. The chaplain can answer these questions in ways that fulfill the commitment of sharing the gospel when invited to do so.

Thus, evangelical chaplains associate their understanding of hospitality with a two-part relationship-building model that potentially opens the door to an opportunity for evangelism. Denominations' desires and the needs of organizations that employ chaplains are met through this model. First, the one seeking care comes to the chaplain with a problem and receives care in relation to this problem. Second, religious or spiritual issues may be addressed in these encounters, in which case the evangelistic desires of the denomination are fulfilled. A guest-host relationship allows for two sides of the chaplains' identity to have their requirements met.

The "Other"

Evangelical chaplains encounter people who are strangers and invite them into sacred spaces, extending hospitality with the hope of eventually bringing the stranger into a faith relationship with Christ. Western philosophy and theology provide an understanding of who this stranger, this "other," is. The simple answer is that strangers or others are people unlike a given person. Evangelical chaplains tend to accept their denomination's definition of who strangers are, which varies from "non-Christians" to "everyone who is not [part of the chaplain's] denomination."[22] The military tends to define the other as the enemy, the terrorist, the traitor, the one who is not part of this community or organization, and this definition is often accepted without question by military chaplains. Outside the military, the other is defined by race, religion, gender, class, or any other difference between people. Chaplains respond to these definitions by accepting the other and incorporating them into the whole. Emmanuel Levinas, however, has expanded the definition of "other" and "Other" to incorporate concepts that put evangelical chaplains' practice of hospitality in tension.

22. Langston, "Establishing the Practical Significance," 223.

Levinas argues that people's egos empty as they engage with the faces of others, who are the people around them.[23] He creates an interplay between the "Other," which appears to be God, and the "other," which people can see in the faces of other human beings. Levinas, a Jewish theologian who lived through World War II, settled in France after the war and rejected much of Western philosophy, saying that the essence of that philosophy was the seedbed for the evil he witnessed during the war. He posits, "My welcoming of the other is the ultimate fact,"[24] as he argues that people have responsibility to the Other, which demands that they care for others. He states, "The Other who dominates us in his transcendence is thus the stranger, the widow, and the orphan, to whom I am obligated."[25] Levinas focuses on the need to allow the Other to be absolutely Other and not a reflection of oneself and one's needs. The face of the Other forces people to look outside themselves in order to encounter the faces of others. In like manner, the face of the other calls people to act ethically and compassionately toward them. They are obligated to respond with care and compassion to those around them.

In recent years, Levinas's stress on the other as obligation has received a new focus, as Europe, Australia, and other parts of the world have begun to struggle with an overwhelming number of immigrants. The postwar period, the time when Levinas began writing, saw one of the largest groupings of refugees that had ever been in Europe. Currently, Europe and the United States are again struggling with "others" who have left their homelands for a better life. Evangelical chaplains often encounter the face of the other in multiple ways that can lead to tension and guilt.

The pluralistic, multicultural environment that exists within chaplain-employing communities makes this understanding of the other a continual challenge for evangelical chaplains. Recently, a person came to me (Mike) for help with a problem, and I welcomed them as a stranger. I wondered, though, if the person were a Christian of the same denomination as me, would I extend the same hospitality, since they would already be saved and part of the Christian community? If so, care could easily have focused strictly on the problem at hand, since the person would not need to return for a possible evangelistic reason. Other questions arise with respect to ethnicity, race, gender, and sexual orientation. The other could come as a married Christian lesbian who is having marital difficulties. In this case, the evangelical chaplain might have concerns

23. Emmanuel Levinas, *Humanism of the Other*, trans. Nidra Poller (Urbana: University of Illinois Press, 2003), 32–33.
24. Emmanuel Levinas, *Totality and Infinity: An Essay on Exteriority*, trans. Alfonso Lingis (Pittsburgh: Duquesne University Press, 1969), 77.
25. Levinas, *Totality and Infinity*, 215.

with both the organization's requirements and the denomination's demands about same-sex marriage. This tension involved in extending hospitality to the other is one that evangelical chaplains have to deal with delicately to continue their ministry.

Thus far we have noted the difficulty in defining the other in chaplaincy settings but have not offered a definition. The determining factor in defining the other comes from the chaplain's christological identity—namely, that of Christ-in-me. This identity defines the other simply as the faces around Christians. Evangelical chaplains seek to imitate Christ in this respect as they extend hospitality to all. The limitations of the denomination and the organization, however, at times limit the hospitality that chaplains can extend. Chaplains can acknowledge that Christ, in Scripture, responds to certain situations with hospitality, but they cannot imitate his action because their denomination or organization refuses to allow an intervention. This tension can cause guilt, shame, and even anger within evangelical chaplains as they are prevented from responding as Christ would have them respond.

Evangelicals differ in their acceptance of people from other denominations, faiths, and groups. Some evangelicals are very exclusive, avoiding people whose faith differs from their own. Evangelical chaplains have a mission from their denominations to evangelize those with whom they come into contact; however, chaplains at times have to work with and respect the practices of people of other religions, causing some strain with people in their denominations who do not understand the chaplain's work.

Dietrich Bonhoeffer, in a book section titled "The Total and Exclusive Claim of Christ," discusses the importance of exclusivism and totality as parallel concepts that are necessary for Christians who wish to follow Christ's example.[26] Commenting on the statements "The one who is not against us is for us" (Mark 9:40) and "Whoever is not with me is against me" (Matt. 12:30), Bonhoeffer explains that each verse has a different claim on the Christian. Jesus speaks the first verse in response to his disciples, who have told a man who was casting out demons in Jesus's name to cease. Jesus says that the man was doing no harm, because, as Bonhoeffer explains,

> wherever the name of Jesus is still spoken, even though it be in ignorance or in the knowledge only of its objective power but without personal obedience, and even though it be only with hesitation and embarrassment, wherever this name is spoken it creates for itself a space to which the revilement of Jesus has no access, a region which still belongs to the power of Christ, where one must

26. Dietrich Bonhoeffer, *Ethics*, ed. Eberhard Bethge, trans. Neville Horton Smith (New York: Touchstone, 1955), 59.

not interfere and hinder but where one must allow the name of Jesus Christ
to do its work. It is an experience of our days that the spoken name of Jesus
alone exercises an unforeseen power; and the effort which it costs to speak this
name is perhaps connected with some faint apprehension of the power which
is inherent in it.[27]

The name of Jesus gives people power and protection, whether or not they are
fully cognizant of that power; thus, those who are not against believers are for
them.

Continuing his argument, Bonhoeffer explains the second verse, which seemingly contradicts the first: "Whoever is not with me is against me" (Matt. 12:30).
He says it is a means of demanding exclusive allegiance to Christ and claims
that the "dangers which threatened the church with inner disintegration and
disruption lay in the neutrality of large numbers of Christians."[28] To counter
this neutrality, Bonhoeffer clearly and directly proposes that having exclusive
allegiance to Christ leads to a knowledge that we are "with Christ."[29]

Bonhoeffer combines the two statements of Christ to present a fullness
to the encounters that Christians have with others in the world. Bonhoeffer
states,

> These two sayings necessarily belong together as the two claims of Jesus Christ,
> the claim to exclusiveness and the claim to totality. The greater the exclusive-
> ness, the greater the freedom. But in isolation the claim to exclusiveness leads
> to fanaticism and to slavery; and in isolation the claim to totality leads to the
> secularization and self-abandonment of the church. The more exclusively we
> acknowledge and confess Christ as our Lord, the more fully the wide range of
> his dominion will be disclosed to us.[30]

Bonhoeffer argues that the more Christians claim exclusive allegiance to Christ
and the more they follow him with their total being, the more freedom they
will have to exercise faith in him and the more they will come to know him.
Evangelical chaplains tend to wrestle with these concepts from Bonhoeffer, but
such chaplains strongly cling to their christological center, sometimes being
fearful to exercise true hospitality among those of other faiths.

Sometimes the trap of exclusivism affects evangelical military chaplains when
they are required to work with imams or mullahs from the Islamic faith in RLE
situations. This chapter has recounted my encounter with the Afghan Hajj and

27. Bonhoeffer, *Ethics*, 59.
28. Bonhoeffer, *Ethics*, 59–60.
29. Bonhoeffer, *Ethics*, 60.
30. Bonhoeffer, *Ethics*, 60.

Islamic affairs minister, which serves as a positive example of encounters with clergy of other faiths. In this encounter, I developed a relationship in which both of us formed a sense of respect for the other and the beliefs that the other held. I realized the Afghan minister's role as host and my own role as guest. This encounter exemplifies Bonhoeffer's concept of holding to exclusivity *with* totality in order to demonstrate allegiance to Christ.

During the Afghan and Iraqi conflicts, RLE required US military chaplains to engage the local imams, mullahs, and other indigenous religious leaders to handle situations as they arose. Senior evangelical military chaplains encountered other evangelical military chaplains who objected to engaging imams. Exemplifying Bonhoeffer's warnings of exclusivity *without* totality, the objecting chaplains cited exclusivist reasons and objected to engaging in an interreligious dialogue, refusing to participate (or participated grudgingly) in public hospitality opportunities that provided no opportunity for evangelism. The tension between perceived denominational issues and the military requirements affected the influence that these chaplains had on the military members around them. The objections from these chaplains limited their view of hospitality and increased tensions due to the perceived arrogance of these American military members and exclusivist Christians who wanted only to be a host and never a guest.

Levinas's concepts of emptying the self and of infinite responsibility to the Other, leading to the natural response, "Here I am,"[31] are in line with Isaiah's "Here I am! Send me" and are also much like Jesus's "Sell all that you have" (Mark 10:21) and "If anyone would come after me, let him deny himself and take up his cross and follow me" (Matt. 16:24). For Levinas, the emptying of the self is the preparatory step for encountering the other. Because of the focus of many evangelical denominations on exclusivism, evangelical chaplains are inclined to regard the other of a multicultural, pluralistic environment as just a person to be saved instead of a guest to be welcomed. This tension exists for chaplains throughout their ministry, especially when they dialogue with their denomination. The same challenge exists in multicultural and international organizations that have evangelical chaplains. Whether working in a hospital, business, park, or sports complex, evangelical chaplains in multicultural settings must decide if they will welcome the other as a guest or turn them away.

In a discussion of current refugee issues, Ross Langmead presents an argument that highlights one of the problems with the Western world's approach

31. Emmanuel Levinas, *Ethics and Infinity: Conversations with Philip Nemo*, trans. Richard A. Cohen (Pittsburgh: Duquesne University Press, 1985), 60.

to hospitality. He argues for an understanding of hospitality as a missiological mandate to seek and share justice and peace, which Christians have learned from the hospitality of God. Langmead speaks of a guest moving into a host position and the host hopefully becoming a guest. At that point, the relationship is viable, and more people become part of the experience. He states, "Perhaps the greatest mystery of Christian hospitality is that in extending God's welcome as a host we so often become the guest, both because our guest becomes our host and because, more profoundly, the Jesus we serve through the poor and hungry (Matt. 25) becomes our host." Langmead describes the divine encounter that results from these engagements.[32] The binary of host and guest becomes a confusing concept at this point. When is one a guest? When is one a host? If a host creates a safe and sacred space for a guest but the guest is Christ—who brought the safe and sacred space—then who is the host and who is the guest? This example reveals a weakness in the host-guest binary that will be discussed in the following section.

Chaplains often view themselves as hosts to those in need. The caring, comforting, and serving roles that they perform reinforce the view of the host position. If, however, evangelical chaplains truly seek to extend hospitality as Jesus did, they have to strive to empty themselves and allow Christ to work through them as they stand between the profane and the holy. This tension is at the heart of chaplaincy.

People who come to a military, first responder, or prison chaplain with a problem can arrive with literal and figurative blood on their hands. Standing between the profane and the sacred, the human and the divine, the chaplain may have to welcome the other who has just taken one or more lives— sometimes those of innocents. Attending to the wounds of the other, related as tales of urban battles and killings, of death and loss, of wrecks and shootings, chaplains encounter the profane interlocked with the sacred. How can chaplains embrace this participation in the profane, the evil of this world? Military members, first responders, and others in these circumstances come to chaplains as foreigners—people who are foreign to themselves and those they have left at home. Chaplains offer care and comfort that is centered in Christ's hospitality and not in evangelism. Christ offers a radical hospitality that stems from the Father in heaven and often removes the roles of host and stranger from consideration, and the chaplain becomes a "vessel" for this hospitality.

32. Ross Langmead, "Refugees as Guests and Hosts: Towards a Theology of Mission among Refugees and Asylum Seekers," *Exchange* 43 (2014): 29–47, http://doi.org/10.1163/1572543X -12341301.

An Ethic of Hospitality

Extending hospitality as care and comfort becomes an invitation to God's banquet of salvation. As bearers of the presence of God, evangelical chaplains view themselves as hosts welcoming guests so that they can provide care and comfort for people as the good Samaritan did for the wounded traveler. Evangelical chaplains have to be aware of the dichotomy between host and guest that can easily pull them from God's banquet table to their own table, as they focus on their roles as hosts, bearers of God's presence, Americans, military officers, evangelical Christians, head chaplains, and so on.

In interviews from the Langston study, unlimited hospitality was shown to be continual for evangelical chaplains.[33] Andrew Shepherd summarizes the struggle as follows:

> What are the implications of this doctrine of sin for our understanding of human personhood and identity? While created by the hospitable God, and designed to participate in the communion of the divine persons by receiving and offering the gift of hospitality, as sinful people there appears an inward drive, an inherent bias, to seek to comprehend and control what is Other than ourselves. In doing so, not only do we do damage to the human—and non-human—Other, but we also damage ourselves. But is the human experience to be understood as an unending tension between our desire for experiencing genuine hospitality, and our tendencies to overcome and devour the Other, to assimilate them to the Self?[34]

The struggle to provide hospitality for the other can lead chaplains to the self-focused role of host. However, focusing on emptying themselves daily, as Christ instructed and as Levinas encourages, allows chaplains to focus on Christ-in-me as host. When the other comes to the evangelical chaplain, the chaplain provides a safe space that becomes sacred because the chaplain is the bearer of the presence of God. If, however, the chaplain focuses on the other as the Other—that is, as Christ—then the chaplain becomes the guest of the holy. The safe space becomes a sacred space because of the presence of the chaplain (Christ-in-me) and the guest (Christ). Abraham and Sarah entertained angels unaware (Gen. 18:1–22; Heb. 13:2), and the men on the road to Emmaus provided hospitality to Christ without being aware of who he was (Luke 24:13–35). In like manner, evangelical chaplains focusing on the other can experience the Other in their presence to avoid the pitfalls of ego and arrogance.

33. Langston, "Establishing the Practical Significance."
34. Andrew Shepherd, *The Gift of the Other: Levinas, Derrida, and a Theology of Hospitality* (Eugene, OR: Pickwick, 2014), 128.

Albert Schweitzer provides an excellent summation of a focus on the other. In a passage based on Luke 5:1–11, he writes:

> He comes to us as One unknown, without a name, as of old, by the lakeside. He came to those men who knew Him not. He speaks to us the same words: "Follow thou me!" and sets us to the tasks which He has to fulfill for our time. He commands. And to those who obey Him, whether they be wise or simple, He will reveal Himself in the toils, the conflicts, the sufferings which they shall pass through in His fellowship, and, as an ineffable mystery, they shall learn in their own experience Who He is.[35]

Thus, it is the bearer of the presence of God and Christ whom the believer meets. The safe space becomes sacred as much because of the guests (i.e., others), who reveal themselves at a later point to be Christ, as because of the host (chaplain), bearer of the presence of God. The chaplains within the Langston study often mentioned that they were blessed by their encounter with the other. Christ revealed himself to them through the face of the other.

In today's world, where military chaplains may encounter violence through terrorists or other people, they struggle with offering hospitality to those who have vowed to eradicate them. During the war in Iraq, chaplains were targeted for capture and execution. They were not welcome in many Middle Eastern countries because of the people's Islamic beliefs. Thus, the act of entertaining the other through RLE was a threat to the lives of chaplains. As Amos Yong discusses, Jesus's radical hospitality led to his death, and if chaplains are to follow him, then the hospitality they offer to the other has to encompass the same possibility. Divine hospitality is offered to people through the death of Jesus Christ, and chaplains are called to offer hospitality in the same way that Christ did.[36]

Evangelical chaplains have to accept the limitations that come from their denominations, their organizations, and their own physical, mental, and emotional capabilities. This balance is an ongoing concern for chaplains as they seek to provide for all needs but find themselves limited by their denomination and organization. In this sense, chaplains often feel that they have not fulfilled the hospitality requirements that Christ has set forth. As the chaplains throughout the Langston study reported, the spiritual disciplines of prayer, Bible study, quiet time, and fellowship with other chaplains assisted them in determining the limitations of the hospitality they offered.[37]

35. Albert Schweitzer, *The Quest of the Historical Jesus* (New York: Macmillan, 1956), 403.
36. Amos Yong, *Hospitality and the Other: Pentecost, Christian Practices, and the Neighbor* (Maryknoll, NY: Orbis Books, 2008), 131.
37. Langston, "Establishing the Practical Significance."

Arthur Sutherland discusses "seeing" as a way to imitate Christ through hospitality. In order to respond in a hospitable way, one must be "conditioned to seeing."[38] In the Gospels, Jesus sees illness, hurt, and pain in the people around him. Sutherland emphasizes that Jesus does not set out to see—that is, to find someone to heal or help. "Jesus' hospitality to the displaced and distressed is not calculated but casual. It is as though Jesus lived his life as a present participle: as he is going, Jesus saw."[39] Chaplains report that as they move among the people of their organizations, they see their needs. This type of casual hospitality—which involves seeing as they are moving through an area—is hospitality that comes from Christ-in-me. Nurturing this response is a way to be mindful of hospitality.

Bonhoeffer's ethic of exclusivity with totality guides evangelical chaplains in their attempts to develop an ethic of hospitality amid the tensions that are part of their identities.

> As Jesus' helpers, the effectiveness of the disciples is grounded in the clear commandment of their Lord. It is not left up to them to decide how to undertake and understand their work. The work of Christ they are to do forces the messengers completely into the will of Jesus. Blessed are they who have such an authority given them for their office and who are freed from their own discretion and calculation![40]

This christological approach to offering hospitality provides a focus for evangelical chaplains as they practice their belief that God has offered hospitality to Christians and that they, in turn, can share this hospitality in his kingdom work.

Conclusion

Evangelical chaplains' identities are formed by their evangelical theology, their denominations, and the organizations they are serving, yet one of their primary focuses is caring for, comforting, and serving the people they encounter. Like Jesus, evangelical chaplains move through their organizations, offering a casual hospitality that invites people to seek out the chaplain for care. Evangelical chaplains' vocation of caring for those around them allows them to encounter

38. Arthur Sutherland, *I Was a Stranger: A Christian Theology of Hospitality* (Nashville: Abingdon, 2006), 78.

39. Sutherland, *I Was a Stranger*, 70–79.

40. Dietrich Bonhoeffer, *The Cost of Discipleship*, trans. R. H. Fuller, rev. ed. (New York: Macmillan, 1963).

the other, whose presence brings the chaplain into an encounter with the divine Other through the ethic of hospitality that chaplains extend. Thus, Christ-in-me leads to the Holy Spirit touching those around the chaplain, which in turn leads to the chaplain experiencing God through the work of caring, comforting, and serving. Christ-in-me leads evangelical chaplains to deny themselves, take up their crosses daily, and follow Christ (Matt. 16:24).

10

Chaplaincy Leadership

Leadership is key to the service that all chaplains are called to do by the Lord and hired to do by their employers. One can have all the required education and skills in preaching, teaching, counseling, and caring, but without the ability to lead well, the chaplain will fall short of the goal. Often, chaplains strive to climb the ladder of success but then find themselves struggling to get others to follow them. This chapter discusses the foundations of leadership and presents four areas of concern every chaplain needs to focus on to become an effective leader: calling, character, competence, and connection. Additionally, this chapter introduces three models of leadership: transformational, relational, and servant leadership.

The Foundations of Chaplaincy Leadership

The Bible shows that excellent leadership should be faithful to God and the Scriptures, guided by the Holy Spirit, visionary of his kingdom, wise in discernment and decisions, ethical in its practices, and personal in its application. Most modern scholars writing on the topic indicate that leadership is all about influence. Peter Northouse writes, "Leadership is a process whereby an individual influences a group of individuals to achieve a common goal."[1] Another definition takes the concept further, stating that "leadership is the ability to influence others in a way that inspires them to change, transform and orient their knowledge, skills, abilities, focused on achieving the stated objectives

1. Northouse, *Leadership*, 6.

of the organization."[2] Paul Hersey, Kenneth Blanchard, and Dewey Johnson describe leadership as "any attempt to influence the behavior of an individual or group."[3] James M. Burns says that leadership is "a relationship that raises the vision, values, and aspirations of both the leader and the follower to new levels of expectations."[4] Walter Wright opines that leadership is "a relationship in which one person seeks to influence the thoughts, behaviors, beliefs, or values of another person."[5] All of these definitions agree that leadership is a process of influencing others to follow or get in step with a certain pattern or direction in order to accomplish common goals and missions.

Calling

The chaplain's calling is vital to their leadership. The chaplain's call is first a call to follow Christ and then a call to lead others as an undershepherd of Jesus. Jesus illustrates this principle when he rebukes Peter for trying to usurp his authority and then turns to his disciples and says, "If anyone would come after me, let him deny himself and take up his cross and follow me" (Matt. 16:24). In this passage, it becomes clear that following Jesus means an all-embracing commitment, even if that includes death. Complete allegiance to Christ is foundational to becoming a leader for Christ. The idea that chaplaincy might be a good career choice for any other reason than to follow Christ wholeheartedly is ill-conceived.

A commitment to follow Christ will result in a search for clarity as to God's specific direction for one's life. The Scriptures instruct, "Trust in the LORD with all your heart, and do not lean on your own understanding. In all your ways acknowledge him, and he will make straight your paths" (Prov. 3:5–6). James reminds his readers that life is too short to squander time attempting to accomplish one's will and that doing so will cause one to miss God's will (James 4:13–15). Once an individual chooses to follow the Lord no matter what, God will direct their path and calling. This commitment to Christ is the beginning point for a call to chaplaincy.

The call to lead others as a chaplain flows not just from a heart's desire to follow Christ but also from an overwhelming desire to help others know the love of God and experience the joy of serving him. Leading people to Christ when invited to do so is the most important kind of leadership a chaplain will

2. Michael W. Langston, "Leadership" (lecture, Naval Chaplaincy School and Center, Fort Jackson, SC, September 15, 2010).
3. Paul Hersey, Kenneth H. Blanchard, and Dewey E. Johnson, *Management of Organizational Behavior*, 6th ed. (Boston: Pearson College, 2007), 5.
4. James MacGregor Burns, *Leadership* (New York: Harper, 1978), 9.
5. Wright, *Relational Leadership*, 8.

ever engage in. To leave a person in their sins without seeking to share the re-demptive good news of Jesus misses the mark of the chaplain's high calling to bear the presence and message of Christ. Therefore, a call to lead as a chaplain is a call to engage, ethically, in evangelism.

Finally, a call to chaplain leadership is a call to a sacrificial life. It is a call to serve others and not oneself. It is a call to be humble and hold others in higher esteem than oneself (Phil. 2:3–4). Many occupations are about seeking one's own good and gain, but the calling of a chaplain is to sacrifice one's life for God and others. It is a call to lose one's life in Christ and to live a sacrificial life for the glory of God (Matt. 16:25). It may be a call into harm's way, tragic situations, emergen-cies, and painful settings. Even so, the chaplain is called to the "Valley of Baca" (i.e., the "valley of tears," Ps. 84:4–7) to bring the hope and healing of Christ.

Character

The chaplain's character is vital to leading as a chaplain, and this standard is established by certain biblical requirements. The individual who is "blame-less" (1 Tim. 3:10), "above reproach" (3:2), and "well thought of by outsiders" (3:7) is morally fit to be a chaplain. The moral requirements of the chaplain are high but necessary, as chaplains have the opportunity to lead vast numbers of people in secular and sacred situations. Sometimes people have the idea that if a person is not morally qualified to be a pastor, then maybe they should become a chaplain. This idea is entirely incorrect. If a person is called to be a chaplain, this person is called to be a minister and needs to have the kind of godly character that represents Christ well to the world.

Evangelical chaplains seek to emulate the character of Christ in their leader-ship. The pathway to such character begins with salvation and a total surrender to the will of God (Rom. 12:1). Once this foundation is laid, the chaplain needs to seek a transformed mind (Rom. 12:2). The transformation of one's mind does not happen at the moment of salvation. When one receives Christ as Lord and Savior, that person becomes a new person in Christ with a new nature (2 Cor. 5:17), and the new nature brings new desires for Christlikeness. A transformed mind is foundational to godly character and requires a daily commitment of practicing various spiritual disciplines. These disciplines should include Scrip-ture reading and memorization, meditation, prayer, worship, and journaling. God's Word is powerful and is the key agent in acquiring a Christlike mind, so chaplains should immerse themselves in it. Further, meditating on what God declares to be true and beautiful will assist one in developing Christlike think-ing and character (Phil. 4:8).

Evangelical chaplains are best able to be "the salt of the earth" when rooted in Christlike character (Matt. 5:13). In context, Jesus is calling his disciples to serve as preservatives of God's righteousness for an ungodly world. Likewise, God calls chaplains to be of such character. Being a preserving agent in a culture that is quickly rotting is not an easy task but is indeed what God expects of his chaplains. With the spiritual decline of American culture, it is not popular to speak up and declare God's standards of righteousness, whether in relation to marriage, family, or gender. Doing so might lead to persecution or rejection or prevent job promotion. In fact, Jesus warns of such persecution right before he encourages the disciples to be the salt of the earth (Matt. 5:10–12). Nevertheless, God calls chaplains of Christlike character to speak up and declare God's standards as true and right.

Evangelical chaplains are best able to be "the light of the world" when rooted in Christlike character as well (Matt. 5:14). Chaplains seek to be the light of Christ by bearing the presence and message of Christ. Yet they are sometimes expected to hide the light of Christ, particularly in pluralistic, secular settings. This obscuring of the light might look like avoiding the name of Jesus in public prayers or deciding not to share the gospel in hospital rooms. Lots of people have ideas about how Christian chaplains should minister, but the only opinion that matters is God's, and he has made clear that he wants his name and message to be declared to the world. Chaplains of Christlike character will not put a covering over the light of Christ as they seek to bear his presence and his Word.

Sometimes chaplains are expected not only to hide their light but also to stifle the flame. They may be encouraged to ignore their doctrine, practice of ministry, ordination vows, and endorser's requirements. In these situations, the chaplain of godly character will seek wisdom from the Lord to serve and speak as Christ would in the same situation and to do all for the glory of God (Col. 3:17). God cannot deny himself, and no chaplain should deny him either. The chaplain of godly character will lead others in truth and righteousness with the fear of God and not men (Matt. 10:28; Acts 5:28).

Competence

Preparation for chaplain leadership begins with a call to follow Jesus, is followed by a commitment to Christlike character, and proceeds with a desire to prepare to lead. Formal training, ministry experience, godly mentors, and personal study are invaluable in becoming a competent chaplain leader. Competence in ministry is vital to leading as a chaplain, no matter the type of chaplaincy. A lack of competence will leave needy individuals without effective chaplain care and may destroy the chaplain's reputation and opportunities for future chaplain ministry.

The best examples of competent leadership are found in the Scriptures, with Jesus being the supreme example. No discerning believer would question Jesus's competence to lead. Knowing Jesus has complete knowledge and understanding makes trusting and following him easy. On a lesser plane, the same point might be made of a competent, well-educated, experienced chaplain. A professional who has taken time to complete seminary and to apply that formal education to ministry is a person who can more readily be trusted and followed.

The need for competence is a reason that chaplain endorsers and employers have educational and experience requirements. Completing a degree is important, but it alone does not make one competent. Experience is equally important in gaining competence as a chaplain. Sometimes individuals complete an MDiv degree and feel they are ready to serve as a chaplain, but the military and most healthcare systems require the person to put the acquired knowledge into practice before they can attain full acceptance as a competent qualified professional. As stated in chapter 6, the military and most endorsers require at least two years of full-time pastoral experience following seminary, and healthcare chaplains are normally required to complete four units of CPE and be board-certified.

Chapter 7 has already discussed mentors, which are an invaluable resource for growing in competence. They can provide experiential wisdom to help aspiring or new chaplains lead well, can assist in applying scriptural principles to resolve ethical dilemmas, and can provide practical insights to help the protégé avoid pitfalls and stay on course.

Finally, the personal study of Scripture and Christian authors will undergird chaplains' constant desire to improve their competency and serve well as a chaplain. There is no substitute for the daily study of God's Word (2 Tim. 2:15). Aspiring and new chaplains should allow God's Word to permeate their minds and guide their words and actions. They should make it a lamp to their feet and a light to their path (Ps. 119:105) as they grow in knowledge and competence for the glory of God.

Connection

The chaplain's ability to connect with others is vital to leading well as a chaplain. A person who is unable to relate to people will not be effective in leading others. The ability to connect has become known as emotional intelligence, or EQ. However, from a biblical basis, one may see the ability to connect with others as relational wisdom, or RW.[6] This type of wisdom is rooted in God,

6. Walter C. Wright, *Relational Leadership: A Biblical Model for Influence and Service*, 2nd ed. (Downers Grove, IL: IVP Books, 2009), 34; Peter Northouse, *Leadership: Theory and Practice*, 9th ed. (Los Angeles: SAGE, 2022), 38.

who at his core is an emotional, spiritual being in relationship with himself, Father, Son, and Holy Spirit. In his divine wisdom, he has chosen to create men and women in his image (Gen. 1:26–27), and this creation in the divine image entails the ability to relate to God and one another emotionally and spiritually. Thus, relational wisdom is essential in seeking to lead.

The chaplain's leadership challenge is to emotionally relate to *everyone*. Thankfully, the Holy Spirit is readily available to direct one's emotions (Gal. 5:16). Daniel Goleman, Richard Boyatzis, and Annie McKee describe emotional leadership as "primal leadership" and say that a leader must tap into their emotions and seek to resonate with the emotions of their followers. Good leaders ignite the passions of their followers to accomplish the mission.[7] From a biblical perspective, we understand that God is the source of our emotions and that he desires to control those emotions through his Spirit. To accomplish this goal, the Lord calls followers to crucify "the flesh with its passions and desires" and to "live by the Spirit" (Gal. 5:24–25). Ken Sande challenges Christian leaders to exercise their emotions with relational wisdom and to seek to connect with people by exercising God's love and care for them.[8]

To connect and lead people well, the chaplain needs to follow Jesus's example of engaging emotionally with people by loving them selflessly (John 21:15–17) and befriending them wholeheartedly (Luke 7:34–50). I (Steve) remember, during my first assignment, being called out by another chaplain for giving him the cold shoulder. He said, "I've been trying to reach my hand out to you in friendship, only to be emotionally shut out. Jesus doesn't do that!" Following the shock of being bluntly confronted, I humbly admitted he was right, and I apologized. Since that defining moment, I have sought to connect emotionally with every person and, like Jesus, to open my heart to them (1 Pet. 1:22). To serve and lead well, the chaplain will be wise to follow Jesus's example and to lead with their heart, to love selflessly, and to befriend wholeheartedly (John 11:33–35).

Leadership Styles

Leadership styles form a continuum, ranging from the most controlling (transactional) to the most freewheeling and open (laissez-faire). The five leadership styles are transactional, relational, servant, transformational, and laissez-faire (see fig. 10.1).

7. Daniel Goleman, Richard Boyatzis, and Annie McKee, *Primal Leadership: Unleashing the Power of Emotional Intelligence* (Boston: Harvard Business School Press, 2012).
8. Ken Sande, "Discovering Relational Wisdom 2.0," YouTube video, 2:00:06, posted by FOCL-Online, https://youtu.be/1P_X_cF2r4s.

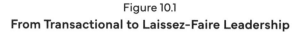

Figure 10.1
From Transactional to Laissez-Faire Leadership

| Transactional | Transformational | Relational | Servant | Laissez-Faire |
| Leadership | Leadership | Leadership | Leadership | Leadership |

Adapted from Bernard M. Bass and Ronald E. Riggo,
Transformational Leadership, 2nd ed. (New York: Psychology Press, 2006), 9–11.

The leadership continuum illustrates the complexity and the distinct characteristics within each style. On the far left is transactional leadership, which describes a very autocratic, authoritarian leader. The followers have few choices, and the choices they do have are not necessarily aligned with their needs, their interests, or their desire to be engaged by the leader. On the far right of the continuum is laissez-faire leadership. This term describes a carefree style of leading. It creates an almost free-for-all environment, and followers do as they think best in the performance of work activities.

The three leadership styles in the middle of the continuum are all focused on the leader inspiring the individuals by exemplifying positive traits. Each style includes a sense of strong involvement in the relational, caring, and serving aspects of leadership. These attributes increase the willingness of people to follow the leader. These three middle leadership styles fit well in chaplaincy. While each one has its drawbacks, the combined positive aspects of the three leadership styles give the leader a powerful skill set that leads to positive outcomes. Each of these leadership styles is discussed and developed in more detail in the following sections.

Transformational Leadership

In any given workplace, a chaplain might find evidence of low morale, which many people attribute to poor leadership in those workplaces. Leadership is, in reality, only one factor; many things contribute to employee morale, such as pay, organizational structure, supervisory support, community relationships, and manpower.[9] Indeed, keeping morale up within any organization is almost

9. Olivia Johnson, "8 Ways Police Leaders Can Improve Morale," Police1, September 27, 2019, https://www.police1.com/police-leader/articles/8-ways-police-leaders-can-improve-morale-0uISJ wQrAdGSWc0e.

a Sisyphean task, involving so many moving parts that people find they cannot change it. Yet leadership problems are a factor, and chaplains can help in this regard. They have the unique ability to talk to every person at every level, from the CEO and president to the department head, supervisor, and line chief, all the way down to the lowliest rookie just entering the workforce. Chaplains are gifted in their ability to listen, are bound by both civil and religious law to maintain confidentiality, and are often able to give advice that is taken seriously by those with whom they have spent time building a relationship. Through the principles of transformational leadership, a chaplain has the potential to influence professionals and the workforce in such a way as to effect change and improve the overall morale of an organization.

Northouse explains transformational leadership's main focus as being "concerned with emotions, values, ethics, standards, and long-term goals. It includes assessing followers' motives, satisfying their needs, and treating them as full human beings."[10] This style of leadership involves the leader—in this case, the chaplain—exerting their influence in a way that causes followers to reach their full potential and motivates followers beyond the expected. This transformation "occurs when one or more persons engage with others in such a way that leaders and followers raise one another to higher levels of motivation and morality."[11] Northouse lists four factors of transformational leadership: idealized influence, inspirational motivation,, intellectual stimulation, and individualized consideration.[12]

The first of these factors, again, is *idealized influence*. This is "the emotional component of leadership." In this factor, the leader sets an example that is so strong that the followers have a driving desire to imitate what they see and identify with. Through their charisma, the leader can effect change in individuals simply by providing a strong guiding example. The second factor, *inspirational motivation*, "is descriptive of leaders who communicate high expectations to followers, inspiring them through motivation to become committed to and a part of the shared vision in the organization." This factor inspires followers to be dedicated to the mission of the organization they are a part of and encouraged by the progress that is being made. The third factor, *intellectual stimulation*, "includes leadership that stimulates followers to be creative and innovative and to challenge their own beliefs and values as well as those of the leader and the organization." Through such stimulation, the leader encourages and facilitates the improvement of the followers to inspire their efforts to come up with new and unique ways of accomplishing the organization's mission.

10. Northouse, *Leadership*, 185.
11. Burns, *Leadership*, 20.
12. Northouse, *Leadership*, 190–95.

Finally, *individualized consideration* is "representative of leaders who provide a supportive climate in which they listen carefully to the individual needs of followers. Leaders act as coaches and advisers while trying to assist followers in becoming fully actualized." This factor is a very important aspect of discipleship in the Christian faith: a mentor disciples the follower and helps them realize their full potential as a follower of Christ. So, too, does the transformational leader mentor, encourage, and educate followers so that they can realize their full potential within the organization.[13]

Chaplains can use this model of leadership to facilitate change and encourage the people they are serving. For example, by setting an example as a person who has integrity and holds to the organization's values in the face of confusing and traumatic circumstances, the public safety chaplain can inspire law enforcement officers to maintain their integrity and values, both personal ones and those inherent in the badge, under the most intense personal and professional pressures. Chaplains can encourage officers to remain dedicated to the organization by broadening their view of situations through additional insights from command staff or from the community. The chaplain can also provide officers with ideas and challenge their presuppositions about various circumstances so as to inspire them to think innovatively in tackling problems, both internally and externally. And finally, the chaplain can spend time mentoring and building relationships with individual officers so that the officers feel validated in their professional lives and have a safe place to vent to someone who truly understands, is required to keep their confidence, and can provide those special insights that can come only from a clergyperson.

The Christian faith is based on the idea of transforming lives and the greater world. The very act of making disciples of all nations is an effort of transformational leadership: it is the mission of discipling and mentoring individuals so that their lives are transformed to be more and more like Christ (Matt. 28:19–20). As Robert Coleman articulates, the Christian transformational leadership model involves individualized consideration as modeled by Christ in his selection of the apostles and his personal involvement in their development (see, e.g., Matt. 4:18–22).[14] He provides an example of how to do ministry that will transform the lives of those one ministers to by teaching the Word (e.g., Matt. 5–7); healing the sick (e.g., Matt. 8:1–4, 14–17); reaching out to outcasts to inspire them to change their lives (Matt. 9:9–13); dedicating time in prayer, both alone (Matt. 14:23; Mark 1:35; 6:46; Luke 5:16; 6:12) and in public; and teaching disciples

---

13. Northouse, *Leadership*, 192–94.

14. Robert E. Coleman, "Preparing Transformational Leadership the Jesus Way," *Knowing and Doing*, Summer 2008, https://www.cslewisinstitute.org/wp-content/uploads/KD-2008-Summer -Preparing-Transformational-Leadership-the-Jesus-Wa-649.pdf.

how to pray (Matt. 5:5–15). Christ presents himself as the purest example of transformational leadership.

How, though, does the chaplain use transformational leadership to change the morale of an entire department when morale is dependent on so many factors? Through the practice of idealized influence, the chaplain sets an example for the personnel to follow, from the newest hire all the way to the senior leadership of the organization. By holding on to their values, by being uncompromising, and by holding themselves to a high standard, the chaplain can influence and inspire the people within the organization to improve their own standards and to uphold an uncompromising commitment to their own personal and professional values. The chaplain uses inspirational motivation to challenge the workforce personnel across the organizational levels to be better members of their departments as a whole and helps them see that if they can be a better workforce, they will make the organization better, which will in turn increase morale. Through intellectual stimulation, the chaplain can encourage the workers to improve themselves and facilitate this improvement. The chaplain can direct individuals to various educational and training programs that will improve their résumés and help them get promotions, thus improving their job performance and increasing upward mobility in the organization. This, too, will increase morale. Finally, through individualized consideration, the chaplain can build relationships with the whole workforce, and through these relationships the chaplain can mentor and disciple others and help them become better leaders and simply better men and women in general. By increasing the number of these relationships, the chaplain can influence more and more of the organization toward improvement, thus increasing morale across the board. The influence of the chaplain through the ministry of presence is far-reaching, bringing about change and improvement to the organization through careful, caring ministry and friendships.

Relational Leadership

Another style of leadership that is conducive to chaplaincy is relational leadership. Relational leadership is a compassionate, encouraging, and ethical way to lead others. Chaplains build relationships with the people they are serving, who in turn follow them and are influenced by their leadership qualities. These leadership qualities and components are addressed in the following paragraphs.

Basics of Relational Leadership

A relational style of leadership means leading from the bottom up in that the leader will guide others by fostering relationships, practicing a personal kind of management, and caring for others. Leaders can act as a model in nurturing relationships, being humble, and empowering teams. This leadership style is "a relational, ethical process of people attempting to accomplish positive change."[15] Susan R. Komives, Nance Lucas, and Timothy R. McMahon describe relational leaders as inclusive, empowering, ethical, and having purpose.[16] "Inclusivity" refers to the knowledge of one's role, listening skills, interpersonal skills, and attitudes that are relational. Empowering others is the way relational leaders encourage people and come alongside them as helpers to support them in their drive toward a common goal. Leaders are "co-creators in the help process."[17] Knowledge alone is not enough for a leader; it is a clear shared goal that empowers leaders to influence those they lead. The purpose of leadership is to maintain ethical, quality relationships while seeking positive changes within people and within the workplace. Relational leaders find their purpose within the process of producing change, as well as in implementing that change. Influencing others toward a clear vision produces purpose within the process.

Relationships are paramount in the human experience, and the same is true for ministry. Chaplains and pastors share some characteristics when dealing with people in their ministries. "We might not always like specific congregants, but our quest to love them is essential to our well-being and effectiveness as a pastor and to our ability to bring out the best in our partnerships within our congregations."[18] "Healthy ministry is a matter of intentionality and mindfulness" when dealing with relationships vocationally and privately.[19] There is a strong need for all humans, especially those in relational ministry, to be needed by others. That is why self-care, which allows people to replenish their energy and maintain a balance in life, is essential for those in relational ministry.[20]

The Scriptural Foundation of Relational Ministry

God created man and woman in his image (Gen. 1:26–27), a design rooted in his triune nature. Scripture reveals that God's triune nature is relational among

15. Susan R. Komives, Nance Lucas, and Timothy R. McMahon, *Exploring Leadership for College Students Who Want to Make a Difference*, 3rd ed. (Hoboken, NJ: Jossey-Bass, 2013), 14.

16. Komives, Lucas, and McMahon, *Exploring Leadership*, 2.

17. Komives, Lucas, and McMahon, *Exploring Leadership*, 115–19.

18. Bruce Epperly, *The Center in the Cyclone: Twenty-First Century Clergy Self-Care* (Lanham, MD: Rowman & Littlefield, 2014), 147–48.

19. Epperly, *Center in the Cyclone*, 148.

20. Roy M. Oswald, *Clergy Self-Care: Finding a Balance for Effective Ministry* (Washington, DC: Alban Institute, 1991), 14.

Father, Son, and Holy Spirit (Luke 3:21–22; 2 Cor. 13:14). God created Adam
and Eve to be in relationship with him. Further, God created Adam and Eve to
be in relationship with one another (Gen. 2:18, 21–25). Sin broke the relationship
with God and with one another (Gen. 3:1–6). That alienation remains to this day.
Nevertheless, God sent Jesus to restore the relationship (John 3:16). God values
relationships above all else, which was made clear on the cross and through the
Great Commandment, to love God and to love one another (Matt. 22:36–39).

Scripture is replete with examples in which God heals and reconciles relationships that had been lost. His triumphs give us hope that relational restoration
is possible. Chaplains not only exude this hope but put it into action as they
build transformative relationships in the power of the Holy Spirit (Ps. 147:3).

A relational-ministry model cannot exclude the ministry of presence, which is
"characterized by suffering alongside the hurting multitudes and the oppressed.
It is here we see a being rather than a doing or telling."[21] This model is remi-
niscent of Job's friends sitting with him in silence for seven days (Job 2:11–13).
They meet Job where he is, just as Jesus meets all people where they are. Jesus
keeps the twelve disciples close, and he ministers with them and encourages
them as a team in a relational model of leadership. Building a relationship is
how God enacts salvation through Christ Jesus. An eternal relationship with
God is a gift of grace, but it required that Jesus die on the cross.

God works in people's lives through relationships to comfort, encourage, and
give more abundant purpose. God's way of loving comes through a personal
relationship. He originally intended for humans to walk with him in the cool-
ness of the evening in the garden (Gen. 3:8). But by their sins, people broke
the relationship, and since that time God has planned, through his redemptive
purposes and by establishing faith relationships in and through Jesus, to restore
their right relationship to him. Relational leadership is essential in ministry
because it is vital to the way God communicates his support for us.

Servant Leadership

The servant leadership model was developed by Robert Greenleaf and first articulated in his book *The Servant as Leader*, published in 1970.[22] It was here that
the term "servant leadership" was popularized, and Greenleaf's work started
a new leadership focus.

21. Winnifred F. Sullivan, *A Ministry of Presence: Chaplaincy, Spiritual Care, and the Law* (Chicago: University of Chicago Press, 2014), 178.
22. Robert K. Greenleaf, *The Servant as Leader* (1970; repr., South Orange, NJ: Greenleaf
Center for Servant Leadership, 2015).

The concept of servant leadership is vital for successful chaplain ministries. It can seem disorienting because the two words that make up its title seem contradictory, yet the term was coined with reference to the example Jesus gives when he washes his disciples' feet (John 13:1–17). In verse 15, he challenges his disciples, "I have given you an example, that you also should do just as I have done to you." Therefore, this is an area of ministry in which chaplains should want to excel.

A servant leader is a person of character who puts people first, is a skilled communicator, is a compassionate collaborator, demonstrates foresight, is a systems thinker, and leads with moral authority. These descriptions are also known as the seven pillars of servant leadership. Within each of these pillars, there are several competencies that the chaplain must have, and these competencies will manifest themselves in several attributes that are observable by those the chaplain works with.

Servant leadership may sound like a strange concept to someone who has not been exposed to Jesus's teachings. Jesus taught by his words and his example that a true leader leads by being a servant to all (Matt. 20:25–28). In contrast to many leadership styles, a servant leader's mission is to lead by serving. Servant leadership is conducted by example and is very concerned with personal character.

The Culture and the People

The concept of a leader who performs his leadership through service is foreign to most contexts and cultures. It was foreign to the culture that Jesus lived and taught in, as evidenced by his comparing the authoritarian leadership of the gentile rulers to servant leadership in Matthew 20:25–28. A countercultural paradigm such as servant leadership is an asset to the chaplain in ministry because it draws attention to the dichotomy between the power structures in most organizations in which a chaplain might serve and the person-centered approach of the ministry of presence.

A leader is only effective as a leader when they have people following them. One antecedent condition of servant leadership is the receptivity of those who are following. Some people are more willing to follow than others. The chaplain will have to determine the receptivity of those they are called to lead through personal relationship and observation. Certain individuals will require more time and effort to lead effectively.

Behavioral Traits of Servant Leadership

Seven leadership behaviors are essential for the servant leader:

1. Conceptualizing—that is, understanding and explaining the vision and mission of the organization

2. Offering emotional healing—caring about the concerns of others and taking the time to address them

3. Putting followers first—prioritizing the needs of followers over one's own

4. Helping followers grow and succeed—knowing others' personal and professional goals and encouraging them in their pursuits in order that they might succeed

5. Behaving ethically—having a high ethical code that drives the desire to do the right thing in the right way

6. Empowering—building up the confidence of followers and providing opportunities for them to succeed and be self-sufficient

7. Creating value for the community—connecting what the leader does at the organization with what they do for the community[23]

The chaplain who practices these servant-leader characteristics will be a highly effective leader who follows in Christ's footsteps within the workplace.

Putting followers first is likely the most important behavioral trait for servant leadership. Attending to the well-being of others is at the very heart of what it means to be a proper servant. A leader who holds others in higher esteem than themselves (Phil. 2:3–5) will craft a vision for the organization and the future, effectively heal emotional wounds, encourage followers to grow and succeed, behave ethically, empower those working around them, and create value for the organization and community.

Characteristics of the Servant Leader

Servant leaders demonstrate the following characteristics:

1. Listening—hearing and being receptive to what others have to say

2. Empathy—standing in the shoes of another person and attempting to see the world from their point of view

3. Healing—caring about the personal well-being of their followers

4. Awareness—being in tune with one's physical, social, and political environments

5. Persuasion—using clear and persistent communication to convince others to change

6. Conceptualization— thoroughly understanding the organization and its mission

23. Northouse, *Leadership*, 261–63.

7. Foresight—making reasonable and insightful predictions about the future

8. Stewardship—taking responsibility for the leadership role entrusted to the leader

9. Commitment to the growth of the people—helping individuals grow personally and professionally

10. Community building—fostering the development of the community

In our opinion, empathy is the most significant characteristic for servant leaders because they must be able to understand the struggles of others. A well-developed sense of empathy informs and develops many of the other characteristics listed here. A servant leader who is highly empathetic will be an active listener, concerned about the healing of others, aware of the needs of others and therefore more aware of themselves, persuasive in a nonmanipulative way, intentional about stewarding well and knowing the impact of stewardship on others, committed to people's growth, and effective in building community. The only characteristics not directly affected by empathy are conceptualization and foresight.[24]

The Outcomes of Servant Leadership

Three outcomes of servant leadership demonstrate its effectiveness: follower performance and growth, organizational performance, and societal impact. These outcomes build on one another and interact with one another once established. Servant leadership prizes the welfare of the followers as the highest priority. With this focus on follower well-being, effective servant leadership will encourage growth and development within the individuals of the organization. This growth and development will, in turn, lead to high performance and the overall success of the organization. When an organization thrives and succeeds, it can positively affect the surrounding community and the society at large.

Conclusion

This chapter delved into the foundations of chaplain leadership, presented four areas of concern for effective leaders (calling, character, competence, and connection), and introduced three models of leadership style (transformational, relational, and servant leadership). A solid calling, character, competence, and

24. Northouse, *Leadership*, 225.

ability to connect are vital for effective leadership. Additionally, building one's leadership capabilities is a necessary goal for all chaplains. Leadership influences individuals or groups in the choices they make. Becoming competent in one's leadership foundations, styles, and capabilities allows chaplains to lead effectively for the good of individuals, families, and organizations for the glory of God.

PART 2

Ten Functional Areas of Chaplaincy

Understanding the theological underpinnings and the theory of chaplaincy within the realm of practical theology is essential to chaplain ministry. Part 1 has provided these underpinnings, explaining the theological concepts that are foundational to a strong chaplain ministry. Part 2 describes the application of this foundation within the ten functional areas of chaplaincy throughout the United States and the rest of the world. Moving into workplaces and other settings as bearers of the presence and message of God, chaplains bring a whole-life ministry that is religious, spiritual, personal, and organizational to those they serve.

Full-time employees spend at least eight hours a day, forty hours a week, and over three-hundred days a year in their workplaces. The majority of their waking lives is spent in the workplace, with their personal and professional problems and challenges accompanying them. To address this need, this part of the book explores the types of ministry available to chaplains. We have delineated ten functional areas of chaplaincy, divided into four categories, which reflect similarities in the formality of requirements to become a chaplain in the field, the rigidity of guidelines to work in the field, and the location of the ministry setting, as follows:

1. Professional organization chaplaincy includes corporate, healthcare, and military chaplaincies. Each of these chaplaincies expects chaplains to perform according to certain guidelines established by the workplace.

2. Institution chaplaincy includes education and prison chaplaincies, in which ministry is done in an institutional setting.

3. Community assistance chaplaincy is focused on community settings for ministry. This category includes community, disaster relief, and public safety chaplaincies.

4. Sports and recreation chaplaincy addresses the increasing role that leisure plays in society. Sports chaplains work with teams and leagues supporting the players and their organizations. Leisure chaplains work in national and state parks, recreational vehicle parks, cruise ships, and more. These chaplains realize the needs of the people that emerge while traveling, on vacation, or during leisure.

The chapters in this section are written or sourced by chaplains who have worked or are currently working in the functional area. These chaplains understand firsthand the dynamics of their unique ministry areas. Thus, this section provides an inside look at each functional area of chaplaincy. The authors share information that explains the requirements to become a chaplain in each functional area, the ministry opportunities within the area, and how chaplains can serve within that area. Understanding the opportunities available assists new chaplains or chaplains who are changing fields in finding the ministry position God has called them to. The opportunities available to chaplains extend beyond these ten functional areas, but the ministries explained in this part of the book can prepare future chaplains for their chaplaincy work in the kingdom of God.

11

Corporate Chaplaincy

Jeff Brown, Robert Terrell, Rick Higgins, and Donnie Jenkins

Unlike ministers serving in churches, hospitals, or the military, corporate chaplains minister to Americans as they work in the same place for at least eight hours a day, five days a week. Usually, on the surface, employees complete their job responsibilities and seem to be well. Behind their facades, however, the closed doors of factories, offices, and truck docks scattered across the nation hide these employees' struggles. They face all the problems that are encountered in any other part of society, such as aging parents and teenager issues, marital and financial problems, physical and mental health challenges, and a myriad of other difficulties. In most of these situations, employees have spiritual questions involving *why* they face these struggles, and they long for someone to support them.

One reality that most businesses have learned is that the problems of an employee often become the problems of the employer. Corporate chaplains are great resources for addressing hurting people right where they spend most of their waking lives—at work. Corporate chaplains work with adults in the workplace, discussing problems and bringing care into their lives. These chaplains usually cover one large business or several smaller businesses. This chapter explains the requirements for becoming a corporate chaplain, the cautions that corporate chaplains need to be aware of, and the subareas within which corporate chaplains work.

The History of Corporate Chaplaincy

The history of corporate chaplaincy reaches back to the beginning of the United States. "Pastors have long hung out with employees. During the Industrial Revolution, they would preach from factory floors. Nineteenth-century Catholic teachings declared it the Church's duty to support the working poor. And in the Great Depression, industry titans hired chaplains to visit employees on the Hoover Dam."[1] Key individuals had an impact on the corporate-ministry movement over the past few centuries. Men such as Jeremiah Lanphier in the 1850s and business owners of the Christian Business Men's Committee in the 1930s played significant roles. Even passionate Christian soldiers coming back from World War II took their faith into the corporate world after the war.

In 1954, the Second Assembly of the World Council of Churches stated, "The real battles of the faith today are being fought in factories, shops, offices, and farms, in political parties, and government agencies, in countless homes, in the press, radio, and television, in the relationship of nations."[2] The assembly addressed the idea that the church should enter businesses in the United States and throughout the world, and they called on the laity to begin bringing their faith into their workplaces.[3]

Over time, the laity began to reach into the business world. Organizations like Marketplace Ministry, founded in Dallas in 1984, and Corporate Chaplains of America, founded in Wake Forest, North Carolina, in 1996, began sending chaplains into the corporate world. "Both Marketplace and Corporate Chaplains of America are chaplain staffing organizations that employ chaplains to serve as pastoral support (daily walkthroughs, crisis care, and more) for employees. Businesses then contract with the staffing organizations directly to obtain these chaplaincy services for their employees."[4] These chaplain staffing organizations have grown in the previous few decades.

In the 1990s, some businesses and corporations began to hire their own chaplains without using the chaplain staffing organizations. Tyson Foods is

---

1. Emma Green, "Finding Jesus at Work," *The Atlantic*, February 17, 2016, https://www.theatlantic.com/business/archive/2016/02/work-secularization-chaplaincies/462987.
2. Cited in Gage Arnold, "How Workplace Chaplains Are Changing the Face of Corporations," Faith Driven Entrepreneur, accessed January 19, 2023, https://www.faithdrivenentrepreneur.org/blog/how-workplace-chaplains-are-changing-the-face-of-corporations.
3. Arnold, "Workplace Chaplains."
4. Arnold, "Workplace Chaplains."

an example of a publicly traded company that has an in-house chaplaincy program, which started in 1990.[5] They have probably the largest private-sector corporate-chaplaincy program. Corporate chaplaincies have become established as separate jobs in the past few decades so that organizations do not have to rely on regular employees to provide informal support to each other.

The Culture and Ethos of Corporate Chaplaincy

American employees bring their personal problems to work with them. Whether blue collar or white collar, all employees face life issues that ultimately affect their work. Impacts include degradation in morale and job satisfaction, lack of productivity, poor attendance, lessened quality of work, and continuing recidivism. These employees need help, and the businesses want to help them in order to improve productivity, morale, and other aspects of the business. Corporate chaplains step into this gap between employees and productivity by providing care and help for the employees. Jesus said, "The fields are white for harvest" (John 4:35), and corporate chaplains discover that crisis care and effective ministry in the business world reap a great harvest. As America becomes more post-Christian, the opportunities for fruitful Christian influence in the corporate world are increasingly apparent.[6]

Chaplaincy is not something just for organizations that are specifically religious in their nature or mission. For example, chaplains perform services for companies that are open about their faith, businesses that are more subtle about the faith of the owners, and business leaders and companies that do not endorse or support faith in the corporate world. These latter companies offer chaplaincy to their employees simply because they believe such care helps the company's profitability. What is important is not the faith stance of the company but the desire of the company to meet the needs of their employees. Businesses that hold a more holistic view of employment, understanding that their employees bring many of life's struggles with them to work, benefit greatly from corporate chaplaincy.

Corporate chaplains are typically employed by a nonprofit ministry or chaplain organization. The ministry or organization approaches a prospective client with an offer to provide chaplain services, and if an agreement is reached, the client pays the ministry or organization, not the chaplain, for the services.

5. Green, "Finding Jesus at Work."
6. "The Most Post-Christian Cities in America: 2019," Barna Group, June 5, 2019, https://www.barna.com/research/post-christian-cities-2019.

Some organizations attract full-time career chaplains, while other ministries hire bivocational chaplains on a part-time basis. In rare cases, companies hire internal chaplains and add them to their own payroll.

Revenue to sustain the chaplain program is typically based on a fee-for-service model. In this model the client will pay a certain fee per employee per month. This fee includes the overhead necessary to sustain the program, which includes finances for the back office, training, supplies, and future growth. The largest percentage of the fee pays the salary and benefits of the serving chaplain or chaplains. Chaplains' pay may take the form of a monthly salary or, for part-time employees, an hourly wage. Most large chaplaincy organizations will provide competitive pay and benefits to the chaplains as professional and highly trained caregivers.

The company's culture is the single most important factor concerning whether corporate chaplaincy will work effectively within a specific company or not. A culture in which employees genuinely trust that their employer cares for their well-being will lead to an effective implementation of corporate chaplaincy on the company's part. Such a culture will encourage employees to approach the chaplain for needs; reaching out will not be seen as a negative action for the employee.

A strong culture of employee care also helps when there is a seeming conflict of interest on the chaplain's part. Even though a chaplain is indirectly compensated by the employer, the chaplain still must practice confidentiality when having privileged conversations with employees. A robust culture of employee care will help the employees believe that the chaplain will protect their conversations. However, in the recent past, many states changed their priest-penitent laws. (For more information on confidentiality and priest-penitent privilege, see chap. 4.) Corporate chaplains must check these laws because they may have to report information to local legal authorities. The chaplain organization can assist with understanding the confidentiality laws in each area they cover.

A vigorous company culture of care and trust allows chaplains to be effective by being involved in as many areas of the company's work as possible. The company trusts chaplains enough to enable them to join various meetings and other activities that might not be open to the typical nonemployee of the company. Such activities give chaplains greater insight into the employees' needs and also increases the presence of chaplains. This increased presence has a direct impact on chaplain effectiveness. This ministry of presence opens many doors for chaplains, allowing them to influence the decisions of the company.

The concept of a ministry of presence comes from God's character of being "the God who is there."[7] By being present, the chaplain serves as a physical reminder of the God who is always present. The chaplain's presence helps others to see the reality that has always been true: God is with them. Chaplains are also the bearers of the presence of God, which is part of the ministry of presence. This presence is the reason chaplains should attend employees' life milestones, both mundane and monumental. Bearing God's presence brings the holy into the mundane.

In corporate chaplaincy, the ministry of presence begins with doing rounds. Chaplains must regularly be involved in the work life of the employees of the company by completing the following:

- Walking around the facility and checking in on employees in a nondisruptive manner
- Chatting with employees at lunch and other down times
- Remembering the names of employees' family members
- Following up with sick employees
- Asking how things are going with family, projects at home, and other parts of the employees' lives
- Attending company meetings and picnics
- Sending out communication to all those involved in the company in every means possible, being skilled with social-media usage, though always checking company policy before posting

The most important precondition for effective corporate chaplaincy is for the chaplain to be there. When chaplains are there, they act as the bearers of the presence of God, thereby opening the door for them to introduce employees to God when invited to do so.

Vibrant corporate ministries need to be grounded in the building of caring relationships. In the context of a relationship, chaplains are given permission to enter into all aspects of an employee's life. Ministry opportunities in the context of an established relationship may pertain to any crisis, concern, or need in the life of the employee. The following are examples of how chaplains can be involved in corporate ministry:

- Employees dealing with health issues often share those concerns with a friend. As the chaplain becomes a friend, the chaplain is drawn into the

7. Francis A. Schaeffer, *The God Who Is There* (1968; repr., Downers Grove, IL: InterVarsity, 2020).

person's inner circle and is informed about the health issues. The difference is that the chaplain brings professional care and comfort. Whether
the issue is a health concern, hospital stay, or surgery, a friendly chaplain is often called on to attend to the person.

- All aspects of family difficulty can be addressed by the chaplain. These
  issues may include wedding and marriage planning, marriage strife,
  small children with high needs, troubled teens, or the family budget
  and finances. Professional chaplains can even provide triage care for
  domestic abuse situations as well as divorce care. The chaplain can
  then refer these cases to professionals.
- Corporate chaplains are equipped to provide care for those dealing
  with heavy emotional concerns, including stress, anxiety, and depression. Although not a professional counselor, the caregiving chaplain can
  give initial direction and help with serious matters like mental illness
  and even suicidal ideation.
- Chaplains are able to assist the business in conflict resolution, communication, supervisor-subordinate relationships, and even terminations
  and layoffs.
- Corporate chaplains can help with serious issues related to jail and
  court. They can attend a court hearing and provide emotional support for those involved, and they can visit family members who are
  incarcerated.
- Corporate chaplains can be indispensable in all matters related to grief
  care. They work closely with grieving families and assist them in funeral arrangements, meetings with funeral directors, and even the conducting of the funeral. Grief care is especially helpful because a growing
  majority of employees do not have a consistent church home or access
  to a pastor.

Chaplains often hear the question "Is this legal?" Since the concept of a
chaplain in the corporate world is not widely understood, the fear of the unknown always raises questions about the legality of the chaplain's ministry. The
short answer is a resounding yes. Private businesses are free to offer a wide
array of benefits and support for their employees, including the support of a
chaplain. Providing chaplains is another way many employers are recognizing
the whole person and providing individual care to employees with personal or
professional struggles. Corporate chaplaincy does not raise questions about
the separation of church and state, as this doctrine has no bearing on private
businesses. Even private businesses that receive public funding are permitted

to have chaplains, so long as public funds are not directly used to pay for the chaplain.

Chaplains should be trained in employee interactions to avoid anything that could violate Title VII employment discrimination laws or comparable state laws. Title IX laws should also be familiar to chaplains. Chaplain services should be provided to employees on a voluntary basis, with no requirement that an employee utilize the services. Likewise, an offer of assistance must be accepted by the employee before a chaplain can take action. Typically, this offer takes the form of a simple question such as "Can I pray for you on that matter?" An affirmative response allows the chaplain to proceed, but a negative response requires the chaplain to refrain from praying. In either case, the chaplain will continue building the relationship and caring for the person to the level and degree the employee desires. Essentially, the company is providing an employee benefit at no cost to the employee. As with any benefit, employees can opt in or out. If the company abides by these guidelines, employees have no legal grounds to object to chaplaincy. They have no power to demand the elimination of a chaplain simply because they object to the chaplain's presence. Moreover, a company's observance of these guidelines encourages employees to trust the chaplain and therefore supports an effective chaplaincy program.

Most corporate chaplain organizations are well grounded in biblical principles. Therefore, their ministries follow biblical mandates of unconditional love, servanthood, forgiveness, and even outreach. The chaplain recognizes the brokenness of this world and the underlying principles of the human sin nature. Helping people solve their problems without a recognition of these foundational truths will yield only temporary results and will provide no long-standing life change on the part of the employee.

The ultimate solution provided by the Christian chaplain ministry is the power of the gospel. In the gospel, there is power for healing, help, hope, and salvation. In this sense, evangelism is the mandate for every Christian outreach ministry. However, this evangelism should be done only in the context of voluntary, permission-based, confidential relationships. When these three principles are observed, an employee who is interested in the Christian faith may have a life-altering encounter with the gospel of Jesus Christ.

Failing to follow the three principles will result in a perpetuation of the negative perceptions of evangelism and will lead to what is essentially proselytism. When the gospel is forced on an unsuspecting employee, they will feel betrayed and develop a negative view of the program and even more so of Christianity in general. To be truly loving, care must be given in a way that respects the wishes of the employee.

Employees discover that corporate chaplaincy is a benefit not just for themselves but also for their families. Therefore, the company's culture of care will expand from the employee to those the employee cares about. Employers who have added chaplains learn that they, too, appreciate the chaplain's services. Unlike many other company benefits, chaplaincy tends to become an essential part of company culture. Chaplaincy is thus different from most other employee benefits.

Working as a Corporate Chaplain

Corporate chaplaincy lacks subareas. Businesses decide what duties they want chaplains to perform, and these duties can differ from business to business. The main factor that affects a corporate chaplain's duties is whether they work for a nonprofit, a chaplain organization, or a company itself. The following information consists of guidelines that prepare chaplains to work within most businesses.

Once corporate chaplains are assigned to their respective companies (mission fields), they meet with the owner and/or the human resources (HR) manager to gain insight into the functionality of the company's hours of operation. Then chaplains begin to coordinate their weekly schedules according to what the company needs and wants. For example, in a 24/7 environment, chaplains need to check in with each employee multiple times during the week. When serving multiple companies or locations, chaplains coordinate additional scheduling efforts to serve each company or location consistently across time.

A chaplain's work schedule follows the pattern of the company or companies they serve. If one company closes on a holiday and the other companies do not, the chaplain is responsible for visiting with those other companies if the holiday falls on a day when the chaplain would typically visit. Chaplains can always check with the companies to work out other arrangements, but they should be aware of the expectations of the companies they serve.

Chaplains must adhere to whatever safety protocols a company has in place for its employees. If safety glasses, earplugs, or steel-toed shoes are mandatory for employees, then they are mandatory for chaplains as well. Companies can be fined if employees and others in work zones do not have the proper safety gear.

Chaplains must avoid situations that appear to be inappropriate. Some chaplains avoid meeting with employees of a different gender in private places, to avoid giving the appearance of impropriety. Chaplains must protect both their reputation and that of the employee. A chaplain might choose to meet in an open area with proper visibility or in a room with clear windows, though in the latter case, chaplains might arrange to have someone monitor the meeting through the glass. Chaplains should avoid physical contact, though handshakes, fist bumps, and similar greetings are acceptable. Many people are no longer comfortable with any physical contact, and chaplains should honor those preferences.

In some cases, employees are not physically present at a job site, so chaplains use remote chaplaincy to meet their needs. Remote chaplaincy presents challenges, because face-to-face interactions are replaced with phone calls, texts, emails, or communication mediated by computer screens, which are less effective means of communicating. Often, remote chaplaincy involves weekly correspondence with employees. In some cases, chaplains interact in real time through a video-call service such as Zoom. Hospital visits, counseling, and Bible studies can be conducted this way. Other means of remote communication include YouTube videos, podcast episodes, or Facebook posts that offer encouragement for the employees and are accessible anytime. Devotions can also be delivered in any of these formats. In each of these virtual mediums, a chaplain still needs permission from employees to interact with them.

Corporate chaplains should avoid some behaviors. Even if employees give an invitation, chaplains should avoid the following situations:

- *Becoming involved in operations.* The vast majority of corporate chaplains have a background and experience in a secular work environment. In some cases, chaplains have worked in the corporate world for decades, accumulating a vast amount of operational knowledge and skill. The temptation for some chaplains can be to put on a business consultant hat: "Have you thought about adding another shift?" "You might get better results if you changed to this particular production software." Examples such as these fall outside the chaplain's primary purpose of connecting with and caring for individual employees. Chaplains can, however, refer leaders and decision makers to trustworthy sources of information.

- *Interfering with people doing their jobs.* Chaplains make every effort to get plenty of consistent one-on-one time with each employee. Typically, the interactions are brief. On many occasions, employees continue to perform their jobs safely and effectively while carrying on a short conversation with the chaplain. However, the chaplain must maintain situational awareness at all times. At times, even a quick "Good morning, Joe. How are you today?" can jeopardize the flow of production or safety. On the other end of the spectrum, an employee may want to go into great depth about a particular personal problem or struggle. If it appears that a conversation may require more than a brief exchange, the chaplain has some options. These options include getting permission from the employee and supervisor to address the matter on the spot (perhaps in a vacant room) or making arrangements with the employee to discuss the matter when the employee has completed work. Business owners and managers hire people to accomplish specific tasks. Ultimately, the chaplain should be viewed as helping productivity, not hindering it.

- *Coming between supervisors and employees.* Chaplains look forward to the day when employees freely share whatever is on their minds. Building relationships that allow such freedom fosters increasing trust as well as greater opportunities to provide care when needed. In light of this, a potential danger exists when an employee opens up about a grievance regarding the work environment. Examples include conflict with management or problems with procedure. Here the chaplain's primary role is to listen and, if need be, refer. On many occasions, the employee simply wants to discuss the issues. At other times, the chaplain can remind the employee about the company's protocol for expressing complaints; encouraging the employee to use that system, which may include seeking assistance from the HR office; using the company's suggestion program; or taking advantage of a boss's open-door policy. The chaplain can even ask the employee for permission to share the grievance with a supervisor in a way that does not jeopardize anonymity. What a chaplain must avoid is any appearance of taking sides with either management or the employee. The chaplain is an advocate for harmony and conflict resolution, not discord and division.

Chaplains should also be cautious in matters related to HR. Employees' roles and responsibilities are not always clear. When it comes to the chaplain's interactions with HR personnel, an abundance of discernment is in order. For example, let's imagine that HR informs a chaplain about an employee issue in general terms and with the person's permission. But when the chaplain speaks with the employee, the conversation is privileged and protected by confidentiality laws. The employee has to give the chaplain permission to inform HR of the conversation they had.

Chaplains are hired to perform specific, agreed-on tasks in a business. They must always remain vigilant to stay within the boundaries of the job, even if they have other knowledge or experience or if they feel sympathetic with one party or another in a workplace conflict.

Requirements for Becoming a Corporate Chaplain

All professional chaplaincy requires preparation in chaplaincy, theology, and ministry skills, and corporate chaplaincy has formalized requirements that people must meet before entering a business setting. Corporate chaplains need to have the following KSAs to help them succeed in their ministry:

- *Knowledge:* This includes a knowledge of chaplaincy, theology, counseling, and leadership training, which is gained through higher education and CPE. Corporate chaplains also need knowledge of business functions.
- *Skills:* These include excellent interpersonal skills; pastoral skills, such as caring and showing compassion; leadership skills; and counseling skills. Corporate chaplains may have long-term counseling with some employees, so skills in marital conflict management, conflict resolution, and other such areas are important. Skills in short-term crisis intervention, spiritual counseling, and support counseling are needed. Additionally, compassion, empathy, and listening skills are important for this type of chaplaincy.
- *Abilities:* These include capacities to comfort people in times of crisis, care for employees and management in routine or crisis times, work well with teams, and provide spiritual care for others.

Aspiring corporate chaplains can obtain these KSAs by completing the requirements in this section and volunteering in ministry settings. To qualify for chaplaincy within most corporate chaplaincy organizations, chaplains must meet certain criteria. In some cases, corporate chaplain organizations are extremely selective in who they hire, so as not to damage their reputation in the mission fields. While this sounds selfish, a larger concern comes from the fact that some businesses have a low level of trust for Christians. Selectivity is necessary to ensure that chaplain selection organizations can maintain their ability to provide care for those businesses. The requirements for becoming a corporate chaplain are formalized, but they can differ slightly between chaplain organizations.

Business experience. Candidates must have several years' experience working in corporate America apart from full-time ministry. This additional experience allows the chaplain to connect with employees better, whether on a shop floor or in the office. Most people do not understand the concept of vocational ministry, so corporate or business experience is preferred. The chaplain could have been anything from a truck driver, secretary, or car salesman to a manager, vice president, CEO, or even president of a company.

Ministry. Applicants must also have extensive ministry experience, and they must have the life experience of dealing with and recovering from a major life event (e.g., cancer, loss of a child or spouse, loss of employment, marital issues, caregiving to a parent). These kinds of experiences allow chaplains to bring experiential knowledge to their ministry, which increases their credibility with employees.

Education. A theological education is preferable, with preference going to an accredited MDiv or MA degree in chaplaincy, counseling, theology, or a similar concentration. The minimum educational requirement a chaplain will need to meet is the completion of a bachelor's degree in a relevant field from an accredited college or university.

Calling. Corporate chaplains need to have received a spiritual call and to have made a commitment to long-term one-on-one corporate chaplaincy.

Ordination or licensing. Corporate chaplains need to be licensed or ordained as a minister. Ordination typically comes through a local church that extends support to the candidate. For some faith groups, the ordination process can take six to twelve months. During this time, the ordination committee considers various aspects of the individual, such as integrity, church attendance and involvement, tithing, and so on.

Endorsement. As with those serving in the other functional areas of chaplaincy, corporate chaplains should be ordained by their faith group so that they can get support and backing for their theological decisions from the faith group's endorser.

Ethical standards. A candidate for chaplaincy must be willing to adhere to the professional ethical requirements and standards that the corporate ministry has established. Each applicant must be willing to go through an extensive interview process that may include the following elements: a background check, including criminal, credit, and Department of Motor Vehicles components; a temperament assessment test; multiple telephone and face-to-face interviews; and willingness to agree with the organization's statement of faith and mission.

Professional Organizations for Corporate Chaplains

The organizations listed below represent opportunities for corporate chaplains. These organizations support corporate chaplains and offer training and networking opportunities. Some of these groups provide chaplains for businesses.

- Business Chaplains of America
- Chaplaincy Institute
- Corporate Care, Inc.
- Corporate Chaplains Network
- Corporate Chaplains of America
- Corporate Chaplains Outreach Canada
- Frontline Chaplains
- International Chaplains Association
- Marketplace Chaplains USA
- National Institute of Business and Industrial Chaplains
- Seaport Chaplaincy
- Trucker and Transportation Chaplains
- Trucker Chaplains
- Workplace Chaplaincy Scotland
- Workplace Chaplains

Leadership as a Corporate Chaplain

Leadership positions offer opportunities to influence senior leadership and the course of a department. Corporate chaplains often serve on teams, influencing policies and decisions for small groups or large corporations. As transformational leaders, they can work to reach the goals set by the business, while remaining ethical in the planning. Thus, chaplains can model decision-making processes that will then influence how the leaders make decisions.

Among employees, chaplains can be relational leaders who develop relationships with employees in order to care for them and assist them in resolving issues. Corporate chaplains can also be servant leaders by helping employees develop into strong leaders with a deep spiritual sense. Chaplains in the business world can indeed be influential leaders.

Summary

Corporate chaplains minister to people in businesses throughout this country and the rest of the world. All day, every day, corporate chaplains have the opportunity for one-on-one ministry as people spend eight or more hours a day in their place of work. Whether chaplains choose to work for the business itself or with one of the chaplain placement groups, corporate chaplains care for, serve, and counsel people within businesses of various kinds. Ultimately, corporate chaplains bring the peace and love of Christ into an environment that may be hospitable—or may be hostile—to the gospel message. Chaplains stand in the gap between the problems of life and the love of Christ.

12

Healthcare Chaplaincy

Juliana Lesher

ealthcare chaplaincy falls within the professional organization category of the ten functional areas of chaplaincy. Healthcare chaplains
work in hospitals, centers, homes, and offices where people's physical
health or mental health (or both) are the focus of care. Chaplains bring hope,
comfort, and care as they seek to meet the spiritual needs of patients. This type
of chaplaincy involves caring for patients, family members, and staff members
who work with patients in healthcare institutions.

Healthcare chaplaincy can change pace rapidly depending on the chaplain's
location within a facility. Chaplains can work in highly energized atmospheres
such as trauma units, or they can work in lower-energy care facilities for geriatric memory-loss patients. Within hospitals, chaplains can move from high-
energy emergency rooms to lower-energy general medicine wards in the span
of a morning. This type of chaplaincy thus offers a wide variety of pacing and
patient care from which chaplains can choose.

This chapter explains the history of healthcare chaplaincy, the culture and
ethos of the field, different types of healthcare chaplaincy and the skills needed
to be successful in them, requirements for healthcare chaplains, professional
organizations available to healthcare chaplains, and leadership opportunities
for healthcare chaplains.

The History of Healthcare Chaplaincy

Healthcare chaplaincy's roots extend to the earliest days of Christianity, when Christian leaders visited the sick, prayed over them, and offered assistance to various families. When sick people began to go to modern hospitals in the late nineteenth century, priests and pastors visited the members of their congregations. The secular hospitals did not have formalized chaplain requirements, leaving the work to active and retired clergy members; however, private hospitals established by religious groups (such as Catholic hospitals) usually had clergy members visit and support patients and their families. In the early twentieth century, the "religion and health" movement began to utilize theological students in caring for hospital patients.

During this time, Congregational minister Anton Boisen and Presbyterian minister Seward Hiltner developed what has become known as clinical pastoral education (CPE), in which ministers are trained specifically for healthcare work. Boisen was diagnosed with schizophrenia and experienced three stays in mental hospitals. He began to question how much of various illnesses resulted from medical issues and how much resulted from spiritual needs. Boisen and Hiltner developed programs that became the early beginnings of healthcare chaplaincy. The concepts of providing care for "living human documents" (explained in the overview of CPE later in the chapter) and the use of self as pastoral care are part of Boisen and Hiltner's approach. Hospitals changed as a result of their work, and modern CPE programs emerged.

Since that time, healthcare chaplaincy has expanded from hospitals to care facilities to trauma centers and many other health facilities. Healthcare chaplaincy is one of the older types of chaplaincy and is well developed, with many chaplains specializing in certain types of healthcare chaplaincy.

The Culture and Ethos of Healthcare Chaplaincy

Healthcare chaplaincy includes ministry in general, pediatric, VA, and other hospitals; same-day-surgery, trauma, and specialty centers; mental health hospitals and treatment centers; rehabilitation and long-term care facilities; and home, hospice, and telechaplaincy care. When working in healthcare, chaplains are paid by the institution for which they work, receiving insurance, holidays, and other benefits from the institution. This section explains the culture and ethos of healthcare settings, which is the collective spirit within which healthcare providers work.

Healthcare chaplains work with two groupings of people: (1) hospital staff members and (2) patients and their families. When working with staff members, chaplains can function as workplace chaplains in that they are meeting people where they work. In doing so, they are carrying out a ministry of presence. Staff members utilize chaplains for help with marital problems, spiritual questions, and other issues. Like employees in other places, staff members bring their personal problems to the workplace and seek out help from chaplains.

The primary focus of healthcare chaplains, however, is patients and families in times of crisis. Chaplains meet the patients where they are, develop relationships if possible, and provide care and comfort for people who are facing traumatic occurrences. As bearers of the presence of God, chaplains visit rooms, sit with patients awaiting tests, and pray with those who so request. Most relationships are short-term, as patients move into and out of the hospital rapidly. Some relationships, however, can last longer in care facilities, rehabilitation hospitals, and mental hospitals.

Healthcare chaplains should avoid participating in any medical procedures that are outside chaplaincy certifications. The liability issues for the healthcare institution prevent chaplains from being involved in medical services. Additionally, chaplains should avoid interfering in interactions between supervisors and staff members or between staff members and patients. However, if a chaplain is asked to participate in conflict resolution, then involvement is acceptable. Staff meetings and team meetings are appropriate times for chaplains to present issues, as long as chaplains stay within the confidentiality requirements. Chaplains who follow the rules and regulations of the workplace earn the respect of the staff members with whom they work.

Subareas for Ministry in Healthcare Chaplaincy

The various subareas of healthcare chaplaincy share some KSAs; however, they also require some specialized skills. Expectations for chaplains who serve in general medicine hospitals may differ from expectations for chaplains in mental health hospitals or other settings. This section explains the different types of healthcare chaplaincy and lists specialized KSAs needed in each setting.

General Medicine Hospitals

In general medicine hospitals, chaplains encounter patients with a wide range of illnesses and medical needs, from routine procedures, such as appendectomies, to specialized procedures, such as heart surgery or advanced COVID care. Chaplains have the opportunity to meet people at some of their most vulnerable times and bring the comfort and care of Christ to the patient, family, and staff.

194 Ten Functional Areas of Chaplaincy

General KSAs in providing comfort, listening actively, and offering spiritual care are necessary in general medicine hospitals.

In these settings, patients can face crisis times, such as receiving news that what they thought was a routine procedure is much more serious or complex. Thus, they may have to transfer to a specialized setting or be subjected to advanced tests. These are the times when chaplains can become a refuge for a patient to express his or her fears and anger about the uncertainties that lie ahead. Family members who need to express their emotions can turn to chaplains, who then have the opportunity to bring comfort through spiritual care and listening. Asking permission to pray with the patient and family can be comforting to them. At these vulnerable times, patients can be more open to discussing matters of faith, providing them with a sense of peace and assurance that the Divine Physician understands people's bodies better than even the most advanced medical doctors.

Chaplains may face difficult decisions as they enter into the pain and suffering of others, and they often struggle to discern how Jesus would respond to a hurting person while remaining faithful to their theological beliefs. This kind of struggle can arise when a traumatic incident occurs, such as the death of a newborn baby. The distraught parents and heartbroken nursing staff may desperately want to honor the fragile and unresponsive baby through baptism. For many chaplains, baptizing infants who are going to die is part of their faith group's theological stance. In these cases, chaplains practice the skill of providing for those people within their own denomination or who have similar theological beliefs. Providing for those who share similar beliefs is one of the skills needed for effective chaplaincy. In this example, the chaplain will baptize the baby and then care for and support the parents and staff.

Some chaplains belong to faith groups that do not baptize infants, and certain others belong to faith groups that do indeed baptize infants but assign to baptism a meaning that would not allow it in this instance. For example, in some faith groups of the latter category, the practice of infant baptism is a witness of the parents and church family to faithfully raise the child in the Christian religion until the child is of age to make his or her own confirmation of faith. The issue for chaplains who follow this interpretation and practice of infant baptism is that if the child has died, the parents are not able to raise their newborn in the Christian faith. Thus, when the parents request baptism for their deceased baby, chaplains are faced with a choice. If the chaplain cannot in good conscience fulfill the request, they will help find someone who can meet the families' needs.

The chaplain also may not be able to baptize the baby because of theological and denominational boundaries. This example shows how a chaplain can cooperate without compromise. The chaplain still has the responsibility to care for the family's needs, so the chaplain utilizes the skill of facilitation by contacting another chaplain who is able to baptize the baby. Facilitation means that when the chaplain cannot provide the requested action, that chaplain contacts another clergy member who can. The family and staff receive the comfort and care they need while the chaplain maintains their denominational identity. Chaplains need to be able to discern God's will within their convictions as they both provide for those who share their beliefs and facilitate for people who have needs outside what the chaplains' beliefs and commitments allow.

Pediatric Hospitals

Pediatric hospitals serve the needs of children from the neonatal stage through their eighteenth year. Chaplain skills for working with children often involve playing, either freely or in games, and reading stories. The hope is that children will learn to trust the chaplain and will discuss their fears. However, young children often are unable to voice what they feel. Thus, chaplains must understand the developmental needs of children in order to be able to communicate with them. Praying and discussing spiritual issues can be very natural for children, whereas adults can find the issues uncomfortable. Chaplains, when working with children, need to understand how they approach spirituality.

The chaplain's role as bearer of the presence of God follows Jesus's example of letting the little children come to him (Matt. 19:14). Children are often much more spiritually aware than adults. Thus, they more easily come into the presence of God when the chaplain is near; they respond to God working through the chaplain. However, children are often unable to voice this occurrence.

Parents and staff are also a focus for pediatric hospital chaplains. Listening to parents' fears, hopes, and dreams as they face the reality of their children's circumstances is part of the ministry opportunity. Comforting them and the staff in difficult times is part of the ministry as well. Faith challenges for chaplains include assisting parents and children in understanding why God allows innocent children to suffer. The issues of death and dying are also commonly raised. Pediatric chaplains need to work well with children, parents, and staff in hospitals.

Mental Health Hospitals and Treatment Centers

While in most settings chaplains care for those who are suffering from physical illnesses, not all sicknesses and wounds are visible to the human eye. Many deep-seated hurts lie within the mind and spirit of a person. Often, churches and people of faith have upheld judgmental stigmas about mental illness, with the result that people suffering from mental illnesses sometimes feel shamed and guilty about their conditions. Chaplains must be aware of the preconceptions of spiritual representatives that patients in mental health settings may have.

Historically, mental healthcare and pastoral care have been divided; however, mental health providers are increasingly acknowledging the importance of spiritual care in treatment. Spiritual care addresses soul wounds of guilt and shame and is valued along with the traditional psychotropic drug treatments for mental illnesses.[1] Patients in mental health hospitals have shorter stays, while patients in mental health treatment centers stay for longer periods to address behavioral and addictive problems.

Often, chaplains host spiritual discussion groups for patients in mental health hospitals and treatment centers. The facilitation of these discussion groups can be challenging for new chaplains, as they need to have a strong foundational faith of their own and skills to facilitate group discussions on matters of faith. The patients involved typically hold a wide range of beliefs and may have varying levels of cognitive ability. Chaplains who have completed CPE have acquired the skills needed for effective and meaningful group discussions: creating safe places for all viewpoints to be equally voiced in the group, ensuring no one person dominates or dictates the direction of the group, and safeguarding in such a way that each person is genuinely respected and honored in the group.

VA Hospitals

The Veterans Health Administration's primary mission is to provide comprehensive care for veterans and their families and caregivers. Patients within VA hospitals are unique in feeling stronger connections to other patients and providers than patients in other hospitals typically do. This trait works as a positive for any group counseling that chaplains may provide. Worship services can also reflect this sense of community as veterans connect with each other physically, mentally, and spiritually in their struggles.

To be effective, VA chaplains must understand military culture in order to show respect to the veterans with whom they work. Trusting civilian workers is difficult for veterans because of the cultural gap that exists between the military and civilian worlds. Many veterans in VA hospitals have physical injuries, but they can also struggle with posttraumatic stress disorder, moral injury, spiritual injury, and other challenges. Chaplains should be acquainted with the latest research in these areas in order to minister effectively to veterans. For

---

1. H. Koenig, N. Boucher, R. Oliver, N. Youssef, S. Mooney, and J. Currier, "Rationale for Spiritually Oriented Cognitive Processing Therapy for Moral Injury in Active Duty Military and Veterans with Posttraumatic Stress Disorder," *Journal of Nervous and Mental Disease* 205 (2017): 147–53.

example, veterans who have moral injuries suffer shame, guilt, and feelings of worthlessness. These feelings translate into their spiritual lives, as they feel God cannot forgive them for actions they have done. Chaplains can walk alongside these veterans if they understand the injury and refrain from offering platitudes.

Trauma Centers

Chaplains serving in level-one trauma centers, particularly in large cities, often run on the adrenaline produced from the constant and extreme trauma continually entering the center. Chaplains in these facilities deal with many issues, from patients with bodies that are destroyed to family members demanding answers about the patient, even to staff distancing themselves from the intensity of gruesome situations before them. People who come to check on patients can be from gangs and other dangerous groups. Trauma teams tend to cope by dehumanizing patients until the weight of the horror breaks through the barrier they erect. Chaplains are there to comfort family members and to help trauma teams remain effective in this fast-paced environment.

Amid family members with spiraling, almost out-of-control emotions and frantic staff attempting heroic efforts, chaplains can be the calm reminder that the living God meets broken humanity, enters people's chaos, and offers comforting peace where there is only tumultuous agony. In these settings, chaplains must be aware of the pluralistic culture that surrounds them, being ready to facilitate patients' and families' needs when required. If an area has both Hindus and Catholics, evangelical chaplains need to understand the requirements of each group in regard to death and dying so they know how to respond. They also need to construct a list of resources in the local area so that they can request help and therefore meet the needs of a patient or family.

Specialized Medical Units

Specialized medical units exist within hospitals and provide transplants, chemotherapy or other cancer treatments, heart or other organ treatment, and similar care. Patients receive care as inpatients, outpatients, or both, depending on the treatment cycle. The patients in these units share certain characteristics, one being emotional roller-coaster rides concerning effectiveness of treatments, living and dying, and other highly charged topics. Recurring theological questions include why God allows suffering, why he heals some and not others, and where God is in the midst of dying.

As with many other settings, chaplains who work in these units minister to both staff and patients. Many of the patients are in their last stages of life;

some, for example, are dying because they cannot get a new organ or a life-saving treatment. Staff members stand by as treatments fail and patients die. They need the comfort of prayer and support that chaplains bring. Chaplains in these settings need to have a theology of suffering and of death and dying. A compassionate approach to those who are suffering, as well as to those who watch the patients suffer, allows the chaplain to convey the presence of God to patients and staff alike.

Care Facilities and Rehabilitation Centers

Healthcare chaplains also minister to people living in care facilities and reha-bilitation centers. People in care facilities are referred to as residents and gener-ally live full-time in the facility. The population within these facilities includes, among other people, geriatric patients who need help with physical care, mental acuity, or social experiences. Younger patients may be in care facilities for long-term physical therapy. Rehabilitation centers focus on physical rehabilitation for all ages. Residents live in these facilities and then move to outpatient treat-ment. The similarities include long-term care and more attentive nursing care.

Chaplains in these facilities provide regular worship services in a chapel or church setting, and they also visit residents in their rooms. In many facilities, chaplains can develop long-term relationships with residents. Involving resi-dents in regular worship services allows chaplains to assist in maintaining the social and religious aspects of residents' lives. To work in these facilities, chap-lains must be comfortable ministering to the aging, discussing death and dying, and having disruptions in their services. Chaplains bring peace and comfort to residents of care facilities and rehabilitation centers.

Hospice or Palliative Care

End-of-life care, also known as hospice or palliative care, may be offered in an institutional setting or a home-health setting. Palliative care, meaning "comfort care," attempts to keep a patient as comfortable as possible, especially when there is no medical cure for a patient's condition. In caring for hospice patients, chaplains are often involved in difficult family discussions about end-of-life care options for a loved one. Many times, family members may have differing opinions about the courses of action for the patient, which range from sustaining life at all costs to wanting only to keep the patient as comfortable as possible. Chaplains often mediate between these family members to maintain existing relationships within the family and to provide a peaceful environment for the patient. If a patient has assigned a healthcare power of attorney and completed do-not-resuscitate instructions, then the family is eased from these decisions. However, chaplains often mediate in situations in which no final wishes have been formalized.

Chaplains need to know not only their own position on sensitive topics but also the approaches of other faith groups to medical situations and death and dying. Chaplains come alongside the patients and families to support them in their faith decisions as they stand against possible perceived pressure from the medical community. Staff members turn to chaplains for workplace issues as well as death-and-dying issues. Hospice chaplains walk with people in some of the most difficult times of life.

Home Health

In the last decade home healthcare has greatly increased, with hospital stays becoming shorter and people choosing to return home for their final days. Some home healthcare agencies employ chaplains as part of their interdisciplinary healthcare team. Chaplains need to work well with teams and be timely with their reporting of home visits. Interpersonal skills with families and with co-workers are important as well.

Home health chaplaincy is unique because chaplains enter patients' personal spaces—their homes. While home healthcare agencies assess the safety of homes, chaplains can encounter situations that require intervention inside them. Chaplains should refrain from judgmental statements about the home, which might upset the patient and family members, but should report any unsafe or unhealthy situations they notice. Safety is more of a concern when one enters a home than when one enters a public space. Chaplains should establish safety practices when visiting homes, such as texting a supervisor when arriving and then again when leaving. Home healthcare allows chaplains to enter personal spaces and bring spiritual comfort to the people there.

Telechaplaincy (Virtual Care)

A newer modality of medical care is telemedicine, or virtual healthcare, in which the healthcare provider enters patients' homes through computer screens. Healthcare chaplaincy is traditionally viewed as bringing "high-touch" and "in-person" pastoral care to people. When the ministry of presence is mediated through a screen, it does not include these elements; however, it provides care for those who are too distant or too sick to come to a chaplain. Chaplains have to develop skills to overcome the virtual distance. Skill sets for virtual care include creating safe and sacred sharing spaces with patients through a virtual connection. Many methods can achieve this, but relational openness and empathetic understanding in particular help patients feel valued and heard. Chaplains need to close the distance that screens create.

When COVID-19 caused widespread lockdowns in 2020, telechaplain care became the norm for healthcare chaplaincy. It was used for patients who were hospitalized with COVID and in isolation. Chaplains were able to connect patients and families through telechaplaincy as well. In hospice units, chaplains have been able to connect dying patients virtually with distant family members for end-of-life family reunions. Healthcare chaplains need to be familiar with managing phone calls and handling large groups in virtual family meetings. For most people, virtual meetings are awkward, so skill sets must include maintaining a comfortable presence in such meetings.

Requirements for Becoming a Healthcare Chaplain

Professional chaplaincy requires preparation in chaplaincy, theology, and ministry skills. Healthcare chaplaincy has formalized requirements that chaplains must complete before entering a healthcare setting. Healthcare chaplains need to have the following KSAs in order to succeed in ministering in a clinical setting:

- *Knowledge:* This includes a knowledge of chaplaincy, theology, counseling, and leadership training, which is gained through higher education and CPE.
- *Skills:* These include excellent interpersonal skills; pastoral skills, including the conducting of services; leadership skills; and counseling skills. While healthcare chaplains are not long-term counselors, they do benefit from having skills in short-term crisis intervention, spiritual counseling, and support counseling. Additionally, compassion, empathy, and listening skills are important for this type of chaplaincy.
- *Abilities:* These include capacities to comfort people in times of crisis, care for staff and patients in routine or crisis times, work well with teams, and provide spiritual care for others.

Aspiring healthcare chaplains can obtain these KSAs by completing the requirements in this section and volunteering in healthcare settings. The requirements are as follows.

Education. To become a healthcare chaplain, applicants must have a minimum of a bachelor's degree, though many healthcare settings prefer MDiv and

MA degrees. Because not all healthcare chaplains are Christians, the education requirements are broad.

- At the bachelor's and master's levels, students may study chaplaincy, religious studies, counseling, psychology, or related fields.
- If one gets a master's degree, the major of the bachelor's degree is not very important. But the major of a master's degree is always important.
- Master's programs often involve CPE, which is required for healthcare chaplaincy.

Calling. Healthcare chaplains need to have received a spiritual call and to have made a commitment to work with medical personnel, patients, and families in healthcare settings.

Ministry experience. Applicants must also have some ministry experience, which is often gained through CPE.

Ordination or licensing. Prospective healthcare chaplains should seek ordination by a local church. Some churches do not offer ordination, in which case chaplains should seek licensure.

Ecclesiastical endorsement. Healthcare chaplains are required to receive ecclesiastical endorsement from their faith group. By providing endorsement, the denomination or other faith group approves the person as a clergy member. Through the endorsement process, the person is set apart for ministry and sent forth to represent the faith group in the healthcare setting. The endorsement serves to set the person apart for a specific ministry before God and to remind that clergyperson of their faith commitment. While ordination is not required in many settings, endorsement by a faith group is highly advisable.

In recent years, movements to change healthcare chaplaincy from a ministry to a secular entity have come and gone. Viewing the chaplain as a compassionate caregiver allows for this broader interpretation of the work of the chaplain. This interpretation omits God and provides for the social needs of the patients and staff but omits their spiritual needs.[2] Endorsement allows chaplains to remain faithful to the traditions of their denomination while ministering effectively in God's name.

CPE. All healthcare chaplains must complete CPE, through which they develop listening and helping skills. Usually, four or more units of CPE are required for chaplains in the healthcare field. CPE allows people to work in a clinical setting under a supervisor in order to improve their skills in ministering to

2. T. Thorstenson, "The Emergence of the New Chaplaincy: Re-defining Pastoral Care for the Postmodern Age," *Journal of Pastoral Care and Counseling* 66, no. 2 (2012): 1–6.

suffering people. Anton Boisen, the pioneer of CPE, focused on studying "living human documents."[3] During a hospitalization for mental illness, Boisen experienced a divine call that led him to incorporate religious care into the medical treatment of patients. Boisen believed seminary students were challenged to think more deeply when they were allowed to engage and study living human documents firsthand. These living documents were patients struggling with declining health, broken spirits, and life-threatening illnesses.[4] Boisen's concept of studying the living human document emphasizes that broken patients need chaplains who are trained to observe, study, and hear their heartfelt laments. CPE provides intense training to help chaplains develop the KSAs needed for ministering in a healthcare setting.

CPE is built on the action-reflection-action model of practical theology. Action begins as students are given hands-on opportunities to engage with patients in various settings, to dialogue with them about their spiritual needs, and to provide pastoral care for them. After providing direct pastoral care, students reflect by writing verbatims, where students record, to the best of their memory, the exact statements the patients said to them and the exact statements the students said to the patients. In the record of the exchange, students note the emotions expressed by the patients, the emotions the students themselves felt, the nonverbal exchanges that occurred, and the physical surroundings of the patient-care encounter.

The reflection process continues as students bring their verbatims to a group-learning environment composed of other students and a certified clinical pastoral educator. The patient-and-chaplain dialogue of the verbatim is read within the group, and the group members then discuss how the student chaplain may have effectively engaged the patient or how the student may have missed a critical concern raised by a patient. From this group reflection process, the student then returns to action by engaging more patients as the action-reflection-action model continues. These reflection and discussion sessions assist students in developing skills for healthcare chaplaincy, such as empathy, compassion, care, provision of comfort, service, self-care, and listening.

Ideally, this action-reflection-action model used by students in CPE becomes a natural part of the rest of their ministry career. CPE requires students to be vulnerable, humble, open to learning, and willing to grow. By being vulnerable and willing to share about their weaknesses, they may gain new insights about how perceived weaknesses can become strengths.

3. Glenn H. Asquith Jr., "Anton T. Boisen and the Study of 'Living Human Documents,'" *Journal of Presbyterian History* 60, no. 3 (1982): 244–65.

4. Anton Boisen, *Out of the Depths* (New York: Harper, 1960).

Through CPE, student chaplains learn a set of skills that are categorized into three primary areas: pastoral formation, pastoral competence, and pastoral reflection. Within each of these areas of focus, there are Level I Outcomes and Level II Outcomes. Students are required to achieve these outcomes in order to become board-certified (see below). CPE students must fully demonstrate Level I Outcomes before pursuing Level II Outcomes.

The pastoral-formation outcomes focus on students' awareness of themselves as ministers, how students' attitudes affect their pastoral care, and how students seek support and guidance for their pastoral functioning. The ACPE lists the following as outcomes that comprise the primary area of pastoral formation:

1. Articulate the central themes and core values of one's religious/spiritual heritage and the theological understanding that informs one's ministry (Level I).
2. Identify and discuss major life events, relationships, social location, cultural contexts, and social realities that impact personal identity as expressed in pastoral functioning (Level I).
3. Initiate peer group and supervisory consultation and receive critique about one's ministry practice (Level I).
4. Articulate an understanding of the pastoral role that is congruent with one's personal and cultural values, basic assumptions, and personhood (Level II).[5]

The pastoral-competence outcomes emphasize an understanding of how students' social conditions, religious heritages, and behavioral sciences affect their pastoral care and counseling. CPE outcomes comprising the primary area of pastoral competence include the following:

1. Risk offering appropriate and timely critique with peers and supervisors (Level I).
2. Recognize relational dynamics within group contexts (Level I).
3. Demonstrate the integration of conceptual understandings presented in the curriculum into pastoral practice (Level I).
4. Initiate helping relationships within and across diverse populations (Level I).

---

5. "Objectives and Outcomes for Level I/Level II CPE," ACPE Manuals, ACPE, accessed September 20, 2023, https://www.manula.com/manuals/acpe/acpe-manuals/2016/en/topic/objectives -and-outcomes-for-level-i-level-ii-cpe.

5. Use the clinical method of learning to achieve one's educational goals (Level I).

6. Provide pastoral ministry with diverse people, taking into consideration multiple elements of cultural and ethnic differences, social conditions, systems, justice and applied clinical ethics issues without imposing one's own perspectives (Level II).

7. Demonstrate a range of pastoral skills, including listening/attending, empathic reflection, conflict resolution/transformation, confrontation, crisis management, and appropriate use of religious/spiritual resources (Level II).

8. Assess the strengths and needs of those served, grounded in theology and using an understanding of the behavioral sciences (Level II).

9. Manage ministry and administrative function in terms of accountability, productivity, self-direction, and clear, accurate professional communication (Level II).

10. Demonstrate competent use of self in ministry and administrative function, which includes: emotional availability, cultural humility, appropriate self-disclosure, positive use of power and authority, a non-anxious and non-judgmental presence, and clear and responsible boundaries (Level II).[6]

The pastoral-reflection outcomes focus on students' abilities to apply the clinical method of learning to their ministry for the purposes of care and evaluation. The CPE outcomes that comprise the primary area of pastoral reflection include the following:

1. Formulate clear and specific goals for continuing pastoral formation with reference to one's strengths and weaknesses as identified through self-reflection, supervision, and feedback (Level I).

2. Establish collaboration and dialogue with peers, authorities, and other professionals (Level II).

3. Demonstrate self-supervision through realistic self-evaluation of pastoral functioning (Level II).

4. By the end of Level II, students will be able to demonstrate awareness of the Common Qualifications and Competencies for Professional Chaplains (Level II).[7]

6. "Objectives and Outcomes."
7. "Objectives and Outcomes."

CPE programs in which students enroll should be accredited by the US Department of Education. Various organizations offer healthcare systems CPE that they can use as they train clergy for clinical chaplaincy, but only the ACPE and the Institute for Clinical Pastoral Training are accredited by the US Department of Education.

Board certification. Prospective healthcare chaplains must serve in a healthcare environment that is characterized by distinct medical modalities and clinical practices. Having a board-certified chaplain designation upholds the core clinical professionalism and standardized clinical accountability of a healthcare chaplain. Without clear clinical competencies and standards that must be met by chaplains in a medical environment, there is the risk of well-meaning people without a clear comprehension of the complexities of a healthcare system causing unintentional harm.

In a healthcare system, all clinical professionals, such as physicians, nurses, therapists, social workers, and dietitians, are required to have clinical state licenses. Because clergy cannot have a clinical state license owing to the separation of church and state, the board-certified chaplain designation serves in the place of the clinical state license. The thirty-one board-certified chaplain competencies ensure competent pastoral care by addressing the following overarching areas: the integration of theory and practice, professional identity and conduct, professional-practice skills, and organizational leadership.

Some of the board-certifying bodies do not require ecclesiastical endorsement. Chaplains who pursue board certification should consider a body that does. Currently, the following bodies require ecclesiastical endorsement: the Association of Certified Christian Chaplains, the Association of Professional Chaplains, the National Association of Catholic Chaplains, and the National Association of Veterans Affairs Chaplains.

Professional Organizations for Healthcare Chaplains

Healthcare chaplaincy has many professional organizations to which chaplains can belong. Some of these organizations are faith-group or organization specific, while others are open to all chaplains. They include the following:

- American Association of Pastoral Counselors
- Association for Clinical Pastoral Education
- College of Pastoral Supervision and Psychotherapy
- HealthCare Chaplaincy Network
- National Association of Catholic Chaplains

- National Association of Veterans Affairs Chaplains
- Neshama: Association of Jewish Chaplains
- Pathways to Promise: Ministry and Mental Illness

These groups provide community for chaplains and continuing professional-development opportunities. Many denominations also have organizations for the chaplains they endorse. Becoming involved in professional organizations allows chaplains to maintain a professional standing and to form community for support as they, in their ministries, provide for others.

Leadership as Healthcare Chaplains

Healthcare chaplains can serve in leadership roles that include leading and managing a chaplain service, overseeing groups of chaplains, and leading CPE programs. While many chaplains do not seek positions of leadership and management, they can find themselves in those positions and should prepare so that they will be effective in them. Before accepting or rejecting leadership positions, healthcare chaplains should consider the following key principles that are essential to being an effective chaplain who is also a leader.

First, prayerfully approach the position. Healthcare chaplains are called by God to a distinct ministry (including a ministry of leadership) and must be sure of the calling. When chaplains serve from a posture of being called by God to the position of leadership, they are equipped to endure even the toughest challenges that may arise. If chaplains are not called by God but seek a leadership role for their own desire and benefit, they are less capable of being resilient and weathering the numerous problems that demand their attention.

Second, chaplains should be led by deep convictions as to what is right and honorable for the patients they serve and the chaplains they lead. The right decisions may not always be popular. Chaplain leaders should be aware of the tendency to employ a gentle pastoral approach for a problematic situation when a firmer approach is needed. Chaplains should hold themselves and the chaplains they lead to the same high standards of accountability, which means being willing to administer disciplinary measures as required and recognizing positive contributions from other chaplains.

Third, chaplains should understand fiscal accountability and the organizational side of healthcare. Chaplains who have little to no training in healthcare need to develop the associated skills through courses and reading. Developing effective time management and organizational skills allows leaders to manage the organization effectively. Taking time to develop business skills allows chaplains to fulfill the roles in which God places them.

Summary

Healthcare chaplains often explain suffering and loss to patients and families as they struggle to accept devastating health news that medical staff deliver to them. To be effective in healthcare settings, chaplains must come to terms with the theological topics of death and dying, suffering and pain, and anger at God. Chaplains do not need to have all the answers, but they need to be comfortable with their own beliefs so that they can walk alongside people who are experiencing difficult times and asking difficult questions. Healthcare chaplains serve people in healthcare settings for varied time periods, depending on the illnesses at hand. Developing relationships with staff is a way for chaplains to serve those with whom they work for a longer period.

Healthcare chaplains must stay readily available to serve as God wills amid the unexpected circumstances and unprecedented situations that may arise in their professional lives. When medical science and the financial world do not provide the security people seek, people develop an increased interest in matters of faith as they pursue existential answers, comforting grace, and eternal hope that are beyond the temporal things of this world. First Peter 3:15 states, "Always be prepared to give an answer to everyone who asks you to give the reason for the hope that you have. But do this with gentleness and respect" (NIV). Healthcare chaplaincy allows chaplains to fulfill this verse daily.

The COVID-19 pandemic provided increasing opportunities for healthcare chaplains not only to provide pastoral care for patients and their family members but also to provide pastoral care for healthcare leaders during extremely challenging situations. God has used telechaplaincy and chaplain phone calls in ways that were rejected in prepandemic times. God has worked powerfully in the last few years through healthcare chaplains and continues to do so as they serve on the cutting edge of changes in chaplain ministries.

13

Military Chaplaincy

Keith Travis

As part of the professional organization category of the functional areas of chaplaincy, military chaplaincy is one of the most formalized kinds of chaplaincy among the ten functional areas. Military chaplains work for both the US military and for their faith group. Those entering military chaplaincy must meet certain physical, educational, and experiential requirements before they can be accepted into the Army, Navy, or Air Force Chaplain Corps. After ordination, their faith group must also endorse them for military chaplaincy. Once they fulfill those requirements, chaplains must pass basic courses in military formalities that teach them how to be military officers. All branches require these courses.

Military life requires time away from home, frequent moves, and changes in job positions. Military chaplains work with military members, family members, and DOD civilians who work in the chaplain's assigned area. If chaplains are assigned to chapels, they also care for retired military members and their families who attend the chapel. Military chaplains work with military units, in hospitals, in chapels, and in many other places on military bases. This chapter explains military life, job expectations, educational requirements, and leadership opportunities for military chaplains.

The Culture and Ethos of Military Chaplaincy

Military chaplains serve full-time with the Army, Navy, Marine Corps, Coast Guard, Air Force, and Space Force. The National Guard, Air National Guard, and reserve units of the branches have chaplains who are part-time like the other members of these groups. Military chaplains serve in a multitude of commands, and that service can include air, land, sea, shore, and overseas duties. For some assignments, chaplains can be in chapels, where they conduct services, or in hospitals, where they work with patients and staff. Other jobs include serving with air wings, on submarines, with infantry units, with artillery units, on aircraft carriers, and with any unit that the military branches have. The military expects chaplains to deploy when the unit leaves. Deployment means that the chaplain is away from home for anywhere from a few days to a year, depending on the assignment.

Most military members are between ages eighteen and twenty-five, and the families are young as well. Most of the ministry of chaplains occurs with this age grouping, as its members learn to deal with life, death, and a highly structured lifestyle. Social media, video games, and pop culture are the focus of many in this group. Working with military members requires an understanding of social media and the ability to use it effectively, as well as the ability to discuss the pop-culture interests of young adults. Building relationships opens doors for chaplains to reach those who are seeking spiritual understanding.

Moving from place to place and changing communities (from aircraft carriers to infantry to staff) are constants in military life. Chaplains and their families move often, which means changing friends, schools, and homes. The US government pays military chaplains and provides housing allowances, health insurance, dental insurance, and retirement plans. Military chaplains also have opportunities to further their education through tuition assistance and GI Bill benefits. When chaplains enter the military, they enter a community that has a culture unlike that of civilian life. Chaplains must learn and embrace that culture in order to be effective in military ministry.

The culture within the military is much stricter and more "bureaucratic, hierarchical, and dominated by instrumental rationality" than most other institutions in which chaplaincy is practiced.[1] The military is highly structured and designed to form its adherents into a unified, organizational whole that follows orders explicitly. The cultural practice within the military requires that people are thrown together to form a cohesive unit while being stripped of their

1. Kim Philip Hansen, *Military Chaplains and Religious Diversity* (New York: Palgrave Macmillan, 2012), 13.

individuality. This cohesion involves a sense of mission and solidarity to which members subscribe. Within the military setting, there is no democratic nature that allows debate and compromise, and members do not have the ability to walk away if they feel inclined to do so.[2] This cultural formation is unique to the military, and military members often struggle with it. Within this cultural setting, chaplains can often have a voice as commanders learn to trust the chaplain's moral and spiritual guidance; however, chaplains must first earn the trust of the command staff.

Military chaplains are required to adopt and adapt to this hierarchical design in the same way that other military members do.[3] There are three unique cultural distinctives that military chaplains must be able to negotiate in order to serve the military community:

- *A diverse, pluralistic community:* Military chaplains serve a very religiously diverse population, containing members of most of the world's religious and nonreligious communities.

- *Divided loyalties:* Military chaplains serve with a sense of divided loyalties as they serve both the US military authority and their respective religious community's authority. This leads to a potential "role conflict," as chaplains are ordained clergy or certified religious providers endorsed by their faith group, and they are also commissioned officers in the US military's armed services.

- *First Amendment issues:* Military chaplains face issues of legitimacy; however, the First Amendment of the Constitution of the United States mandates the provision of religious care to members of the military.[4]

The Geneva Conventions' Article 22 and Article 24, section 28, and the Geneva Protocols of 1977 identify chaplains as protected personnel in their

2. Hansen, *Military Chaplains*, 14.
3. Hansen, *Military Chaplains*, 13.
4. Eric Patterson, ed., *Military Chaplains in Afghanistan, Iraq, and Beyond: Advisement and Leader Engagement in Highly Religious Environments* (Lanham, MD: Rowman & Littlefield, 2014); Michael Whittington and Charlie N. Davidson, *Matters of Conscience: A Practical Theology for the Evangelical Chaplain* (Lynchburg, VA: Liberty University Press, 2013), 39–41, 44–48; John Witte Jr. and Joel A. Nichols, *Religion and the American Constitutional Experiment*, 4th ed. (New York: Oxford University Press, 2016), 120–21; Hansen, *Military Chaplains*, 39–40; Robert D. Crick, *Outside the Gates: The Need for, Theology, History, and Practice of Chaplaincy Ministries*, with Brandelan S. Miller, rev. ed. (Oviedo, FL: HigherLife Development Services, 2011), 8–9; and John D. Laing, *In Jesus' Name: Evangelicals and Military Chaplaincy* (Eugene, OR: Resource, 2010), 69–70.

function and capacity as ministers of religion.[5] Specific service regulations further prohibit chaplains from bearing arms and classify chaplains as non-combatants.[6] Thus, chaplains have to negotiate the areas between combat training, unit readiness, and spiritual needs.

One of the more problematic cultural issues for military chaplains is the rank that they wear. The US Constitution, law, and policy support the free exercise of religion. For example, Title 10, United States Code (U.S.C.), sections 3073, 5142, and 8067, provide for the appointment of officers as chaplains in the Army, Navy, and Air Force. The Navy directs its Chaplain Corps to provide chaplains for the Marine Corps, Coast Guard, and Merchant Marine. Chaplains normally have rank without command (e.g., Title 10, U.S.C., sections 3581 and 8581) and function in the dual roles of religious leader and staff officer. Department of Defense Instruction 1300.17, *Accommodation of Religious Practices within the Military Services*, describes the commander's responsibility for religious accommodation.[7] Military chaplains are commissioned officers in the US Armed Forces and wear the rank insignia of their pay grade, such as lieutenant, captain, major, lieutenant colonel, and colonel, which are recognized in the Army, Marine Corps, and Air Force. In the Navy and Coast Guard, the relevant ranks are ensign, lieutenant junior grade, lieutenant, lieutenant commander, commander, and captain.[8] Ranks are important for chaplains to learn as they prepare for military service.[9]

One exception exists to the standard military policy of chaplains having no command authority. At the Naval Chaplaincy School in Newport, Rhode Island, the senior chaplain, a Navy captain (O-6), is the commanding officer of the school. As the commanding officer, that chaplain has all the rights, responsibilities, and authority as all Navy commanding officers. This person is the only chaplain serving in the US military who has that kind of operational authority and responsibility.

All military personnel must wear uniforms. The uniforms display information about the wearer's branch of service, rank, job, and special awards.

5. Pauletta Otis, "Understanding the Role and Influence of U.S. Military Chaplains," in *Military Chaplains in Afghanistan, Iraq, and Beyond: Advisement and Leader Engagement in Highly Religious Environments*, ed. Eric Patterson (Lanham, MD: Rowman & Littlefield, 2014), 26–27.

6. Hansen, *Military Chaplains*, 7, 27, 42.

7. Chairman, Joint Chiefs of Staff, "Joint Guide 1-05 for Religious Affairs in Joint Operations," February 1, 2018, I-1, https://www.jcs.mil/Portals/36/Documents/Doctrine/jdn_jg/jg1_05.pdf.

8. Angela L. Caruso-Yahne, "Spiritual, but Not Religious: Fostering Conversations in the Military System," Upaya Zen Center, December 2013, 8, https://upaya.org/uploads/pdfs/CarusoYa hneThesisFinal.pdf.

9. A list of ranks across the branches of the military can be found at Chad Storlie, "How to Understand US Military Rank Structure," Medium, December 21, 2016, https://medium.com /@combattocorp/how-to-understand-us-military-rank-structure-b817b63fdbe5.

Military members wear ribbons and medals that they have received for missions they have performed or as special recognition of work they have completed. All military members can "read" the ribbons and medals and understand the military history of the person with whom they are speaking (something like a curriculum vitae). Additionally, chaplains wear religious symbols that designate their faith-group affiliation, such as the Christian Latin cross, the Jewish tablets of the Ten Commandments, the Muslim crescent moon, the Buddhist dharma wheel, and the Hindu om.[10]

One of the hardest cultural misunderstandings to dispel fully is the idea that military chaplains are nothing more than an "ecclesiastical pawn of the government who is directed to preach a watered-down gospel that supports their policies and social engineering in an effort to appease the Washington DC bureaucrats."[11] This negative myth continues to be promulgated by members of the clergy who do not understand chaplaincy and how it functions within the military or other institutions that employ chaplains.[12]

Military chaplains are the protectors of religious liberty and the right to worship freely.[13] They minister in a pluralistic environment in which they should be open to and accepting of religious differences among others. Chaplains learn to facilitate for those who are not of their faith group, and they provide for people within their faith group. Oftentimes, chaplains can call on other chaplains to meet the needs of military members.

Military chaplains meet the needs of military members, their families, and civilian workers on the military institutions. When serving in chapels or performing services in the field, Protestant military chaplains conduct services according to their faith background (liturgical, nonliturgical, etc.). Catholics and other groups have services for their own members. A chapel can be shared by many faith groups because the building belongs to the commander of the base.

Humanist chaplains are not yet serving as part of the military chaplain corps. Such chaplains are being considered for inclusion in the ranks of established chaplains. As military chaplaincy evolves and forms to meet military adherents' needs, it faces the challenge that the military prefers a chaplaincy that is ecumenical and staffed in a way that is flexible and open-minded toward people and the needs of the military's mission. Kim Hansen has intimated that the military likes "broad, generic chaplains [who] can meet more religious needs than narrower ones can. Ecumenically minded chaplains are less likely to be

10. Caruso-Yahne, "Spiritual, but Not Religious," 8.
11. Whittington and Davidson, *Matters of Conscience*, 87.
12. Whittington and Davidson, *Matters of Conscience*, 87.
13. Hansen, *Military Chaplains*, 2–3, 14, 40–44.

distracted by theological bickering."[14] Yet evangelical military chaplains must cooperate without compromise as they represent their faith groups as well as the US government.

As chaplains follow the leadership of their respective faith groups, they are guided on what they can do in ministry. For example, some faith groups do not support prayers for the dead. It may come about that a military member requests that a chaplain pray a special prayer for a deceased person. If the chaplain's faith group rejects the practice of this kind of prayer, then the role of the chaplain is to find someone who can administer it. The chaplain in this case would be engaging in facilitation. In like manner, if the chaplain is asked to perform a same-sex wedding and their faith group does not allow this, then the military chaplain's role is to recommend a person who can perform the wedding. Military chaplains need to maintain an active list of other chaplains, civilian ministers, lay ministers, and others on whom they can call for assistance in providing the ministry that they cannot perform.

Chaplains serve many positions within commands. In some commands, the chaplain serves on the commander's staff, advising the commander on issues pertaining to religion, morale, and the command environment in general. Chaplains, as staff officers, are expected to be present at all staff meetings and functions (staff call, officers' call, and other functions). Chaplains should also attend birthday balls and similar functions. By attending these functions, chaplains are able to support the members of the command and make themselves visible as a caring presence.

Some issues chaplains encounter pertain to religious liberty. Chaplains today serve in a multicultural, multireligious (or nonreligious) secular environment. Chaplains must fully understand the complexities of religious liberty within the context of the military. One place the chaplain might go for help in this area is the endorser. Most endorsers provide training that will help the chaplain understand the issues and learn how to minister and maneuver within the environment.

Two other issues of great importance for chaplains are praying in Jesus's name and sharing their faith (evangelism). Chaplains serve every military member in the unit: those of like faith, those of other faith backgrounds, and those of no faith. Praying in Jesus's name can insult and alienate people if they are not believers. By building bridges and showing respect, chaplains can choose other ways to begin and end prayers.[15] In this way, chaplains show care and love for those who have different belief systems.

14. Hansen, *Military Chaplains*, 165.
15. See chap. 8, under "Public Prayer."

Chaplains need to develop relationships, choose their timing, and rely on the Holy Spirit to guide them in evangelizing. By building relationships, chaplains act as the bearers of the presence of God. Cultivating trusting relationships is therefore part of the ministry of presence. Evangelism also involves bearing the message of Christ. Chaplains who develop relationships with people can answer questions of faith when asked. In such cases, the safe space of the chaplain's office becomes a sacred space where Christ is present and the Holy Spirit works.

Subareas of Ministry in Military Chaplaincy

Chaplains serve in each branch of the military on active or reserve duty. Congress laid out the responsibilities for chaplains in Title 10, section 3547, of the United States Code, which states, "Each chaplain shall, when practicable, hold appropriate religious services at least once on each Sunday for the command to which he is assigned, and shall perform appropriate religious burial services for members of the Army who die while in that command."[16]

Military chaplains must choose a branch and a level of commitment before they can begin serving. There are three branches to choose from: Army, Navy, and Air Force. Navy chaplains serve the Navy, Marine Corps, and Coast Guard. Air Force chaplains serve the Air Force and Space Force. The commitment level is either full-time or part-time. Active-duty chaplains serve full-time, while reservists or National Guard chaplains serve part-time. Part-time work involves one weekend a month and two weeks of training each year. However, recent years have shown that the part-time work can require longer periods that extend up to a year as the National Guard and reservists are called up to fill in for regular military when resources are strained.

While military chaplains share many aspects across the branches, each branch has its specific ways of performing ministry that chaplains should learn. The following paragraphs explain the ways the different kinds of military chaplains serve, the ministries they perform, and the ways they interact with military members and their families.

Navy

The US Navy serves on land, in the air, on the sea, and under the sea. Navy chaplains, religious personnel, doctors, nurses, corpsmen, dentists, and dental assistants can serve in the Navy, Marine Corps, and Coast Guard. Religious personnel, who are not chaplains, are enlisted members who work in the chap-

16. 10 U.S.C. (2012), § 3547, https://uscode.house.gov/browse/prelim@title10&edition=prelim.

lain's office. They set up for services, assist with events, and act as force protection for the chaplain in combat zones. Chaplains and religious personnel work closely together.

Navy chaplaincy is unit-based, with chaplains serving and deploying aboard ships, with air wings, or with other units. Navy chaplains work in the following areas: chapels, hospitals, family service centers, counseling centers, ships, submarines, planes, staffs, and other areas on bases. They serve on larger ships, from destroyers to aircraft carriers. When the ship goes to sea, the chaplain sails with it. Often, the men and women aboard these ships seek out chaplains when they are at sea, but they would not in port. Ministry opportunities for chaplains include counseling; preaching; mentoring; conducting weddings and funerals; leading Bible studies, vacation Bible schools, and Sunday schools; and carrying out any other service that a pastor or counselor would perform.

Navy chaplains are the bearers of the presence of God when they walk into a room. The collar or sleeve of their uniform displays an emblem of their religion so that everyone can see that they are a chaplain. The uniform itself announces that a ministry of presence is at work. Chaplains need listening, counseling, and caring skills. To reach military members, chaplains must run and do the physical training with the other members of the unit. Many bridges are built by a chaplain who can beat most of the military members in their daily physical training runs. Additionally, chaplains who wear the uniforms of the group with whom they are working make great strides in establishing relationships. Uniforms are purchased during basic courses in Newport, Rhode Island. For ship and shore duties, these uniforms are sufficient; however, if chaplains serve a squadron in the air wing, then they can buy the flight suits that the pilots wear. A caution, however, is that chaplains should wear the uniforms correctly lest they be isolated from the crews.

Navy bases are generally on the coasts of the United States and also in other countries such as Italy, Japan, South Korea, and Spain. Individual assignments can take a chaplain to England, Germany, Australia, and other countries around the world. Often, chaplains circumvent the globe aboard ships as they sail from the East Coast and then from the West Coast. Navy duty divides into sea duty and shore duty. Sea duty usually means deployments, while shore duty is often on a staff or in a chapel. Chaplains serving with the Navy should enjoy the sea and traveling.

Marine Corps

Navy chaplains also serve with the Marine Corps as unit-based chaplains. They serve with a unit and deploy when that unit does. The culture of the

Marine Corps is difficult to be accepted into because of the ethos of the corps. Marines have basic training that is more difficult than any other branch. This training breeds a long line of pride and culture that is not as open to outsiders. Understanding the culture of the Marine Corps, attending events, and being able to keep up with physical training are important for establishing relationships with marines.

When reporting for duty, chaplains will want to have Marine uniforms and wear them correctly. Discipline is high in the Marine Corps, with emphasis on neatness and order. Thus, uniforms should be ironed, and shoes should be polished. Otherwise, chaplains risk being marginalized within the culture. Chaplains find it difficult to form relationships with marines, but respecting what is important to them can be a relationship builder. Many marines are strong Christians and work to support chaplains. However, chaplains have to work to gain the respect of other marines.

Marines train for combat, and their tasking is to be the first to respond. They are a rapid-response group and can deploy swiftly. Therefore, marines sometimes leave their families without preparation. When deployments occur, many family issues that have been hidden come to the surface. Marital problems and problems with teenagers or younger children can emerge with little to no way to work them out until the deployment is over. Chaplains can help in these situations. If the chaplain is stationed on a Marine base, they can support families. If the chaplain is deployed with the unit, they can support marines trying to handle these situations from a distance. Counseling skills are important for Marine chaplains.

Marines train for desert, jungle, and urban warfare. Planes and helicopters make up part of the Marine Corps as well. When marines need to move in large masses, they use Navy ships to move supplies and people. Learning the marines' system and acronyms is important so that chaplains can build relationships with them and affect their lives.

Coast Guard

Navy chaplains can also be stationed with the Coast Guard as unit-based chaplains. They work in the Coast Guard stations and may accompany the guardsmen on a trip to sea; however, they usually do not deploy in the same way that they do with the Navy and Marine Corps. The opportunities to work with the Coast Guard are fewer than Navy and Marine billets (jobs), but the positions require buying Coast Guard uniforms. Coast Guard bases line the coasts of the United States, and guardians deploy to other areas at times. Their main tasks are to search for drugs coming in through coastal areas and to rescue immigrants crossing the seas. Coast Guard bases are also on the Great Lakes.

Chaplains serving with the Coast Guard lead chapel services, care for families, and tend to the spiritual and emotional needs of their units. They work with the unit commander to meet the needs of the crews, and they influence decisions by reminding commanders of the moral and spiritual compasses of decision-making. Coast Guard boats can deploy, as they did in the wars of the past few decades, but they usually stay in coastal areas around the United States.

Army

The Army has the largest chaplain corps of all the military branches. Army chaplains are unit-based and deploy when the unit deploys. During the last few wars, the Army and Marine Corps deployed more often and for longer periods than the other branches did. Many family problems arose amid these rapid deployments, and many military members developed stress-related injuries from their rapid-deployment schedules. All chaplains working with military members should be aware of the stress-related injuries that they suffer. Chaplains should prepare, through counseling coursework, to help those with such injuries.

Army chaplains can work in chapels and hospitals, with air and ground units, and on staffs throughout the world. Army chaplains work with families, counsel military members, and conduct marriage counseling and other family-related ministries. The work in chapels includes a full range of church programs, depending on the available volunteers. Often, military retirees in the area continue to attend chapels and will help with programs for families.

Bases are found throughout the United States and in Europe and Asia. Army chaplains can also go to other places in the world when they accompany a unit. As with the other branches, Army chaplains should wear their uniforms correctly and know the military language. Understanding the Army's culture is important in reaching people where they are.

Air Force

Air Force chaplaincy uses a chapel-based model for ministry. The senior chaplain is stationed in the base chapel with the other chaplains. As needs arise with units, chaplains are assigned to those units to meet the needs. When the needs are met, the chaplain returns to the chapel offices to await the next assignment. Chaplains will deploy with the units, but these deployments are usually shorter and less frequent than in other branches.

In between assignments, Air Force chaplains run chapel programs such as worship services, Bible studies, Sunday school classes, children's and youth programs, and music programs. Counseling families and military members is a large part of an Air Force chaplain's job; therefore, CPE is an important part of preparation for this kind of ministry.

Space Force

Some Air Force chaplains moved to the Space Force when it was established in 2019. They brought the model of chapel-based ministry from the Air Force to the Space Force. This newest branch of the military offers an opportunity for different kinds of ministry as it begins to fulfill its mission. Currently, however, Space Force members are still facing the problems and struggles of this planet, problems that chaplains can assist them with. For that reason, Space Force chaplains rotate to the Space Force and then back to Air Force assignments.

Reservists and National Guard

Chaplains who want to become part-time military members should consider entering the Army, Navy, or Air Force reserves. These federal groups require less commitment than full-time active duty. Chaplains interested in the reserves should understand the following:

- The preparation requirements are the same as for active duty.
- The work requires a weekend per month for drill. (For chaplains with weekend church responsibilities, the days can possibly be negotiated.)
- The work requires two weeks during the year for extended training.
- Retirement opportunities and other benefits are possibilities.

Many pastors and other ministers serve their nation part-time as reserve chaplains. Reservists should be aware that they can be called to active duty if the nation needs more chaplains. They cannot back out if their schedule does not allow the full commitment. When chaplains become reservists, they do so with the knowledge that they may have to serve full-time. If chaplains desire, they can apply to augment to active duty at some time during their career.

Chaplains in the National Guard or Air National Guard are paid by the states in which they serve. Their preparation requirements and training are the same as those for reservists. They also have benefits and retirement opportunities, including pensions, healthcare benefits, and use of base facilities. These groups respond to emergencies in the states, such as hurricanes, flooding, and tornadoes. Chaplains work with the guardsmen, but they also can work with the people affected by natural disasters. National Guard units can be federalized and sent to other areas within the United States. Chaplains, then, would accompany the units at these times. Generally, if the chaplain is a pastor or staff member of a local church, that church will need to approve the part-time chaplaincy request.

These part-time opportunities provide added income and additional outreach opportunities for chaplains. Of course, the rules for active-duty chaplains concerning counseling and evangelism apply to reservist and National Guard chaplains as well.

Special Concerns with the Military

Special concerns when working with the military include understanding post-traumatic stress disorder, moral injury, and spiritual injury, as well as working with people who are suffering from them. People desiring to become military chaplains should take coursework in counseling so they will be prepared to recognize and refer those with these injuries.

Another concern for chaplains is the prominence of sexual assault within the military. Many military members carry the trauma of sexual assault. Chaplains should be aware of this problem and learn of various ways to help victims of this kind of trauma.

In today's climate, suicides among military members have risen to an alarming rate. Chaplains need to understand how to maintain confidentiality while also providing help for military members overwhelmed with life. Knowing when to refer and recognizing the signs of suicidal ideation are important skills for chaplains to have when working with military members. Additionally, chaplains often teach workshops on suicide prevention for different units. Thus, preparation in this area would be beneficial for those entering military chaplaincy.

Requirements for Becoming a Military Chaplain

Professional chaplaincy requires preparation in chaplaincy, theology, and ministry skills. Military chaplaincy also has formalized requirements that chaplains must complete before entering this kind of service. Military chaplains need to have the following KSAs in order to succeed in ministering in the military:

- *Knowledge:* This includes a knowledge of chaplaincy, theology, counseling, and leadership training, which is gained through higher education and CPE. It also includes knowledge of military ranks and branches.
- *Skills:* These include excellent interpersonal skills; pastoral skills, including the conducting of services; leadership skills; and counseling skills. Military chaplains can be short- or long-term counselors, depending on where they are stationed. Thus, they should have counseling skills. Additionally, compassion, empathy, and listening skills are important for this type of chaplaincy.
- *Abilities:* These include capacities to comfort people in times of crisis, care for military members and families in routine or crisis times, work well with teams, and provide spiritual care for others. Military chaplains also need the ability to run a full chapel program and to care for military personnel in combat zones.

Aspiring military chaplains can obtain these KSAs by completing the requirements in this section and volunteering in churches, hospitals, and military bases (if nearby).

The formalized requirements for entry into military chaplaincy begin with meeting the medical, physical, and age requirements of the branch that the chaplain is considering. While the age requirements have changed in recent years, the medical and physical rigors have not. Checking with chaplain recruiters of the branch of choice is the best way to secure the current requirements. The importance of using chaplain recruiters is that the age range for chaplain positions differs from the age range for other jobs within the military. With the requirement of a master's degree and experience, chaplains are typically older than others when they enter. The following requirements are approved by the Department of Defense and apply to all prospective chaplains.

DOD requirements. The DOD requires the following education and experience from people who want to be chaplains:

- A bachelor's degree in any subject.
- An MDiv (or similar degree) with seventy-two credit hours of study from a DOD-approved seminary. Chaplaincy studies should be a part of the graduate program, as should theology and counseling.

- Two years of ministry experience after seminary. CPE can be part of the experience for some faith groups. CPE is an excellent addition to the military chaplains' pursuit of the listening and counseling skills that are part of the job.
- Experience leading at least one funeral and one wedding. This requirement may be waived by the endorser if candidates acquire quality ministry experience while in seminary or at other times in their lives.
- Endorsement from a DOD-approved religious endorser.

Calling. Prospective military chaplains must receive a call to serve as a chaplain in the military, and they must commit to long-term work with military members and their families.

Chaplain-candidate programs. Each branch has a chaplain-candidate program for people desiring to be chaplains. The program is available to prospective chaplains who are in graduate schools. In the program, chaplain candidates work on military bases (in their branch of choice) during school breaks and may attend basic courses during that time as well. They also undergo periods of on-the-job training under the direction of a full-time military chaplain. This experience is excellent.

Once selected for service as a chaplain in a particular branch, prospective chaplains attend chaplains' school. Each branch has a separate chaplains' school that prepares chaplains for military culture and for the ministry they will conduct. The Navy school is at Naval Base Newport in Rhode Island; the Army school is at Fort Jackson, Columbia, South Carolina; and the Air Force school is at Maxwell Air Force Base, Montgomery, Alabama. These chaplains' schools do not teach theology but rather teach chaplains to be officers in the branch in which they will serve. Chaplains learn basic military functions like rank structure, marching, saluting, running, physical training, and individual sailor's, airman's, and soldier's tasks. Chaplains are taught how to navigate the diverse, secular culture in which they are serving. They also learn to wear uniforms properly.

Because of the First Amendment, the DOD cannot favor one religion over another. Thus, when chaplains report to their basic courses, they are expected to be religious leaders within their own faith group. Each branch has expressed this philosophy in its own manner:

- The Army Chaplain Basic Course has the vision "to transform civilian religious leaders into influential, adaptive, and critically thinking military religious leaders capable of meeting the religious support needs of the Army."[17]

- The Navy has a similar mission: "To train, develop, and inspire chaplains . . . to pursue excellence as they strengthen the soul of the warfighter, the family, and the fleet. . . . Religious ministry and compassionate pastoral care are characterized by cooperation, tolerance, mutual respect, and respect for diversity, as well as an emphasis on understanding the pluralistic military environment."[18]

- The vision of the Air Force chaplain school is to equip "the Air Force Chaplain Corps through training and education to care for Airmen more than anyone thinks possible."[19] This is done by training and educating the prospective candidate to serve faithfully the airmen and families within the Air Force.

The basic schools introduce chaplains to the military, and later military schools emphasize concepts and ideas that military chaplains need to know. Chaplains attend military schools throughout their careers to learn about new skills, new projects, and leadership responsibilities for new jobs.

Professional Organizations for Military Chaplains

Professional organizations exist for US military chaplains. Most chaplain corps, however, have professional organizations within their branch of service. Often, the chaplains on a particular base, fort, ship, or elsewhere meet weekly or monthly to network and address issues they may have. The hierarchical structure provides mentoring for new chaplains. Each branch's chaplain corps offers routine training through schools and workshops. If chaplains are from large faith groups, they will meet at certain times with other chaplains in the area who are from their faith group. Networking and social events among chaplains provide professional support.

Professional organizations for military chaplains include the following:

17. "Chaplain Basic Officer Leader Course (CHBOLC)," US Army Institute for Religious Leadership, accessed April 12, 2023, https://usairl.tradoc.army.mil/courses/chbolc.

18. James Stockman, "Naval Chaplaincy School, Center Uses Virtual Training for Mission Success," America's Navy, U.S. Navy Office of Information, October 19, 2020, https://www.navy.mil/Press-Office/News-Stories/Article/2385571/naval-chaplaincy-school-center-uses-virtual-training-for-mission-success.

19. "Air Force Chaplain Corps College," Air University, United States Air Force, accessed January 19, 2023, https://www.airuniversity.af.edu/Eaker-Center/AFCCC.

- Military Chaplains Organization
- National Association of Veterans Affairs Chaplains

Military chaplains network with other chaplains from a variety of nations when they are deployed to or with other countries. Building professional chaplain networks assists military chaplains in being effective in their ministries.

Leadership as a Military Chaplain

Leadership positions offer opportunities to influence senior leadership and the course of a department or unit. Military chaplains lead by being the moral and spiritual compasses on the command's leadership teams, which means they have the responsibility of reminding the leaders of their moral and spiritual responsibilities with respect to the decisions that the command makes.[20] With an evangelical chaplain influencing the direction in which leadership moves, the moral and spiritual compasses point true.

As military chaplains are promoted, they begin to direct other chaplains and influence decisions of top-ranking military personnel. Chaplains can mentor and guide newer chaplains so that they understand the goals of chaplaincy in relation to leading command teams. Military chaplains have ample opportunities to lead during their time in the military.

Summary

Military chaplaincy offers a unique platform for ministry among younger people who share a goal to protect the United States. By influencing their choices and building relationships with them, chaplains help military members focus on their missions while knowing that the chaplain supports them. Whether on a ship, in a plane, on the ground, in a chapel, or in a combat zone, military chaplains are stationed around the world to support military members and aid them in their spiritual struggles.

On May 1, 1946, Fleet Admiral Chester Nimitz gave the closing remarks at the annual meeting of the General Commission on Army and Navy Chaplains in Washington, DC. He stated:

> My own esteem for the chaplains is not so much based upon deeds of valor as it is appreciation for their routine accomplishments. No one will ever know how

20. Ed Waggoner, "Taking Religion Seriously in the US Military: The Chaplaincy as a National Strategic Asset," *Journal of the American Academy of Religion* 82, no. 3 (2014): 717–18.

many young men were deferred from acts of desperation by a heart-to-heart talk with the "Padre."

"Man cannot live by bread alone," to be sure, and neither can man's spiritual needs be wholly satisfied by ritual. By his patient, sympathetic labors with the men, day in, day out, and through many a night, every chaplain I know contributed immeasurably to the moral courage of our fighting men.

None of that effort appears in the statistics. Most of it was necessarily secret between the pastor and his confidant. It is for that toil in the cause of God and country that I honor the chaplains most.[21]

21. Kenneth D. Perkins, review of The History of the Chaplain Corps, United States Navy, Volume Two, 1939–1949, by Clifford M. Drury, Historical Magazine of the Protestant Church 20, no. 2 (June 1, 1951): 308–9.

14

Education Chaplaincy

Michael W. Langston

M any colleges and universities have offices for chaplains within their communities. With the rise of suicide and other serious mental issues related to self-harm on postsecondary campuses, chaplains are in positions to provide confidential conversations and help for students who are struggling. COVID-19 seriously affected postsecondary students who were unable to attend classes or social events at their institutions. Their isolation and loneliness brought to the forefront many issues that students thought they had outgrown. Students in colleges and universities face many challenges to their lives, beliefs, and morals. Chaplains working in these institutions have opportunities to influence the next generation of adults as they struggle with forming an identity, belonging to a community, and moving into an unknown future. Chaplains also have the ability to support faculty and staff as they struggle with the challenges of holding onto faith within the world of higher education.

Part of the institution chaplaincy category, education chaplains work in higher education throughout the United States. Brian Konkol, an education chaplain at Syracuse University, issues the following call to action for education chaplains as he discusses the current crises on college campuses:

> Crisis can spark clarification. The more significant the crisis, the more substantial the potential for clarity. In this time of sustained crises surrounding COVID-19,

anti-Black racism, anti-Semitism, political dysfunction, mental illness and countless other personal and public traumas, what seems to be increasingly clear is that
chaplains are essential for the heart and soul of higher education.[1]

Education chaplains are the heart and soul of higher education. They bring
peace and pastoral counseling to students, faculty, and staff who are overwhelmed with personal and social issues as they search for meaning. This
chapter presents the history of education chaplaincy, its culture and ethos, its
subareas, the required preparation, relevant professional organizations, and
leadership opportunities for education chaplains.

The History of Education Chaplaincy

The history of education chaplains traces back, as all chaplain histories do, to
St. Martin of Tours. For education chaplaincy, however, the path is more of a
hidden history, since early education in the United States was usually offered for
religion and medicine, with chapel services being a required part of all studies.
The early Puritans and settlers established colleges to educate their ministers.
Thus, the faculty members were pastors, chaplains, and campus ministers, as
well as professors.

In the early twentieth century, however, colleges and universities lost their
religious emphasis as they embraced humanism as a guiding philosophy and
began rejecting the influence of religion. Religion was pushed into departments,
chapel services were canceled, and other influences from the religious sector
were minimized. As a result, students, faculty, and staff experienced a gap as
they sought to incorporate meaning in their lives and their studies.

Currently, many colleges and universities are filling these gaps by hiring
chaplains to provide pastoral care, to support people in their struggles, and to
help them find meaning in their lives. Chaplaincy in public institutions is an
area that some groups oppose because of the separation of church and state;
however, this opposition has not changed the commitment of colleges and
universities to provide chaplains for their students, faculty, and staff.

The Culture and Ethos of Education Chaplaincy

Education chaplains offer educational institutions unique perspectives as leaders and influencers. In the current "mental, emotional, and spiritual health

1. Brian E. Konkol, "Chaplains Are Essential for Higher Education's Heart and Soul," Inside
Higher Ed, December 14, 2020, https://www.insidehighered.com/views/2020/12/15/importance
-chaplains-and-why-colleges-should-support-them-opinion.

crisis amongst college students," chaplains are in unique positions not only to provide pastoral care to students but also to assist them in finding meaning within their lives. Education chaplains' "positions on campus and pastoral care training make them especially qualified to help individuals find meaning, build communities, and foster a sense of belonging." As campuses seek to "build inclusive, diverse, and equitable campus communities," chaplains bring a spirit of acceptance and openness to these goals.[2] Chaplains build relationships with faculty and staff so they can influence the moral and spiritual discussions that occur at the institutions while these institutions seek to produce more open environments.

To be effective, education chaplains must go where students are and not wait for them to come to them. Chaplains find students in the gym, at coffee shops, at athletic events, at cafeterias, outside classroom buildings, and throughout the campus. To develop trust with students, chaplains engage them in conversation and fun. Students in today's universities and colleges are very aware of mental health and the crises in their culture. They also are aware of stereotypes of religious people and Christians, which can cause distrust of chaplains. Through patience and relationship building, education chaplains can break down those barriers.

Education chaplains differ from campus ministers in that campus ministers often represent one faith group and engage in evangelism and proselytism. They share their faith with students with the hope that students will join their faith group. For chaplains, by contrast, proselytism is not allowed. Education chaplains are hired by the institution to resist proselytizing and instead build relationships, offer care and comfort, and serve the students, staff, faculty, and administration. While education chaplains also spread the gospel, their main focus is relationships that develop into permission to share the gospel. Also, chaplains fall under confidentiality laws, while the case may not be as clear-cut with campus ministers.

Education chaplains work with the entire college or university community, including faculty, staff, and students. Because of this diverse community, education chaplains need to understand the pluralistic culture of the campus. "Cooperation without compromise" is a guiding principle for chaplains. Depending on where chaplains serve, the pluralistic culture can vary greatly. Chaplains should learn the demographics of the campus in order to understand the religious beliefs and needs of the people who work and live there. Helping individuals

2. Varun Soni, "The Future of Campus Chaplains as Leaders in University Life," Henry Luce Foundation, May 25, 2021, https://www.hluce.org/news/articles/future-campus-chaplains-leaders-university-life.

from all faiths is part of the chaplain's caregiving. Below are just a few examples of an education chaplain's responsibilities:

- *Facilitating religious and spiritual practices:* Education chaplains should be familiar with the religious and spiritual practices of students, faculty, and staff at their institution. Chaplains can plan services on holy days for different religions by having a clergy member come to campus. They can also facilitate, rather than provide, spiritual care when a request falls outside the limits of their own beliefs and practices. Education chaplains often encounter world religions as students from other countries and cultures attend the college or university.
- *Counseling and mentoring:* Education chaplains provide counseling for all members of the community. Chaplains are required to be nondiscriminatory in their counseling.
- *Helping develop policies and curriculum:* Education chaplains can serve on diversity-and-equity committees to give input on creating welcoming environments. They also can assist in the development of religious curriculum. Chaplains need to be aware that they may face opposition to inclusion on committees.
- *Serving their unique demographic:* Educational institutions have unique demographics with professors, supporting staff, students, and administrators. Education chaplains can guide faculty members to be more sensitive to student issues and can educate faculty and staff about current issues students are facing. They can also guide students in solving problems and searching for meaning in their lives.[3]

These responsibilities allow education chaplains to minister effectively to the communities they serve.

The skills that education chaplains need in order to accomplish these tasks include the following:

- *Interpersonal skills*—being able to listen carefully to and advise students and others clearly about their worries and fears, faith issues, and responses to grief and other crises
- *Spiritual skills*—understanding different spiritual perspectives and religious traditions

3. "What Is a University Chaplain?," AdventHealth University, September 23, 2021, https://www.ahu.edu/blog/university-chaplain.

- *Emotional skills*—understanding and responding with empathy to the emotions that students and others experience, offering support and encouragement
- *Analytical skills*—interpreting signs of crisis and knowing how and when to intervene[4]

With the suicide rates increasing rapidly in college and university populations, recognizing and interpreting the signs of crisis is an important skill. The section below titled "Requirements for Becoming an Education Chaplain" outlines the training people need in order to acquire all these skills.

Education chaplains also need networking skills in order to fulfill their duties properly. Chaplains need contacts in various parts of the college or university community, including the health system, the disabilities office, campus security, the ombuds office, advising offices, diversity-and-equity offices, Title VII and IX offices, and other campus offices that provide support for students. They also need resources from the city or town in which the school is located.

By learning the confidentiality laws within the state where they work, education chaplains can gauge what they are required to share and what they should not share from priest-penitent conversations. The confidentiality laws now vary from state to state, so updating their knowledge is a requirement for education chaplains. Additionally, education chaplains need to understand the state's laws for being a mandatory reporter on certain issues. Most postsecondary institutions require employees to announce to students that they are or are not mandatory reporters before students share information. Education chaplains should research the laws and the institution's policies regarding mandatory reporting. Chaplains are responsible for knowing federal and state laws on these policies and standing by those laws.

Colleges and universities embrace diversity and inclusion. They welcome students from other countries and cultures, providing international offices and teams to help these students adjust. Education chaplains have opportunities to work with these offices in welcoming international students and faculty. Providing resources that meet the students' beliefs and customs can build bridges with these newcomers, who are adjusting to a new culture.

Konkol provides insight into the role of education chaplains by explaining the current climate on university campuses:

Chaplains serve alongside people of diverse religious, spiritual, moral and ethical backgrounds. By inviting learners into the fullness of life, chaplains are called

4. "What Is a University Chaplain?"

upon to draw from various traditions and practices to build community, provide guidance, lead rituals, facilitate interfaith cooperation and offer unconditional care. As college students are now increasingly pressured to succeed despite the instability of situations that surround them—and within a historical era of conflict, change and isolation—one can credibly contend the role of chaplain has never been more important.[5]

The challenges of American culture have disrupted students' lives in ways that they are not mature enough to understand yet. Chaplains who understand current ideas and trends on campus can assist students in understanding and forming their own opinions on current issues. The insertion of faith into the discussion is also part of the chaplain's task as students struggle to find meaning in their lives and in the world.

Konkol addresses another major issue on college campuses: the pressure to succeed. Students in colleges and universities today fill their time with volunteer work, internships, intensive studying, and social clubs, with the hope of attaining a prestigious job or entering a graduate program upon graduating. Success was worked into American culture long before the birth of today's students, but it is the lifeblood of many of them. The pressures and stresses they endure in order to succeed have physical, mental, emotional, and spiritual costs of which they are unaware. Education chaplains, by building relationships and listening to their struggles, can guide students to a better perspective that is spiritually based instead of materially based.

Continuing in his message to chaplains, Konkol explains that chaplains should view students as being "worthy of awe and respect." As St. Martin of Tours found the robe to be sacred, education chaplains should view students as sacred. Konkol states, "The hopes of our students are sacred. The dreams of our students are sacred. The affirmations, questions, curiosities, fears, faiths, doubts and failures of our students are all wonderfully sacred."[6] Realizing that students explore ideas they learn in class and walking with them through their faith struggles, their doubts, their fears, and their lives, education chaplains convey to students their sacredness to God.

In today's colleges and universities, employees and students focus on identity, diversity, acceptance of other ideas, and many other concepts. Students with religious backgrounds can approach education chaplains for help in discerning how to adapt these concepts and ideas into their faith. This growth helps students determine their own faith, in distinction to what they may

5. Konkol, "Chaplains Are Essential."
6. Konkol, "Chaplains Are Essential."

have been taught at earlier stages of their lives. Education chaplains stand
in a unique place to usher students from an inherited faith to a faith that is
their own. Through the following practices that Konkol discusses, chaplains
can assist students, staff, and faculty in dealing with the acceptance of new
ideas.

1. *Exploring and honoring identity:* Education chaplains often begin
   learning by exploring who they are, deciding who they might become, and using that information as a foundation for all that follows.
   Often, a chaplain's calling is part of this process. Seminary and CPE
   further assist in this discovery. By being aware of and focusing on
   the Spirit within them, chaplains provide students with freedom and
   an example of how to focus on the Spirit as they encounter new
   ideas.[7]

2. *Creating and cultivating community:* Being present is a skill that chaplains develop and fine-tune in CPE. When chaplains are present
   with others, they create safe spaces in which students can feel that
   they belong. Amid the rapid-paced and changing postsecondary
   education environment, chaplains serve as a "living reminder that
   humans being are, at their core, relational beings. By accompanying diverse learners through the twists and turns of their dynamic
   lives, chaplains link becoming to belonging and provide a reminder
   that being present alongside others can hold tremendous power and
   possibility."[8]

3. *Illuminating and igniting purpose:* "In the midst of significant and turbu-
   lent times like crises, chaplains seek to link identity (Who am I?) with
   community (Where am I?) to offer a greater understanding of purpose
   (Why am I?)." Chaplains help students "nourish a lifelong discernment
   of vocation—or a sense of shared responsibility that embraces opportunity and encompasses multiple areas of life in service to our common
   good."[9] Offering students a concept of vocation also introduces them
   to the power of God in their lives as they move out from the university
   and into the world.

Education chaplains can affect the lives of students as they consider the sacredness of each student and the power of vocation in their lives.

7. Konkol, "Chaplains Are Essential."
8. Konkol, "Chaplains Are Essential."
9. Konkol, "Chaplains Are Essential."

Subareas of Ministry in Education Chaplaincy

Subareas of education chaplaincy are not as distinct as those of some other functional areas of chaplaincy; however, the differences are still worth exploring. Junior colleges and major research universities, private and public schools, and small and large institutions attract students with differing interests and needs. Understanding the differences allows education chaplains to minister more effectively.

Large Public Universities

Public university employees and students can often face problems pertaining to religion because of misunderstandings about the separation of church and state. Education chaplains need a full understanding of the laws and arguments so they can clearly defend their right to be on campus. Ministry in large universities requires staff with counseling centers that can help handle the student population.

Building relationships with students can begin as early as move-in day, with chaplains assisting students with their boxes, continuing with video games at the student center, and later including tailgating at football games. Attending other sporting events and intramural games, working out in the gym, hanging out in libraries, and being a presence on campus are ways to invite students to investigate the chaplaincy program on campus.

Education chaplains need to be versatile on social media. Students expect social media usage. Podcasts, videos, and other online communications are necessary with today's students. Education chaplains must be able to utilize these platforms to be current in the education world.

Engaging in committee work and teaching classes are ways for chaplains to encounter faculty and staff. Visiting workplaces and sending notes of congratulations for achievements posted in campus papers are other ways to begin building relationships. The main challenge for education chaplains on large campuses is the overwhelming number of people on the campus.

Small Public Universities

Small public universities often have students who want to be in or whose parents want them in an environment where they will not be overwhelmed by people. Chaplains have an easier job establishing relationships in this setting because students often desire mentoring relationships with faculty or staff. The reason for their choice of a smaller school is to be known.

Chaplains can utilize that desire to be known by forming small group meetings and other community activities. The ideas for ministering in larger schools discussed above are also effective in smaller schools, though chaplains are not as overwhelmed by the numbers. Chaplains have access to a larger percentage of the student and employee population in smaller schools because they can physically cover more of the campus areas than they can in larger schools.

Private Colleges and Universities

Often in private colleges and universities, chaplains are confused with campus ministers or pastors. This confusion occurs in Christian institutions that place the education chaplain in a precarious position. By law, chaplains have to maintain the confidentiality of information told to them in confidence. They can be taken to court for breaching confidentiality. Yet when a student has an issue and is sent to the education chaplain for counseling, administrators may expect the chaplain to share what the student discusses. Chaplains cannot share this information without the student's permission. Campus ministers, by contrast, can.

While not all private postsecondary institutions are Christian, many of them, as well as many of their students, are. These students still face the typical struggles of non-Christian students, as they are away from home while exploring new experiences and new ideas. Chaplains can guide and assist them as they challenge their childhood beliefs and explore a faith of their own.

Virtual Education

Chaplains can be virtual chaplains. This can involve podcasts, social media, online devotional videos, and other such means. During the COVID-19 pandemic, chaplains began to meet with students through video chats and other formats. Education chaplains also provide care for online students in some postsecondary programs. This care extends worldwide, and chaplains must be comfortable with video meetings. Virtual-education chaplaincy is a new and developing part of an education chaplain's work.

Requirements for Becoming an Education Chaplain

Professional chaplaincy requires preparation in chaplaincy, theology, and ministry skills. Education chaplaincy has less formalized requirements than some other functional areas, but those who pursue it need to have the following KSAs in order to succeed:

- *Knowledge:* This includes a knowledge of chaplaincy, theology, counseling, young-adult development, and leadership training, which is gained through higher education and CPE. Chaplains can benefit from courses in drug and alcohol awareness as well as training in short-term mental health interventions.

- *Skills:* These include excellent interpersonal skills; pastoral skills, including the conducting of services; leadership skills; and counseling skills. Education chaplains can be short- or long-term counselors, so they benefit from training in short-term crisis intervention, spiritual counseling, and support counseling. Additionally, compassion, empathy, and listening skills are important for this type of chaplaincy.
- *Abilities:* These include capacities to comfort people in times of crisis; care for faculty, staff, and students in routine or crisis times; work well with teams; and provide spiritual care for others.

Aspiring education chaplains can obtain these KSAs by completing the requirements in this section and volunteering in college or university settings. In order to qualify for chaplaincy within most educational institutions, chaplains must meet certain criteria. The requirements for becoming an education chaplain are less formalized than those of most other types of chaplaincy because they differ between institutions. But overall the requirements are similar. To become a professional education chaplain, people should prepare as follows.

Education. Those pursuing education chaplaincy should complete the following educational requirements:

- A bachelor's degree in any field.
- An MDiv or MA degree with a concentration in chaplaincy studies. Counseling and theology courses are beneficial, as are courses focused on the needs of young adults. Courses in drug and alcohol awareness and training in short-term mental health interventions are helpful as well. Degrees should be earned from regionally accredited colleges or universities.
- Preferably at least one unit of CPE, which provides supervision of and feedback on chaplains' provision of pastoral care.

Calling. Education chaplains need to have received a spiritual call and to have made a commitment to long-term work with students, faculty, and staff in college or university settings.

Ministry experience. Applicants must have some ministry experience, which is often gained in student ministry or in chaplaincy.

Ordination and licensing. Education chaplains should be licensed and ordained as ministers. Local churches ordain and license people for ministry. This bond between chaplain and church provides support for the chaplain and ministry opportunities for the church.

Endorsement. As with chaplains in the other nine functional areas, education chaplains should be officially endorsed by their faith group so that they can get support and backing for their theological decisions. Endorsing agents provide support to chaplains in the field and assist with theological and practical issues that arise in chaplains' ministries.

Professional Organizations for Education Chaplains

While chaplains have worked in education for many years, professional organizations have not yet formalized this functional area. The list below contains professional interfaith organizations:

- Association for Chaplaincy and Spiritual Life in Higher Education
- National Campus Ministry Association

Many denominations have their own professional organizations as well, with which chaplains should connect for both networking and training opportunities. Additionally, education chaplains can find networking and training opportunities in organizations aimed at student ministry.

Leadership as an Education Chaplain

Education chaplains can serve as the moral compass and spiritual voice throughout their schools. By forming relationships with the administration, faculty, and staff—and by being a relational leader—chaplains can influence the leadership within postsecondary institutions. Chaplains can serve on committees, influencing how policies are developed and applied. They can also transform the school's understanding of acceptance of those who are different.

Chaplains can model what it means to care for students in their struggles at their institutions. They can also, without breaking confidentiality, inform college or university officials of disturbing or harmful trends in the student population, whether they come from social media challenges or are created by the students. In this way, chaplains can model care without breaking confidentiality and can influence leaders within the systems. The opportunities to lead and influence others are unending in postsecondary culture.

Summary

Konkol contends, "By accompanying students through their increasingly complex educational journeys, chaplains deserve to be considered indispensable within the ever-changing context of higher education."[10] Education chaplains provide care, support, and confidentiality as they assist students in navigating through new ideas to a place where they find meaning in their lives. Faculty and staff also benefit from the moral and spiritual guidance that education chaplains bring to the institution. Education chaplains enrich college and university campuses throughout the United States.

10. Konkol, "Chaplains Are Essential."

15

Prison Chaplaincy

Michael W. Langston

Prison chaplaincy belongs to the institution category of the ten functional areas, and it involves working with people who are eleven years old or older and are incarcerated in federal, state, and local prisons. In the United States, prisons range from local jails to low, medium, and high security federal or state facilities. Juvenile facilities house youth from eleven years old to their eighteenth birthday. Prison chaplaincy in these different facilities requires varying preparations. The federal prison system has formalized requirements for chaplains desiring to work in its prisons, while local jails may have no requirements other than a desire to work with inmates.

Prison chaplaincy includes working not just with people who are incarcerated but also with their families and the staff at the prison. In larger prisons, chaplains are responsible for organizing services and volunteers. Volunteer staffs can be somewhat large if nearby churches focus on local prison ministry. This chapter provides information on different kinds of prison chaplaincies, the preparation required for each, and special considerations when applying to prisons or jails.

The History of Prison Chaplaincy

Prison chaplaincy has a long past, as pastors have routinely visited those in prison throughout history. Biblical references to caring for prisoners are in both the Old Testament and the New Testament. The prophet Isaiah says:

> The Spirit of the Sovereign LORD is on me, because the LORD has anointed me to proclaim good news to the poor. He has sent me to bind up the brokenhearted, to proclaim freedom for the captives and release from darkness for the prisoners, to proclaim the year of the LORD's favor and the day of vengeance of our God, to comfort all who mourn, and provide for those who grieve in Zion—to bestow on them a crown of beauty instead of ashes, the oil of joy instead of mourning, and a garment of praise instead of a spirit of despair. They will be called oaks of righteousness, a planting of the LORD for the display of his splendor. (Isa. 61:1–3 NIV)

These verses discuss the proclamation of good news to prisoners so they can be released from darkness and become "oaks of righteousness." In the well-known passage Matthew 25:34–40, Jesus says that he was "in prison and you came to me" (v. 36). The Bible expects believers to visit those in prison.

Throughout history, pastors have made visits to prisons. In the early years of Christianity, prisoners were often church leaders who were in prison for preaching about Christ. In the early years of the Puritans and settlers, churches imprisoned members who broke sacred laws. However, when the United States was formed in 1776, people were imprisoned for breaking the laws of the country or of the state. The number of religious imprisonments fell significantly as the country moved away from an explicitly Christian basis.

Pastors and church members have routinely visited prisoners since the founding of the United States. Often, these pastors and church members have prayed with prisoners and offered practical help. Prison chaplains were one of the "first organized groups of corrections professionals." In the early days, "community clergy would visit inmates primarily to 'save souls,'" and they would give sermons that "were hollered down the hall to inmates locked in cells."[1]

Prison chaplains appeared in the nineteenth century. They changed the formula for visiting prisoners from the early model of hollering evangelistic messages down halls to providing counseling, religious programming, and activities for prisoners, families, and staff. Chaplains also assisted prisoners in the free exercise of religion, which was impeded by their being incarcerated.

1. Judith Coleman, "Chaplains: God's Partners in Prison," *Corrections Today* 65, no. 7 (2003): 122–25.

Thus, prison chaplaincy formed on the basis of a combination of evangelistic visits and the upholding of the First Amendment.

The Culture and Ethos of Prison Chaplaincy

"Today, religious people still play an important role in the US criminal justice system. Almost all of the nation's more than 1,100 state and federal prisons have at least one paid chaplain or religious services coordinator, and collectively they employ about 1,700 professional chaplains." Ranking first in incarceration in the developed world, the United States has men, women, and teens in prisons throughout the country. Chaplains enable people to practice their religion "even if they are behind bars. [This right] has been affirmed by courts and bolstered by federal legislation, and the first duty of prison chaplains is to help meet the religious needs of inmates."[2] This section discusses the duties of prison chaplains and the cultures within which they work.

Prison chaplaincy involves counseling inmates and leading religious services. Chaplains usually supervise volunteers and provide or facilitate religious programs within the prison.[3] Facilitating may be more difficult for prison chaplains than for other chaplains because not all clergy can access the institutions. They still need to have a list of resources to help with religious programs for those outside their faith group. Chaplains provide services for prisoners and staff from their own faith group, often finding many prisoners who are willing to help with services.

Prison chaplains counsel prisoners and often find that they seek forgiveness for their crimes. In most cases, confidentiality applies within the prison walls as it does outside them. Any communication between chaplains and prisoners in a counseling or confession setting is protected by priest-penitent laws. In recent years, however, states have passed laws overriding federal priest-penitent laws. Chaplains should fully understand the requirements of their states before sharing confidential information with prison authorities, lawyers, families, or other interested parties.

Prisons have a variety of people within them, including teenagers and adults, women and men, short-term and lifetime prisoners, mental hospital prisoners, and others. People of all faiths and no faith, as well as people of different races and ethnic groups, are in prison. Those who have committed heinous crimes

2. "Religion in Prisons: A 50-State Survey of Prison Chaplains," Pew Research Center, March 22, 2012, https://www.pewresearch.org/religion/2012/03/22/prison-chaplains-preface.
3. "Becoming a Prison Chaplain," Pastoral Counseling, accessed January 19, 2023, https://www.pastoralcounseling.org/career/prison-chaplain.

and those who have merely shoplifted can be in a jail that a chaplain visits. Some prisoners are in solitary confinement, while others are allowed to move freely throughout the jail. Chaplains bring a ministry of presence to jails and prisons as they work to bring peace, care, and forgiveness to this population.

The prisoners to which chaplains bear the presence of God include people who have received death sentences. Chaplains who work with these prisoners can possibly "facilitate discussions between the inmate and their family or between the inmate and the family of those who were hurt. Some on death row do want to ask forgiveness from the families of their victims, and such a discussion often needs the help of a chaplain to make sure it goes smoothly."[4] These discussions are difficult and require great care from chaplains, but bearing the presence of God to these men and women is a holy work.

Prison chaplains often supervise volunteers in their religious-ministry programs. The populations of large prisons require a whole prison chaplain staff. Thus, multiple prison chaplains may work within the prison, offering a variety of programs for inmates. Prison chaplains oversee these programs, which can be offered through volunteer chaplains or ordained ministers from the surrounding community.

Prisons also offer new or experimental programs through chaplains' offices that require chaplain participation. In the federal system, a pilot program called the Life Connections Program is currently in place in five locations. Chaplains are part of this reintegration effort for prisoners. The program's description is as follows:

> The Life Connections Program (LCP) [offers] inmates the opportunity to improve critical life areas within the context of their personal faith or value system. LCP is a multifaith residential reentry program that is available at five sites across the country at low, medium, and high security levels. It is an intensive, multi-phase program which instills values and character through a curriculum of personal, social, and moral development. The LCP program utilizes various faith communities nationwide who serve as support group facilitators or mentors at program sites and release destinations to enhance community reintegration.[5]

This program is an example of chaplains' involvement in all aspects of prisoners' lives and not just in providing services.

The work of prison chaplains varies, depending on the type of prison and the population of the prison in question. The following list gives an overview

4. "Becoming a Prison Chaplain."
5. "Religious Programs," Federal Bureau of Prisons, accessed January 19, 2023, https://www.bop.gov/inmates/custody_and_care/religious_programs.jsp.

of the responsibilities of prison chaplains, though some of the items may not apply in particular cases and some prisons may have other requirements.

- Administer religious programs.
- Cooperate with other members of the clergy and faith teams to provide a variety of accessible worship experiences.
- Lead worship services and other services.
- Work with external faith-based groups.
- Advise correctional staff on religious issues.
- Be prepared to speak with offenders after release.
- Supervise and train volunteers.
- Provide support and counseling for staff.
- Facilitate interfaith dialogue.
- Administer secular rehabilitation services.
- Follow up with former inmates after their release.
- Help offenders examine their behaviors and decisions.
- Facilitate the process as offenders discover new ways of living.
- Help offenders find peace of mind.
- Facilitate the acceptance of responsibility for their actions.
- Help offenders safely reintegrate into communities.
- Ensure that offenders of all traditions are offered equal opportunities to practice their faith.
- Perform administrative tasks.
- Facilitate communication between families and inmates.
- Offer regular pastoral counseling.
- Offer crisis pastoral counseling to offenders in need.
- Coordinate pastoral volunteer services.
- Visit with inmates and their families as appropriate.
- Obtain an official ecclesiastical endorsement from their denomination or faith group.
- Help inmates explore questions related to spirituality, religion, vocation, and life purpose.[6]

Again, this list does not cover all the potential duties of a prison chaplain, but it is an excellent introduction to those duties.

6. "Becoming a Prison Chaplain."

Subareas of Ministry in Prison Chaplaincy

Federal Prisons

Federal prisons have prisoners from throughout the United States and even other countries. People who have been found guilty of breaking federal laws are incarcerated in federal prisons. These people are of different genders, races, ethnic groups, and ages. They have different financial standings in the outside world. Additionally, prisons range from low security to maximum security and have varying levels of amenities, such as workout rooms and educational opportunities offered to prisoners.

Each state in the US houses federal prisons. The guidelines for becoming a federal chaplain are highly formalized and must be followed as people prepare for chaplaincy in the federal system. Federal prison chaplains are paid by the federal government.

State Prisons

State prisons house people who have been found guilty of committing crimes at the state level. As with federal prisons, state prisons house people of all genders, religions, beliefs, races, and ethnic groups. They also have varying levels of security, from minimum to maximum security. The amenities vary with state prisons as well.

One distinction of state prisons is that, depending on the size of the state, family members may live close enough to visit. Prison chaplains can then involve the families in services and other activities and counsel them as necessary.

The requirements for state prison chaplaincy vary from state to state, but they tend to be more formalized than other areas of chaplaincy. State prisons often use volunteer chaplains and incorporate church volunteers into their ministry endeavors.

Jails

Jails are short-term facilities in which prisoners reside while awaiting trial. When someone is arrested for committing a crime, they are placed in a jail to await a court decision. People may not be guilty and yet be in jail for a night or two. Prison chaplains can provide short-term ministry for people who are in jails.

Often, cities and counties do not have funding to pay chaplains. Therefore, volunteer chaplains work in jails, providing for the needs of the inmates. Many church groups also support jail ministries.

Youth Prisons

Youth prisons, sometimes referred to as juvenile detention centers, house youth from eleven to seventeen years of age. These young people attend school within the facility and often have other tasks that they are required to accomplish. Families often visit them if possible. Prison chaplains have ample opportunities to minister to the youth and their families. Chaplains interested in working in youth prisons should take some coursework in teenage ministry.

Mental Health Prisons

Prisoners who have been placed in mental health sections of a prison or a prison hospital often require the counseling skills of a professional. Prison chaplains, however, can be the bearer of the presence of God to such people. A peaceful, caring presence can bring respite to those prisoners whose struggles are within their minds. Chaplains should be cautious about what they share with prisoners in order to avoid confusion with what professional counselors may have told prisoners.

Requirements for Becoming a Prison Chaplain

Professional chaplaincy requires preparation in chaplaincy, theology, and ministry skills. Prison chaplaincy has both formalized requirements and less formalized requirements that chaplains must complete before entering this kind of ministry. The prison system to which chaplains apply affects the formalization of the requirements for chaplaincy. The federal system is highly formalized, while local jails allow anyone to minister as a chaplain. Prison chaplains need to have the following KSAs to help them succeed in ministering to the incarcerated, their families, and staff in prison settings:

- *Knowledge:* This includes a knowledge of chaplaincy, theology, counseling, and leadership training, which is gained through higher education and CPE.
- *Skills:* These include excellent interpersonal skills; pastoral skills, including the conducting of services; leadership skills; and counseling skills. Prison chaplains can be short- or long-term counselors. They benefit from having training in short-term crisis intervention, spiritual counseling, and support counseling. Additionally, compassion, empathy, and listening skills are important for this type of chaplaincy. Prison chaplains also need organizational skills in order to plan multifaith services, organize volunteers of all faiths, and plan a full program of events.

- *Abilities:* These include capacities to comfort people in times of crisis; care for the incarcerated, their families, and staff in routine or crisis times; work well with teams; and provide spiritual care for others. Forgiving and accepting the prisoner are important abilities for prison chaplains as well.

Aspiring prison chaplains can obtain these KSAs by completing the requirements in this section and volunteering in local prisons. To qualify for chaplaincy within federal and state prison systems, chaplains must complete certain criteria. The following requirements apply generally to prison chaplaincy. The federal requirements are listed afterward. Each state's requirements vary, so people desiring to be chaplains in state or local systems should check those systems' requirements.

Education. Aspiring prison chaplains should complete the following educational requirements:

- A bachelor's degree in any field. Psychology, chaplaincy, or counseling are beneficial.
- An MA degree with a concentration in chaplaincy, counseling, or similar studies. An MDiv degree is beneficial but not required at all levels of prison chaplaincy. Degrees should be earned at regionally accredited colleges or universities.
- Preferably at least one unit of CPE, which provides supervision of and feedback on chaplains' provision of pastoral care.

Calling. Prison chaplains need to have received a spiritual call and to have made a commitment to long-term work with prisoners, families, and prison staff.

Ministry experience. Applicants must also have ministry experience, which is often acquired in church settings; however, local jails and prisons are also places where applicants can obtain ministry experience.

Ordination and licensing. Prison chaplains should be licensed and ordained as ministers. This bond between chaplain and church provides support for the chaplain and ministry opportunities within the prison system for the church. Ordination is not required for some prison-chaplain positions.

Endorsement. As with those serving in the other functional areas of chaplaincy, prison chaplains should be endorsed by their faith group so they can get support and backing for their theological decisions. Endorsing agents provide support to chaplains in the field and assist with theological and practical issues that arise in chaplains' ministries. Endorsement is not required for some prison-chaplain positions.

Federal prison requirements. Those pursuing a chaplaincy position in the federal prison system have higher requirements:

1. An undergraduate degree from an accredited college or university
2. An MDiv degree or the equivalent from an American Theological School–accredited residential seminary or school of theology, including the following elements:
    a. Twenty graduate hours of theology
    b. Twenty graduate hours of sacred writings
    c. Twenty graduate hours of church history or comparative religions
    d. Twenty graduate hours of ministry courses

Other requirements. Prison chaplaincy also requires the following:

1. A willingness to provide and coordinate programs for inmates of all faiths
2. Necessary credentials and the ability to provide worship services from the perspective of one's faith tradition
3. Age limits: between the ages of twenty-one and thirty-seven at the time of hire (age waivers may be granted)
4. At least two years of autonomous experience as a religious or spiritual leader in a parish or specialized ministry setting[7]

Professional Organizations for Prison Chaplains

There are many professional organizations that provide networking opportunities and continuing education opportunities. Joining these organizations allows chaplains to stay abreast of new ideas within prison chaplaincy and to connect with mentors. Some of these organizations are as follows:

- American Association of Pastoral Counselors
- American Correctional Chaplains Association
- International Prison Chaplains Association
- Pastoral Counseling
- Prison Fellowship

Chaplains can find support and answers to their questions within these organizations.

7. "Chaplain," Federal Bureau of Prisons, accessed January 19, 2023, https://www.bop.gov /jobs/positions/index.jsp?p=Chaplain, s.v. "Qualifications."

Leadership as a Prison Chaplain

Prison chaplains have ample opportunities for leadership as they oversee volunteers, organize programs, and meet with administrators. By providing a moral and spiritual interpretation of ideas, chaplains can influence courses of action within prisons as leaders work to prevent recidivism. Overseeing the volunteers and other chaplains allows prison chaplains to develop leadership abilities and to help steer the course of the prison.

Summary

Prison chaplaincy is one of the few types of chaplaincies that are directly mentioned in the Old and New Testaments. Visiting prisoners is a command that the church has followed throughout its history. Prison chaplaincy offers chaplains ways to comfort and care for prisoners while bringing the good news to them and their families. Prison chaplains bring a ministry of presence into buildings full of guilt and shame. They bring the presence of God to those struggling with their past deeds, and they open the door to eternal forgiveness through Christ.

16

Community Chaplaincy

Leroy Gilbert

P art of the community assistance chaplaincy category, community chaplaincy involves ministry to people in the communities where they live and work. By serving sections of a city or town, community chaplains are strategically positioned near people in order to provide immediate, relevant, hands-on pastoral care. Most people are familiar with chaplaincy in the military, VA, hospitals, prisons, police and fire departments, and colleges and universities; however, few may be aware of community chaplaincy. Nevertheless, ministry to neighborhoods and communities may be one of the earliest forms of chaplaincy.

According to a Gallup survey, US church membership is constantly in decline. In 1937, 73 percent of Americans were church members, while in 2020 church membership had declined to 47 percent of the population.[1] Today, even fewer Americans are in church or connected with a church community in any way. The Great Commission's target today is on the mission field, which is found in communities throughout the nation. Community chaplaincy has become a rapidly growing mission field, as God has given believers insight and vision on how to win souls to Christ and provide for the "least of these" (Matt. 25:40).

1. Jeffrey M. Jones, "US Church Membership Falls below Majority for First Time," Gallup, March 29, 2021, https://news.gallup.com/poll/341963/church-membership-falls-below-majority -first-time.aspx.

This chapter describes how community chaplaincy has evolved into a productive, exciting ministry.

The History of Community Chaplaincy

Community chaplaincy in America has its origin in churches, organizations, and individuals throughout the country who had a zeal to be "good neighbors" and to take care of the needs of the people outside the walls of the church. Initially, ministry to the community was not an organized initiative but was performed by people who saw a need in their community and responded accordingly. As the service to the community expanded, the ministry became more intentional, organized, and purposeful.

From the eighteenth century through the mid-twentieth century, aid for communities was usually provided by churches. Depending on the tasks, women's groups or men's groups would provide the needed aid. If people needed clothing, then women would generally collect it. If a roof needed repair, then men would provide the aid. People in churches would also provide tutoring and other educational services through women's missionary societies. Churches cared for their communities.

There are many examples of churches establishing aid societies to help certain groups in communities. An example of this type of society comes from freed slaves. In 1787, the first African American mutual aid society, the Free African Society, was formed in Philadelphia by Richard Allen and Absalom Jones. The mission of the group was to provide fellowship, a place of worship, and monetary support for members and their families in cases of sickness or death.[2] In 1808, the New York African Society for Mutual Relief supported ill or unemployed members and, if they died, their widows and orphans. The society also provided a form of health and life insurance for its members and their families.[3]

Many other aid societies were formed to support people struggling to obtain food, education, medical care, housing, and other needs. Immigrants of different ethnic origins developed mutual aid societies to assist people migrating to the United States. Catholic priests in neighborhoods with large immigrant populations provided aid as needed. Other churches in these communities helped as well. These groups provided much care and comfort for those in

2. W. E. B. Du Bois, *The Negro Church* (Atlanta: Atlanta University Press, 1903).

3. James Sullivan, "The New York African Society for Mutual Relief (1808–1860)," BlackPast .org, January 22, 2011, https://www.blackpast.org/african-american-history/new-york-african -society-mutual-relief-1808-1860.

need, similar to the way in which community chaplaincy seeks to help people in today's world.

Today, the existence of commuter churches means that people drive in from other areas and that churches are not as concerned about their immediate communities. As church membership has declined, aid to the community has also declined. Communities, even if churches exist within their neighborhood boundaries, are seeking care and help for people in need. Community chaplaincy is providing chaplains to meet those needs.

The Culture and Ethos of Community Chaplaincy

Community chaplaincy incorporates a variety of locations and ministries. Any community can establish a chaplaincy to meet the needs of people in their environment. Therefore, community chaplaincy is defined as a ministry that provides specified religious coverage, pastoral care, help, and support to neighborhoods or areas of cities and towns. Working within a geographical setting, community chaplains provide ministry to anyone who lives or works there: shop owners, retirees, people who commute into the area for work, homeless people, and others.

One of the struggles with this functional area of chaplaincy is that its definition is in flux. Different faith groups define the term in different ways, and other functional areas may be included in the term as well. For example, the Church of God Chaplains Commission's Community Service Chaplaincy program describes community chaplaincy in this way:

> Community Service Chaplains are men and women who are dedicated to the spiritual, emotional, and physical well-being of the employees, residents, patients, or inmates of the institution or agency wherein they provide ministry. A chaplain may be professional clergy or a layperson dedicated to serve outside the four walls of a church, most often in a volunteer capacity.[4]

This definition incorporates several of the functional areas of chaplaincy into one division. Thus, people pursuing community chaplaincy should not simply look for opportunities that use this term. The definition of the term is always important and must be ascertained.

Community chaplaincy is often formed by a person, group, or organization in a community that is aware of a need for a particular ministry in a designated

---

4. "Community Service Chaplaincy," Church of God Chaplains Commission, accessed January 19, 2023, https://www.cogchaplains.org/about.

area. For instance, a community in an urban area may be frustrated and be-wildered by escalating crimes and violence. A group of concerned citizens may get together and decide to work with a community chaplain to prevent crimes and save youth from being killed. An example of this type of group is Fo-cused Community Services in Atlanta. It requires chaplains to live within the neighborhoods they serve so they can model being a good neighbor as Christ commanded. Chaplains work to eradicate the violence in Atlanta by using a community approach of bringing hope.

The communities within which chaplains work are pluralistic, comprised of multiple faith groups, ethnic groups, ages, races, sexual preferences, and gender identities. In some cases, most residents may be atheists or people who have no knowledge of Christianity. If the community includes many homeless people, chaplains may work to provide care for their physical and mental needs. If the community includes young professionals, then providing care takes the form of meeting emotional needs. Listening and assessing needs are skills needed for this type of chaplaincy. Community chaplains must be accepting of all people and must avoid discriminating as they work to help those within the community.

Chaplains raise their own money through donations from people within their area of ministry, nonprofit organizations, and others who want to sup-port their work. People desiring to organize a community chaplaincy should conduct research to find monetary and personnel support from local churches, grants, governmental agencies, and businesses. They should also be aware that when funding comes from churches, the latter can sometimes expect prosely-tism from the chaplain. Chaplains should be clear that they will not pressure people to join the church.

The number of hours and days that community chaplains work fluctuates, since chaplains are available when people are in the area. Thus, a senior com-munity would require a daytime ministry, while a young adult community would be more receptive to an evening ministry. Chaplains provide care to those who are within the community and meet them where they are and when they are there.

Many examples from Scripture support the mission of community chaplains, who are bearers of the presence of God in the community. Jesus's mandates include loving one's neighbor and caring for widows, orphans, the needy, the destitute, and the least among a community. Matthew 25:34–40 exemplifies Jesus's instructions on this subject:

> Then the King will say to those on his right, "Come, you who are blessed by my Father, inherit the kingdom prepared for you from the foundation of the world. For I was hungry and you gave me food, I was thirsty and you gave me drink,

I was a stranger and you welcomed me, I was naked and you clothed me, I was sick and you visited me, I was in prison and you came to me." Then the righteous will answer him, saying, "Lord, when did we see you hungry and feed you, or thirsty and give you drink? And when did we see you a stranger and welcome you, or naked and clothe you? And when did we see you sick or in prison and visit you?" And the King will answer them, "Truly, I say to you, as you did it to one of the least of these my brothers, you did it to me."

Community chaplaincy may have many approaches and missions, because it is multifaceted and the community's needs may vary. However, community assistance chaplaincy has theological roots in the biblical concepts of being a good neighbor, showing Christian charity, and bearing one another's burdens (Gal. 6:2).

Evangelism is part of a community chaplain's services and ministry in the community. At its best, evangelism is usually done outside the walls of the church. Tom Shanklin, a renowned evangelist, says that Jesus's mission statement was "to seek and save the lost."[5] Spending little time in the synagogue or temple, Jesus primarily conducted his ministry in the community because the people he targeted lived, worked, and associated in a community. In like manner, community chaplains spend their time in the community because that is where people live, work, and otherwise spend their time.

Chaplains engaged in evangelism see more than souls needing salvation; they also see people needing food, shelter, and other necessities of life. In their ministry of presence, chaplains are aware of more than just spiritual needs as they move among the people, and they find ways to fill those needs. Jesus's model of evangelism often includes feeding the poor and hungry before talking to them about the bread of life. The Bible often depicts God as feeding the hungry. Mary sings, "He has filled the hungry with good things" (Luke 1:53). The psalmist praises God by saying that he "executes justice for the oppressed" and "gives food to the hungry" (Ps. 146:7). In Isaiah 58:10, God tells the nation of Israel that feeding the hungry is an important part of true religion. John the Baptist urges the Jews who came to him by saying, "Whoever has two tunics is to share with him who has none, and whoever has food is to do likewise" (Luke 3:11). The community chaplain expresses a ministry of presence by meeting the physical needs of people in the community. Historically, taking care of the community's needs was the seed that grew into community chaplaincy.

The duties of community chaplains may vary, depending on the community's needs, values, concerns, problems, and challenges. A general list of community

5. Tom Shanklin, "Jesus' Mission Statement: He Came to Seek and Save the Lost," Tom Shanklin Ministries, November 6, 2018, https://shanklinministries.org/jesus-mission-statement.

chaplains' duties includes the following; however, the opportunities for ministry are unlimited.

- *Meeting spiritual needs:* Leaders have learned that organizations cannot provide care for the whole self without involving the spiritual dimension. Community chaplains provide for the spiritual needs of the people who live and work in the community.
- *Ministering to real people with real problems:* Whether ministering to homeless people, businesspeople, or those who live in the area, community chaplains address problems that people encounter in their daily lives, such as a lack of food and healthcare, family issues, and financial problems.
- *Providing immediate, in-person, spiritual triage ministry:* If a store is robbed, if someone is shot or killed in the street, if a senior citizen receives disturbing news, or if apartment dwellers are involved in a critical incident—such as an apartment fire, a fall down the stairs, or a burglary—a trained chaplain becomes crucial and necessary. Crisis ministry training is important coursework for community chaplains to complete.
- *Providing a ministry of presence and availability:* A ministry of presence simply entails being present and accessible, which sends a message of love and care. Community chaplaincy is a ministry of involvement and hands-on experience. It involves identifying with people by working, speaking, and being present with them.
- *Serving as a source of help and referrals:* Chaplains who have the skills to identify problems and who have knowledge of helpful resources are valuable in the community. A list of resources, including agencies, nonprofits, and people, is useful when people in the community encounter serious problems.
- *Offering pastoral care and religious services:* With the decline in church membership in America, there will always be unchurched people who are not knowledgeable of the role of clergy in religious, familial, and personal matters. The community chaplain is a known resource for people to use when they need reassurance, help with problems, or a pastoral service such as wedding officiation.
- *Coordinating programs and activities:* Chaplains may coordinate programs and activities designed to build community, unity, and teamwork. Programs may center on holidays, whereas activities may include neighborhood cleanups and other such projects. This area has unlimited potential for community chaplains.

- *Hosting Bible studies, training, and personal-enrichment seminars:* Chaplains may lead these learning opportunities, or they may use people on their resource list.
- *Offering private, confidential services:* Like other chaplains, the information that community chaplains learn from people in a confessional or counseling setting is protected by confidentiality laws. People will often seek out a chaplain because of the opportunity for protected communication.
- *Performing various other duties:* Community chaplains can be directed to focus on certain tasks by the nonprofits and other groups that are supporting their ministry. They can also aid leaders in the community, such as politicians, business owners, and lawyers, by performing tasks that need to be completed, such as collecting trash, planting trees and flowers, and raising funds to help the homeless. In this way chaplains can become a true part of the community.

Subareas of Ministry in Community Chaplaincy

Community chaplaincy is often defined by a geographical area instead of an institution or organization. Imagine, for example, that in a major city, a certain neighborhood exists in an area marked off by two highways and two rivers. That area, Neighborhood A, can be a community chaplain's area of work, where the chaplain responds to specific needs in the community. The community chaplain serving in Neighborhood A ministers to the small businesses along the main road. Many of the business owners live above their businesses and rent out living space to others. An area that was formerly used for warehouses is now becoming filled with upscale apartments for young professionals who are new to the city. In another section, teens socialize at a park, playing basketball and other games until the park closes at 11:00 p.m. Neighborhood A has some churches within its borders, but most people in the neighborhood no longer attend, and the church members drive in from suburban areas of the city. The community chaplain of this neighborhood meets the business owners, hangs out with the young people, helps people move in, checks on the elderly, and brings the presence of God into Neighborhood A by caring for and serving its people in many other ways. Thus, community chaplains serve all ages and ethnic groups in their communities.

The following are some subareas of community chaplaincy, but the subareas of this functional area of chaplaincy are limited only by the needs of the people in a chaplain's region.

Field-Based Community Chaplaincy

Field-based community chaplaincy focuses on a certain area instead of a faith-based organization. The "field" is the area that the chaplain covers. The boundaries of that area are established by the people who desire to have a chaplain. These people might be part of an organization or a neighborhood group. Chaplains in field-based chaplaincy minister in a variety of settings.

Community Chaplaincy for Faith-Based Organizations

A faith-based organization is a group of people who share a faith commitment to provide services to meet the needs of community members. Often, the activities that faith-based organizations engage in are primarily secular rather than religious. For example, food kitchens, shelters, and free clinics can be practical ministries of faith-based organizations. Some examples of faith-based organizations include Catholic Charities and Lutheran Services. These organizations were founded on the tenets of their faith with the purpose of serving those in need. Other organizations can be interdenominational.

Community chaplains can become part of that work by offering a ministry of presence to the people who come to the organizations and by being a liaison between the organization and the people. This liaison position allows the chaplain to build relationships that open doors for spiritual conversations in the future. Chaplains can also provide for the needs of the people working in the faith-based organization.

Community Chaplaincy in Neighborhoods

Communities in the United States are becoming more isolated and exclusive as the number of gated and private communities rises. Churches often do not have access to these communities, which are only for residents, unless a member of their church lives in the community. Many communities even have rules against churches and other groups accessing the people in the neighborhood. Another, more general problem is the widespread disinterest in Christianity among today's American population. Many people claim to be spiritual but choose not to affiliate with churches.

Community chaplaincy has advantages over the church because chaplains in neighborhoods are often insiders who live in the community, have accessibility, and are not identified with some of the negative feelings people have about churches and church members. To become a chaplain in a neighborhood, chaplains should discuss the concept with a community association, an apartment-building manager, or a group of concerned neighbors. These contacts may provide chaplains the credibility they need to begin ministry within the area and advertise the service in the neighborhood newsletter and other community media networks.

Community Chaplaincy to Senior Citizens

One of the core values of the early church was to take care of vulnerable people, including senior citizens. Paul writes, "In all things I have shown you that by working hard in this way we must help the weak and remember the words of the Lord Jesus, how he himself said, 'It is more blessed to give than to receive'" (Acts 20:35). Residential communities for senior citizens are a growing business. Many new communities for people fifty-five and older are being built throughout every city in America. These communities have a variety of focuses, along with assisted-living care, which allow seniors to move in with others their age and continue their activities while managing any memory or physical issues they may have.

Chaplains can provide services, visits, and activities for people within these groups. Many seniors living in such communities still drive, shop, play golf, and travel. Some communities have "step-up" care, which is administered when people, as they age and their need for physical help increases, move to new areas in the community. Senior communities differ from one to the next in the care they offer to their residents, but most of them welcome chaplains, since seniors often face debilitating illnesses, loneliness, and feelings of worthlessness. Community chaplains can establish the relationships for which these people long and provide a ministry of presence to them.

Other Areas of Community Chaplaincy

Community chaplains also work in airports, with government at all levels, and in various other areas. The opportunities for community chaplains are expanding, and the concept is growing in importance as people struggle to find help for their spiritual needs.

Requirements for Becoming a Community Chaplain

Professional chaplaincy requires preparation in chaplaincy, theology, and ministry skills. Community chaplaincy has less formalized requirements for chaplains to complete before entering the ministry setting. These requirements are typically set by the organization or organizations for which the chaplain works. Even so, community chaplains, whether volunteers or paid

staff, need to have the following KSAs if they are to succeed in ministering in
community settings:

- *Knowledge:* This includes a knowledge of chaplaincy, theology, counseling, and leadership training, which is gained through higher education
  and CPE. Community chaplains also need knowledge of the geographical area in which they will work.
- *Skills:* These include excellent interpersonal skills; pastoral skills,
  such as the conducting of services and the running of support programs; leadership skills; and counseling skills. Community chaplains
  may have long-term counseling with some people in the community,
  so conflict resolution for marital conflict and other issues is part of
  the needed training. Skills in short-term crisis intervention, spiritual
  counseling, and support counseling are needed. Additionally, compassion, empathy, and listening skills are important for this type of
  chaplaincy.
- *Abilities:* These include capacities to comfort people in times of crisis,
  care for people in routine or crisis times, work well with teams, and
  provide spiritual care for others.

Chaplains can acquire the needed KSAs by fulfilling the following other basic
requirements.
Education.

- A bachelor's degree, preferably in a closely related field, such as religion, divinity, counseling, psychology, or theology
- An MDiv or MA in chaplaincy, religion, or theological studies. Coursework in chaplaincy, crisis ministry, and pastoral care is
  desirable.
- Preferably at least one unit of CPE, which prepares chaplains for dealing with people in crisis situations, counseling people, and providing
  pastoral care

Church and faith-group support.

- A call from God in order to work in this area
- Ordination and/or licensing from a church
- Endorsement

Certifications.

- Preferably one of the various certifications available for different areas
  of community chaplaincy, which are optional but helpful

There is a growing number of schools, institutions, and organizations providing professional training, certification, and employment for community chaplains. Community chaplains should attend accredited schools.

Professional Organizations for Community Chaplains

Professional organizations provide support for chaplains through networking and the sharing of ideas. The following are examples of professional organizations for community chaplains:

- American Chaplains Association
- International Alliance of Chaplain Corps

The following list provides examples of community chaplaincy operating in different states and cities. The websites of the organizations below are excellent resources that may provide ideas for and models of community chaplaincy. Community chaplains can use these organizations to build community with other chaplains and to share ideas for ministry.

- Associated Ministries of Tacoma Pierce County (Tacoma, Washington), focusing on homelessness and economic issues
- Chaplains on the Way (Waltham, Massachusetts), emphasizing homeless communities
- Community Chaplain Services (Norton, Ohio), focusing, through a coffee house, on community needs
- Community Chaplains' Outreach (Columbia, South Carolina), an example of meeting the needs of people in its community
- Community Strategies Urban Ministry (Focused Community Strategies; Atlanta, Georgia), emphasizing life within the community to model what it means to be a good neighbor
- London Community Chaplaincy (London, Ontario), focusing on the provision of chaplains for all community needs
- Street Chaplains (United Kingdom), an example of teaming with business and professional organizations and utilizing volunteers in community chaplaincy
- US Community Chaplains Association (various locations), focusing on multiple community needs
- Washington Community Chaplain Corps (Sumner, Washington), stressing work within communities to meet needs

Leadership as a Community Chaplain

Community chaplains are leaders within the community. They are servant leaders, focused on caring and providing for people. As they develop relationships with people and begin to influence their lives, community chaplains work as transformational leaders. Serving on teams with the organizers of the community chaplaincy project, community chaplains are relational leaders, influencing the course of action within the community and the leadership. Through these means, community chaplains act as leaders within the community as they influence people in the ways of God.

Summary

This chapter is a starting point for preparing for and working within community chaplaincy. A rapidly expanding and changing ministry, community chaplaincy provides people in communities with help, support, and ministry that churches at large used to provide. Community chaplains operate in the center of the communities they serve, providing relevant, meaningful, and spiritual ministry where people live, work, and play. The COVID-19 pandemic has underscored the value of ministry outside the walls of the church. The focus of ministry in the future will be mostly in the communities where people spend most of their time.

17

Disaster Relief Chaplaincy

Michael W. Langston

P art of the community assistance category of the ten functional areas, disaster relief chaplaincy involves providing care after hurricanes, tornadoes, train derailments, earthquakes, plane crashes, blizzards, and other disasters. Chaplains who answer the call to disaster relief chaplaincy provide care for the people at the scene of a disaster. They can work with adults and children, healthy and injured people, family members, and anyone else who is present. They also provide debriefing care for first responders who are overwhelmed from working at a major disaster.

Many faith groups and nonprofit organizations have disaster relief teams who respond with immediate and long-term relief for people. Disaster relief chaplains often accompany these teams or respond to a call from the Red Cross to provide care and comfort to people who are in shock. This chapter offers an introduction to this type of ministry and the preparation that is required.

The History of Disaster Relief Chaplaincy

Disaster relief efforts have always been part of the church's function within communities. Giving people specialized training so they can support disaster relief efforts, however, is a newer concept for many faith groups. The United Methodists and Southern Baptists formed disaster relief groups in the mid-twentieth century, while the Church of God and other groups formalized their disaster relief efforts in the 1990s. The need for formalized chaplain training has come to the forefront in recent times.

In the late 1990s, the National Transportation Safety Board became over-whelmed as they worked to support victims of air disasters and their families. When Rabbi Stephen Roberts became aware of the struggle, he approached the Red Cross concerning the establishment of an alliance that would address the spiritual needs of disaster victims, along with their families. From the efforts of this agency, Disaster Spiritual Care was born in New York in 2000. This organization was finalized and placed into action in New York City during the first week of September 2001. The next week, the 9/11 tragedy occurred. "With disaster protocol ready to be implemented, more than 800 chaplains volunteered their time and skills over the next nine months of rescue and recovery efforts. [As] the largest multifaith chaplaincy effort ever in the United States, the program had an immediate impact."[1]

The Red Cross now runs a nationwide chaplaincy list to assist in relief as disasters occur. Many faith groups also have a disaster response team with people who can build, clear, and do other manual labor, as well as a chaplain who can assist in processing disaster issues that the team may encounter.

The Culture and Ethos of Disaster Relief Chaplaincy

Disaster relief chaplains specialize in responding to major disasters and bringing spiritual care to the people involved in them. The Red Cross, which becomes involved in major disasters, has developed courses and chaplaincy coverage for most of the United States. Many other groups, such as the Southern Baptist Convention, the United Methodist Church, the Church of God, and Samaritan's Purse, have large, well-funded disaster response teams. These teams have chaplains who take care of the spiritual needs of victims and workers. Disaster chaplains are the first-line triage for those involved in or affected by a disaster, referring them to experts who can assist them in recovery.

Chaplains offer a ministry of presence to people at disaster scenes. "A vital aspect of disaster chaplaincy is 'the ministry of presence.' A major premise of care amid crisis is presence. The care of souls first requires being there. Simple,

---

1. "Crises," Chaplaincy Innovation Labs, accessed January 19, 2023, https://chaplaincyinnovation.org/resources/by-sector/crises.

empathic, listening presence is a primary pastoral act, the presupposition of all other pastoral acts."[2]

When disasters occur, people ask spiritual questions and look to chaplains to help them create meaning from what has happened. Tim Serban, who works as a chaplain with the Red Cross in Oregon, explains the circumstances of people at a disaster site: "Most disaster victims need more than just a meal and a safe place to sleep. They also need emotional and spiritual support to help them get through an ordeal that threatens to tear their lives apart. They already know what happened. Now they want to know why it happened and why such a terrible thing happened to them."[3] These statements summarize what people want from a disaster relief chaplain. These statements summarize the psychological first-aid concept that chaplains use.

When chaplains are present, people can ask questions about God, suffering, and tragedy. Disaster relief chaplains can prepare for these conversations by developing a strong theology of suffering and of God's presence. Often, people just need someone to listen to their doubts, anger, and confusion. As bearers of the presence of God, disaster relief chaplains listen to the cries of the people, caring for them in their suffering.

Chaplains at scenes of disasters must guard against platitudes that provide little to no comfort for people waiting for news on a loved one. Understanding the depth of the ministry of presence and of active listening is essential if chaplains are to fully care for people amid chaos.

When disasters happen, first responders, whether in the police, fire, or medical category, rush to the scene. Often, these groups have their own chaplains, called public safety chaplains, who provide care for the first responders and the people at the scene. There are therefore two kinds of chaplaincy that overlap when disaster strikes. Disaster relief chaplains need to communicate with public safety chaplains to work out shifts for long-term responses and to extend coverage to everyone at a scene.

Disaster relief chaplains can help protect first responders and disaster relief workers against a danger of their job: exhaustion. Working on a disaster scene is difficult, and responders can become overwhelmed with the situation. They initially work on adrenaline but find themselves becoming more and more tired with time. These personnel can also become overwhelmed with the emotions that they have held back. Disaster relief chaplains watch for signs of exhaustion

2. "Crisis Response Chaplains," Tuff Services Ministries, accessed January 19, 2023, https://www.tuffservices.org/crisis-response-chaplains.

3. "Meeting Emotional and Spiritual Needs," American Red Cross, October 14, 2017, https://www.redcross.org/local/oregon/about-us/news-and-events/news/Meeting-Emotional-and-Spiritual-Needs.html.

so they can offer a ministry of presence to people in these situations. A reminder to rest for a few minutes or sleep for a few hours may be a word of wisdom that the workers need amid the stress of their work. Showing care and compassion for relief workers and first responders means noticing their condition and reminding them to care for themselves.

Chaplains on the scene of a disaster may be asked to inform families of the death of loved ones, or they may be asked to be present when someone else informs the family. Understanding how people respond to the news of a loved one's death and being able to offer comfort are skills that disaster relief chaplains need to develop. Sharing the news of a death is not an easy task. Disaster relief chaplains should consult other chaplains to learn how to do this and then prepare the words to use in these situations.

Disaster relief chaplains may spend anywhere from several hours to several weeks in a disaster area. A limit in funding for volunteer or part-time chaplains may restrict the amount of time they remain on the scene, and some chaplains may be required to move on because of the requirements of their job. Chaplains should prepare their families for the possibility of long absences. They also should have gear prepared so they can leave rapidly if needed. If they work on a disaster relief team, chaplains will usually be provided with the equipment they need.

Disaster relief teams are often made up of psychologists, medical doctors, nurses, and others with skills that are useful when disasters happen. Chaplains can work with people from many faiths, races, and belief systems; they are guaranteed to work in a pluralistic environment. Being open to those of other faiths and no faith is required of disaster relief chaplains. The primary task of the disaster relief chaplain is not evangelism; it is providing care and comfort through a ministry of presence. As people ask questions, chaplains can respond with answers based on their faith perspective. Of course, they are bound to follow priest-penitent rules about confidentiality.

Disaster relief chaplains serve for the length of time of the disaster. While a few organizations maintain full-time employees, most disaster relief chaplains are employed elsewhere and leave that job during the disaster. For example, a hospital chaplain would leave the hospital to help people after a devastating hurricane. Then that chaplain would return to the hospital when the disaster work was completed.

Disaster relief chaplains work with people at some of the worst times of their lives. Disasters are overwhelming, unsettling, and chaotic. Chaplains bring a sense of peace and care as they act as bearers of the presence of God amid the chaos. Disaster relief chaplaincy requires chaplains to meet people in times of tragedy and answer spiritual questions that come from the events. Chaplains must place high emphasis on self-care in the midst of such environments, lest they become casualties themselves.

Subareas of Ministry in Disaster Relief Chaplaincy

Disaster relief chaplaincy lacks subareas, except in terms of events and organizations. The Red Cross has a nationwide list of chaplains who respond to disasters. Many denominations and groups, such as Samaritan's Purse, train and fund chaplains on their disaster relief teams. Chaplains desiring to work in disaster relief should consider aligning with established groups throughout the country.

Requirements for Becoming a Disaster Relief Chaplain

Professional chaplaincy requires preparation in chaplaincy, theology, and ministry skills. Disaster relief chaplaincy has less formalized requirements than some other kinds of chaplaincy. Yet disaster relief chaplains need to have the following KSAs if they are to succeed in ministering in the crisis and chaos of disasters:

- *Knowledge:* This includes a knowledge of chaplaincy, theology, counseling, and leadership training, which is gained through higher education and CPE.
- *Skills:* These include excellent interpersonal skills; pastoral skills, including caring and showing compassion; leadership skills; and crisis-counseling skills. While disaster relief chaplains are not long-term counselors, they do benefit from having skills in short-term crisis intervention, spiritual counseling, and support counseling. Additionally, compassion, empathy, and listening skills are important for this type of chaplaincy.
- *Abilities:* These include capacities to comfort people in times of crisis; care for staff, injured people, and their families in times of crisis and chaos; work well with teams; and provide spiritual care for others.

Aspiring disaster relief chaplains can obtain KSAs by completing the requirements listed below and volunteering in healthcare or public safety settings. The requirements for becoming a disaster relief chaplain are less formalized because many pastors and laypeople volunteer to be chaplains during disasters. The length of the chaplain ministry equals the period that first responders, the Red Cross, the Federal Emergency Management Agency, and others are at the scene of the disaster. If a chaplain desires to be professional, the following criteria would assist in that goal.

Education. Aspiring disaster relief chaplains would benefit from postsecondary training. This includes the following:

- A bachelor's degree in any field, but chaplaincy, psychology, or counseling are beneficial. If a chaplain desires to work in disaster relief, some classes in crisis counseling would also be beneficial.
- An MA or MDiv with a concentration in chaplaincy, counseling, or a similar field. Degrees should be earned from regionally accredited colleges or universities. Chaplains should take courses on death and dying, suffering and sin, and other such matters so they can develop a theology of these subjects.
- Preferably at least one unit of CPE, which provides supervision of and feedback on chaplains' provision of pastoral care. Disaster relief chaplains deal with people in shock and with overwhelmed first responders. CPE helps chaplains develop skills that are useful for this ministry.

Theological education is important for disaster relief chaplains because they need to have worked out their theologies of death, dying, and suffering. People ask questions about God's presence in their lives and about his allowance of suffering and sin, and chaplains must be prepared to answer. A general theology of chaplaincy is an effective base that disaster relief chaplains should have before they begin their ministry. They should also prepare by completing crisis and disaster courses.

Calling. Disaster relief chaplains need to have received a spiritual call and to have made a commitment to work with people during disasters.

Ministry experience. Disaster relief chaplains must also have ministry experience, which is often gained in church settings. This requirement assists chaplains by allowing them to learn ministry skills in less chaotic settings. They can then apply these experiences to hectic disaster scenes.

Ordination and licensing. Disaster relief chaplains should be licensed and ordained as ministers. This bond between chaplain and church provides support for the chaplain and ministry opportunities for the church when disasters occur in their local area. Ordination is not required for some disaster relief chaplaincy positions.

Endorsement. As with those serving in the other functional areas of chaplaincy, chaplains in disaster relief ministry should be endorsed, though endorsement is not required for some positions.

Professional Organizations for Disaster Relief Chaplains

Disaster relief chaplains have fewer professional organizations focused on their functional area than most other areas of chaplaincy. The following professional organization offers disaster relief chaplains access to networking and educational opportunities:

- Disaster Chaplaincy Services

Disaster relief chaplains can also find information on this organization's website for help with chaplaincy questions.

Leadership as a Disaster Relief Chaplain

Disaster relief chaplains in some of the larger programs have opportunities for leadership as they oversee volunteers, organize projects, and meet with administrators. By providing a caring and calm environment at disaster sites, chaplains can reduce the overall anxiety of first responders and other people working there. Chaplains can also lead amid the chaos of a disaster by suggesting ideas that others are too upset to consider. Through a peaceful presence and a caring countenance, disaster relief chaplains can exercise servant leadership at the scene of a disaster.

Summary

Disaster relief chaplains work in chaotic contexts of destruction and injury. Chaplains in this field should consider becoming a part of one of the many faith groups or nonprofit organizations that have large, well-funded teams that respond to disasters. By working with these groups and organizations, chaplains can focus on bringing the presence of God into the chaos as well as answering the questions about God that come from disasters. Disaster relief chaplaincy offers an important bridge between suffering people and the peace of God.

18

Public Safety Chaplaincy

Chris Wade

Part of the community assistance category, public safety chaplaincy can be one of the most exciting and rewarding jobs in ministry. Opportunities to serve in law enforcement, emergency medical services (EMS), and fire and accident protection and prevention draw many interested men and women. These jobs, however, come with inherent risks. First responders move into situations that most people avoid. Between 2011 and 2015, more than eight hundred first responders died from injuries on the job.[1] Every year, some first responders are shot and killed, are wounded in assaults and accidents, or die trying to protect life and property. Public safety chaplains minister to first responders, their families, and the staff of various departments.

First responders experience some of the worst sides of humanity, witnessing the consequences of person-on-person violence and the neglect of children and senior citizens. They also witness horrendous accidents, both man-made and natural, that disfigure and destroy the human body. These experiences may leave first responders with physical scars and emotional and spiritual damage that many cannot easily overcome. Chaplains whose ministry is in public safety

---

1. "Fatal Occupational Injuries to Emergency Responders," Injuries, Illnesses, and Fatalities, U.S. Bureau of Labor Statistics, last modified December 5, 2019, https://www.bls.gov/iif/factsheets /archive/fatal-occupational-injuries-emergency-responders-2011-15.htm.

work alongside and support the men and women serving in these dangerous jobs. This chapter will offer an overview of public safety chaplaincy for those who may consider pursuing this area of service.

The History of Public Safety Chaplaincy

The earliest known public safety chaplains in the United States served the fire department of York, Pennsylvania, around 1898.[2] In 1906, New York City police commissioner Theodore A. Bingham established a group of chaplains to collaborate with the police department.[3] The modern EMS system began taking form in the 1960s and was usually covered by local fire departments and served by fire chaplains.[4]

In New England, some of the early chaplains were recruited from the Catholic Church and were invited to minister to the predominantly Irish Catholic police officers and firefighters. In the same way, local fire and law-enforcement departments in other regions would seek various services from local clergy, sometimes formalizing the relationship by naming a clergyperson as the department chaplain. Professional public safety chaplaincy with formalized job descriptions and standards for ethics and training emerged more recently and has been promoted primarily through two organizations: the International Conference of Police Chaplains, which was formed in the 1970s, and the Federation of Fire Chaplains, which was established in the 1980s.

In 1973, three Internal Revenue Service agents were killed in a late-night automobile accident in Washington, DC. Chaplain Joseph Dooley became very frustrated when he was unable to contact other chaplains to help deliver death notifications to families living outside the DC area. He recognized the need for a network of law-enforcement chaplains. Thus, a letter was created and sent out to 175 police chiefs, police associations, and chaplains across the United States, with two goals: to create a directory of chaplains, listing their contact information and police affiliations, and to build a community of chaplains from the United States and Canada for fellowship and the dissemination of information. In October of that year, a group of chaplains went to Washington, DC, and formed the International Corporation of Police Chaplains, which would

2. "A Sermon to the Goodwill," *York Daily*, January 31, 1898.

3. Pascal Storino Jr., "What's the Deal With: The 'Genesis' of the NYPD's Police Chaplains," History of Policing in the City of New York, April 26, 2018, http://nypdhistory.com/whats-the -deal-with-the-genesis-of-the-nypds-police-chaplains.

4. Manish N. Shah, "The Formation of the Emergency Medical Services System," *American Journal of Public Health* 96, no. 3 (March 2006): 414–23, http://doi.org/10.2105/AJPH.2004 .048793.

later be called the International Conference of Police Chaplains, or ICPC. In this way, law-enforcement chaplaincy became a formalized entity that had the ability to call on members for assistance when needed.

In 1978, a group of chaplains in the Fort Worth, Texas, area met to share their ideas concerning chaplaincy in the fire service. This was the beginning of the Fellowship of Fire Chaplains, which would grow into the Federation of Fire Chaplains (FFC). In 1992, the federation was incorporated as a nonprofit professional organization. Its purpose was to bring together those interested in providing effective chaplain ministry for the fire service and facilitating the exchange of ideas and concerns that affect the quality of life for all fire-service members and their families. Most chaplains in the federation, as well as fire chaplains in general, fall into one of three categories:

1. Local clergy who volunteer their time with the fire department
2. Firefighters who serve as chaplains while also fulfilling other duties
3. Firefighters who are full-time paid chaplains

Often, these fire chaplains respond to EMS calls as well; however, distinct EMS chaplains are a growing group. Counting or estimating the number of public safety chaplains in the United States is difficult because many volunteer their time and may not be counted in labor statistics.

The Culture and Ethos of Public Safety Chaplaincy

Firefighters, emergency medical technicians, and law-enforcement officers tend to work long shifts. A twelve-hour shift is typical in law enforcement, while many firefighters prefer the "Kelly" shift: twenty-four hours of work followed by forty-eight hours off. Long shifts help first responders develop a sense of camaraderie with their coworkers, but these shifts can lead to exhaustion and burnout, especially for busy stations and precincts. These long hours affect job safety.[5] Those who use their unusual schedule to pick up another job on the side are even more vulnerable to exhaustion.

When an emergency call comes in, first responders may have to act within minutes or seconds. The resulting hypervigilance and adrenaline rush have

5. "Firefighter Burnout and Workplace Safety," Industrial Safety and Hygiene News, August 3, 2018, https://www.ishn.com/articles/109094-firefighter-burnout-and-workplace-safety; Todd D. Smith, Kevin Hughes, David M. DeJoy, and Mari-Amanda Dyal, "Assessment of Relationships between Work Stress, Work-Family Conflict, Burnout and Firefighter Safety Behavior Outcomes," Safety Science 103 (March 2018): 287–92, https://doi.org/10.1016/j.ssci.2017.12.005.

their appeal and keep first responders alert. Chaplains often respond as well, accompanying the first responders on the call. In the long term, being on edge and waiting for the next call are hard on both mind and body. For the volunteer firefighters who make up 65 percent of US firefighters,[6] those calls can come anytime they are within the boundaries of the district they serve and not just when they are on a shift. Therefore, they are always on call and required to respond from work or home, both day and night. This work schedule means that they miss many meals, holidays, and family events because of emergency calls. The interruption of activities can cause stress for chaplains and their families. Developing skills to deal with the unexpected is necessary in public safety chaplaincy.

Like other workers, firefighters and law-enforcement and EMS employees bring their personal issues to work. They struggle to separate their personal lives from their work lives when they report to the job. Many public safety workers have issues with their marriage, with parenting, and with finances because of the hours they work. Sometimes the work itself evokes personal struggles or fears, as when they help a child victim who reminds them of their own child or when they respond to a cardiac arrest that reminds them of the death of a parent. Thus, chaplains must learn to listen to these first responders while counseling them through difficult situations.

Scripture offers many examples in the life and teachings of Jesus that are beneficial for public safety chaplains. The parable of the good Samaritan (Luke 10:25–37) offers some parallels to this type of chaplaincy. Jesus tells the story of the Samaritan who stops to assist someone who is physically injured. The Samaritan provides care and comfort following a crisis in the stranger's life. The Samaritan is not bothered that the injured man is a Jew and that Samaritans and Jews avoid each other. He sees the needs of the suffering man and, through a ministry of presence, provides for those needs. When he is unable to stay with the injured man, the Samaritan facilitates for his needs by paying the innkeeper for a room, food, and medical attention. The Samaritan makes sure he is safe before leaving to complete his own journey. Selfless service without judgment is the spirit behind professional public safety chaplaincy.

Public safety chaplains build relationships with first responders as they talk with, work alongside, and support them. As a result, chaplains can be those whom first responders approach for help with life issues. For example, a first

6. Rita Fahy, Ben Evarts, and Gary P. Stein, *US Fire Department Profile 2020* (National Fire Protection Association, September 2022), https://www.nfpa.org/-/media/Files/News-and-Research/Fire-statistics-and-reports/Emergency-responders/osfdprofile.pdf.

responder may have difficulty separating themselves from unpleasant work experiences. Often, they dwell on their experiences at home but do not share this with their spouse. The spouse does not understand, and disagreements emerge. Some first responders develop substance abuse, depression, and sleep issues due to an inability or unwillingness to deal with what they have experienced. When chaplains observe this behavior, they can empathetically listen to the first responder because they have previously built the relationship. By caring and listening, the chaplain can provide counseling, and the door can open for the sharing of the gospel. Chaplains can also pray with the first responder and offer him or her hope.

In public safety chaplaincy, the ministry of presence may take the form of making rounds; visiting stations; attending drills, training sessions, roll calls, and other gatherings; going out on emergency calls when invited; and riding along with law-enforcement officers. Such activities help establish chaplains as faithful and available and, therefore, increase the likelihood that people will seek them out to talk about shared experiences or the challenges they face in their work or at home. The chaplain must earn their trust.

First responders come from many faith groups and even from no faith group at all. As with other kinds of chaplains, public safety chaplains meet the needs of people but only when doing so aligns with their beliefs and practices. In other cases, they facilitate for people's needs. For example, an evangelical chaplain would call a Catholic priest to perform rites and prayers that the Catholic Church reserves for its priests. The chaplain could pray for a Catholic individual requesting the service but would not stand in as a priest.

In situations where chaplains rely on other clergy to meet religious needs, chaplains can be tempted to use the crisis as an opportunity to proselytize the person in need. Building relationships first is a cornerstone of public safety chaplaincy. Once the relationship is built, then chaplains can ask permission to share their faith and answer questions about their faith. In these moments of evangelizing, chaplains stand in safe spaces that become sacred spaces graced with the presence of God. However, chaplains who try to force their own beliefs or faith perspective on first responders usually alienate them.

Chaplains also practice facilitation when they are not qualified to perform a required service. For example, if a public safety chaplain is not a licensed counselor or therapist, then they should offer a referral for a person dealing with abuse, suicidal ideation, or other serious issues of like nature. Keeping lists of community resources, religious groups, mental healthcare providers, and even sources of legal or financial help assists chaplains as they facilitate for others.

Most public safety chaplains are expected to offer prayers at banquets, memorials, and other ceremonies. Weddings are not part of their official duties, but chaplains can be asked to perform weddings for those with whom they work. They may participate in or conduct funerals for first responders, their families, or people the first responders served at an emergency scene. As noted, first responders are killed in the line of duty every year. Responding to a line-of-duty death or another death among those serving in the department is often part of chaplains' duties.

Public safety chaplains may be part of teams that go to homes to notify next of kin. When appropriate, they also attend and report at critical-incident stress debriefings. Chaplains counsel survivors and families as needed. Teams of chaplains are often called on when many people are involved in an incident. If first responders have experienced grief and loss, chaplains are often called to assist them as well. A first responder may refuse to talk to the chaplain, but expressions of compassion such as meals and other practical help are usually welcome. Through this ministry of presence, chaplains develop relationships with first responders.

Chaplains engage in conflict resolution among first responders as well. In these cases, chaplains need to apply counseling skills to assist in finding a resolution. They may be asked to come alongside a first responder showing signs of reckless behavior, anger, dissatisfaction, or other issues that are causing problems in the department. In these incidents, chaplains must remember the confidentiality requirements that apply.

When they are on a call, chaplains can serve as peacemakers or a pastoral presence for members of the public. They can also serve as liaisons between the department and the public. If chaplains serve in this role, they need to consult with the department leaders about the information they should and should not share.

Each of these challenges offers public safety chaplains the opportunity for ministry—as they serve first responders and their families and, when appropriate, serve alongside first responders to assist victims and families in crisis. Chaplains listening to trauma and pain will themselves feel the trauma and pain. They therefore need a developed theology of pain and suffering, death and dying, and caring for the hurting. Bearing the trauma of others wears chaplains down over time. They need to practice self-care and have people with whom to discuss matters, though they must, of course, follow confidentiality laws as well.

While many chaplain responsibilities are similar to those of pastors within local churches, significant differences exist between chaplains and pastors. Table 18.1 lists these distinctions.

TABLE 18.1

Distinctions between Pastors and Chaplains

	Pastor	Public Safety Chaplain
Hiring / Ministry Organization	Works for local churches or congregations. Usually ordained by faith group.	Works for government agencies, businesses, or private organizations. May be ordained or licensed by faith group. It is advantageous to be ordained as a vetted clergy person.
Focus of Ministry	Is concerned about ministering to those in their own faith group or helping convert people to their faith.	May be from any faith group. Works with people of many faiths. Is not focused on proselytizing. Is free to discuss their faith just as anyone else is.
Location of Ministry	Works mostly within the church walls or at least with people of like-minded faith. Speaks on behalf of the congregation.	Works in the marketplace among people of many faiths. The chaplain is not expected to "check their faith at the workplace door" when they come to work but cannot impose it on others.
Ministry Skills	Deals with doctrines, rituals, and beliefs specific to a faith group. May deal with counseling that reflects their faith tradition.	Deals more with caring, serving, and crisis response. Listens more than they talk, though counseling is a part of the job. Walks with people as they live out their lives in the workplace.
Religious Freedom	Performs a role seen by the government as primarily religious in nature.	Performs a role seen by the government as a bona fide clergyperson with all rights and privileges in the performance of their duties.
Denominational Responsibilities	Deals with religious ministry as defined by the local church, denomination, or faith group.	Provides for those of one's own faith group. Facilitates for those of other faith groups. Cares for all. Advises senior leadership on religious and spiritual issues.
Response Expectations	Usually has to stay outside an emergency response situation.	Is part of the police or fire response and is free to move within the emergency response situation as training and protocols allow. The chaplain is often trained in crisis response and trauma.

Source: Michael Langston, "Religious Freedom, and the Constitutionality of Chaplaincy" (lecture, Columbia Biblical Seminary, Columbia, SC, 2021) (slightly modified).

Subareas for Ministry in Public Safety Chaplaincy

Public safety chaplains often work among first responders as part of the response team. Some responders view the presence of the chaplain as a reminder that God is on the scene. Others take comfort knowing someone is looking out for them while they are focused on victims or criminals. Some chaplains operate more in the background and may be seldom seen, but they often are well known to the staff of the organizations they serve.

Department leadership decides the duties of public safety chaplains. Sometimes there is a job description with a set of standard operating procedures or guidelines, but often there is no job description whatsoever. Senior officers and executives may have a limited understanding of what chaplains can and should do. A series of dialogues between the chief and the chaplain, as well as sample documents from other departments, may help establish the job requirements. One of the biggest decisions that should be clarified is whether the chaplain will serve the people of the department only or also members of the public. The decisions about the job requirements depend on the abilities, availability, and training of the chaplain. The duties may change, however, as the chaplain receives additional training or as additional chaplains are added to the team.

In the field, first responders deal with the mechanics of broken bodies, fires, accidents, and crime scenes. Chaplains comfort victims, connect with family members, locate community resources for victims and families, provide ethical counsel, and offer spiritual guidance and direction. When chaplains are available at the scene, first responders can focus on their own responsibilities. Chaplains also fulfill some tough responsibilities that first responders do not necessarily want to deal with, such as staying on the scene to comfort a grieving widow, assisting the coroner, or caring for someone having an emotional outburst.

Public safety chaplains can be found within all levels of law enforcement, the fire service, EMS, and the dispatch (911) system.

Law Enforcement

Law enforcement encompasses police, sheriff, and highway patrol departments. Some states have differing kinds of law enforcement at the state level, which also offer opportunities for chaplaincy. At the federal level, law-enforcement chaplains work in the Federal Bureau of Investigation, Customs and Border Protection, the US Marshals Service, and other agencies. Local law enforcement, depending on the budget, often uses volunteers from local churches to fill chaplain positions. These volunteers may be pastors or other ministers, but they can also be laypeople. Larger localities and state and federal organizations require chaplains to be ordained by local churches and endorsed by their denominations.

Working with law-enforcement officers can be challenging for chaplains. For officers, the work itself involves extended periods of routine riding and paperwork, punctuated by periods of action. Law-enforcement officers are aware of the dangers that come with each call they answer. Chaplains develop relationships with law-enforcement officers by caring for them, listening to their problems without judgment, and supporting them in challenging times. Discussing death and dying is a common practice.

A career in law enforcement can breed marital problems because of long hours that can include the night shift, low pay, and stressful work environments. Chaplains need active listening skills and some marriage-counseling training to work successfully with law-enforcement personnel. When chaplains "ride along" with law enforcement, they accompany officers in vehicles or on foot throughout their shifts. Ride-alongs not only show officers that their work is important to chaplains; they also allow chaplains to better understand the challenges officers face. During this shared experience, chaplains become confidential listeners who can add perspective to the officers' struggles.

Chaplains are available for people at the scene of a crime or accident. While law enforcement takes statements, chaplains can watch children or sit with a frazzled witness. Chaplains should avoid encouraging witnesses and those involved to make statements. They should also avoid interfering with law enforcement as they complete their tasks. While chaplains should undergo some training to understand the terminology and procedures used by law enforcement, chaplains should always remain in their roles as chaplains.

The Emergency Dispatch Center (911 Operation Center)

Emergency dispatch centers often have chaplains who work in their area of operation. Depending on the size of a center, phone calls may consume all of the dispatchers' time, leaving them few opportunities to talk with a chaplain. Still, law-enforcement chaplains often have an emergency dispatch center as part of their ministry field and, thus, will check in with the employees at certain times during the week.

Emergency dispatchers struggle with the same life challenges that other people face. They also bring their problems to work, as employees in other professions do. These dispatchers, however, have high-stress jobs, as they work to save lives by directing first responders to specific locations. Dispatchers have to understand and assess what someone is saying on the phone and then pass that on to the appropriate first responders. They also have to deal with people in imminent danger (e.g., a robbery, a fire) or amid health crises (e.g., a heart attack).

The work of assessing and categorizing emergencies and dispatching first responders is highly taxing. Chaplains need to be present with people without feeling the need to speak all the time. There is power in providing safe space for dispatchers who have been involved in crises that did not end well. As a dispatcher sits with a chaplain and God's presence fills the room through the chaplain, the safe space can become a sacred space. If the person gives permission, the chaplain can pray with them. The chaplain can be a powerful presence in the workplace.

The Fire Department

Firefighters often live in the firehouse when they are on duty. Chaplains can have long talks and even some counseling sessions with firefighters in these settings; however, it simply is not appropriate to engage them at the scene of a fire or during some other crisis. Building bridges of trust and communication are essential to ministering to firefighters, who, as a group, can be resistant to accepting chaplains as part of their unit.

Chaplains must find ways to bridge the gaps. One main way to build trust is by working alongside the firefighters. A ministry of presence means the chaplain is physically at the firehouse or on the scene. This presence can include cleaning the firehouse, washing the trucks, and performing other routine tasks. With these acts, chaplains show that they want to be part of the team and that they will be there for the work that is less glamorous. Having casual conversation while working can build trust across time. Firefighters who experience chaplains working at a fire or accident can also begin to trust them and eventually confide in them. Chaplains who only say prayers at functions or fulfill other official duties will be unable to build relationships with firefighters. Relationships build trust, which can lead to questions about God and Christ.

A Specialized Area of Concern: First Responders' Traumatic Incidents

Firefighters, law-enforcement officers, and EMS personnel are rarely on the job for very long without witnessing distressing situations, such as murder, suicide, untimely and gruesome deaths, and other realities of living in a broken world. At times, these first responders need to take a break from the scene and talk out the situation with someone who listens with compassion and care. A department chaplain, if well equipped, is able to provide that care, while a peer may not be able to do so. Serving as a sounding board and allowing first responders to tell their story and talk about their own responses are often what they need. At other times, crisis debriefing of some type is required. Chaplains with special training in crisis ministry can play important roles in helping first responders deal with their responses to the traumatic incidents they have witnessed and endured.

Responding to one traumatic incident or a series of them may leave a first responder with posttraumatic stress disorder, compassion fatigue, burnout, or moral injury. Chaplains who are familiar with the distinctions between them and the signs of each can help first responders get the help they need. This is another reason why chaplains should include crisis-ministry training in their education and take refresher courses throughout their career.

Each year, more first responders die by suicide than are killed in the line of duty. This tragic situation has been true in the United States for a number of years.[7] Even more widespread with first responders are addiction, depression, and anxiety, which can lead to suicide. First-responder studies report the following statistics:

- 37 percent of EMS professionals have had suicidal ideation.
- 47 percent of firefighters have had suicidal ideation.
- 25 percent of female and 23 percent of male law-enforcement officers have had suicidal ideation.[8]

Chaplains can play a significant role in raising awareness of this issue at every level, recognizing and responding to mental health issues as soon as possible and offering first responders practical tools they can use in getting help for themselves or for others.

Requirements for Becoming a Public Safety Chaplain

Professional chaplaincy requires preparation in chaplaincy, theology, and ministry skills. Public safety chaplaincy has less formalized requirements than some

7. Kelly Powers, "Firefighters Are Heroes, but Who's Watching Out for Them When It Comes to Suicide?," Delmarva Now, September 23, 2019, https://www.delmarvanow.com/story/life/2019/09/23/firefighter-suicide-mental-health-culture-maryland-delaware-virginia-salisbury/1300515001; David Lohr, "For Third Straight Year, Police Suicides Outnumber Line-of-Duty Deaths," Huffington Post, January 2, 2019, https://www.huffpost.com/entry/for-third-straight-year-police-suicides-outnumber-line-of-duty-deaths_n_5c2d110de4b05c88b70542fa.

8. Substance Abuse and Mental Health Services Administration, "First Responders: Behavioral Health Concerns, Emergency Response, and Trauma," Disaster Technical Assistance Center Supplemental Research Bulletin (May 2018), https://www.samhsa.gov/sites/default/files/dtac/supplementalresearchbulletin-firstresponders-may2018.pdf.

other kinds of chaplaincy do. Public safety chaplains need to have the following KSAs in order to succeed:

- *Knowledge:* This includes a knowledge of chaplaincy, theology, counseling, and leadership training, which is gained through higher education and CPE. Public safety chaplains should also have basic knowledge of first aid and fire safety before working with first responders.
- *Skills:* These include excellent interpersonal, pastoral, leadership, and counseling skills. Public safety chaplains can be short- or long-term counselors; therefore, they benefit from having skills in short-term crisis intervention, spiritual counseling, and support counseling. Additionally, compassion, empathy, and listening skills are important for this type of chaplaincy.
- *Abilities:* These include capacities to comfort people in times of crisis; care for first responders, victims, and families in routine or crisis times; work well with teams; and provide spiritual care for others. Public safety chaplains should also have the ability to be present at gruesome accident scenes and other traumatic scenes.

Aspiring public safety chaplains can obtain these KSAs by completing the requirements in this section and volunteering in ministry or public safety settings. There is no standard path leading to work in this field. Most federal and state law-enforcement organizations have standardized requirements for chaplains. Many law-enforcement agencies establish their own requirements, though many follow the requirements that the ICPC recommends. Likewise, fire departments establish their own requirements, though many follow the recommendations of the FFC. EMS and dispatch-center chaplains lack a professional organization, and the individual departments establish the requirements for chaplains. The requirements for public safety chaplains include the following.

Calling. As with all other areas of chaplaincy, the first step to becoming a public safety chaplain is receiving a calling from God. When God calls someone to public safety chaplaincy, that person has to begin doing research to discover the requirements for local, state, or federal departments and agencies.

Education. Most public safety chaplains have completed a bachelor's degree. Many public safety chaplains have an MDiv or an MA, as well as CPE training, and have been ordained and/or licensed by a church. Some of these chaplains receive endorsement from their faith groups as well. Public safety chaplaincy, however, differs from some other forms of chaplaincy because the department chiefs appoint chaplains. These chaplains are often pastors of local churches or retired pastors who bring a church model to the department. Because of these appointments, public safety chaplains can have a greater disparity in levels of training, professionalism, and proficiency than chaplains in other functional areas.

Completing theological education is important for public safety chaplains because they need developed theologies of death, dying, and suffering. People ask questions about God's presence in their lives and his allowance of suffering and sin, and chaplains need to be prepared to answer. A theology of chaplaincy is also important for public safety chaplains to develop before they begin their ministry, and they should complete crisis and disaster response courses as well.

CPE is effective in helping chaplains develop strong listening and ministry-of-presence skills. These skills are foundational to effective ministry with first responders. CPE also assists with crisis training for chaplains. The four units of CPE required in some functional areas may be more than the public safety chaplain needs or finds useful, but completing at least one unit would be a wise choice.

Ordination or licensing. Local churches can offer highly effective support teams for first responders when mass-casualty or other large-scale crises occur. Churches that have ordained or licensed chaplains who can work with first responders readily answer the call for help during these crises, whether it involves providing food, shelter, or other support. Additionally, chaplains who have been sent out by churches and denominations remain grounded in their theologies as they walk with first responders through the challenges in their lives and careers.

Endorsement. Endorsement assists public safety chaplains in being anchored to their faith group as they minister in a pluralistic setting. The support of an endorser in facing theological and other questions can be highly beneficial to a public safety chaplain.

On-the-job training. Chaplains should participate in on-the-job training opportunities when they arise. They should develop professional skills for public safety, along with chaplaincy skills. Competence in areas such as CPR and basic first aid allows chaplains to assist at the scene if necessary. Chaplains should also consider obtaining an Emergency Medical Responder (EMR) certification. These preparations provide chaplains with skills that can be welcomed at emergency scenes; however, chaplains must be aware of and stay within the boundaries placed on them by departments.

Professional-development opportunities. Ongoing professional-development opportunities allow chaplains to complete online courses and participate in conferences and associations designed for first responders. As part of the response team, chaplains should be aware of public safety operations and should, if possible, train alongside first responders during in-house training and drills. In this way, chaplains gain perspective on the jobs that first responders perform.

Basic Courses

A number of chaplain courses are offered nationally. The following is a list of organizations that offer these courses, together with the courses themselves, which allow chaplains to network and continue their education:

- FFC
  - Essentials of Fire Chaplaincy, a sixteen-hour course recommended for all fire department chaplains
  - Advanced Fire Chaplain, a certificate requiring five years of chaplaincy experience. It acknowledges college credits earned and requires completion of a number of advanced courses.
  - Additional courses, such as Emotional Resilience; Ethics; and Dealing with Difficult Deaths[9]
- ICPC 12 Basic Courses, an introduction to police chaplaincy[10]
- Federal Emergency Management Agency free online courses that are appropriate and may be required for some chaplains. There are courses about the agency's incident command system and national incident management system (IS-100, IS-200, IS-700), the inclusion of people with disabilities in disaster operations (IS-368), and religious and cultural literacy competence in disaster situations (IS-505).
- International Critical Incident Stress Foundation courses suggested for chaplains and required for the advanced certificate from the FFC (Assisting Individuals in Crisis; Group Crisis Intervention; Advanced Assisting Individuals in Crisis; Advanced Group Crisis Intervention; Pastoral Crisis Intervention I & II)
- National Child Traumatic Stress Network's Psychological First Aid, a free four-hour online course that equips participants to help victims in the immediate aftermath of a crisis, such as a natural disaster or terrorist attack

9. "Federation of Fire Chaplains Training Institute," Federation of Fire Chaplains, accessed January 19, 2023, https://ffc.wildapricot.org/Institute.

10. "ICPC Basics Course Descriptions," Indiana State Police, accessed January 19, 2023, https://www.in.gov/isp/3204.htm.

Professional Organizations for Public Safety Chaplains

Within the field of public safety chaplaincy, several professional organizations hold annual conferences, conduct training, and provide websites for chaplains. These organizations include the following:

- Association of Law Enforcement Chaplains
- Federation of Fire Chaplains (FFC)
- International Conference of Police Chaplains (ICPC)
- International Police and Fire Chaplains Association
- Regional fire and police chaplain organizations
- Regional public safety chaplain organizations
- State fire and police chaplain organizations
- State public safety chaplain organizations

These organizations provide support, networking, and additional training for public safety chaplains. Some organizations are not focused specifically on public safety chaplaincy, but chaplains may find that they still provide relevant training and service opportunities and also allow chaplains to form relationships with colleagues.

Leadership as a Public Safety Chaplain

Leadership positions offer opportunities to influence senior leadership and the course of a department. Chaplains act as relational leaders as they build relationships with first responders of every rank and position. Through these relationships, chaplains can influence the moral decisions and spiritual direction of the department or unit. As servant leaders, chaplains can exemplify "something different" by completing tasks that few want to do. They can influence others by example. Ultimately, servant leadership works hand in hand with relational leadership in strengthening relationships so that others come to chaplains to ask why they are different. The door is then opened for sharing the gospel.

Chaplains can serve on leadership teams and use the opportunities afforded to effect changes that transform the morale and culture within departments. Through transformational leadership, chaplains can influence the consideration of employee needs and other concerns. Chaplains can, then, utilize leadership skills to encourage improvements in public safety departments. When leadership positions are offered, chaplains should be open to them.

Summary

While public safety chaplains' responsibilities are defined at the local level, assistance is provided by national, state, and local professional organizations, which offer recommendations. Preparing for this ministry includes training in crisis intervention, counseling, and listening. Public safety chaplains benefit from understanding how to care for, comfort, and come alongside those to whom they minister. The greatest challenge for many chaplains who enter this functional area is the pluralistic nature of the workplace. Learning to cooperate without compromising their own beliefs is a challenge for chaplains who work with other clergy and with first responders claiming no religion.

Public safety chaplains provide safe spaces that can become sacred spaces as chaplains bear the presence of God in public safety work environments. Providing that presence is the ministry that chaplains offer within stations, crime or accident scenes, and any other places where first responders are. Public safety chaplains experience some of the worst of humankind but bear the greatest of presences in these contexts.

19

Recreation Chaplaincy

Michael W. Langston

S ailing the seven seas remains a dream for many people in the world. Yet recreation chaplains sometimes sail with cruise ships, usually receiving a room in exchange for conducting services and counseling people if necessary. If messages with tragic news are delivered to the cruise ship, chaplains deliver the news to families. People on cruise ships are of all ages and come from all backgrounds, so chaplains minister to a diverse mix of travelers.

Recreation chaplaincy is included in the sports and leisure chaplaincy category. In addition to service on cruise ships, recreation chaplaincy includes work in national and state parks—in particular, the leading of services on holy days and on the weekends—and in county and city recreation centers. Park-chaplaincy positions are usually seasonal and filled by volunteers, but chaplains might be able to find church sponsors. Chaplains who work with county recreation departments are often paid to work year-round. This chapter offers an introduction to recreation chaplaincy for those who may consider working in this functional area.

The History of Recreation Chaplaincy

Many church groups in the nineteenth and twentieth centuries held services or revivals in the areas that became national parks. The Great Smoky Mountains

National Park is one example. Church groups, escaping summer heat, would hold revival services while camping in the Appalachian Mountains. People set up campsites with tents, campfires, and chairs, and they fished and hunted between services. Whoever came into one of the areas was welcomed to services. Later on, many churches in these areas maintained the *tradition* of holding summer services in the mountains, even after the areas became national parks. These events often attracted visitors to the parks.

Since that time, recreation chaplains have emerged in volunteer capacities throughout the United States. In 1951, A Christian Ministry in the National Parks began working with visitors and employees in Yellowstone National Park. They now work in over forty-five national parks, using over two hundred people to provide care for more than thirty thousand people. This ministry has influenced many states to provide chaplain services in their state parks. Chaplains in parks hold services for people camping or staying in nearby hotels and assist in crises that may happen.[1]

Seafaring shore-based associations have provided care for sailors since the United States began. These organizations, located in port cities, have opened up to cruise-ship passengers as the cruise industry has grown. Cruise ships have volunteer chaplains conduct services while they are at sea, especially during holiday seasons. These chaplain programs are less documented than many other chaplaincy programs.

The Culture and Ethos of Recreation Chaplaincy

Recreation chaplains work in national parks, state parks, recreational vehicle parks, county or city recreation centers, and cruise ships. Centers for sailors and mariners in cities with old ports often have chaplains as well. These chaplains minister to the sailors who come into the ministry center, which is usually on the harbor.

Chaplains working in state and national parks usually camp or stay within the park, though sometimes they live close to the park and can be called on if needed. Their duties include providing services and being present to people in the parks during crises. Tourists in national parks are often internationals from different cultures and religions. They may come to services out of curiosity and then have questions afterward. Chaplains answer their questions and meet their needs without proselytizing. If necessary, chaplains facilitate for those of other faiths by contacting other clergypersons in the community.

1. "About," A Christian Ministry in the National Parks, accessed January 19, 2023, https://acmnp.com/about.

State parks usually have fewer international visitors (depending on the park and its location), but the people can be just as pluralistic in their beliefs as the international visitors in national parks. Recreation chaplains, while conducting services according to the practices of their own tradition, must have resources for people in need of a clergyperson from another faith group. This facilitation is a way to have a ministry of presence among the people in the state park.

Chaplains in state and national parks also work with park rangers and staff. If the park has hotels and restaurants, then chaplains can minister to the people who work there. Counseling and caring for the employees allows the chaplains to build relationships that will enable them to help when people are in need. Oftentimes, park rangers and employees in state and national parks attend services that are offered within the parks if they are unable to attend their own churches.

Chaplains in recreation centers work with the people who come to the center—perhaps seniors in the morning, children in the afternoon, and teens in the evening. By building relationships and offering a ministry of presence, chaplains become part of the lives of the people they encounter. Over time, chaplains develop relationships that allow people to trust them, and this trust allows chaplains to share their faith when invited. Chaplaincy in recreation centers shares many aspects of community chaplaincy.

Even though recreation chaplains are mainly volunteers, they still need to be aware of the confidentiality laws of their state and how these laws apply to their chaplaincy. When chaplains are ministering in national parks, they are on federal land and come under federal confidentiality laws. When chaplains counsel people in a counseling or confessional setting, priest-penitent laws apply. Chaplains must treat the person's communication as confidential and cannot share it with anyone unless the person gives permission. Recreation chaplains do not counsel as much as other chaplains, but they should still be aware of the laws pertaining to confidential communications.

Requirements for Becoming a Recreation Chaplain

Professional chaplaincy requires preparation in chaplaincy, theology, and ministry skills. Even though recreation chaplaincy has few formalized requirements, recreation chaplains need to have the following KSAs in order to succeed:

- *Knowledge:* This includes a knowledge of chaplaincy, theology, counseling, and leadership training, which is gained through higher education and CPE.

- *Skills:* These include excellent interpersonal skills; pastoral skills, including the conducting of services; leadership skills; and counseling skills. While recreation chaplains are not long-term counselors, they do benefit from having skills in short-term crisis intervention, spiritual counseling, and support counseling. Additionally, compassion, empathy, and listening skills are important for this type of chaplaincy.
- *Abilities:* These include capacities to comfort people in times of crisis, care for staff and other people in routine or crisis times, work well with teams, and provide spiritual care for others.

Aspiring recreation chaplains can obtain these KSAs by completing the following requirements and volunteering in parks, recreation areas, or other ministry settings.

Education. Aspirants should consider completing the following education:

- A bachelor's degree in any field, but psychology, chaplaincy, or counseling are beneficial. If a chaplain desires to work in parks, classes on outdoor-related subjects such as first aid and land navigation would be beneficial.
- Preferably an MA with a concentration in chaplaincy, counseling, or a similar area. An MDiv degree is beneficial but not required for recreation chaplaincy. Degrees should be earned from regionally accredited colleges or universities.
- Preferably at least one unit of CPE

Calling. Recreation chaplains need to have received a spiritual call and to have made a commitment to work in city or county recreation areas, in state or national parks, or on cruise ships.

Ministry experience. Applicants must also have ministry experience, which is often gained in church settings.

Ordination/licensing. Recreation chaplains should be licensed and/or ordained as ministers. This bond between chaplain and church provides support for the chaplain and ministry opportunities for the church when chaplains need assistance with events in the parks. Ordination is not required for some recreation-chaplain positions.

Endorsement. As with those serving in the other functional areas of chaplaincy, recreation chaplains should be endorsed, though endorsement is not required for some recreation-chaplain positions.

Professional Organizations for Recreation Chaplains

There are fewer professional organizations devoted to recreation chaplaincy than there are organizations devoted to some other areas of chaplaincy. However, many states and national and state parks have networking opportunities for chaplains. The following are professional organizations that recreation chaplains can join for networking and educational opportunities:

- A Christian Ministry in the National Parks
- International Christian Maritime Association

Recreation chaplains can also find information on these organizations' websites for assistance with chaplaincy questions.

Leadership as a Recreation Chaplain

Recreation chaplains have opportunities for leadership as they oversee volunteers, organize programs, and meet with administrators. By providing a moral and spiritual interpretation of ideas, chaplains can influence courses of action within parks, recreation centers, and cruise ships. Though many recreation chaplains are volunteers, they still have opportunities to influence decisions made by leaders with whom they work.

Summary

Recreation chaplaincy is one of the few chaplaincies that can happen entirely outdoors. Bringing a ministry of presence into forests, campsites, cruise ships, and recreation centers throughout the United States, recreation chaplains primarily provide services for people in recreation settings. Recreation chaplains enjoy the wonder of God's creation as they bring his presence to people through worship or counseling.

20

Sports Chaplaincy

Michael W. Langston

S ports chaplaincy, part of the sports and leisure category of the ten functional areas, is a growing field that involves working with athletes, coaches, family members, staff, and referees. Many colleges and universities have found great value in providing their athletes with access to sports chaplains, and many professional sports teams have chaplains who work with their teams. Organizations in sport areas such as car racing and horse racing also use sports chaplains. These chaplains may travel with the sports group or be assigned to a certain location. The US Olympic team travels with chaplains at all times.

Sports chaplains work with adult athletes who are eighteen years old and older. If an athlete plays for a college, university, or other elite team, it means that athlete is highly successful in his or her sport. Chaplains working with these athletes can celebrate their accomplishments with coaches and fans; however, when a player's sports career is ended because of an injury or some other occurrence, chaplains are present to bring comfort and care as the person grieves the loss and learns to find meaning outside the sport. Sports chaplains therefore bring a sense of care and comfort to athletes who struggle with fame or a fall from fame. This chapter introduces the ministry of sports chaplaincy and explains the requirements for those who want to pursue this kind of ministry.

The History of Sports Chaplaincy

Sports chaplaincy has existed for over fifty years in the United States, with many teams opting for chaplains over the last twenty years. The United States, Australia, New Zealand, Canada, and the United Kingdom have many robust sports chaplaincy programs that have developed since the mid-twentieth century.[1]

A turning point for sports chaplaincy was the 1972 Olympics, when the Israeli team was murdered. The resulting shock, fear, and trauma among other athletes highlighted the need for caring people who could provide counsel to athletes in times of high stress. Since that event, sports chaplaincy has grown to encompass Olympic and other world events, professional and collegiate sports teams, and other sports contexts. Sports chaplaincy is a growing field.

The Culture and Ethos of Sports Chaplaincy

Understanding the culture and ethos of sports chaplaincy requires a broad understanding of athletes, coaches, and competition. Providing care and comfort to athletic staff and players can be challenging, since athletes tend to endure pain without complaining. John Boyers, a retired Manchester United Football Club chaplain, describes what chaplains are not:

> Chaplains are not fans trying to get close to their sporting heroes and heroines. Chaplains are not failed sports people trying to resurrect former dreams through their role. Chaplains are not people seeking status or kudos or significance by their involvements.

Boyers continues by describing chaplains' usefulness in professional sports environments, in which a person can be on top one day and no longer matter the next day:

> [Chaplains] are involved to serve people in a world where hopes are created and dashed in an instant, where many wonder who they can really trust in conversation, where winners are lauded and losers ignored, where people don't give up the game, but rather the game gives up on people. Chaplains are needed in sport. The worth and value of a pastorally trained and experienced minister providing unconditional support to members of the sports club staff is obvious.[2]

1. See, e.g., Beyond Gold's website (www.beyond-gold.org).
2. John Boyers, quoted in "Chaplaincy," Soccer Chaplains United, accessed January 19, 2023, https://soccerchaplainsunited.org/chaplaincy.

Chaplains ministering to sports teams must learn the specific culture of the sport and of the athletes in order to meet the needs of the people they serve.

Sports chaplains are often volunteers, though large venues pay chaplains. The hours that they work depend on the team's game schedule, practice schedule, and season. Semiprofessional soccer teams often play from the late spring until early fall; then the players are released until the next season. Thus, the sports chaplain serving the team would work from late spring through early fall. Sports chaplains, however, are not limited to the season and may stay in touch with players throughout the offseason if they give permission.

Sports chaplains serve in pluralistic settings, with people of all faiths and no faith. Ministering to all, such chaplains refrain from judging others' moral, faith, and life decisions. They support their teams by being caring listeners who help meet the needs of their teams, coaches, staff, referees, and associated families. Sports chaplains who opt to complete a course on world religions will find the knowledge useful.

Several challenges in the sports world affect sports chaplains. The first is the psyche of elite or world-class athletes. These athletes have worked for years and are the best—or almost the best—in the nation or the world. Failure is not something they have experienced often. In many cases, this success translates into their entire lives, and they are resistant to asking for help. They rely on their training to solve problems in their sport. When they face a challenge for which they have no training, such as the death of a loved one, the loss of a friendship, or a season-ending injury, they struggle. At these times, sports chaplains can listen to their frustrations and care for them as the athletes try to make sense of an out-of-sync world. Chaplains who have taken courses in sports psychology are better prepared to deal with top-level athletes. Preparing in advance helps them understand how to offer pastoral care and relationship to these athletes.

Another challenge comes from working for famous coaches or serving a team that has famous players. Sports chaplains can be overwhelmed by people seeking to get close to the coaches and players. Friends and family may pressure the sports chaplain to introduce them. Media personnel and fans may also approach the chaplain for access to these figures. Sports chaplains must have responses prepared for these situations, and they must remember their commitment to provide care for the team. Such care involves protecting the privacy of coaches and players instead of taking advantage of their relationship with them.

Sports chaplains also face challenges during games. Chaplains can cheer for the team, but they are not fans, so they refrain from booing or calling out negative comments to the opposing team. Support for the team is the chaplain's job, but harassing the other team is outside the boundaries of the job. Additionally, sports chaplains need to refrain from yelling at umpires or referees. Shouting at anyone during the game confuses players and coaches, as it makes them see the chaplain as a fan rather than as a chaplain. A single instance of yelling can fracture the existing chaplaincy relationship. Chaplains who used to play the team's sport must be especially careful about controlling their passion for the game.

Sports chaplains must also refrain from coaching. Chaplains who have played the sport have knowledge that other chaplains lack. They also gain respect from players if they played the sport at a high level. However, this experience is not necessary and can actually serve as a negative for a chaplain. If a chaplain was an athlete in the past, then coaching may be a strong temptation. ("If the player just turned his foot this way, then the whole process would flow.") However, the chaplain is with the team as a chaplain and not as a coach. If chaplains forget this fact, players can become confused as to who they should follow for coaching. The coach can then grow irritated because the chaplain is challenging the coach's authority and interrupting the game or practice session.

Practices and games are usually not times to have discussions with players. Players on the sidelines should be following the game or practice so they can step in when called on. Sports chaplains should attend practices and games in a support function and not discuss issues with players. Attendance shows that chaplains care about what is happening with players. Trust is built by chaplains caring enough to watch. However, chaplains can assist players having a difficult time if a coach asks them to do so.

Sports chaplains who attend practices and games are available for players after the practice or game ends. Chaplains who hang out in the locker room or in the areas surrounding the field are often approached by players who want to talk. Part of sports chaplaincy is being available for athletes whenever they are free to discuss what is important to them. Athletes, coaches, and others connected with the team can pose spiritual questions or ask about the ultimate meaning of life. When they have a career-ending injury, athletes can struggle to find that meaning. Marriage counseling and grief care can also be part of the sports chaplain's work. More generally, the job means bringing a calm presence to a highly competitive world.

Sports chaplains conduct Bible studies and services for athletes, who have the option to attend or not to attend. Sports teams are pluralistic, comprised of athletes of different faith groups and others who have no faith. Chaplains need to facilitate religious or spiritual care for team members of different faiths when they desire to worship or consult clergy. This facilitation requires having community resources that can support the athletes' and coaches' spiritual needs. Chaplains can, of course, provide for the spiritual needs of athletes and coaches within their own faith group.

Sports chaplains develop relationships with people connected to the teams they serve. They need to have relationships with team doctors and trainers so they can support injured players. In the context of these relationships, they care for people as they offer counseling and spiritual guidance. If someone expresses a desire to know more about a chaplain's faith, the chaplain can share the gospel with that person. This evangelism should not move into proselytism. In the pluralistic culture of sports, chaplains learn to cooperate with other faiths and beliefs without compromising their own faith and beliefs.

Subareas of Ministry in Sports Chaplaincy

Sports chaplaincy is broad, involving various sports and age groups. Sports chaplains tend to focus on a certain sport and age range, though they are not bound by their initial decision. The following paragraphs introduce some subareas of sports chaplaincy.

Chaplaincy in Various Sports

Sports chaplains must choose a sport within which to minister. Most major sports, such as baseball, soccer, football, hockey, basketball, softball, and stockcar racing, have chaplains. Aspiring sports chaplains should choose a sport they are interested or experienced in. To build credibility, they should understand the rules and how the sport is played. If chaplains used to play a sport, they may want to select that sport. The time of the year when the sport is played may also affect chaplains' choices, as it may conflict with other vocational plans.

College or University Sports Chaplaincy

After selecting a sport, chaplains should choose an age level on which to focus. College and university sports programs vary from highly competitive schools to much smaller colleges in which students are less competitive. Working with postsecondary students entails understanding their stage of life and assisting them in learning to move into adulthood. Working with postsecondary students involves supporting and forming adults. Relationships with athletes are usually limited to four or five years at the most, since students graduate and move to professional sports or the workplace.

Professional Sports Chaplaincy

Many professional sports and teams have chaplains on their staff. These chaplains provide pastoral counseling and spiritual care for players, coaches, families, and staff members. Professional athletes' ego-boosting knowledge of their own prowess can cause them to act as if life contains no consequences. These sometimes-risky choices lead to consequences in other areas of the athletes' lives, which force them to need assistance. Chaplains help them with marriage problems, addictions, alcohol abuse, and other personal struggles and self-destructive behaviors. Many chaplains who work with professional athletes form strong bonds with them that last many years. The chaplain can walk with these players and their families through tough times and great times alike. The relationships tend to be longer term than those with college athletes.

Amateur Sports Chaplaincy

Amateur sports, in which athletes are not paid to compete, also hire chaplains to work with athletes. The Olympics, the World Cup, and other events for amateur athletes include the same challenges and successes as professional sports. However, funding can be an additional problem for amateur athletes; professionals tend not to face that challenge unless they play in the minor leagues. Sports chaplains bring the same skills to amateur teams that they would bring to professional teams, thus caring for athletes at all levels.

Requirements for Becoming a Sports Chaplain

Professional chaplaincy requires preparation in chaplaincy, theology, and ministry skills. Sports chaplaincy has less formalized requirements than those in some functional areas, but sports chaplains still need to have the following KSAs if they are to succeed:

- *Knowledge:* This includes a knowledge of chaplaincy, theology, counseling, and leadership training, which is gained through higher education and CPE. Sports chaplains should also understand the sport in which they work.
- *Skills:* These include excellent interpersonal skills; pastoral skills, including the conducting of services and the leading of Bible studies; leadership skills; and counseling skills. Since sports chaplains can be long-term counselors, they benefit from having skills in short- and long-term crisis intervention, spiritual counseling, and support counseling. Additionally, compassion, empathy, and listening skills are important for this type of chaplaincy.

- *Abilities:* These include capacities to comfort people in times of crisis, care for staff and athletes in routine or crisis times, work well with teams, and provide spiritual care for others.

Aspiring sports chaplains can obtain these KSAs by completing the following requirements and volunteering in ministry settings, including settings that involve sports teams.

Education. Aspirants should complete the following educational requirements:

- A bachelor's degree in any field
- An MDiv or an MA with a concentration in chaplaincy, theology, or counseling studies. Sports chaplaincy classes are beneficial as well. Degrees should be earned from regionally accredited colleges or universities.
- Preferably at least one unit of CPE

Calling. Sports chaplains need to have received a spiritual call and to have made a commitment to long-term work with athletes, coaches, referees, staff, and associated family members.

Ministry experience. Applicants must also have some ministry experience, which is often gained in chaplaincy.

Ordination/licensing. Sports chaplains should be licensed and/or ordained as ministers. This bond between chaplain and church provides not only support for the chaplain but also ministry opportunities for the church.

Endorsement. As with those serving in the other functional areas of chaplaincy, sports chaplains should be endorsed. Endorsing agents provide support for chaplains in the field and assist with theological and practical issues that arise in chaplains' ministries.

Languages. Many teams have athletes from other countries and cultures. If sports chaplains become proficient in other languages, they can converse with athletes in their native languages.

Professional Organizations for Sports Chaplains

Sports chaplaincy is an emerging field and, like several other functional areas of chaplaincy, is still formulating professional organizations. Below are some professional organizations whose websites can assist people who are interested in learning more about this type of chaplaincy. The organizations allow sports chaplains to network and stay current in the field.

- Athletes in Action
- Baseball Chapel, for Major League Baseball
- Beyond Gold (international sports chaplaincy), for Olympic athletics
- Fellowship of Christian Athletes
- Hockey Ministries International
- Major Sports Events Chaplaincy
- Motor Racing Outreach Association, for professional car racing
- Soccer Chaplains United, for professional soccer in England

Different sports have different chaplains' organizations. There are many sports chaplaincy organizations throughout the United States, Canada, England, Australia, and New Zealand.

Leadership as a Sports Chaplain

Sports chaplains act as leaders through relational leadership. They build relationships with and influence athletes, coaches, family members, and staff as these people learn to make ethical and spiritual decisions. Coaches can turn to sports chaplains in meetings and ask them to give input on moral and spiritual matters, thereby creating leadership opportunities for them. When a large team has a staff of chaplains, they are led by one chaplain who delegates work and assignments and who influences the growth of newer chaplains. Leadership is an integral part of the sports chaplain's job.

Summary

Sports chaplaincy is a fast-growing area of chaplaincy that reaches across the world. College, professional, and amateur athletes, all of whom are top performers, are distinctly competitive and hyperfocused. When athletes fail, chaplains can assist them in finding their way through the defeat and can help them make new meaning in their lives outside of sports. Chaplains work with athletes in various sporting contexts, bringing a sense of care and peace to a highly competitive world.

CONCLUSION

The Future of Chaplaincy

The future of Christian chaplaincy in America is bright, but chaplains will face greater challenges as the culture drifts further and further from its biblical foundations. Humanism, secularism, paganism, and individualism have been rapidly replacing God as the center of American culture. Historically, Americans agreed on the existence of God, as noted in the country's founding documents.[1] However, the belief that "we are endowed by our Creator with certain inalienable rights" is now rejected by many citizens, who believe in evolution and not a Creator.[2] The misconception of the "wall of separation" between church and state has left God out of the classroom and the courtroom and allowed the vacuum to be filled with nontheistic philosophies and "religions." America is experiencing the fallout of removing God and his Word from their place as the benchmark of laws and conduct. God's standards for moral conduct, marriage, and family are quickly being replaced by the humanistic, secular, and individualistic idea that each person can determine their own truth and standards (cf. Gen. 3:5). With God replaced by the individual, each person has the opportunity to determine what is right

1. Paul Strand, "America's 'Explicit Covenant with God': How a Nation Pledged to God Can Save a World or Lose It," CBN News, Christian Broadcasting Network, July 1, 2022, https://www1 .cbn.com/cbnnews/us/2019/may/americas-explicit-covenant-with-god-how-a-nation-pledged -to-god-can-save-a-world-hellip-or-lose-it.
2. Jon D. Miller, Eugenie C. Scott, Mark S. Ackerman, Belen Laspra, Glenn Branch, Carmelo Polino, Jordan S. Huffaker, "Public Acceptance of Evolution in the United States, 1985–2020," *Public Understanding of Science* 31, no. 2 (2021): 223–38, https://doi.org/10.1177/096366252110 35919.

in their own eyes (Prov. 21:2). Essentially, this is what the Bible describes as idolatry, making oneself God (Exod. 20:3). Some have even declared that they—and not God—can determine their gender (cf. Rom. 1:28), and still others proclaim that they—and not God—can determine what counts as a human life (see Ps. 139).

Even so, God has called Christian chaplains to bear the light of Christ in the darkness of an increasingly godless society (see Matt. 5:14). Evangelical chaplains can be confident of future opportunities to serve openly and freely because of the United States' commitment to the free exercise of religion as recorded in the First Amendment to the Constitution. Evangelical chaplains can also be confident about the future because they have a clear mission from God to bear the presence and message of Christ whenever and wherever the Holy Spirit opens a door. They understand that the success of the mission relies not on them but on the Lord (Phil. 4:13) and that the Lord will use them for his glory, no matter the situation, conflict, or opposition. They can be sure that God is so powerful that he will bring good from bad situations and challenges (Rom. 8:28). As the culture and society struggle to find purpose and meaning, the Christian chaplain will stand ready to share "the way, and the truth, and the life" (John 14:6). Chaplains will stand with an open heart and open arms, eager to share the love, hope, and care of Jesus. They will be prepared to personally provide biblically based ministry to all who desire it and facilitate the religious needs of all as their faith and conscience allow. Although challenges for Christian chaplains will increase as humanism, secularism, paganism, and individualism expand across society, every person a chaplain encounters should be met with the love, humility, presence, message, power, and commitment of the Lord Jesus Christ.

Challenges for Evangelical Chaplains

Humanism may be defined as "a progressive philosophy of life that, without theism or other supernatural beliefs, affirms our ability and responsibility to lead ethical lives of personal fulfillment that aspire to the greater good."[3] Humanism is a system of thought that views humans and not the divine as the center of life's purpose. It believes in "the denial of any power or moral value superior to that of humanity; the rejection of religion in favor of a belief in the advancement of humanity by its own efforts."[4] Humanists believe that there

---

3. "Definition of Humanism," American Humanist Association, accessed January 19, 2023, https://americanhumanist.org/what-is-humanism/definition-of-humanism.

4. *Collins Dictionary*, s.v. "humanism," accessed August 21, 2023, https://www.collinsdictionary.com/us/dictionary/english/humanism.

are no supernatural beings, that only a material universe exists, that there is no life beyond the grave, that science is the only reliable source of knowledge, and that one's moral code is derived from lessons of history, personal experience, and contemplation.[5]

This system of belief has become more popular over recent years, and some of its leaders have sought to add humanist chaplains to the US military. With an increasing number of self-identified atheists in the larger society, the Military Association of Atheists and Freethinkers claims that they are the rightful overseers of all such persons and should be able to endorse humanist chaplains to the military in order to meet the "religious" needs of atheist personnel.[6] Yet many individuals who might be perceived as falling into the humanist and atheist categories are not certain that there is no God and are open to exploring the possibility of God's existence. These searchers often list their religious affiliation as "no preference" and should not be identified only as humanist or atheist. Others would like to see chaplaincy eliminated from the military altogether, as seen in the legal battle of *Katcoff v. Marsh*.[7] Conversely, evangelical chaplains believe that "without faith it is impossible to please [God], for whoever would draw near to God must believe that he exists and that he rewards those who seek him" (Heb. 11:6).

The term "secularism" comes from a Latin word meaning "of this world." "As a doctrine, then, secularism is typically used as a label for any philosophy which forms its ethics without reference to religious beliefs and which encourages the development of human art and science."[8] Secularism is most often associated with "indifference to or rejection or exclusion of religion and religious consideration."[9] Secularism often embraces the idea that religion has no place in the public square and should be left out of all public forums, including Congress, government agencies, the military, public schools, and courtrooms. This system of belief has been growing while Christian beliefs have been declining among the American population.[10] Conversely, evangelical chaplains believe that God should not be fenced out of the public square, as "there is no authority except from God, and those that exist have been instituted by God" (Rom. 13:1).

5. "Non-Religious Views," Bitesize, BBC, accessed July 3, 2023, https://www.bbc.co.uk/bitesize/guides/zwstxfr/revision/4.

6. Barry Klassel, "Why We Need Humanist Chaplaincies," Humanist Chaplaincies, accessed January 19, 2023, http://humanistchaplaincies.org/are-humanist-chaplaincies-important.

7. Katcoff v. Marsh, 755 F.2d 223 (2d Cir. 1985), https://casetext.com/case/katcoff-v-marsh.

8. Austin Cline, "What Is Secularism?," Learn Religions, updated June 25, 2019, https://www.learnreligions.com/secularism-101-history-nature-importance-of-secularism-250876.

9. "What Does Secularism Mean?," Center for Inquiry, accessed January 19, 2023, https://centerforinquiry.org/definitions/what-is-secularism.

10. Gregory A. Smith, "About Three-in-Ten U.S. Adults Are Now Religiously Unaffiliated," Pew Research Center, December 14, 2021, https://www.pewresearch.org/religion/2021/12/14/about-three-in-ten-u-s-adults-are-now-religiously-unaffiliated.

Further, evangelical chaplains believe that God has sent them into public places outside the church to minister in government agencies, the military, prisons, and hospitals to bear his presence and message (Acts 1:8).

Paganism may be defined as "a polytheistic or pantheistic nature-worshipping religion," and "its adherents venerate Nature and worship many deities, both goddesses and gods."[11] *Merriam-Webster* defines it as "spiritual beliefs and practices other than those of Judaism, Islam, or especially Christianity: such as the spiritual beliefs and practices of ancient polytheistic religions."[12] This system of belief has been increasing in popularity in America. It thrives on the idea that "God does not exist, that the Bible is not divinely inspired, that all religions are equally valid, that absolute values of right and wrong do not exist, and that there is no such thing as sin."[13] Conversely, evangelical chaplains believe that God does exist (Rev. 1:8), that the Bible is divinely inspired (2 Tim. 3:16), that the only true religion is Christianity (John 14:6), that absolute moral values are rooted in the holy nature of God (Exod. 20:1–17), and that sin does exist and has entered the world through disobedience to God (Gen. 3:1–7).

Individualism may be defined as a "belief that the interests of the individual are of the greatest importance" and "the conception that all values, rights, and duties originate in individuals."[14] Individualism, as understood in this light, contradicts the beliefs of evangelical chaplains that all values, rights, and duties of humankind originate with God (Gen. 1:26–31) and that the entire duty of humanity can be summed up as "fear God and keep his commandments" (Eccles. 12:13). Individualism replaces God with oneself (Exod. 20:3–4). It makes the self, not God, the moral authority. It sees the self, rather than God, as the one who brings purpose and meaning to life (Col. 1:16).

Meeting the Challenges

Bearing the Love of Christ (John 3:16)

When confronted with opposition, evangelical chaplains should respond with the love of Christ. There is no more powerful force in the universe than

11. Prudence Jones, "What Is Paganism?," Pagan Federation International, accessed January 19, 2023, https://www.paganfederation.org/what-is-paganism.

12. *Merriam-Webster*, s.v. "paganism," accessed August 21, 2023, https://www.merriam-webster.com/dictionary/paganism.

13. Douglas S. Winnail, "The Rise of Modern Paganism," Tomorrow's World, November-December, 2019, https://www.tomorrowsworld.org/magazines/2019/november-december/the-rise-of-modern-paganism.

14. *Merriam-Webster*, s.v. "individualism," accessed January 19, 2023, https://www.merriam-webster.com/dictionary/individualism.

the love of God. As the Holy Spirit indwells a person's being, they have the capacity to love as Christ loves, to "love [their] enemies and pray for those who persecute [them]" (Matt. 5:44). The natural reaction is to respond with resistance and force, but the supernatural reaction is to respond with God's love. Chaplains should trust the power of God living in them through the Holy Spirit to help them respond to all opposition with a genuine desire to see people come to know Christ and have a personal, saving relationship with him. Indeed, God calls the chaplain to be "sheep in the midst of wolves" for the purpose of bearing the presence and message of Christ and seeing wolves become sheep (Matt. 10:16).

Bearing the Humility of Christ (Phil. 2:1–10)

In a world where everyone seems to be striving for the top of the hill, God calls chaplains to be humble and to "do nothing from selfish ambition or conceit, but in humility [to] count others more significant than [themselves]" (Phil. 2:3). This Christlike attitude is foundational to chaplains' service and effective ministry to believers and nonbelievers alike. Humility is especially surprising to nonbelievers, and they may become curious about the reason for the chaplain's selfless behavior.

Bearing the Servant Heart of Christ (Phil. 2:8)

The ultimate nature of humility is the willingness to give one's life for another. This is exactly what Jesus did when he "emptied himself, by taking the form of a servant. . . . He humbled himself by becoming obedient to the point of death, even death on a cross" (Phil. 2:7–8). The chaplain who is truly humble in spirit will be a valuable servant of the Lord and others. Such humility allows relationships to flourish with nearly everyone for the glory of God.

Bearing the Presence of Christ (Phil. 1:21)

When a chaplain enters a room, the presence of Christ should permeate the space. It is not the chaplain's physical presence that matters most but rather the presence of the Holy Spirit flowing through the chaplain—emanating love, humility, and a servant's heart. Bearing the presence of Christ is the best defense for those confronted with opposition, and it is God's way of presenting himself through the chaplain.

Bearing the Message of Christ (Rom. 1:16; 6:23)

As stated in chapter 2, the chaplain's mission is not only to bear the *presence* of Christ but also to bear the *message* of Christ (Matt. 28:19–20). The good news is an announcement of God's love, humility, and service to all persons, even those who oppose him and his message of salvation (2 Pet. 3:8–10). It is not the chaplain's ability to build relationships that God uses to generate faith in the heart and save souls. Rather, it is his Word that he uses. "Faith comes from hearing, and hearing through the word of Christ" (Rom. 10:17; see Eph. 2:8–9). Bearing the message of Christ is the best offense with all who desire to hear.

Bearing the Power of Christ (Acts 1:8)

The chaplain's mission to bear the presence and message of Christ is formidable because it is God's presence and God's message that the chaplain carries. It is the very presence of almighty God indwelling and speaking through the chaplain (Acts 1:8). Indeed, the chaplain "can do all things through [Christ,] who strengthens" them (Phil. 4:13). There is no challenge too big for the chaplain who is walking with the Lord, because "he who is in [them] is greater than he who is in the world" (1 John 4:4).

Bearing the Commitment of Christ (John 10:11)

Jesus was totally committed to his mission to serve the Father, to die for humanity, to rise again for humanity, and "to seek and to save the lost" (Luke 19:10). Likewise, the Lord calls chaplains to be totally committed to him: "If anyone would come after me, let him deny himself and take up his cross and follow me" (Matt. 16:24). He calls on chaplains, in the words of the apostle Paul, to "present your bodies as a living sacrifice, holy and acceptable to God" (Rom. 12:1). Total, fearless commitment to Christ is what is needed for chaplains to effectively bear the presence and message of Christ to all people, in all places, at all times.

Conclusion

Overcome! Jesus said, "I have said these things to you, that in me you may have peace. In the world you will have tribulation. But take heart; I have overcome the world" (John 16:33). God says through Paul, "Do not be overcome by evil, but overcome evil with good" (Rom. 12:21). We apply these verses to the call and practice of chaplaincy, closing with words from John: "For everyone who has been born of God overcomes the world. And this is the victory that has overcome the world—our faith. Who is it that overcomes the world except the one who believes that Jesus is the Son of God?" (1 John 5:4–5). May evangelical chaplains hold strongly to their faith, overcome the attacks of Satan and the wiles of the world, and be found faithful bearing the presence and message of Christ to the glory of God!

APPENDIX

Subareas of Chaplaincy

1. Corporate Chaplaincy

Chaplains at Work
http://www.chaplainsatwork.com

Corporate Chaplains Network
https://tfcglobal.org/tfc-global-corporate
-chaplains-network

Corporate Chaplains of America
http://chaplain.org

Frontline Chaplains
http://www.frontlinechaplains.com

Marketplace Chaplains USA
http://mchapusa.com

Marketplace Ministries
https://www.mchapcares.com

**National Institute of Business
and Industrial Chaplains**
https://nibic.org

2. Healthcare Chaplaincy

**Clinical Pastoral Education Inter-
national (CPEI)**
https://cpe-international.org

**College of Pastoral Supervision
and Psychotherapy (CPSP)**
https://www.cpsp.org

**Institute for Clinical Pastoral Training
(ICPT)**
https://www.icpt.edu

Hospice

Aging with Dignity
https://www.agingwithdignity.org

American Hospice Foundation
https://americanhospice.org

Americans for Better Care of the Dying
https://caringcommunity.org/resources
/models-research/americans-for-better
-care-of-the-dying

Association for Death Education and
Counseling
https://www.adec.org

Children's Hospice International
http://www.chionline.org

Hospice Foundation of America
http://hospicefoundation.org

International Association for
Hospice and Palliative Care
https://hospicecare.com/home

International Fellowship of Chaplains
http://www.ifoc.org

Jewish Hospice & Chaplaincy Network
https://jewishhospice.org

National Association for Home Care
and Hospice
https://nahc.org

National Association of Catholic
Chaplains
https://www.nacc.org

National Hospice and Palliative
Care Organization
https://www.nhpco.org

National Institute for Jewish Hospice
http://nijh.org

National Prison Hospice Association
https://npha.org

Hospital

Association for Clinical
Pastoral Education (ACPE)
https://www.acpe.edu

Association of Professional Chaplains
http://www.professionalchaplains.org

Hastings Center
http://www.thehastingscenter.org

HealthCare Chaplaincy Network
https://www.healthcarechaplaincy.org

Healthcare Chaplains
Ministry Association
http://www.hcmachaplains.org

National VA Chaplain Services
https://www.patientcare.va.gov/chaplain
/index.asp

Pediatric Chaplains Network
http://pediatricchaplains.org

Mental Health

Associated Ministries
https://associatedministries.org

Episcopal Mental Illness Network
http://www.eminnews.com/wp

Health Ministries Association, Inc.
https://hmassoc.org

Mental Health Chaplaincy
http://mentalhealthchaplaincy.org

National Alliance on Mental Illness
https://www.nami.org

North American Association of
Christians in Social Work
http://www.nacsw.org

Pathways to Promise
http://www.pathways2promise.org

Presbyterian Serious Mental Illness
Network
https://www.presbyterianmission.org
/ministries/phewa/psmin

United Church of Christ Mental Health
Network
https://www.mhn-ucc.org

VA Integrative Mental Health
https://www.mirecc.va.gov/MIRECC
/mentalhealthandchaplaincy/index.asp

3. Military Chaplaincy

Air National Guard Chaplain Corps
https://www.ang.af.mil/chaplaincorps

Army National Guard Chaplain Corps
https://www.nationalguard.com/chaplain

US Air Force Chaplain Corps (Active Duty, Reserve, Chaplain Candidate)
https://www.airforce.com/careers/specialty-careers/chaplain

US Air Force Chaplain Corps College
http://www.airuniversity.af.mil/Eaker-Center/afccc

US Army Chaplain Center and School
https://os56.army.mil/History-Chaplain-Center-and-School

US Army Chaplains Corps (Active Duty, Reserve, Chaplain Candidate)
https://www.goarmy.com/chaplain.html
https://www.army.mil/chaplaincorps
https://www.facebook.com/ArmyChaplain Corps

US Coast Guard Academy Chaplains
https://uscga.edu/cadet-life/cadet-resources/chaplains

US Merchant Marine Academy Chaplains
https://www.usmma.edu/chapel-staff

US Military Academy West Point Chaplains
https://www.usma.edu/chaplain/SitePages/Chaplains.aspx

US Naval Academy Chaplains
https://www.usna.edu/Chaplains

US Naval Chaplaincy Center and School
https://www.netc.navy.mil/ncs

US Navy Chaplain Corps (Active Duty, Reserve, Chaplain Candidate)
https://www.navy.com/careers/chaplain-support/chaplain.html#ft-key-responsibilities
https://www.facebook.com/navychaplain

US Navy Chaplain Corps (Marine Corps)
http://www.hqmc.marines.mil/Agencies/Chaplain-of-the-Marine-Corps

Military Chaplain Support Organizations (Volunteer Opportunities)

Civil Air Patrol Chaplain Corps (US Air Force Auxiliary)
http://capchaplain.com/join
https://www.facebook.com/CAPchaplains

Military Chaplains Association
http://www.mca-usa.org

State Guard Chaplaincy
https://chaplainservices.weebly.com/state-defense-force-chaplains.html
http://www.gotxsg.com/careers.php

U.S. Coast Guard Auxiliary Chaplain Support Directorate
https://wow.uscgaux.info/content.php?unit=g-dept

4. Education Chaplaincy

Albion College Spiritual Life
https://www.albion.edu/offices/spiritual-life

Association for Chaplaincy and Spiritual Life in Higher Education
https://nacuc.net

Harvard University Chaplains
https://chaplains.harvard.edu

International Association of
Chaplains in Higher Education
http://iache.org

Liberty University Shepherd
https://www.liberty.edu/osd/lu-shepherd

National Campus Ministry Association
https://www.natcampusmin.com

Tufts University Chaplaincy
http://chaplaincy.tufts.edu

University of St. Thomas Campus
Ministry
https://www.stthomas.edu/campusministry

Yale University Chaplain's Office
https://chaplain.yale.edu

5. Prison Chaplaincy

American Correctional Association
http://www.aca.org

American Correctional
Chaplains Association
http://www.correctionalchaplains.org

Federal Bureau of Prisons
https://www.bop.gov/jobs/positions/index
.jsp?p=Chaplain
https://www.bop.gov/policy/technical
/5360_02.pdf
https://www.bop.gov/jobs/positions/docs
/chaplain_faq.pdf

Good News Jail & Prison Ministry
https://goodnewsjail.org

International Prison Chaplains
Association
https://www.ipcaworldwide.org

Jail Chaplains
http://www.jailchaplains.com

National Prison Hospice Association
https://npha.org

Prison Fellowship
https://www.prisonfellowship.org

6. Community Chaplaincy

American Chaplains Association
http://americanchaplainsassociation.org

American Legion Chaplains
https://www.legion.org/honor/chaplains

Boy Scouts of America Troop
Chaplains
https://www.scouting.org/programs/scouts
-bsa/troop-resources/troop-chaplain-and
-chaplain-aide-roles
http://usscouts.org/chaplain/faiths.asp

Chaplains on the Way
http://www.chaplainsontheway.us

Community Chaplain Services
http://communitychaplainservices.org

International Alliance of Community
Chaplains
https://iaocc.net

London Community Chaplaincy
(Ontario)
https://londoncommunitychaplaincy.com

Street Chaplains
http://www.streetchaplain.com

7. Disaster Relief Chaplaincy

American Red Cross
http://www.redcross.org
*Search for training in local chapters

Billy Graham Rapid Response Team Chaplains
https://billygraham.org/what-we-do/evangelism-outreach/rapid-response-team/chaplaincy

Chaplain Innovation Lab Disaster / Crisis Response Services
https://chaplaincyinnovation.org/resources/by-sector/crises

Christian Emergency Network
http://www.christianemergencynetwork.org

Disaster Chaplaincy Services
http://www.disasterchaplaincy.org

Disaster Response Ministries International
https://www.drministries.net

Federal Emergency Management Agency (FEMA)
https://www.fema.gov

https://community.fema.gov
https://www.fema.gov/training

International Critical Incident Stress Foundation
https://www.icisf.org

National Disaster Interfaith Network
http://www.n-din.org

National Organization for Victim Assistance
https://www.trynova.org

National Voluntary Organizations Active in Disaster
https://www.nvoad.org

South Carolina Baptist Convention Disaster Relief
http://www.scbaptist.org/dr

Southern Baptist Disaster Relief Chaplaincy/Crisis—North American Mission Board
https://www.namb.net/chaplaincy/disaster-relief

8. Public Safety Chaplaincy

Chaplaincy USA
https://chaplaincyusa.org

Emergency Chaplains
http://www.echap.org

Emergency Services Chaplains
http://www.emergencychaplains.org

Federation of Fire Chaplains (FFC)
https://ffc.wildapricot.org

Fellowship of Christian Firefighters
https://www.fellowshipofchristianfirefighters.org

International Conference of Police Chaplains (ICPC)
http://www.icpc4cops.org

International Police & Fire Chaplains Association
http://www.ipfca.org

Public Safety Chaplaincy
http://www.publicsafetychaplaincy.com

Public Safety Ministries
http://publicsafetyministries.org

9. Recreation Chaplaincy

National and State Parks

A Christian Ministry in the National Parks
https://acmnp.com

Christian Resort Ministries
https://www.crmintl.org

Wilderness Chaplains & Crisis Response Services
https://www.wildernesschaplains.org

Airports

Catholic Civil Aviation Apostolate
https://www.usccb.org/committees/pastoral-care-migrants-refugees-travelers/airport-ministries

Interfaith Airport Chapels of Chicago
http://www.airportchapels.org

International Association of Civil Aviation Chaplains
https://www.iacac.aero

National Conference of Catholic Airport Chaplains
http://www.nccac.us

Sky Harbor Interfaith Chaplaincy (Phoenix)
https://skyharborchapel.wordpress.com

Vatican Guidance for Catholic Aviation Chaplains
http://www.vatican.va/roman_curia/pontifical_councils/migrants/documents/rc_pc_migrants_doc_19950314_avci_directives_en.html
http://www.vatican.va/roman_curia/pontifical_councils/migrants/s_index_civilaviation/rc_pc_migrants_sectioncivilaviation.htm

Cruise Ships, Maritime, Seaports

Apostleship of the Sea of the United States of America
http://www.aos-usa.org

Chaplain Cruise Ship Jobs
http://www.cruiseshipjob.com/clergy.htm

International Christian Maritime Association
http://icma.as/?s=chaplain

North American Maritime Ministry Association
http://www.namma.org

US Merchant Marine Academy (Chapel Staff)
https://www.usmma.edu/chapel-staff

Transportation

FAITH Riders (Motorcycle Ministry)
http://faithriders.com

HonorBound Motorcycle Ministries
https://hbmm-national.org

Railroad Chaplains
https://mchapusa.com/railroad-chaplains-latest-frontier-of-workplace-chaplaincy-expansion/

Trucking Ministries
https://www.namb.net/chaplaincy

Truck Stop Ministries
https://www.truckstopministries.org

10. Sports Chaplaincy

Association of Church Sports and Recreation Ministries
http://www.csrm.org

Athletes in Action
https://athletesinaction.org

Christian Motorsports International
http://teamrfc.org

Fellowship of Christian Athletes
https://www.fca.org

Golden Spur Ministries (Rodeo)
http://www.goldenspur.org

Motor Racing Outreach (NASCAR)
http://www.go2mro.com

Race Track Chaplaincy of America (Horse Racing)
http://www.rtcanational.org

Sports Chaplaincy Australia
https://sportschaplaincy.com.au

Sports Chaplaincy UK
https://sportschaplaincy.org.uk

Sports Chaplains Community
https://www.sportschaplainscommunity.org

Sports Outreach
http://www.sportsoutreach.net

Surfing Chaplaincy
https://www.christiansurfers.net

Categories of Professional Chaplaincy

Professional Organization Chaplaincy
- Corporate chaplaincy
- Healthcare chaplaincy
- Military chaplaincy

Institution Chaplaincy
- Education chaplaincy
- Prison chaplaincy

Community Assistance Chaplaincy
- Community chaplaincy
- Disaster relief chaplaincy
- Public safety chaplaincy (police, fire, EMS)

Sports and Leisure Chaplaincy
- Recreation chaplaincy
- Sports chaplaincy

Note: There are over 165 subareas of chaplaincy that are associated with each of the ten functional areas of chaplaincy. Compiled by Michael W. Langston.

ABOUT *the* AUTHORS

Mark A. Jumper, commander, Chaplain Corps, US Navy (retired), earned a BA in history from Oral Roberts University, an MDiv from Columbia Theological Seminary, and a PhD in humanities from Salve Regina University with a dissertation on justice after war. Having completed the Advanced Course at the Naval Chaplains School as well, he served as a Navy chaplain for twenty-four years, including assignments with the Marine Corps and Coast Guard. He received the Distinguished Service Award as Coast Guard Chaplain of the Year and served as national secretary of the Military Chaplains Association. He is a veteran of the Desert Storm, Iraqi Freedom, and Hurricane Katrina operations. He designed and implemented the Headquarters Marine Corps Warrior Transition program for marines exiting combat and hostile environments, later providing congressional testimony. He then completed his career at the US Coast Guard Academy and the Naval Chaplains School. He served eight years as chaplain endorser for the Evangelical Presbyterian Church and led the Professional Advisory Group for the Clinical Pastoral Education Program at Veterans Affairs Medical Center in Hampton, Virginia. He has trained military chaplains at Kyiv Theological Seminary; presented on chaplaincy at Trinity Evangelical Divinity School, Marine Corps University, and the Armed Forces Staff College; and provided plenary presentations for the annual symposia of the US Navy Medical Service Corps and the Military Chaplains Association. Dr. Jumper is an associate professor and director of chaplaincy and military affairs at the Regent University School of Divinity, with over 270 students in the MDiv and DMin chaplaincy concentration. He and his wife, Ginger, are parents of seven adult children.

Steven E. Keith, chaplain (colonel), US Air Force (retired), was ordained to the ministry in 1981. He earned a BA and MDiv from Bob Jones University, an MA from Air University, and a DMin from Denver Seminary. As an active-duty Air Force chaplain from 1984 to 2014, he served in fourteen assignments worldwide, including deployments to Saudi Arabia, Qatar, and Iraq, where he received the Bronze Star for exceptional ministry while under fire. His other awards include the Legion of Merit, Meritorious Service Medal with six oak leaf clusters, Air Force Commendation Medal, Army Commendation Medal, and Navy-Marine Corps Commendation Medal. He was the first executive director of the Armed Forces Chaplaincy Center, orchestrating the congressionally mandated inauguration of the Center for Chaplaincy, which featured interservice education for the Army, Navy, and Air Force Chaplain Corps, while also serving as the commandant of the Air Force Chaplain Corps College, responsible for the education and training of all active-duty, reserve, and air National Guard chaplains and chaplain assistants. He now serves as executive director of the Center for Chaplaincy at Liberty University and professor of chaplaincy at the Rawlings School of Divinity at Liberty, educating and equipping over seven hundred chaplain students each semester. He is also the ecclesiastical endorser of Liberty Baptist Fellowship, overseeing five hundred chaplains in military, healthcare, and community settings. Dr. Keith is married to Delta (Johnson) Keith, and they have five children and eleven grandchildren.

Michael W. Langston, captain, Chaplain Corps, US Navy (retired), earned a BS at the University of Louisiana in Lafayette, an MDiv at Southeastern Baptist Theological Seminary, a DMin at Bethel Theological Seminary, an MA at the US Naval War College, and a PhD at King's College, University of Aberdeen, in Aberdeen, Scotland. He was a Marine Corps Infantry Officer for ten years, then a Navy chaplain for twenty-six years. He was diagnosed with moderate to severe PTSD after extensive chaplain tours in Afghanistan and Iraq. He was the first commanding officer of the Naval Chaplaincy School and Center at Fort Jackson, South Carolina, and completed his career as executive director of the Armed Forces Chaplaincy Center. He later served as president of the Military Chaplains Association and continues as deputy commander of the South Carolina State Guard, with the rank of brigadier general. He is currently professor of chaplaincy and practical theology at Columbia International University (Columbia Biblical Seminary) in Columbia, South Carolina.

ABOUT *the* CONTRIBUTORS

Jeff Brown earned a BS in mathematics from the United States Military Academy at West Point. An Army veteran, he earned an MA in biblical studies and theology at Luther Rice Seminary and pastored a Baptist church. He became a chaplain with Corporate Chaplains of America in 2005, later moving into various management positions, most recently as senior vice president of quality and strategic initiatives. He and his wife have one adult daughter and several grandchildren.

Leroy Gilbert, captain, Chaplain Corps, US Navy (retired), earned an MDiv from Howard University, an STM from Yale University, an MA in psychology from US International University, and a PhD in organizational leadership from Regent University. His chaplain service included Navy, Marine Corps, and Coast Guard assignments, with highlights as First Marine Division Chaplain and senior chaplain at the US Coast Guard Academy, completing his career as chaplain of the US Coast Guard, directing the chaplain organizational response at the World Trade Center and Pentagon sites after 9/11. He then served for eighteen years as pastor at Mt. Gilead Baptist Church in the District of Columbia. He is an assistant professor at the Regent University School of Divinity.

Juliana Lesher earned a BA in public relations from Messiah College, an MDiv from Evangelical Theological Seminary, and a PhD in ecclesial organizational leadership from Regent University. She is also a certified pastoral educator with the Association of Clinical Pastoral Education. She has ministered for twenty-six years in various settings, including serving as the national director of chaplain service for the Department of Veterans Affairs. She is the author of *A Heart That Sings for Jesus*.

Keith Travis served for twenty-eight years as an Army chaplain. He retired as a chaplain (colonel), US Army, in 2007. Keith served as a foreign missionary with the Southern Baptist Convention (SBC) and as a pastor of a local church. He served eleven years as the SBC's faith-group endorser, with oversight of over 3,800 chaplains. He is now the associate faith-group endorser for Liberty Baptist Fellowship. He also serves as an associate professor at John W. Rawlings Seminary, teaching chaplaincy. He coauthored *Military Ministry: Chaplains in the Twenty-First Century*. He and Pam have been married for forty-three years and live in Orlando, Florida.

Chris Wade earned a BA in missions at Bushnell University and an MDiv at Multnomah University. He is a candidate for a PhD in chaplaincy at Columbia International University. He is certified as an emergency medical technician and as a compassion fatigue professional. He has served six years as a healthcare chaplain and sixteen years as an EMT and fire chaplain, including service as vice president and then president of the South Carolina Public Safety Chaplains Association. He is now a crisis intervention officer-chaplain for Hillsboro Fire and Rescue, Oregon.

FOR FURTHER READING

Ammerman, E. H. Jim, and Charlene Ammerman. *After the Storm*. With Andrew Collins. Nashville: Star Song, 1991.

Baker, Alan. *Foundations of Chaplaincy: A Practical Guide*. Grand Rapids: Eerdmans, 2021.

Bell, Daniel M., Jr. *Just War as Christian Discipleship: Recentering the Tradition in the Church Rather Than the State*. Grand Rapids: Brazos, 2009.

Benimoff, Roger, and Eve Conant. *Faith under Fire: An Army Chaplain's Memoir*. New York: Three Rivers, 2010.

Bergen, Doris L. *The Sword of the Lord: Military Chaplains from the First to the Twenty-First Century*. Notre Dame, IN: University of Notre Dame Press, 2004.

Bieniek, David L. *At the Time of Death: Symbols and Rituals for Caregivers and Chaplains*. N.p.: Apocryphile , 2019.

Bohlman, Brian. *For God and Country: Considering the Call to Military Chaplaincy*. Create Space, 2015.

Bonhoeffer, Dietrich. *The Cost of Discipleship*. New York: Touchstone, 1995.

Bowers, Curt. *Forward Edge of the Battle Area: A Chaplain's Story*. 2nd ed. As told to Glen Van Dyne. Kansas City: Beacon Hill, 1994.

Browning, Jim B., and Jim Spivey. *The Heart of a Chaplain: Exploring Essentials for Ministry*. Irving, TX: B. H. Carroll Theological Institute, 2022.

Budd, Richard M. *Serving Two Masters: The Development of American Military Chaplaincy, 1860–1920*. Lincoln: University of Nebraska Press, 2002.

Cadge, Wendy, and Shelly Rambo. *Chaplaincy and Spiritual Care in the Twenty-First Century: An Introduction*. Chapel Hill: University of North Carolina Press, 2022.

Caperon, John, Andrew Todd, and James Walters, eds. *A Christian Theology of Chaplaincy*. Philadelphia: Jessica Kingsley, 2017.

Carey, Jonathan C. *Community Chaplaincy: Understanding Needs in the Yard*. N.p.: Carey Press, 2023.

Cash, Carey H. *A Table in the Presence*. New York: Ballantine Books, 2005.

Casto, John M. *The Basics of Hospice Chaplain Ministry: Practical Help for the New Chaplain*. N.p.: Hisway Prayer, 2019.

Crick, Robert. *Outside the Gates: The Need for Theology, History, and Practice of Chaplaincy Ministries*. Oviedo, FL: HigherLife, 2011.

Davis, Glenn, and Teresa Cutts. *Embedded First Responder Chaplaincy: Caring for Our Most Valuable and Vulnerable Public Servants*. N.p.: Stakeholder, 2022.

Dees, Robert F. *Resilient Warriors*. San Diego: Creative Team, 2011.

Demy, Timothy J., Jark J. Larson, and J. Daryl Charles. *The Reformers on War, Peace, and Justice*. Eugene, OR: Pickwick, 2019.

Dickens, William E., Jr. *Answering the Call: The Story of the U.S. Military Chaplaincy from the Revolution through the Civil War*. N.p.: W. E. Dickens, 1998.

Dunn, Doyle W., ed. *Chaplains in the Storm*. Camp Pendleton, CA: Division Reproduction Center, First Marine Division, FMF Pac, 1991.

Evans, Keith. *Essential Chaplain Skill Sets: Discovering Effective Ways to Provide Excellent Spiritual Care*. Nashville: WestBow, 2017.

Hannah, John. *Arthur Carl Piepkorn: Chaplain to the Greatest Generation*. Delhi, NY: ALPB Books, 2002.

Hutcheson, Richard G., Jr. *The Churches and the Chaplaincy*. Atlanta: John Knox, 1975.

Jones, David C. *Biblical Christian Ethics*. Grand Rapids: Baker Books, 1994.

Jumper, Mark A. *Serving Those Who Serve: Chaplain Service US Coast Guard*. Washington, DC: US Coast Guard, 2001.

Keith, Bill. *Days of Anguish Days of Hope: Chaplain Robert Preston Taylor's Ordeal and Triumph as a POW in World War II*. Fort Worth, TX: Scripta, 1991.

Kilner, John F. *Why the Church Needs Bioethics: A Guide to Wise Engagement with Life's Challenges*. Grand Rapids: Zondervan, 2011.

Kruizinga, Renske, Jacques Korver, Martin Walton, and Martjin Stoutjesdijk, eds. *Learning from Case Studies in Chaplaincy: Towards Practice-Based Evidence and Professionalism*. Utrecht, Netherlands: Eburon Academic, 2021.

Kurzman, Dan. *No Greater Glory: The Four Immortal Chaplains and the Sinking of the Dorchester in World War II*. New York: Random House, 2005.

Laing, John D. and Page Matthew Brooks, eds. *Don't Ask, Don't Tell: Homosexuality, Chaplaincy, and the Modern Military*. Eugene, OR: Wipf and Stock, 2013.

Laing, John D. *In Jesus' Name: Evangelicals and Military Chaplaincy*. Searcy, AR: Resource Publications, 2010.

Leary, Jeff, ed. *Taking the High Ground: Military Stories of Faith*. Colorado Springs: Victor, 2001.

Lutz, Stephen A. *College Ministry in a Post-Christian Culture*. Kansas City: House Studio, 2011.

Mansfield, Stephen. *The Faith of the American Soldier*. New York: Jeremy P. Tarcher, 2005.

Military Chaplains Association. *Voices of Chaplaincy*. Arlington, VA: Military Chaplains Association, 2002.

Milton, Michael A., *Cooperation without Compromise: Faithful Gospel Witness in a Pluralistic Setting*. Eugene, OR: Wipf & Stock, 2007.

Moore, Stephen K. *Military Chaplains as Agents of Peace: Religious Leader Engagement in Conflict and Post-Conflict Enviornments*. Toronto: Lexington Books, 2013.

Morgan, Terry. *The Chaplain's Role: How Clergy Can Work with Law Enforcement*. CreateSpace, 2012.

Myers, Russell N. *Because We Care: A Handbook for Chaplaincy in Emergency Medical Services*. N.p.: Progressive Rising Phoenix Press, 2021.

Nash, Paul, Mark Bartel, and Sally Nash, eds. *Paediatric Chaplaincy: Principles, Practices, and Skills*. Philadelphia: Jessica Kingsley, 2018.

Nash, Ronald H. *Is Jesus the Only Savior?* Grand Rapids: Zondervan, 1994.

Nolan, Steve. *Spiritual Care at the End of Life: The Chaplain as a "Hopeful Presence."* London: Jessica Kingsley, 2012.

Paget, Naomi K., and Janet R. McCormack. *The Work of the Chaplain*. Valley Forge, PA: Judson, 2006.

Parker, Philip M. *Chaplaincy: Webster's Timeline History 1539–2007*. San Diego: ICON Group, 2010.

Patterson, Eric. *Just American Wars: Ethical Dilemmas in U.S. Military History*. New York: Routledge, 2019.

———, ed. *Military Chaplains in Afghanistan, Iraq, and Beyond: Advisement and Leader Engagement in Highly Religious Environments*. Lanham, MD: Rowman & Littlefield, 2014.

Purves, Andrew. *Reconstructing Pastoral Theology, A Christological Foundation*. Philadelphia: Westminster John Knox, 2004.

Pye, Jonathan H., P. H. Sedgwick, and Andrew Todd, eds. *Critical Care: Delivering Spiritual Care in Healthcare Contexts*. London: Jessica Kingsley, 2015.

Rae, Scott B. *Moral Choices: An Introduction to Ethics*. 3rd ed. Grand Rapids: Zondervan, 2009.

Roberts, Rabbi Stephen B., ed. *Professional Spiritual and Pastoral Care: A Practical Clergy and Chaplain's Handbook*. Woodstock, VT: Skylight Paths, 2012.

Rood, Rick. *A Day in the Life of a Chaplain: Bringing Grace and Hope to Hurting People*. N.p.: Resource Publications, 2022.

Spivey, Larkin. *God in the Trenches: A History of How God Defends Freedom When America Is at War*. Washington, DC: Allegiance, 2001.

Stahl, Ronit Y. *Enlisting Faith: How the Military Chaplaincy Shaped Religion and State in Modern America*. Cambridge, MA: Harvard University Press, 2017.

Stassen, Glen H., and David P. Gushee. *Kingdom Ethics: Following Jesus in Contemporary Context*. Downers Grove, IL: InterVarsity, 2003.

Sullivan, Winnifred Fallers. *Prison Religion: Faith-Based Reform and the Constitution*. Princeton University Press, 2009.

———. *A Ministry of Presence: Chaplaincy, Spiritual Care, and the Law*. Chicago: University of Chicago Press, 2019.

Swift, Christopher, Mark Cobb, and Andrew Todd, eds. *A Handbook of Chaplaincy Studies: Understanding Spiritual Care in Public Places*. Burlington, VT: Ashgate, 2015.

Thiessen, Elmer J. *The Ethics of Evangelism: A Philosophical Defense of Proselytizing and Persuasion*. Downers Grove, IL: InterVarsity, 2011.

Thomas, Scott, and Tom Wood. *Gospel Coach: Shepherding Leaders to Glorify God*. Grand Rapids: Zondervan, 2012.

Townsend, Tim. *Mission at Nuremberg: An American Army Chaplain and the Trial of the Nazis*. New York: William Morrow, 2014.

Trull, Joe E., and James E. Carter. *Ministerial Ethics: Moral Formation for Church Leaders*. 2nd ed. Grand Rapids: Baker Academic, 2004.

VanDrunen, David. *Bioethics and the Christian Life: A Guide to Making Difficult Decisions*. Wheaton: Crossway, 2009.

Walstad, Clarence E. *Pages from a World War II Chaplain's Diary*. CreateSpace, 2019.

White, Walter H. *The Chapel of Four Chaplains: A Sanctuary for Brotherhood*. Philadelphia: Chapel of Four Chaplains, 1979.

Whittington, Michael, and Charlie Davidson. *Matters of Conscience: A Practical Theology for the Evangelical Chaplain*. Lynchburg, VA: Liberty University Press, 2014.

Wilkens, Steve. *Beyond Bumper Sticker Ethics: An Introduction to Theories of Right and Wrong*. 2nd ed. Downers Grove, IL: InterVarsity, 2011.

Wood, Stuart. *Keeping Faith in the Team: The Football Chaplain's Story*. London: Darton, Longman, and Todd, 2011.

Woodard, Whit. *Ministry of Presence: Biblical Insight on Christian Chaplaincy*. North Fort Myers, FL: Faithful Life, 2011.

Index